BEHAVIORAL INTERVENTIONS IN SCHOOLS

SCHOOL PSYCHOLOGY BOOK SERIES

BEHAVIORAL INTERVENTIONS IN SCHOOLS

Evidence-Based Positive Strategies

Edited by

Angeleque Akin-Little, Steven G. Little, Melissa A. Bray, and Thomas J. Kehle

American Psychological Association • Washington, DC

2nd printing, May 2012
3rd printing, October 2015.

Published by
American Psychological Association
750 First Street, NE
Washington, DC 20002
www.apa.org

To order
APA Order Department
P.O. Box 92984
Washington, DC 20090-2984
Tel: (800) 374-2721; Direct: (202) 336-5510
Fax: (202) 336-5502; TDD/TTY: (202) 336-6123
Online: www.apa.org/books/
E-mail: order@apa.org

In the U.K., Europe, Africa, and the Middle East, copies may be ordered from
American Psychological Association
3 Henrietta Street
Covent Garden, London
WC2E 8LU England

Typeset in Goudy by Stephen McDougal, Mechanicsville, MD

Printer: Edwards Brothers Malloy, Inc., North Carolina
Cover Designer: Naylor Design, Washington, DC
Technical/Production Editor: Emily Welsh

The opinions and statements published are the responsibility of the authors, and such opinions and statements do not necessarily represent the policies of the American Psychological Association.

Library of Congress Cataloging-in-Publication Data

Behavioral interventions in schools : evidence-based positive strategies / edited by Angeleque Akin-Little . . . [et al.]. — 1st ed.
     p. cm.
   Includes bibliographical references and index.
   ISBN-13: 978-1-4338-0460-1
   ISBN-10: 1-4338-0460-3
   1. Behavior modification. 2. Problem children—Behavior modification. 3. Problem children—Education. 4. Behavioral assessment. I. Akin-Little, Angeleque.

   LB1060.2.B443 2009
   370.15'28—dc22   2009006715

British Library Cataloguing-in-Publication Data
A CIP record is available from the British Library.

Printed in the United States of America
First Edition

CONTENTS

CONTRIBUTORS

Angeleque Akin-Little, PhD, Behavioral, Educational, and Research Consultants, Auckland, New Zealand

David W. Barnett, PhD, University of Cincinnati, Cincinnati, OH

Melissa A. Bray, PhD, University of Connecticut, Storrs

Jason Burrow-Sanchez, PhD, University of Utah, Salt Lake City

Bobbie Burton, PhD, The University of Tennessee, Knoxville

Lauren Christian, MA, National Autism Center, Randolph, MA

Elaine Clark, PhD, University of Utah, Salt Lake City

Robin M. Codding, PhD, University of Massachusetts–Boston

Clayton R. Cook, PhD, Louisiana State University, Baton Rouge

Raymond DiGiuseppe, PhD, St. John's University and The Albert Ellis Institute, New York, NY

George J. DuPaul, PhD, Lehigh University, Bethlehem, PA

Tanya L. Eckert, PhD, Syracuse University, Syracuse, NY

William P. Erchul, PhD, North Carolina State University, Raleigh

Laura Fisher, PsyD, National Autism Center, Randolph, MA

Kristin A Gansle, PhD, Louisiana State University, Baton Rouge

Frank M. Gresham, PhD, Louisiana State University, Baton Rouge

Renee O. Hawkins, PhD, University of Cincinnati, Cincinnati, OH

Thomas J. Huberty, PhD, Indiana University, Bloomington

William R. Jenson, PhD, University of Utah, Salt Lake City

Nichole Jurbergs, PhD, St. Jude Children's Research Hospital, Memphis, TN

Thomas J. Kehle, PhD, University of Connecticut, Storrs

Mary Lou Kelley, PhD, Louisiana State University, Baton Rouge

Kathleen Lynne Lane, PhD, Vanderbilt University, Nashville, TN

Steven G. Little, PhD, Massey University, Auckland, New Zealand

Jesse Logue, BA, National Autism Center, Randolph, MA

Brian K. Martens, PhD, Syracuse University, Syracuse, NY
Laura Lee McIntyre, PhD, Syracuse University, Syracuse, NY
George H. Noell, PhD, Louisiana State University, Baton Rouge
Jennifer L. Rheinheimer, MS, Syracuse University, Syracuse, NY
Ann C. Schulte, PhD, North Carolina State University, Raleigh
Brandi Simonsen, PhD, University of Connecticut, Storrs
Amy L. Skinner, PhD, The University of Tennessee, Knoxville
Christopher H. Skinner, PhD, The University of Tennessee, Knoxville
Mark W. Steege, PhD, University of Southern Maine, Portland
George Sugai, PhD, University of Connecticut, Storrs
Erin Sullivan, MS, Margaret Murphy Center for Children, Lewiston, ME
Adrea J. Truckenmiller, MS, Syracuse University, Syracuse, NY
T. Steuart Watson, PhD, Miami University, Oxford, OH
Tonya S. Watson, PhD, Miami University, Oxford, OH
Joseph H. Wehby, PhD, Vanderbilt University, Nashville, TN
Lisa L. Weyandt, PhD, University of Rhode Island, Kingston
Susan M. Wilczynski, PhD, National Autism Center, Randolph, MA

ACKNOWLEDGMENTS

The editors are extremely grateful to all of the contributing authors. Each and every one of you made our job incredibly easy. We were gratified that you agreed to work on what we feel is an important book for psychologists, particularly school psychologists. You were prompt with your submissions and revisions, and you wrote excellent manuscripts. We gave you the opportunity to structure the chapters the way you saw fit—you are the experts, after all—and you did not let us down.

This book would not be what it is without the keen eye and creativity of Susan Herman, our development editor at the American Psychological Association (APA). Her ideas for what the book could and should be were excellent and helped us formulate the book we wanted, that is, a book that provides specific, evidence-based interventions for those working with children and adolescents in the educational setting. Actually, we thank everyone from APA who helped with this project. You have all been very kind to us neophytes as we traversed the new territory of editing a book. We would like to give a special thank you to Susan Reynolds, our acquisitions editor from APA Books, who provided great encouragement and gently led us through this process with prompt, detailed responses to any questions. Finally, we thank David McIntosh, the editor of the Division 16 (Applying Psychology to the Schools) book series, for his support and feedback. In the end, this book would not have happened without contributions from everyone. We thank all of you for joining us in this process. We feel the end product is something of which we can all be proud.

BEHAVIORAL INTERVENTIONS
IN SCHOOLS

INTRODUCTION

ANGELEQUE AKIN-LITTLE, STEVEN G. LITTLE,
MELISSA A. BRAY, AND THOMAS J. KEHLE

In the spring of 2002, Angeleque Akin-Little and Steven G. Little decided to develop a miniseries for *School Psychology Review* entitled "Current Status of Behavioral Interventions in Schools." The intent of that miniseries was to address the need for thought-provoking analysis and a summary of best practices as they relate to school-based behavioral procedures. With the assistance of Frank Gresham, the miniseries was developed and was very well received. However, a single edition of a journal cannot come close to encompassing the full range of behavioral interventions in schools. Therefore, after the publication of this miniseries in 2004, Drs. Akin-Little and Little decided that expanding the concept of the miniseries into a more comprehensive book made sense. Although the development of the book took a few years, with the assistance of Drs. Melissa Bray and Tom Kehle, the goal has been reached.

A FOCUS ON BEHAVIOR

Because its foundations are in the philosophical movement of positivism, a focus on behavior has had a strong impact in psychological and educational intervention methodology. The modern term *behaviorism* was initially

3

coined by John Watson in 1914 (Alberto & Troutman, 2006) and indicated a focus on direct observational data. B. F. Skinner's work in operant conditioning and the use of his theoretically derived principles to change human behavior became much more prominent in the 1950s and 1960s with the advent of behavior modification and applied behavior analysis. Early work such as Ogden Lindsley's (1990) successful application of operant methods to the behaviors of psychotic children and adults at his Harvard Behavior Research Laboratory, Bijou's work with reinforcement and extinction in young children (e.g., Bijou, 1957), Lovaas and colleagues' work with children with autism (e.g., Lovaas, Freitag, Gold, & Kassorla, 1965), and Patterson's work with antisocial children (e.g., Patterson & Brodsky, 1966), provided the initial empirical support for this technology.

We now have decades of empirical research supporting the efficacy of behavioral interventions in the classroom. Ayllon and Azrin's (1968), Birnbrauer, Wolf, Kidder, and Tague's (1965), and O'Leary and Drabman's (1971) work with token economies; Barrish, Saunders, and Wolf's (1969) Good Behavior Game; Iwata and colleagues' research in functional analysis (Iwata, Dorsey, Slifer, Bauman, & Richman, 1982); and Litow and Pumroy's (1975) seminal work in group contingencies all have helped firmly established the continued efficacy of behavioral approaches.

In the past 2 decades, meta-analytic studies have provided even further evidence for the efficacy of behavioral and cognitive–behavioral interventions with children and adolescents. Casey and Berman (1985) conducted a meta-analysis on the effects of child and adolescent psychotherapy. Results indicated an overall effect size of .71, but behavioral interventions were found to be more effective than nonbehavioral interventions, with effect sizes (ES) of .91 and .40, respectively. Similar results were found by Weisz, Weiss, Alicke, and Klotz (1987), who obtained a mean effect size of .79 for psychotherapy, with behavior therapy (ES = .88) again being found more effective than nonbehavioral interventions (ES = .44). Stage and Quiroz (1997) conducted a meta-analysis to examine the use of interventions designed to decrease disruptive behavior in public education settings. Their results yielded a mean effect size of –.78, indicating a reduction in disruptive behavior, of a magnitude approaching Cohen's (1977) definition of a large effect size. Behavioral interventions such as group contingencies (ES = –1.02), self-management (ES = –.97), differential reinforcement (ES = –.97), token economies (ES = –.90), and stimulus cues (ES = –.83) all showed evidence of large effects. Meta-analyses have also supported the efficacy of cognitive–behavioral interventions. Bennett and Gibbons (2000) conducted a meta-analysis of child-based cognitive behavior therapy (CBT) for antisocial behavior and found a mean effect size of .48, indicating a moderate effect size in decreasing antisocial behavior. More recently meta-analytic studies have supported the efficacy of CBT intervention with children and adolescents with pediatric obsessive–compulsive disorder (Watson & Rees, 2008), anxiety disorders

(Ishikawa, Okajima, Matsuoka, & Sakano, 2007), and depression (Klein, Jacobs, & Reinecke, 2007).

Thus, with a consistent body of empirical support for behavioral interventions, coupled with the need for school psychologists and other personnel to be equipped with knowledge of these interventions, this book was designed. That is, this volume is intended to inform readers by providing information on evidence-based positive behavioral strategies for use in the schools. Furthermore, we felt it was important to provide that information in a concise, easy-to-read, and understandable format. Hence, chapters are written so that a person who is somewhat new to behavioral interventions would be able to use the techniques presented immediately and easily while experienced practitioners could have a helpful resource to guide their practice. Of course, there may be instances in which readers may need to seek out other resources for more details on specific methodologies, implementation techniques, and so forth.

EVIDENCE-BASED PRACTICE

In August 2005 the American Psychological Association (APA) adopted a policy with regard to evidence-based practice in psychology. The purpose of this policy was and is to promote effective psychological practice by using evidence derived from clinically relevant research (APA, 2005). Specific statements have also been developed by APA's Divisions 16 (School Psychology; Kratochwill, 2003) and 12 (Society of Clinical Psychology; Weisz & Hawley, 2002).

Evidence-based guidelines have created the necessity for practitioners to use interventions (including primary and secondary prevention programs) that have proven effectiveness. The aim is to improve the quality and efficacy of interventions, delivered efficiently and economically, as measured by objective criteria. The evidence-based movement attempts to integrate research-supported techniques into interventions; however, psychologists and others working with children and adolescents recognize the challenges in implementing these types of interventions (APA Task Force, 2008). Each chapter in this volume is predicated on the principles of evidence-based interventions. In this book, empirically supported principles of psychological assessment, case formulation, and intervention are integrated (APA, 2005) with issues and concerns faced by psychologists and other professionals working with children and adolescents in educational contexts.

POSITIVE AND PREVENTIVE APPROACHES TO
BEHAVIORAL INTERVENTIONS

Emotional and behavioral problems of students in the classroom have been rated as a major concern for teachers, administrators, and the public

(Hardman & Smith, 2003; Macciomei, 1999). Without effective behavior management, a positive and productive classroom environment is impossible to achieve. The most effective model for producing behavior change and preventing the development of maladaptive behavior is the behavioral model (Wielkiewicz, 1995). In addition, and as just discussed, behavioral approaches have been found to be very effective in developing effective instructional strategies. However, resistance to the use of behavioral procedures in the classroom has come from a variety of sources, and some individuals have been particularly harsh in their criticism of the use of positive reinforcement (e.g., Kohn, 1993). In spite of this, teachers continually request training in behavior and classroom management techniques (Maag, 1999, 2001).

School psychology has been transitioning from a primarily psychometric orientation to one that focuses much more on both direct and indirect interventions (Fagan & Wise, 2000). As psychologists are involved in interventions now more than ever, a book such as this is needed to provide practitioners with a summary of empirically valid and ecologically sound intervention strategies that recognizes primary, secondary, and tertiary prevention strategies. To effectively cover the breadth of behavioral interventions related to school behavior, it was necessary to maintain a certain level of brevity in our discussions. The book, however, should provide practitioners, students, and trainers with a resource that aids in identifying and understanding the foundations of appropriate interventions and gives direction as to where additional details can be found. No book can provide a complete depth of coverage of the multitude of problems faced in schools today, but we believe this volume gives readers as complete and comprehensive an understanding as possible for a book of this nature.

ORGANIZATION OF THIS BOOK

We have structured the book around four major areas: (a) Foundations for Designing School-Based Behavioral Interventions, (b) Systematic Approaches to Prevention and Intervention, (c) Specific Behavioral Techniques, and (d) Customizing Behavioral Strategies for Special Populations. In developing this book, we strove to recruit the top researchers in each area, and we believe we have put together an impressive array of authors. A PsycINFO search of authors conducted in November 2007 as the book was under development indicated that cumulatively the chapter authors have published 1,043 journal articles, 187 book chapters, and 44 books.

An understanding of the foundations of behavioral interventions is necessary for any intervention to be implemented with integrity and efficacy. Part I, then, focuses on foundations. It includes chapters on behavioral consultation, behavioral assessment, an introduction to functional behavioral assessment, a discussion of treatment integrity, and an overview of the extrinsic reinforcement/intrinsic motivation issue. Chapters 1 through 4 present integral information to readers as they begin the use of behavioral interventions in the school setting. Chapter 5, while not presenting a specific intervention, discusses an issue important to the effective application of behavioral interventions. Many educational professionals have been exposed to an antibehavioral bias from a theoretical standpoint holding that the use of behavioral techniques will decrease intrinsic motivation (see Kohn, 1993). This chapter attempts to clarify this issue and provide further support for the proper use of positive, evidence-based behavioral techniques.

Part II contains chapters on systematic approaches to prevention and intervention. There are chapters on cognitive behavior therapy, reading interventions, positive behavior supports, classroom management, group contingencies, the use of reductive procedures, and generalization and maintenance. It is important to note that this is one of the first books on behavioral interventions that attempts to include cognitive–behavioral approaches. Also, and new to a book on this topic, the importance of generalization and maintenance, often overlooked, is discussed in detail in chapter 12.

Part III provides information on specific behavioral techniques and includes chapters on response to intervention (RTI), the use of daily report cards, and self-modeling. Frank Gresham, the author of chapter 13, is a highly respected author in the new but growing area of RTI. He was instrumental in ensuring that the use of RTI was added to the Individuals With Disabilities Education Act criteria for learning disability eligibility determination and has conducted some of the seminal research in this area. Chapters 14 and 15 discuss the use of daily report cards and self-modeling, two intervention strategies that are both highly successful and easy to implement in the classroom.

Finally, Part IV includes chapters on customizing behavioral strategies for special populations. Chapters 16 through 21 focus on difficult students, externalizing and internalizing disorders, preschoolers, children with autism, and trauma-focused interventions. This part includes topics that are not regularly seen in a book of this nature but that are valuable to anyone working with children in an educational context.

The target audiences for the book are practicing school psychologists, school psychology students, and other psychologists who work with children. All children in the United States and Canada receive compulsory education. Even if intervention services are not taking place primarily in the schools, practitioners cannot ignore the role of the school and the importance of coordinating interventions with the school. The fact is, much of what is discussed in this book is applicable in multiple environments, including schools, homes, residential facilities, and any place children reside or are educated. It is our sincere hope that other audiences (e.g., teachers, administrators, parents) also have the opportunity to avail themselves of the information provided in this book. To maximize the efficacy of interventions, teachers, parents, and school administrators all must be involved with the psychologist in effective implementation. We believe that this book will be particularly useful to regular and special education teachers and school administrators as well as counselors and social workers.

Clearly, behavioral interventions work. There is a great deal of data supporting this contention. This book attempts to bring together a sampling of the top researchers in behavioral interventions in school psychology and education. Although the target audience is psychologists, we believe this book can also benefit all of those working with children and adolescents in an educational context. It provides details of behavioral interventions, grounded in science (i.e., evidence based), in a simple and easy-to-use format, in order to help professionals provide the very best educational environment for children and adolescents. We believe that such an environment is no less than these groups deserve, and we believe that the techniques detailed herein are the best ones to ensure such an outcome.

REFERENCES

Alberto, P. A., & Troutman, A. C. (2006). *Applied behavior analysis for teachers* (7th ed.). Upper Saddle River, NJ: Merrill Prentice Hall.

American Psychological Association Task Force on Evidence-Based Practice for Children and Adolescents. (2008). *Disseminating evidence-based practice for children and adolescents: A systems approach to enhancing care.* Washington, DC: Author.

American Psychological Association. (2005). *American Psychological Association policy statement on evidence-based practice in psychology.* Retrieved September 30, 2008, from http://www2.apa.org/practice/ebpstatement.pdf

Ayllon, T., & Azrin, N. (1968). *The token economy: A motivational system for therapy and rehabilitation.* New York: Appleton-Century-Crofts.

Barrish, H. H., Saunders, M., & Wolf, M. M. (1969). Good behavior game: Effects of individual contingencies for group consequences on disruptive behavior in a classroom. *Journal of Applied Behavior Analysis, 2,* 119–124.

Bennett, D. S., & Gibbons, T. A. (2000). Efficacy of child cognitive-behavioral interventions for antisocial behavior: A meta-analysis. *Child and Family Behavior Therapy, 22,* 1–15.

Bijou, S. W. (1957). Patterns of reinforcement and resistance to extinction in young children. *Child Development, 28,* 47–54.

Birnbrauer, J. S., Wolf, M. M., Kidder, J. D., & Tague, C. E. (1965). Classroom behavior of retarded pupils with token reinforcement. *Journal of Experimental Child Psychology, 2,* 219–235.

Casey, R. J., & Berman, J. S. (1985). The outcome of psychotherapy with children. *Psychological Bulletin, 98,* 388–400.

Cohen, J. (1977). *Statistical power analysis for the behavioral sciences* (Rev. ed.). New York: Academic Press.

Fagan, T. K., & Wise, P. S. (2000). *School psychology: Past, present, and future* (2nd ed.). Bethesda, MD: National Association of School Psychologists.

Hardman, E. L., & Smith, S. W. (2003). Analysis of classroom discipline-related content in elementary education journals. *Behavioral Disorders, 28*, 173–186.

Ishikawa, S., Okajima, I., Matsuoka, H., & Sakano, Y. (2007). Cognitive behavioural therapy for anxiety disorders in children and adolescents: A meta-analysis. *Child and Adolescent Mental Health, 12*, 164–172.

Iwata, B. A., Dorsey, M. F., Slifer, K. J., Bauman, K. E., & Richman, G. S. (1982). Toward a functional analysis of self-injury. *Analysis and Intervention in Developmental Disabilities, 2*, 3–20.

Klein, J. B., Jacobs, R. H., & Reinecke, M. A. (2007). Cognitive-behavioral therapy for adolescent depression: A meta-analytic investigation of changes in effect-size estimates. *Journal of the American Academy of Child & Adolescent Psychiatry, 46*, 1403–1413.

Kohn, A. (1993). *Punished by rewards: The trouble with gold stars, incentive plans, A's, praise, and other bribes.* Boston: Houghton Mifflin.

Kratochwill, T. R. (2003). *Procedural and coding manual for review of evidence-based interventions.* Madison, WI: Task Force on Evidence-Based Interventions in School Psychology.

Lindsley, O. R. (1990). Precision teaching: By teachers for children. *Teaching Exceptional Children, 22*, 10–15.

Litow, L., & Pumroy, D. K. (1975). A brief review of classroom group-oriented contingencies. *Journal of Applied Behavior Analysis, 8*, 341–347.

Lovaas, O. I., Freitag, G., Gold, V. J., & Kassorla, I. C. (1965). Experimental studies in childhood schizophrenia: Analysis of self-destructive behavior. *Journal of Experimental Child Psychiatry, 2*, 67–84.

Maag, J. W. (1999). *Behavior management: From the theoretical implications to practical applications.* San Diego, CA: Singular.

Maag, J. W. (2001). Rewarded by punishment: Reflections on the disuse of positive reinforcement in schools. *Exceptional Children, 67*, 173–186.

Macciomei, N. R. (1999). Behavior problems in urban schoolchildren. In N. R. Macciomei & D. H. Ruben (Eds.), *Behavior management in the public schools: An urban approach.* Westport, CT: Praeger.

O'Leary, K. D., & Drabman, R. (1971). Token reinforcement programs in the classroom: A review. *Psychological Bulletin, 75*, 379–398.

Patterson, G. R., & Brodsky, G. (1966). A behaviour modification programme for a child with multiple problem behaviours. *Journal of Child Psychology and Psychiatry, 7*, 277–295.

Stage, S. A., & Quiroz, D. R. (1997). A meta-analysis of interventions to decrease disruptive behavior in public education settings. *School Psychology Review, 26*, 333–368.

Watson, H. J., & Rees, C. S. (2008). Meta-analysis of randomized, controlled treatment trials for pediatric obsessive-compulsive disorder. *Journal of Child Psychology and Psychiatry, 49*, 489–498.

Weisz, J. R., & Hawley, K. M. (2002). *Procedural and coding manual for identification of beneficial treatments*. Washington, DC: American Psychological Association, Society for Clinical Psychology Division 12 Committee on Science and Practice.

Weisz, J. R., Weiss, B., Alicke, M. D., & Klotz, M. (1987). Effectiveness of psychotherapy with children and adolescents: A meta-analysis for clinicians. *Journal of Consulting and Clinical Psychology, 55*, 542–549.

Wielkiewicz, R. M. (1995). *Behavior management in the schools: Principles and procedures* (2nd ed.). Boston: Allyn & Bacon.

I

FOUNDATIONS FOR DESIGNING SCHOOL-BASED BEHAVIORAL INTERVENTIONS

1

BEHAVIORAL CONSULTATION

WILLIAM P. ERCHUL AND ANN C. SCHULTE

Suppose you are a beginning second-grade teacher who is experiencing great difficulty with a student named Tommy. It seems that Tommy is out of control—disrupting children around him and interfering with your attempts to teach the class. To deal with this situation, you decide to meet with the school psychologist, Dr. Smith. In the first session, Dr. Smith asks you to describe in observable terms what you mean by Tommy being "disruptive" and "interfering." In reply to her series of questions, you inform Dr. Smith that (a) Tommy is generally a capable student but often leaves his seat for several minutes at a time while you are busy working with a small group and he is among the students who are supposed to be doing independent math work, and (b) Tommy repeatedly calls out answers without raising his hand when you are teaching phonics. Dr. Smith then asks you to describe what is going on in the classroom before, during, and after Tommy leaves his seat and blurts out answers. This meeting ends with Dr. Smith's request that you keep track of how often these two problem behaviors occur each day. She also asks to visit your classroom tomorrow to see Tommy "in action."

The following week, a second meeting is held and, through sharing insights gained from the more systematic analysis of Tommy's behavior, you and Dr. Smith note several patterns: (a) Tommy often leaves his seat be-cause Jimmy motions for him to go to the pencil sharpener (i.e., work avoidance, peer attention); (b) You do not have a clear line of sight to the class members doing independent work while you are teaching small group math; (c) Tommy frequently does not finish his math work as a result of leaving his seat; and (d) When Tommy calls out answers in phonics, you often acknowledge his answer (i.e., give him teacher attention) so as not to interrupt the flow of instruction. Armed with this information, you and Dr. Smith brainstorm intervention ideas. What is discussed and agreed to is that you will (a) reposition Jimmy so that he is not in Tommy's line of sight and also change your position during math small group work, thereby modifying some of antecedents to the problem behavior; (b) allow Tommy extra computer time with a friend if he completes his math seatwork, thereby reinforcing a desirable behavior that competes with leaving his seat during math; (c) re-emphasize the existing rules of classroom etiquette, then ignore Tommy's callouts to extinguish this inappropriate behavior during phonics; and (d) positively reinforce Tommy's appropriate behavior by calling on him only when his hand is raised. Before the meeting ends, Dr. Smith and you role-play what you would say to the class as a whole and Tommy in particular to implement this intervention plan. Dr. Smith asks that you continue to keep track of the daily occurrence of the two problem behaviors.

With Dr. Smith's support, you carry out this plan for 2 weeks, and in the next session you meet to assess the plan's impact on the target behaviors. Though far from perfect, it seems that the intervention has succeeded in lowering Tommy's out-of-seat behavior by an average of 50% (i.e., from four to two times each day) and blurting out answers by an average of 67% (i.e., from three to one time per day). You are fairly satisfied with this progress and decide to keep the plan in place a while longer. Dr. Smith then encourages you to start keeping track of the number of times Tommy appropriately raises his hand during phonics instruction, and you agree to do this. Comparing calendars, a final meeting is scheduled for 2 weeks from today.

This case study is an example of *human services consultation*, a helping process in which an intervention is provided to a client (e.g., student) directly by a *consultee* (e.g., teacher, parent) but indirectly by a *consultant* (e.g., school psychologist). Historically, the consultant's primary role has been to support and assist the consultee; in fact, a consultant may never meet face-to-face with a particular client. Along these lines, because the ultimate responsibility for the client's welfare rests with the consultee, it is usually the consultee who carries out the intervention with the client. Consultation has a dual purpose: (a) to help the consultee with a current work problem and (b) to give the consultee added skills and insights that will enhance future professional functioning. It is the latter purpose that promotes consultation as a means to prevent educational and psychological problems. Note that, unlike other interventions described in this volume, consultation involves a *triadic relationship* (i.e., consultant/behavioral specialist–consultee–client) instead of a *dyadic relationship* (i.e., behavioral specialist–client; Brown, Pryzwansky, & Schulte, 2006; Caplan, 1970; Erchul & Martens, 2002).

More specifically, our opening scenario is an example of *behavioral consultation* (Bergan, 1977; Bergan & Kratochwill, 1990; Goodwin & Coates, 1976; Kratochwill, Elliott, & Stoiber, 2002; Martens, 1993; Martens & DiGennaro, 2008). Behavioral consultation is built on a strong foundation of behavioral psychology, emphasizing concepts such as quantification, current environmental causality, and a close association between assessment and intervention (Haynes, 1978). Obviously many interventions selected and implemented within behavioral consultation are those that are described in Part II of this volume.

Our goal in this chapter is to introduce history, fundamental models, research, and critique of behavioral consultation in the context of how school psychologists, such as Dr. Smith in our scenario, apply it in their practice. Of necessity, we limit our focus to case-centered behavioral consultation but recognize that other variations, such as one with a system-wide focus, are also important to consider (cf. Vernberg & Reppucci, 1986). Throughout the chapter, key references are cited that we strongly encourage readers to consult for more detailed information. In offering this introduction to behavioral consultation, we address its origins, fundamental concepts, effectiveness, criticisms, and future.

ORIGINS OF BEHAVIORAL CONSULTATION

At the core of all approaches to human services consultation is the notion of problem solving, and in behavioral consultation, this is decidedly the case (Erchul & Martens, 2002). From an historical perspective, D'Zurilla and Goldfried (1971) offered a precursor to behavioral consultation that used behavior modification procedures within a problem-solving framework. These authors noted that problem solving is a process that offers many potentially viable alternatives, thereby increasing the possibility that individuals will select the most effective one available. Their model advanced the following five stages of problem solving:

1. *General orientation:* Developing attitudes such as acceptance that problems occur in life, recognizing these problems, and inhibiting the tendency to act impulsively or not at all.
2. *Problem definition and formulation:* Defining all elements of the problem in operational terms and identifying important aspects of the situation.
3. *Generation of alternatives:* Brainstorming and combining various options.
4. *Decision making:* Predicting the likely outcomes of each available option.

5. *Verification:* Assessing effectiveness by comparing actual outcomes with predicted outcomes.

In a related way, Tharp and Wetzel (1969) proposed a detailed method of applying principles of behavior modification in human service settings such as schools. Their approach to consultation represents a logical extension of the assumptions of a behavioral approach to treatment. Perhaps most important, Tharp and Wetzel institutionalized the role of direct care providers (e.g., parents, teachers) to serve as behavior change agents in natural settings. Specifically, they delineated three key participants: (a) *consultant*, a person with expertise in behavior analysis; (b) *mediator*, a person who controls reinforcers and can administer them contingent on a target's behavior; and (c) *target*, a person with a problem that can be addressed through behavior modification. Given the terminology used thus far in this chapter, *consultee* is synonymous with *mediator*, and *client* with *target*.

FUNDAMENTAL CONCEPTS OF BEHAVIORAL CONSULTATION

Influenced by behavioral and cognitive psychology (Bergan, 1995) and extending the ideas advanced by D'Zurilla and Goldfried (1971) and Tharp and Wetzel (1969), John Bergan proposed his model of behavioral consultation (Bergan, 1977; Bergan & Kratochwill, 1990). Although there are many variations of the term *behavioral consultation*, today when it is used the chances are very good that it refers to Bergan's specific model. Relative to other topics presented in this volume, Bergan's model combines the strategies and tactics of behavior analysis with a step-by-step problem-solving approach, uses behavioral technology to develop interventions, and uses the technology of behavior analysis to evaluate intervention outcomes (Erchul & Martens, 2002).

Key Assumptions

Bergan (1977) identified seven key assumptions of behavioral consultation. Specifically, his model

- assumes the consultee (e.g., teacher) is an active participant throughout consultation;
- can promote the development of problem-solving skills in the client (e.g., child) by having the consultant work with the client in the same way as the consultee does;
- offers a means through which the consultant can link knowledge producers (e.g., education researchers) with knowledge consumers (e.g., teachers);

- attempts to connect decision making to empirical evidence by using, for example, direct observations of client behavior and scientific findings about changing behavior;
- defines problems presented in consultation as being outside the character of the client, so common diagnostic labels applied to clients (e.g., dyslexic, emotionally disturbed) are not viewed as helpful and generally are not used;
- emphasizes the role of environmental factors in maintaining and changing behavior, such that respondent, operant, and modeling procedures are often used; and
- centers its evaluation on goal attainment and plan effectiveness (i.e., accomplishments) rather than on client characteristics, which often suggest deficiencies. (Bergan, 1977)

Stages, Interviews, and Objectives

Bergan's (1977) model of behavioral consultation is essentially a four-stage, problem-solving process, and the model's stages include three separate interviews, each of which contains specific objectives that the consultant is expected to address. The four stages are problem identification, problem analysis, plan implementation, and problem evaluation. More recently, plan implementation has been called *treatment implementation* (Sheridan & Kratochwill, 2007), and problem evaluation has been called *treatment evaluation* (Sheridan & Kratochwill, 2007) or *plan evaluation* (Kratochwill et al., 2002). These slight name changes notwithstanding, the critical stages of behavioral consultation have remained essentially the same for over 30 years. Next, these stages and their corresponding interviews and objectives are described.

Problem Identification

The first stage involves specifying the problem to be solved as a result of consultation. Problem identification is accomplished through a problem identification interview, which the consultant conducts with the consultee. This interview is a critical point within behavioral consultation because it (a) creates expectations for the use of a behavioral, rather than a medical model, perspective on the client's problems and (b) stresses the role of current environmental events as being primarily responsible for the problem. The following are specific objectives associated with the problem identification interview:

1. Assess the range of consultee concerns.
2. Identify a problem area to target and/or prioritize components of the problem.
3. Define the problem in observable, behavioral terms.

4. Estimate the frequency, intensity, and/or duration of the problem behavior.
5. Inquire about client strengths.
6. Identify tentative goals for behavior change.
7. Begin to identify environmental conditions surrounding the problem behavior (i.e., antecedent, sequential, and consequent behaviors).
8. Establish and agree on data collection procedures and responsibilities.
9. Schedule the next interview.

Before the next interview, typically observations of the client are conducted and baseline (i.e., preintervention) data are collected on the problem behavior to offer a starting point for evaluating the effectiveness of the intervention plan that is to be implemented.

Problem Analysis

During the second stage of behavioral consultation, the problem behavior is examined further and an intervention is designed to solve it. The problem analysis interview has the following six objectives:

1. Determine whether the baseline data are sufficient to document the existence of a problem.
2. Establish goals for behavior change.
3. Continue the analysis of environmental conditions surrounding the problem behavior (i.e., antecedent, sequential, and consequent behaviors).
4. Design and prepare to implement an intervention plan.
5. Reaffirm data collection procedures.
6. Schedule the next interview.

Plan Implementation

Although the third stage of the model does not involve a formal interview, it assumes that the consultant and consultee will continue to exchange information through brief contacts. During plan implementation, the consultant monitors and assists the consultee in implementing the intervention as agreed to by both parties. Following are three specific objectives associated with plan implementation:

1. Determine whether the consultee has the necessary skills to implement the intervention.
2. Monitor data collection and overall plan operations.
3. Determine the need for plan revisions, if necessary.

Problem Evaluation

The final stage of behavior consultation is problem evaluation, which occurs after the intervention has been in place long enough to have a chance to produce a change in behavior (e.g., 1 week or longer). Problem evaluation involves determining the extent to which the problem has been solved and the plan was effective. Problem evaluation is carried out through the problem evaluation interview, which has the following four objectives:

1. Determine whether intervention goals were met.
2. Assess plan effectiveness.
3. Discuss continuation, modification, or termination of the plan.
4. Terminate consultation or schedule additional meetings to recycle through the problem-solving process (Bergan, 1977; Bergan & Kratochwill, 1990; Erchul & Martens, 2002; Kratochwill & Bergan, 1990; Martens, 1993).

Although the foregoing presentation lists the widely recognized steps and consultant tasks found in behavioral consultation, it is worth noting that several individuals have introduced additional stages and/or consultant tasks into the model. For example, realizing the significance of the working relationship between consultant and consultee to promote cooperation and decrease resistance, Kratochwill et al. (2002) advanced an initial stage that they termed *establishing a consultant–consultee relationship*. Similarly, acknowledging that few interventions developed in consultation will succeed unless implemented with integrity (Noell, 2008), Wilkinson (2006) proposed the treatment monitoring interview, which occurs between plan implementation and the problem evaluation interview.

RELEVANT PROCESS AND OUTCOME RESEARCH

Although space limitations preclude a detailed summary, it is useful to highlight some important findings generated from studies of school-based behavioral consultation that have sought to link aspects of consultant behavior to consultation process and outcomes. The following are some selective results: (a) the best predictor of solving a problem presented in consultation is whether the consultant and consultee identify/define the problem in behavioral terms at the close of the first interview (Bergan & Tombari, 1975, 1976); (b) the consultant's use of behavioral cues as opposed to medical model cues leads to higher expectations by teachers about their ability to teach children with academic problems (Tombari & Bergan, 1978); (c) the odds are 14 times higher that a consultee will identify resources needed to implement an intervention plan if the consultant asks for the consultee's ideas (Bergan & Neumann, 1980); and (d) consultant follow-up in the form of daily or weekly performance data to the consultee increases the odds that the consultee will continue to implement the intervention (Mortenson & Witt, 1998). Though clearly dated, these results constitute important bases for the actions of behavioral consultants even today (Martens & DiGennaro, 2008).

DOES BEHAVIORAL CONSULTATION WORK?

Another way of phrasing this question is to ask: Is there scientific evidence indicating that positive effects occur when a behavioral consultant works directly with one or more school staff members who then work directly with one or more students? Before addressing this question, it is important to acknowledge that consultation research is difficult to conduct, and unfortunately, many of the studies supporting it are methodologically flawed. For instance, because behavioral consultation represents a consultant's attempt to improve the performance of a third party (e.g., child client) through change in a second party (e.g., parent), assuring and verifying that the second party carried out interventions precisely as they were discussed in the consultation interviews can be difficult (Erchul & Martens, 2002).

However, there is considerable evidence indicating that behavioral consultation is an effective intervention (Erchul & Sheridan, 2008). Much of this evidence is based on *meta-analysis*, a statistical means of summarizing the impact of an intervention across many research studies that used that particular intervention. For each study included in a meta-analysis, the change in performance that results from the intervention is calculated as the average score of the group receiving the intervention (i.e., treatment) group minus the average score of the control (i.e., no treatment) group divided by the standard deviation of the control group. These effect size (*ES*) statistics are then averaged across all the included studies to specify the overall effectiveness of that intervention. For example, an *ES* of 1.0 in a treatment/control group design indicates that the treatment group outperformed the control group by one standard deviation or z-score unit on a specific outcome measure (e.g., standardized rating scale of student behavior).

Medway and Updyke (1985) presented the results of 18 studies of behavioral consultation published from 1972 to 1982 that together reported 64 consultee and client outcome measures (i.e., changes in attitudes, behavior, and achievement). They found the average *ES* for behavioral consultation to be .44 for consultee effects and .43 for client effects, meaning that the average consultee and client participating in consultation each fell at the 67th percentile relative to the participants in the control group on the same outcome measure. Applying meta-analytic procedures to individual cases wherein a participant's baseline measurement serves as his or her "control," Busse, Kratochwill, and Elliott (1995) reported an average client *ES* of .95 for 23 cases of behavioral consultation with teachers. Though not a meta-analysis, Sheridan, Welch, and Orme (1996) completed a comprehensive review of school consultation outcome studies published from 1985 to 1995 and concluded that 89% of the behavioral consultation studies reported positive results, 11% were neutral, and none were negative. The conclusion to be drawn is that outcome research on behavioral consultation conducted over the past 35 years has consistently illustrated its effectiveness.

CRITIQUE OF BEHAVIORAL CONSULTATION

Given the overview nature of this chapter, it is necessary to present a critique of behavioral consultation at two different levels. At a basic level, a number of strengths and weaknesses of the model can be readily explained and understood. On the positive side, behavioral consultation has been credited with being based on the evidence-based principles of applied behavior analysis; taught frequently in preservice graduate training programs because of its well-specified goals and strategies and structured interview format; implemented widely by school-based professionals; researched more than any other model of school consultation; and regarded overall as an effective model of consultation. On the negative side, however, behavior consultation has been criticized for being underutilized within schools because of its faulty assumptions about how and why teachers may change their behavior; too client-centered, possibly to the detriment of consultees' professional development; not as concerned with treatment integrity as it should be; and overly reliant on consultee self-reports of important dimensions of assessment and intervention (Erchul & Martens, 2002; Erchul & Schulte, 1996; Witt, Gresham, & Noell, 1996b).

A higher level critique of behavioral consultation requires an understanding of some rather complex issues that unfortunately fall outside the scope of this chapter. To resolve this problem, we direct readers to a very interesting debate that appeared in the professional literature from 1996 to 1998. This exchange began when Witt et al. (1996b) asked the provocative question, "What's 'behavioral' about behavioral consultation?" and proceeded to challenge some mainstay aspects of the model. Erchul and Schulte (1996) replied, indicating that behavioral consultation was best viewed as a "work in progress," which was followed by Witt, Gresham, and Noell's (1996a) rejoinder that the opposing points of view were largely a function of the authors' epistemological and philosophical differences. Continuing this dialogue, Noell and Witt (1996) questioned five key assumptions of behavioral consultation, which Kratochwill, Bergan, Sheridan, and Elliott (1998) forcefully rebutted. In the last installment, Noell, Gresham, and Duhon (1998) again cited epistemological differences but went on to specify areas of substantial agreement across camps, which included the need to effectively deliver school-based consultation services and implement evidence-based interventions. We view this scholarly debate as being far from over and expect to see similar discussions in the future.

THE FUTURE OF BEHAVIORAL CONSULTATION

We end this chapter by predicting that the future of behavioral consultation in schools will be bright. This conclusion is based on several observed trends. First, Bergan's (1977) original model continues to evolve and adapt to meet new challenges posed within schools, families, and society. For instance, Sheridan and Kratochwill (2007) have refined and promoted the offshoot of behavioral consultation known as *conjoint behavioral consultation*, a model of helping that engages both school professionals and parents in the problem-solving process. Also, owing to advances in academic assessment and intervention technology, Jitendra et al. (2007) have embedded an intensive data-based academic intervention (IDAI) component into their behavioral consultation work with teachers of children with attention-deficit/ hyperactivity disorder. This IDAI component institutionalizes functional academic assessment of clients, weekly collection of progress monitoring data, and frequent treatment integrity checks within the basic model of behavioral consultation. More generally, behavioral consultation has evolved in many areas, including training of consultants, psychometric criteria, research designs, assessment methods, and outcome measures (Kratochwill, Sladeczek, & Plunge, 1995; Martens & DiGennaro, 2008).

Another indicator of behavioral consultation's favorable prognosis is that the National Association of School Psychologists, an organization of more than 22,000 members, endorsed problem solving—as illustrated by behavioral consultation—as the conceptual foundation of its popular *Best Practices in School Psychology* series (Thomas & Grimes, 2002). Finally, perhaps the clearest evidence for the continued relevance of behavioral consultation is that it is a primary vehicle for carrying out Response-to-Intervention (RtI) activities in U.S. public schools (Erchul & Sheridan, 2008; Kratochwill, Clements, & Kalymon, 2007). Within one model of RtI, a critical step in assessing whether more intensive special education services are needed is evaluating whether children's classroom problems can be effectively addressed through the use of high-quality interventions implemented by following the problem-solving steps delineated in behavioral consultation (Ikeda et al., 2007). Along these lines, it will be interesting to see how behavioral consultants rise to the challenge of integrating evidence-based interventions into their teacher consultations (Martens & DiGennaro, 2008). Although the impact of RtI is just beginning to be observed, we expect it to be a major educational initiative for some time to come, and we expect the status of behavioral consultation to be elevated as a direct result.

REFERENCES

Bergan, J. R. (1977). *Behavioral consultation*. Columbus, OH: Merrill.

Bergan, J. R. (1995). Evolution of a problem-solving model of consultation. *Journal of Educational and Psychological Consultation*, 6, 111–123.

Bergan, J. R., & Kratochwill, T. R. (1990). *Behavioral consultation and therapy*. New York: Plenum.

Bergan, J. R., & Neumann, A. J. (1980). The identification of resources and constraints influencing plan design in consultation. *Journal of School Psychology*, 18, 317–323.

Bergan, J. R., & Tombari, M. L. (1975). The analysis of verbal interactions occurring during consultation. *Journal of School Psychology*, 13, 209–226.

Bergan, J. R., & Tombari, M. L. (1976). Consultant skill and efficiency and the implementation and outcomes of consultation. *Journal of School Psychology*, 14, 3–14.

Brown, D., Pryzwansky, W. B., & Schulte, A. C. (2006). *Psychological consultation and collaboration: Introduction to theory and practice* (6th ed.). Boston: Pearson/Allyn & Bacon.

Busse, R. T., Kratochwill, T. R., & Elliott, S. N. (1995). Meta-analysis for single-case outcomes: Applications to research and practice. *Journal of School Psychology*, 33, 269–285.

Caplan, G. (1970). *The theory and practice of mental health consultation*. New York: Basic Books.

D'Zurilla, T. J., & Goldfried, M. R. (1971). Problem solving and behavior modification. *Journal of Abnormal Psychology*, 78, 107–126.

Erchul, W. P., & Martens, B. K. (2002). *School consultation: Conceptual and empirical bases of practice* (2nd ed.). New York: Kluwer Academic/Plenum.

Erchul, W. P., & Schulte, A. C. (1996). Behavioral consultation as a work in progress: A reply to Witt, Gresham, and Noell. *Journal of Educational and Psychological Consultation*, 7, 345–354.

Erchul, W. P., & Sheridan, S. M. (2008). Overview: The state of scientific research in school consultation. In W. P. Erchul & S. M. Sheridan (Eds.), *Handbook of research in school consultation: Empirical foundations for the field* (pp. 3–12). New York: Taylor & Francis Group/Routledge.

Goodwin, D. L., & Coates, T. J. (1976). *Helping students help themselves*. Englewood Cliffs, NJ: Prentice-Hall.

Haynes, S. N. (1978). *Principles of behavioral assessment*. New York: Gardner Press.

Ikeda, M. J., Rahn-Blakeslee, A., Niebling, B. C., Gustafson, J. K., Allison, R., & Stumme, J. (2007). The Heartland Area Education Agency 11 problem-solving approach: An overview and lessons learned. In S. R. Jimerson, M. K. Burns, & A. M. VanDerHeyden (Eds.), *Handbook of response to intervention: The science and practice of assessment and intervention* (pp. 255–268). New York: Springer.

Jitendra, A. K., DuPaul, G. J., Volpe, R. J., Tresco, K. E., Vile Junod, R. E., Lutz, J. G., et al. (2007). Consultation-based academic intervention for children with attention deficit hyperactivity disorder: School functioning outcomes. *School Psychology Review, 36*, 217–236.

Kratochwill, T. R., & Bergan, J. R. (1990). *Behavioral consultation in applied settings*. New York: Plenum.

Kratochwill, T. R., Bergan, J. R., Sheridan, S. M., & Elliott, S. N. (1998). Assumptions of behavioral consultation: After all is said and done more has been done than said. *School Psychology Quarterly, 13*, 63–80.

Kratochwill, T. R., Clements, M. A., & Kalymon, K. M. (2007). Response to intervention: Conceptual and methodological issues in implementation. In S. R. Jimerson, M. K. Burns, & A. M. VanDerHeyden (Eds.), *Handbook of response to intervention: The science and practice of assessment and intervention* (pp. 25–52). New York: Springer.

Kratochwill, T. R., Elliott, S. N., & Stoiber, K. C. (2002). Best practices in school-based problem-solving consultation. In A. Thomas & J. Grimes (Eds.), *Best practices in school psychology–IV* (pp. 583–608). Bethesda, MD: National Association of School Psychologists.

Kratochwill, T. R., Sladeczek, I., & Plunge, M. (1995). The evolution of behavioral consultation. *Journal of Educational and Psychological Consultation, 6*, 145–157.

Martens, B. K. (1993). A behavioral approach to consultation. In J. E. Zins, T. R. Kratochwill, & S. N. Elliott (Eds.), *Handbook of consultation services for children: Applications in educational and clinical settings* (pp. 65–86). San Francisco: Jossey-Bass.

Martens, B. K., & DiGennaro, F. D. (2008). Behavioral consultation. In W. P. Erchul & S. M. Sheridan (Eds.), *Handbook of research in school consultation: Empirical foundations for the field* (pp. 147–170). New York: Taylor & Francis Group/Routledge.

Medway, F. J., & Updyke, J. F. (1985). Meta-analysis of consultation outcome studies. *American Journal of Community Psychology, 13*, 489–505.

Mortenson, B. P., & Witt, J. C. (1998). The use of weekly performance data to increase teacher implementation of a prereferral academic intervention. *School Psychology Review, 27*, 613–627.

Noell, G. H. (2008). Research examining the relationships among consultation process, treatment integrity, and outcomes. In W. P. Erchul & S. M. Sheridan (Eds.), *Handbook of research in school consultation: Empirical foundations for the field* (pp. 323–341). New York: Taylor & Francis Group/Routledge.

Noell, G. H., Gresham, F. M., & Duhon, G. (1998). Fundamental agreements and epistemological differences in differentiating what was said from what was done in behavioral consultation. *School Psychology Quarterly, 13*, 81–88.

Noell, G. H., & Witt, J. C. (1996). A critical evaluation of five fundamental assumptions underlying behavioral consultation. *School Psychology Quarterly, 11*, 189–203.

Sheridan, S. M., & Kratochwill, T. R. (2007). *Conjoint behavioral consultation: Promoting family-school connections and interventions* (2nd ed.). New York: Springer.

Sheridan, S. M., Welch, M., & Orme, S. F. (1996). Is consultation effective? A review of outcome research. *Remedial and Special Education, 17,* 341–354.

Tharp, R. G., & Wetzel, R. J. (1969). *Behavior modification in the natural environment.* New York: Academic Press.

Thomas, A., & Grimes, J. (Eds.). (2002). *Best practices in school psychology–IV.* Bethesda, MD: National Association of School Psychologists.

Tombari, M. L., & Bergan, J. R. (1978). Consultant cues and teacher verbalizations, judgments, and expectancies concerning children's adjustment problems. *Journal of School Psychology, 16,* 212–219.

Vernberg, E. M., & Reppucci, N. D. (1986). Behavioral consultation. In E. V. Mannino, E. J. Trickett, M. F. Shore, M. G. Kidder, & G. Levin (Eds.), *Handbook of mental health consultation* (pp. 49–80). Rockville, MD: National Institute of Mental Health.

Wilkinson, L. A. (2006). Monitoring treatment integrity: An alternative to the "consult and hope" strategy in school-based behavioural consultation. *School Psychology International, 27,* 426–438.

Witt, J. C., Gresham, F. M., & Noell, G. H. (1996a). The effectiveness and efficiency of behavioral consultation: Differing perspectives about epistemology and what we know. *Journal of Educational and Psychological Consultation, 7,* 355–360.

Witt, J. C., Gresham, F. M., & Noell, G. H. (1996b). What's behavioral about behavioral consultation? *Journal of Educational and Psychological Consultation, 7,* 327–344.

2

BEHAVIORAL ASSESSMENT
IN THE SCHOOLS

T. STEUART WATSON AND TONYA S. WATSON

From a traditional perspective, *behavioral assessment* has been viewed as a means of measuring one of the four dimensions of behavior (i.e., frequency or rate, latency, intensity, and duration; Bellack & Hersen, 1988). Although there is considerable merit in developing procedures and methodologies for measuring the dimensions of behavior, there are other assessment activities that are subsumed under a much broader definition of behavioral assessment, particularly as it is applied in the school setting. This expanded scope of behavioral assessment includes (a) measuring the dimensions of behavior as well as (b) analyzing antecedent events (i.e., structural analysis), (c) analyzing extra-environmental events (e.g., setting events, motivating operations), (d) conducting a functional behavior assessment, and (e) using single-subject methodology to promote data-based decision making. This chapter covers all five of these areas, as each makes substantial contributions that compose a thorough behavioral assessment. We begin, however, by briefly discussing the premises of behavioral assessment and general assessment methods.

PREMISES OF BEHAVIORAL ASSESSMENT

Prior to conducting a behavioral assessment, it is important that practitioners understand the basic premises that underlie the overall process and the various methodologies. It should be noted that these premises are based on a practical application of behavioral assessment methodologies and subsume some of the psychometric assumptions noted by Gresham and Lambros (1998).

The first of these premises is that assessment should be linked to intervention and/or decision making. That is, data from the assessment should help further operationalize or clarify target behaviors, provide a reliable and valid estimate of problem strength, yield information useful for determining whether intervention is necessary, and be useful for intervention planning and for evaluating the outcome of treatment.

The second premise is that low-inference methods (e.g., direct observation, functional assessment) are preferred over high-inference methods (e.g., rating scales and interviews). That is, the more direct one can be in assessing behavior, the more likely it is that accurate decisions will be made at each step of the process.

Third, a thorough assessment should provide an explanation for why the behavior occurs. This explanation is derived on the basis of assessing and understanding the role of multiple variables in the existing environment (e.g., motivating operations, temporally proximate antecedents, consequences) and how these variables interact with the individual and/or organismic variables.

The fourth premise is based on the assumption that behavior is lawful. That is, behaviors do not occur randomly and haphazardly, even when they seem to occur "out of the blue." The task, then, is to identify the variables that are having a direct impact on the student's behavior.

Fifth, repeated measurements of behavior allow for more definitive statements about the causal environmental variables. Behavior assessment involves collecting samples of behavior. Each observation, for example, is a sample of behavior in that particular environment. As the number of samples increase, so do the reliability and validity of conclusions about the student–environment interaction.

Sixth and finally, information from a variety of sources and methods is preferred so that the practitioner can obtain *convergent validity*. Convergent validity refers to the degree to which information from the various sources and methods yield the same general results. When multiple assessment methods point to the same conclusion, one can be more reasonably assured in his or her determination of important variables. Disconvergent data (i.e., multiple methods yield multiple hypotheses) are an immediate cue to the practitioner that more data needs to be collected prior to hypothesizing about person–environment relationships and about treatment direction.

METHODS OF ASSESSMENT

A number of reliable and valid behavioral assessment methods are available to the school practitioner. One of the methods most often utilized by school practitioners is *direct behavior observation* (Cone, 1978; Shapiro & Heick, 2004). Briefly, direct behavior observation refers to observing, monitoring, and recording a behavior as it actually occurs in real time. Direct behavior observation is considered to be one of the foundations of school-based behavioral assessment and is a low-inference methodology. Although there are a wide variety of direct observation coding systems, covering each is beyond the scope of this chapter. For a recent, in-depth review, the reader is referred to Volpe, DiPerna, Hintze, and Shapiro (2005). Prior to actually observing behavior, one must first operationally define the target behavior, determine when and where observation will occur, choose a method for recording behavior (i.e., frequency, duration, interval recording, time sampling), and choose a recording instrument (e.g., paper/pencil, personal digital assistant [PDA], laptop, or one of the published direct behavior coding systems that are available).

For various reasons, it is not always possible to directly observe behavior as it occurs, as is often the case with children who exhibit low-frequency, high-intensity behaviors (i.e., "behavioral earthquakes"). For this and other practical reasons, practitioners might often rely on indirect methods, such as interviews, to obtain information from those in the student's environment who have had the opportunity to observe the behavior. There are many different kinds of interviews available to the practitioner, including those that are semistructured, structured, and a part of a multimethod assessment protocol (e.g., the Achenbach System of Empirically Based Assessment [ASEBA]; Achenbach & Rescorla, 2001). Other interview formats are more dynamic and fluid and are related to discerning the function of a particular behavior (e.g., the Behavioral Stream Interview, Watson & Steege, 2003; the Functional Assessment Informant Record–Teacher, Edwards, 2002). Regardless of the interview format, the overriding goals in a behavioral assessment are to identify (a) the conditions under which the behavior occurs, (b) the contextual factors that may contribute to the problem, (c) extraenvironmental variables, (d) the peer's and teacher's responses to the behavior, (e) related skill and/or performance deficits, and (f) previous and/or ongoing interventions. Although the interview can be beneficial in providing information not readily observed, the information provided by the respondents is limited by their own set of biases about the student and the behavior and the limited scope of their own observations (i.e., subjectivity) and is generally regarded as a high-inference methodology.

As a supplement to direct observations, checklists and rating scales may also be used to identify problem behaviors and to estimate any of the four dimensions of behavior. It is important to remember that rating scales are subject to many of the same biases inherent in interviews. Although practitioners can select from a seemingly endless array of checklists and rating scales, there are a few that have moderate to robust psychometric properties. For instance, the Sutter-Eyberg Student Behavior Inventory (SESBI; Eyberg, 1992; Funderburk & Eyberg, 1989; Funderburk, Eyberg, Rich, & Behar, 2003) allows the teacher to estimate the intensity of 36 disruptive behaviors typically seen in the classroom setting and to determine whether a behavior is problematic in that setting for that teacher. The Child Behavior Checklist, which is part of the ASEBA (Achenbach & Rescorla, 2001), and the Behavior Assessment Scale for Children–Second Edition (Reynolds & Kamphaus, 2004) are norm-referenced instruments that have multiple scales for parents, teachers, and the students themselves and can be used as part of a behavioral assessment to estimate frequency of a wide range of behaviors.

With the proliferation and miniaturization of technology, a number of behavioral constructs may be measured, albeit indirectly, via the computer, PDA, or other video-based means. The primary purpose of many of these computer-based assessments is to assist in diagnosing versus identifying areas in need of intervention (Cawthorpe, 2001). Perhaps the most common constructs measured using computer technology are those that are linked to attention-deficit/hyperactivity disorder (ADHD; i.e., impulsivity and attention). One of the first measures of attention and impulsivity was the Gordon Diagnostic Test, and it is still widely used today (Gordon, 1983). Only two studies, to date, have examined the extent to which computer-based assessments accurately predict these behaviors in the natural environment (Hoerger & Mace, 2006; Solanto et al., 2001). Taken together, the results of these two studies showed that the results obtained from the computerized assessments were significant predictors of impulsivity (i.e., self-control) and classroom behavior (i.e., gross motor behavior, inappropriate vocalizations, inattention, and inappropriate use of materials) among children diagnosed with ADHD. When conducting a comprehensive behavioral assessment, computerized measures may be considered a useful adjunct and another sampling technique in the assessment armamentarium. However, one should not rely on these measures over more direct, classroom-based observations because there may be questions about their psychometric characteristics as well as the influence of computer contextual variables that may affect performance (Kveton, Jelinek, Voboril, & Klimusova, 2007).

MEASURING THE DIMENSIONS OF BEHAVIOR

As mentioned earlier, the dimensions of behavior refer to the frequency or rate of behavior, the duration of a behavior, the relative intensity with which a behavior occurs, and the latency of a behavior. Although each is important, probably the most salient for school-based practitioners are rate and duration of behavior. *Frequency* refers to the absolute number of times that an event occurs (e.g., the number of times that one child hits another). To use a frequency measure most effectively, the target behavior must have a discrete beginning and end (i.e., it must be easy to discern when the behavior starts and stops), and it should not occur at an excessively high rate because it is difficult to accurately record occurrences of behaviors that occur very rapidly.

Rate refers to the number of times per minute that an event occurs (e.g., hitting occurred 12 times in 5 minutes, resulting in a rate of 2.4 hits per minute). Different units of time (seconds, hours, days) may be applicable for various target behaviors. Rate measures are particularly useful because they allow for comparisons across observations of unequal lengths and are considered a direct measure of behavior (Johnston & Pennypacker, 1993). For instance, a school psychologist observes a student during a group reading lesson on 4 separate days. The lengths of the group lessons are 18, 21, 20, and 25 minutes, respectively. By carefully recording the frequency of the target behavior during each of these observations, the school psychologist can convert the frequency to a rate measure (e.g., 2.1 times per minute for Observation 1, 2.6 times per minute for Observation 2, and so on) and compare the measurements across observation periods.

Duration is measured by one of four methods: (a) partial-interval recording, (b) whole-interval recording, (c) momentary-time sampling, and (d) real-time recording. Of these four, the most accurate is real-time recording. In real-time recording, a sample of time is selected (e.g., 45 minutes) and the teacher or psychologist uses a stopwatch to record the actual amount of time the student engages in a target behavior and then converts the resulting amount to a percentage of time. For example, if a student is out of her seat for 29 minutes of the 45-minute observation period, the student is said to be out of her seat 64% of the time. Real-time recording, like rate measures, allows one to make comparisons across observations of unequal lengths. The primary drawbacks to using real-time recording are that it is time intensive and requires considerable response effort on behalf of the observer. Perhaps the most commonly used method for measuring duration is partial-interval recording. When using partial-interval recording, an observation period is divided into equal time units (typically 10 seconds) and the behavior is scored as occurring if it occurs at any point during that interval. The difference between partial and whole interval is that, with whole interval, the behavior must occur during the entire 10-second interval to be scored as occurring. The number of intervals in which the behavior occurred is divided by the total number of intervals to yield a percentage of intervals. Thus, one can say that the behavior occurred during X% of the intervals for any given observation. A percentage of intervals statement does not really give information about rate or frequency and is considered to be an indirect measure of duration.

Intensity is difficult to operationalize and measure in a school setting. That is, how does one quantitatively measure the relative intensity of a tantrum or a student's screaming? It would be difficult and cost prohibitive to purchase a decibelometer to measure the loudness of a child's tantrums or calling out in the classroom. Perhaps the most parsimonious means of measuring intensity is through the use of a subjective rating scale (e.g., a 1–10 scale in which 1 is the least intense and 10 is the most intense). These types of subjective scales have been shown to be useful and valid for rating the intensity of pain behaviors (Allen & Matthews, 1998) as well as behaviors that occur in a classroom setting (e.g., the SESBI). As part of the behavioral assessment process, a teacher can be asked to rate the intensity level of multiple behaviors at any given time using an informal scale, which adds another dimension to an existing assessment and provides another criterion against which to evaluate the effectiveness of treatment. For instance, a student may still disrupt the class seven times per day, but the intensity of each disruption has decreased from 9 (highly intense disruption) to 2 (very low-disruptive intensity). Adding an assessment of intensity may, as this example illustrates, effect decisions about the efficacy of treatment.

Although *latency* is an important behavioral dimension, it is probably not often assessed. To better understand the role and importance of latency, consider the situation in which a student is referred for noncompliance, yet observations show that the student is almost always eventually compliant. To illustrate this point, consider the case of a teacher who tells a student to return to his seat and begin working on an assignment that was just given to him. The student walks slowly around the class, talks to peers, picks up and looks at objects, sharpens his pencil, and returns to his seat to begin working. The problem described is one of latency. That is, an excessive amount of time elapses between giving an instruction and either initiating behavior that is consistent with the instruction or completing the instruction. The obvious disadvantage of measuring latency is that the observer is required to closely monitor and record the instruction given, the behavior during the latency period, and the behavior that is consistent with the direction. In some instances, this may take 10 or 15 minutes. The primary advantage is that the link between assessment and intervention is very clear in the sense that the target will be to reduce the latency, which could then eliminate the irritating behaviors that occur during the latency period.

ANALYSIS OF ANTECEDENT EVENTS

Antecedent events are those stimuli that occur immediately before an identified target behavior occurs. Functionally, they can be thought of as triggers or cues for a behavior. The obvious advantage to identifying and measuring antecedents is that by doing so, the practitioner can manipulate them so as to change the likelihood that a particular behavior will occur. In schools, such broad events as task difficulty, transitions, physical proximity, and verbal instructions may act as antecedents for interfering behavior.

There are a number of different methodologies for identifying these events and assessing their role in triggering a behavior. This process of analyzing antecedents may be referred to as a *structural analysis* (Watson & Steege, 2003). One such methodology is identifying a possible antecedent, such as task difficulty, and then measuring the interfering behavior under differing levels of task difficulty using a recording instrument such as the Task Difficulty Antecedent Analysis Form (Watson & Steege, 2003). Recording the occurrence of interfering behavior under differing levels of task difficulties allows one to make statements about the conditions that precede behavior. For example, one could say that interfering behavior was five times as frequent when the student was presented with a very difficult task when compared with either moderate or easy tasks. The same basic methodology can be applied to almost any event that is temporally proximate and prior to the target behavior.

Analysis of antecedent events can be incorporated into other behavioral assessment methodologies such as direct behavioral observation and interviews. When conducting a behavioral observation, for example, one can note the stimuli that are temporally proximate to the interfering behavior and look for patterns in terms of either the specific stimulus or the stimuli that share common features. Although one cannot make causal statements about the relationship between the stimulus event and interfering behavior on the basis of such an observation, the information does allow one to begin formulating hypotheses about the conditions that trigger the interfering behavior, hypotheses that can be more formally tested using other methodologies. When conducting interviews, questions about when and where the behavior occurs, what other events are co-occurring with the target behavior, and what the peers and teacher were doing right before the behavior also allows one to identify possible cues for the interfering behavior.

ASSESSING EXTRA-ENVIRONMENTAL EVENTS

In terms of assessing behavior, one of the most difficult tasks is assessing the impact of events that are proximally and temporally distant from the target behavior. These proximally and temporally distant events compose a special class of antecedents called *setting events* and *motivating operations*. Although there is a robust conceptual and theoretical basis for these events (Friman & Hawkins, 2006), there is less empirical research on assessing and manipulating setting events and motivating operations for changing behavior. Although there is considerable disagreement on what actually constitutes a setting event (Bijou, 1993; Kantor, 1959; Kennedy & Meyer, 1998;

Leigland, 1984; Smith & Iwata, 1997; Wahler & Fox, 1981), in this chapter we use the term *setting events* to refer to the broad set of contextual variables that influence the relative strength of an antecedent stimulus that ultimately impacts behavior (Ray & Watson, 2001). This definition is consistent with Bijou and Baer's (1978) definition in which they described setting events as "environmental events or conditions which or suppress established behavior-environment relationships by altering the reinforcing strengths and characteristics of the particular stimulus and response functions involved in an interaction" (p. 26).

In practical terms, motivating operations are events that motivate a student to engage in a particular behavior and make the resulting consequences either a more potent reinforcer or a punisher. It is important to remember that, by definition, motivating operations exert momentary, not permanent, influences on behavior and its consequences. Although assessment of setting events and motivating operations is not part and parcel of every school-based behavioral assessment, it can be a useful procedure when results from other assessment methodologies are providing inconclusive or conflicting results. For example, Ray and Watson (2001) presented results from three school-based experimental functional analyses of normally developing students that were initially inconclusive (i.e., results were highly variable and demonstrated no clearly discernible controlling function). However, when the results of the functional analysis are examined according to whether or not an idiosyncratic motivating event occurred at home, the results of the functional analysis became clear. In this study, motivating operations were measured by the parents and researchers completing a checklist of possible events. Examples of motivating operations for these three students included sleeping less than 5 hours the previous night, waking up late in the morning before school, and engaging in a morning clean-up routine as a result of nocturnal enuresis.

To accurately assess the potential role that motivating operations may play in the occurrence of interfering behavior at school, one must first determine—through functional assessment procedures—that more temporally proximate events (i.e., antecedents and consequences) cannot adequately explain the behavior. Second, the psychologist should conduct interviews with parents and teachers to detect patterns of variability so that possible motivating events can be identified. And third, some type of checklist, such as that employed by Ray and Watson (2001), can be used to correlate the occurrence/nonoccurrence of interfering behavior with specific motivating events.

A number of other researchers have used procedures similar to those of Ray and Watson (2001) to identify motivating operations and subsequently treat interfering behavior. O'Reilly (1995), for instance, found that sleep deprivation was associated with an increased frequency of aggressive behavior in a 31-year-old adult with a severe developmental disability. Kennedy and Meyer (1996) found that sleep deprivation and allergy symptoms were associated with increases in problem behavior for two students and one student, respectively, with developmental disabilities. An interesting study by Northup, Fusilier, Swanson, Roane, & Borrero (1997) showed that the selection and effectiveness of edibles as reinforcers was adversely affected by the presence of methylphenidate (i.e., methylphenidate momentarily altered the reinforcing effectiveness of edibles as reinforcers). Taken together, these studies illustrate the potential advantages of including the assessment of motivating events in some, but not necessarily in all, cases. As mentioned previously, the effort required to go beyond temporally proximate stimuli and assess motivating events should probably be limited to those situations in which the assessment yields equivocal and/or uninterpretable results.

FUNCTIONAL BEHAVIOR ASSESSMENT

Since the publication of seminal work by Bijou, Peterson, and Ault (1968); Carr (1977); and Iwata, Dorsey, Slifer, Bauman, and Richman (1982/1994), there has been tremendous interest in assessing behavioral function and designing treatment on the basis of the identified function. Although functional analysis methodology was pioneered on individuals with severe developmental disabilities, it has been extended to individuals with mild, moderate, and no disabilities. Although a number of methods are subsumed under the broad category of functional assessment—including functional analysis—the term *functional assessment* typically refers to assessment procedures that are not an experimental functional analysis of behavior.

As Watson and Steege (2003) noted, there are three general categories of functional assessment methodologies: (a) direct behavior observation, (b) indirect assessment, and (c) direct descriptive assessment. Before a behavioral observation is conducted, an interview should be scheduled with the referring person to identify and operationally define target behavior(s), select a time for observation, and perhaps collect preliminary information about possible antecedents and consequences. Direct observation, at least as part of functional assessment, involves more than merely measuring one of the dimensions of behavior. When conducting a direct behavior observation in an attempt to discern function, the observer must carefully note the antecedents (e.g., time; setting; immediate behavior of student, teacher, and peers) and consequences (e.g., behavior of the student, teacher, peers; effect of the consequences on the targeted dimension of the interfering behavior) that are temporally proximate to the target behavior.

Indirect assessment, as the term implies, involves assessing student behavior without directly measuring the target behavior. Typically, indirect assessment takes the form of interviews (e.g., the Behavioral Stream Interview; Watson & Steege, 2003) and forms that preliminarily identify antecedents (e.g., Antecedent Variables Assessment Form; Watson & Steege, 2003), consequences (e.g., Consequence Variables Assessment Form; Watson & Steege, 2003), and the individual variables (e.g., Individual Variables Assessment Form; Watson & Steege) that may be related to the interfering behavior. Indirect assessment may also involve the use of ancillary methodologies such as those described in the computerized assessment section of this chapter.

Direct descriptive assessment involves more than merely observing behavior as described above. Although measurement of behavioral dimension is one component, there are additional activities that make this procedure more comprehensive and provide information about functional variables. For instance, the Task Difficulty Antecedent Analysis Form that was described earlier is one example of a direct descriptive procedure that specifically seeks to assess the relationship between a specific antecedent (i.e., task difficulty) and interfering behavior. Another useful procedure is to complete the Conditional Probability Record (CPR), whereby the observer can record the occurrence of a range of antecedents and consequences and derive probability estimates on the basis of the data. For example, one may discover after completing the CPR that the probability of interfering following a teacher-issued verbal reprimand is .82, whereas the probability of interfering behavior following a teacher reminder is only .08. In addition, the CPR also provides similar probability estimates for consequence variables. Although information obtained from the CPR is not unequivocally causal in nature, repeated observations can provide robust information about the likelihood of interfering behavior following specific antecedent events as well as the likelihood of those behaviors resulting in specific reinforcing consequences.

When conducting a functional assessment, the school psychologist must be careful to avoid the following five typical errors when evaluating the data:

- *Recency error of perception*, which typically occurs during interviews, refers to instances whereby the most recent incident of the interfering behavior is recalled and the function of the behavior is inferred on the basis of the most recent incident.
- *Primacy error of perception*, which also typically occurs during interviews, refers to instances whereby the first incident of the interfering behavior is recalled and the function of all subsequent occurrences of the behavior are inferred on the basis of that first incident.
- *Error of inaccurate functional behavioral assessment*, which can occur during any functional assessment procedure, most typically occurs when only very cursory procedures are used to determine function. Simply, this error refers to hypothesizing the incorrect function because of incomplete data.
- *Error of misplaced precision*, which typically occurs during behavioral observations, involves undue emphasis on data collec-

tion that requires considerable effort (e.g., frequency counts of multiple behaviors) but yields little to no information regarding controlling variables, patterns, or relationships among the multiple behaviors.

- *Error of association*, which can occur during any behavioral assessment or functional assessment procedure, occurs when two events are noted/observed to be "associated" but with no additional evidence that there is a causal relationship.

SINGLE-SUBJECT METHODOLOGY

One of the basic premises of behavioral assessment is that the data collected assist in making decisions about the necessity and effectiveness of treatment. When determining whether treatment is necessary, school psychologists can conduct direct behavioral observations of the target student's behavior and compare it with the data collected for another student in the same classroom. For instance, a referred student who is out of her seat an average of 63% of the time during math instruction may, at first glance, appear to be problematic. However, comparison data show that the average amount of time that her peers are out of their seats during the same time period is 57%. Collecting baseline data for both the referred student and the comparison students allows the school psychologist to answer several questions, such as the following:

- Does the referred student's behavior differ from that of his or her peers?
- Do the data indicate that an individual or larger scale intervention is needed?
- Is the behavior for the target student stable, getting worse, or getting better without intervention?
- Are there other problems occurring concurrent with the referral problem?

A thorough behavioral assessment should yield data that answers these basic questions. Repeated, brief observations of the target behavior allow one to establish a baseline level on any of the four dimensions of the behavior prior to intervention. This baseline level then provides the standard against which treatment effects will be measured. The simplest means of evaluating treatment effectiveness is through the use of an A-B design. An A-B design consists of a baseline phase (A) followed by a treatment phase (B). Data between the phases are compared to determine whether the intervention is impacting the target behavior in the desired direction. Shriver and Watson (2005) noted that, although this design does not allow one to draw conclusive statements regarding the controlling function of treatment, it does allow one to make decisions on the basis of data gathered in the natural environment. Barlow and Hersen (1973) also noted that the A-B design is well suited for applied settings, such as schools, in which the practitioner may not have the luxury of conducting more extensive, methodologically rigorous designs. Foster, Watson, Meeks, and Young (2002) recommended a number of other simple designs that school-based practitioners can use to increase accountability for practice, such as the A-B-A-B, multiple baseline, and changing criterion designs. All of these designs are particularly suited to assessing the effects of interventions in schools and typically require less effort than other more rigorous single-subject designs.

CONCLUSION

The development of functional assessment methodology has greatly expanded the scope of behavioral assessment. School psychologists must still measure the dimensions of behavior so that data-based decisions may be made about whether treatment is indicated and, if so, the effectiveness of treatment. Going further, however, the school-based practitioner should use the methodologies described in this chapter to generate hypotheses about the probable function of behavior. Treatment can then be implemented while measuring the impact of the intervention on the target behavior using the single-subject methodology previously described. Perhaps the most important aspects of behavioral assessment that one should remember are the following:

- Direct measures of behavior are preferable over indirect methods.
- The use of low effort measures and procedures may help maximize compliance with monitoring and recording.
- The use of data to drive decision making about both the need for and the effectiveness of intervention is a best practices model.

Behavioral assessment is the cornerstone of behavioral interventions in the schools. Without conducting a thorough assessment, one cannot identify the most salient variables that are impacting a student's behavior in school and cannot determine whether that student's behavior is significantly different from that of his or her peers. Furthermore, without conducting a behavioral assessment, one cannot make empirical decisions about the efficacy of an intervention.

REFERENCES

Achenbach, T. M., & Rescorla, L. A. (2001). *Manual for the ASEBA school-age forms and profiles*. Burlington: University of Vermont, Research Center for Children, Youth, and Families.

Allen, K. D., & Matthews, J. R. (1998). Behavior management of recurrent pain in children. In T. S. Watson & F. M. Gresham (Eds.), *Handbook of child behavior therapy* (pp. 263–286). New York: Plenum.

Barlow, D. H., & Hersen, M. (1973). Single-case experimental designs: Uses in applied clinical research. *Archives of General Psychiatry, 29*, 319–325.

Bellack, A. S., & Hersen, M. (1988). *Behavioral assessment: A practical handbook* (3rd ed.). New York: Pergamon.

Bijou, S. W. (1993). *Behavior analysis of child development.* Reno, NV: Context Press.

Bijou, S. W., & Baer, D. M. (1978). *Behavior analysis of child development.* Englewood Cliffs, NJ: Prentice-Hall.

Bijou, S. W., Peterson, R. F., & Ault, M. H. (1968). A method to integrate descriptive and experimental field studies at the level of data and empirical concepts. *Journal of Applied Behavior Analysis, 1*, 175–191.

Carr, E. G. (1977). The motivation of self-injurious behavior: A review of some hypotheses. *Psychological Bulletin, 84*, 800–816.

Cawthorpe, D. (2001). An evaluation of a computer-based psychiatric assessment: Evidence for expanded use. *CyberPsychology and Behavior, 4*, 503–510.

Cone, J. D. (1978). The behavioral assessment grid (BAG): A conceptual framework and taxonomy. *Behavior Therapy, 9*, 882–888.

Edwards, R. P. (2002). A tutorial for using the Functional Assessment Informant Record–Teachers (FAIR-T). *Proven Practice: Prevention and Remediation Solutions for Schools, 4*, 31–38.

Eyberg, S. (1992). Parent and teacher behavior inventories for the assessment of conduct problem behaviors in children. In L. VandeCreek, S. Knapp, & T. L. Jackson (Eds.), *Innovations in clinical practice: A sourcebook* (Vol. 11). Sarasota, FL: Professional Resource Press.

Foster, L., Watson, T. S., Meeks, C., & Young, J. S. (2002). Single subject research design for school counselors: Becoming an applied researcher. *Professional School Counseling, 6*, 146–154.

Friman, P. C., & Hawkins, R. O. (2006). Contributions of establishing operations to antecedent intervention: Clinical implications of motivating events. In J. K. Luiselli (Ed.), *Antecedent assessment and intervention: Supporting children and adults with developmental disabilities in community settings* (pp. 31–52). Baltimore: Paul H. Brookes.

Funderburk, B. W., & Eyberg, S. M. (1989). Psychometric characteristics of the Sutter-Eyberg student behavior inventory: A school behavior rating scale for use with preschool children. *Behavioral Assessment, 11*, 297–313.

Funderburk, B. W., Eyberg, S. M., Rich, B. A., & Behar, L. (2003). Further psychometric evaluation of the Eyberg and Behar rating scales for parents and teachers of preschoolers. *Early Education and Development, 14*, 67–81.

Gordon, M. (1983). *The Gordon Diagnostic System.* DeWitt, NY: Gordon Systems.

Gresham, F. M., & Lambros, K. M. (1998). Behavioral and functional assessment. In T. S. Watson & F. M. Gresham (Eds.), *Handbook of child behavior therapy* (pp. 3–22). New York: Plenum.

Hoerger, M. L., & Mace, F. C. (2006). A computerized test of self-control predicts classroom behavior. *Journal of Applied Behavior Analysis, 39,* 147–159.

Iwata, B. A., Dorsey, M. F., Slifer, K. J., Bauman, K. E., & Richman, G. S. (1994). Toward a functional analysis of self-injury. *Journal of Applied Behavior Analysis, 27,* 197–209. (Reprinted from *Analysis and Intervention in Developmental Disabilities, 2,* 3–20, 1982)

Johnston, J. M., & Pennypacker, H. S. (1993). *Strategies and tactics of behavioral research* (2nd ed.). Hillsdale, NJ: Erlbaum.

Kantor, J. R. (1959). *Interbehavioral psychology* (2nd ed.). Bloomington, NJ: Principia Press.

Kennedy, C. H., & Meyer, K. A. (1996). Sleep deprivation, allergy symptoms, and negatively reinforced problem behavior. *Journal of Applied Behavior Analysis, 29,* 133–135.

Kennedy, C. H., & Meyer, K. A. (1998). Establishing operations and the motivation of challenging behavior. In J. K. Luiselli & M. J. Cameron (Eds.), *Antecedent control: Innovative approaches to behavioral support* (pp. 329–346). Baltimore: Paul H. Brookes.

Kveton, P., Jelinek, M., Voboril, D., & Klimusova, H. (2007). Computer-based tests: The impact of test design and problem of equivalency. *Computers in Human Behavior, 23,* 32–51.

Leigland, S. (1984). On "setting events" and related concepts. *The Behavior Analyst, 7,* 41–45.

Northup, J., Fusilier, I., Swanson, V., Roane, H., & Borrero, J. (1997). An evaluation of methylphenidate as a potential establishing operation for some common classroom reinforcers. *Journal of Applied Behavior Analysis, 30,* 615–625.

O'Reilly, M. F. (1995). Functional analysis and treatment of escape-maintained aggression correlated with sleep deprivation. *Journal of Applied Behavior Analysis, 28,* 225–226.

Ray, K. P., & Watson, T. S. (2001). Analysis of the effects of temporally distant events on school behavior. *School Psychology Quarterly, 16,* 324–342.

Reynolds, C. R., & Kamphaus, R. W. (2004). *Behavior Assessment System for Children* (2nd ed.). Circle Pines, MN: American Guidance Service.

Shapiro, E. S., & Heick, P. (2004). School psychologist assessment practices in the evaluation of students referred for social/behavioral/emotional problems. *Psychology in the Schools, 41,* 551–561.

Shriver, M. D., & Watson, T. S. (2005). Bridging the great divide: Linking research to practice in scholarly publications. *Journal of Evidence Based Practices for Schools, 6,* 5–18.

Smith, R. G., & Iwata, B. A. (1997). Antecedent influences on behavior disorders. *Journal of Applied Behavior Analysis, 30,* 343–375.

Solanto, M. V., Abikoff, H., Sonuga-Barke, S. B., Schachar, R., Logan, G. D., Wigal, T., et al. (2001). The ecological validity of delay aversion and response inhibition as measures of impulsivity in AD/HD: A supplement to the NIMH multimodal treatment study of AD/HD. *Journal of Abnormal Child Psychology, 29*, 215–228.

Volpe, R. J., DiPerna, J. C., Hintze, J. M., & Shapiro, E. S. (2005). Observing students in classroom settings: A review of seven coding schemes. *School Psychology Review, 34*, 454–474.

Wahler, R. G., & Fox, J. J. (1981). Setting events in applied behavior analysis: Toward a conceptual and methodological expansion. *Journal of Applied Behavior Analysis, 14*, 327–338.

Watson, T. S., & Steege, M. W. (2003). *Conducting school-based functional behavioral assessments: A practitioner's guide.* New York: Guilford.

3

INTRODUCTION TO FUNCTIONAL
BEHAVIORAL ASSESSMENT

GEORGE H. NOELL AND KRISTIN A GANSLE

Functional assessment is an approach to the assessment and treatment of behavioral concerns that grew out of behavior analysis. Like behavior analysis, functional assessment focuses on how the environment influences behavior (Kinch, Lewis-Palmer, Hagan-Burke, & Sugai, 2001). Its goal is to determine why an individual engages in a behavior and to use that information to develop an intervention that is matched to the needs of the individual. The focus is commonly on what environmental variables, such as work demands, set the occasion for challenging behavior and what the consequences are that maintain that behavior (Ingram, Lewis-Palmer, & Sugai, 2005). For example, functional assessment of a challenging behavior might reveal that a student does so because disruptive behavior results in escape from aversive academic work demands (e.g., McComas, Hoch, Paone, & Elroy, 2000).

Perhaps the most fundamental difference between functional assessment and traditional, nomothetic, norm-referenced assessment is their assessment targets. Traditional assessment commonly has focused on the assessment of traits of individuals that have been thought to be stable within individuals across long (e.g., IQ; Humphreys, 1992) or moderately long (e.g., anxiety; Lowe, 2007) time frames but that vary across individuals. In contrast, functional assessment has sought to identify the environmental events that regulate the occurrence of specific behaviors (Iwata, Dorsey, Silfer, Bauman, & Richman, 1994). The relationship between environment and behavior is conceptualized as variable both within individuals and across time.

The fundamental differences between the assessment targets of traditional and functional assessment lead naturally to several additional critical differences. First, nomothetic or traditional assessment has emphasized normative comparisons with a resulting emphasis on making distinctions between individuals. In other words, how does this individual compare with the other individuals who have been assessed? In contrast, functional assessments typically have emphasized comparisons within individuals, such as discovering that challenging behavior is more evident when it leads to peer attention than when it does not. In other words, why is this individual's behavior more challenging in this situation than in that one? Second, within traditional assessment, variability in performance across occasions or items has commonly been regarded as measurement error relative to the true score of the underlying construct (Ghiselli, Campbell, & Zedeck, 1981). Individuals are considered to possess characteristics that could be represented accurately by one true score that would not vary, if only all sources of error that cause the score to fluctuate in nonmeaningful ways could be removed. In contrast, in functional assessment, variability in performance within the individual across assessments is important and worthy of attention. In fact, the essential goal of the functional assessment is to identify the environmental variables that will account for those differences (Iwata et al., 1994). A third difference emerges naturally from the different treatment across assessment approaches of individual variability. Norm-referenced assessment typically has focused on an assessment of the construct of interest at a single point in time, whereas sound functional assessment requires repeated measures across time. Finally, the different approaches of functional versus traditional assessment to the number of assessment occasions, the standard the behavior is compared to (i.e., norms versus within person), and what is being assessed has led to utility for different purposes. Most technically sound, norm-referenced instruments have evidence to support their adequacy for differentiating among individuals, which may contribute to classification and screening decisions. In contrast, functional assessments do not provide data that may contribute to diagnostic decisions, but they have accumulated considerable evidence for their utility in treatment planning (Hanley, Iwata, & McCord, 2003).

Although it has intuitive appeal for treatment design because of its capacity to figure out the "Why?" and suggest the "What's next?", functional assessment is not without controversy. Concern has been raised that the support for its use has been liberally extrapolated from initial positive evidence with individuals with severe disabilities and with young children to children in schools, and that its methods are too cumbersome to be adapted to many school contexts (Sasso, Conroy, Peck Stichter, & Fox, 2001). Additionally, concern has been raised that when examined at the group level, function-based interventions may not be more effective than other environmentally based interventions (Gresham et al., 2004).

Ironically, the one domain in which functional assessment is legally mandated is also the context in which it may be most impractical to conduct, and in which we have less evidence about its effectiveness (disciplinary action against students protected under the Individuals With Disabilities Education Act [IDEA]; see Witt, Daly, & Noell, 2000). IDEA 2004 mandates that a student with a disability whose placement has been changed as a result of inappropriate behavior shall "receive a functional behavioral assessment . . . designed to address the behavior violation so that it does not recur" (IDEA, 2004). It is within the context of the requirements of Public Law 101-476 (Education of the Handicapped Act Amendments of 1990 [the 1990 reauthorization of IDEA]) that the term *functional behavioral assessment* (FBA) was actually coined. In many cases of school suspension and expulsion, the student is removed from the school setting before it is clear that a FBA is needed. In that case, meaningful information about the behavior and the environment(s) in which it occurs is impossible to collect. Furthermore, in many instances of suspension and expulsion, the target behavior is a very low-frequency behavior or a singular event for which valid FBA methods have yet to be developed. To our knowledge, FBA studies examining assessment and treatment of important and disturbing behaviors such as physical fighting between typically developing adolescents, gang-related activity, and children and adolescents bringing weapons to school have not been published.

Space limitations preclude a full discussion of the issues and arguments surrounding the use and misuse of FBA. Part of the challenge inherent in developing such a discussion is that FBA is not a single assessment methodology but a family of methods that share a common goal. These methods range from procedures that are easily implemented but have limited evidence of validity, to complex methods whose utility may be limited to select settings and populations (Sasso et al., 2001). In considering the more demanding FBA tools, we argue that FBA is a tool that has limited but important uses. It may be somewhat like surgery in that it is frequently expensive, complex, includes risk, is not useful for many diagnoses, and yet may be critical to achieving positive outcomes for the child. It also may be similar to surgery in that it requires an elaborate set of professional competencies that not all psychological and educational practitioners may possess (Iwata et al., 2000). We also argue that FBA need not be the tool of choice for all or even most of the referrals in applied psychology or education. For many common referral concerns, interventions have been developed that, when matched to that referral concern, are effective for many individuals without consideration of the consequences that may have maintained the behavior prior to intervention (Gresham et al., 2004; Weiss & Weisz, 1995). We would argue that FBA may be best conceptualized as a general method for approaching referrals and as a specific assessment model for more difficult referrals that have not responded to less intensive assessment and/or intervention efforts.

CONCEPTUAL FRAMEWORK OF FBA

The conceptual framework underlying FBA was developed within the behavior analytic tradition and includes the critical assessment of behavior variations over time and between environments at the level of the individual. An FBA commonly will focus on why behavior occurs at some times under some conditions but never, rarely, or less often at other times under different conditions. FBA is not the approach for attempting to understand dimensions of individuals that may be considered constant. For example, FBA would not be helpful in understanding why a student who is blind does not see or why a student with Down Syndrome learns more slowly than peers. FBA can be useful for assessing why a student with a developmental delay or a sensory impairment may act out at some times but not at others. One of the defining characteristics of FBA is that it seeks to identify the factors that control the occurrence or nonoccurrence of behavior. It is encouraging that this focus on the variability in behavior and how changeable environmental events influence it aligns well with educational environments. Educators commonly seek to arrange environments to achieve a change in behavior, be it reading, social skills, or aggression.

Although applied behavior analysis is based on a wider range of defining features (see Baer, Wolf, & Risley, 1968), FBA draws in particular on four fundamental, reasonable assumptions that have strong empirical support. First, FBA is based on the assumption that how an individual behaves is strongly influenced by his or her environment. The tremendous volume and variety of research demonstrating the environment's influence on human behavior is difficult to argue against. Second, FBA is based on the assumption that how the environment influences behavior is idiographic; in other words, how the same environmental events will affect individuals differently. For example, a student may exhibit more challenging behavior when given difficult task demands without prior instruction than if he or she is provided instruction regarding the task before it is presented (Ebanks & Fisher, 2003). Similarly, one student may find teacher attention highly reinforcing whereas for another, escape from work demands may be far more potent (e.g., Marcus, Vollmer, Swanson, Roane, & Ringdahl, 2001). Third, FBA is based on the assumption that despite strong individual differences in how specific elements of the environment may influence people, there are strong underlying principles that influence all people. For example, although one student may be reinforced by attention and another by escape from work demands, the fundamental principle of reinforcement remains the same. Finally, changing the environment is a powerful way to change behavior. A wealth of data suggests that by changing teaching contexts or providing interventions that change the environment, it is possible to change student behavior (Swanson & Hoskyn, 1998). In fact, for children and youth, environmentally based interventions generally have the strongest empirical support (Weiss & Weisz, 1995).

Although function-based assessment technologies have been extended in a number of ways, the seminal work in this area began with the implementation of functional analyses (described below) to identify the environmental events that maintained the occurrence of self-injury exhibited by individuals with developmental disabilities (Iwata et al., 1994). These functional analyses attempted to clarify why the challenging behavior occurred. In doing so, they drew together the four fundamental assumptions previously described to guide development of a powerful assessment technology. Specifically, the functional analyses examined how the environment influenced behavior through a common principle of behavior (reinforcement) that was expressed differently across individuals (idiographic reinforcers) and that maintained challenging behavior. Subsequent research has demonstrated that interventions that are derived from such data can be extremely successful in reducing severe problem behavior (e.g., Functional Communication Training; Carr & Durand, 1985).

The balance of this chapter describes functional assessment tools, the data they provide, the issues in their implementation, and the issues in their interpretation. However, it is important to first address two considerations. First, educators, parents, and youth adopt widely varying theories as to why people behave as they do. Common theories include thought processes, personality, spiritual factors, and biological differences. It is not a necessary prerequisite of functional assessment that parents, educators, and youth adopt a behavior analytic view. It is often sufficient to focus on the data and their frequently intuitive implications. For example, an assessment result that indicated that a student was acting out when he was presented with instructional materials above his instructional range was interpreted by his teacher as a lack of ability, by his mother as a lack of self-esteem, and by the first author as escape from aversive demands. However, despite our divergence regarding what the data meant, all three were in nearly perfect accord regarding what needed to be done about the situation. The student needed an adjustment in assignments coupled with supports that would allow him to succeed. It is interesting that although we arrived at the same conclusion from the data, we had somewhat different ideas as to why challenging assignments occasioned acting out.

Second, due to the brevity of this volume, it is not possible to provide the reader with either a detailed description of the principles of FBA or of appropriate supporting materials. Those interested in a thorough introduction to applied behavior analysis might consider the highly readable volume by Cooper, Heron, and Heward (2007). Readers interested in procedural guides to conducting FBA with supporting materials might consider O'Neill et al. (1997); Umbreit, Ferro, Liaupsin, and Lane (2006); Watson and Steege (2003); or Witt et al. (2000).

FUNCTIONAL BEHAVIORAL ASSESSMENT: WHAT IS ASSESSED?

The target of assessment within FBA is the relationship between environmental events and behavior. The goal is to develop a hypothesis about a functional relationship between environmental variables and behavior: How does the occurrence of the target behavior change as a function of specific environmental events (Johnston & Pennypacker, 1980)? For example, assessment data might indicate that a student engages in disruptive behavior in contexts in which disruption is followed by teacher attention, but not in those environments in which disruption is not followed by the same. This description suggests that disruptive behavior occurs as a function of the availability of attention. Stated another way, disruptive behavior continues to occur because it is reinforced by the attention it occasions.

Although functional assessment can attempt to identify any type of connection between alterable dimensions of the environment and behavior, as a practical matter, the available research is dominated by investigation of one type of relationship: the consequences that maintain problematic behavior (Hanley et al., 2003). This type of relationship has dominated the functional assessment research for several good reasons. First, behavior that persists is assumed to persist for a reason. Behavior analysts commonly assume that the reason is reinforcement. Essentially, behaviors that produce consequences that the individual finds reinforcing will be sustained. It is important to bear in mind that reinforcers are idiosyncratic. One student may find teacher attention reinforcing, whereas another may not (Broussard & Northup, 1995). Second, volumes of research have demonstrated that once the consequences that maintain challenging behavior have been identified, changing those consequences can be used to decrease challenging behavior and teach desirable behavior (Carr & Durand, 1985). Third, although subtle and complicated person–environment–behavior interactions have been demonstrated and can be important (e.g., O'Reilly, 1995), for many referred individuals, research has demonstrated that the effects of reinforcement are exceedingly overt and testable. In sum, FBA research typically has focused on the reinforcement contingencies for problem behavior because they are assumed to maintain the behavior, are readily testable, and are powerful tools for changing the problem behavior.

Functional assessment research has generally focused on identifying the reinforcement contingencies that maintain challenging behavior. Positive reinforcement occurs when behavior results in something being added to the environment that increases the occurrences of that behavior in the future. For example, attention that occurs as a result of acting out may reinforce that behavior. Negative reinforcement occurs when a behavior results in the removal of a stimulus or avoidance of a stimulus and this contingency is reinforcing. A classic example in schools is when students escape from work demands by engaging in disruptive behavior (e.g., Burke, Hagan-Burke, & Sugai, 2003). A third type of contingency, automatic reinforcement, is sometimes described in the literature but rarely is tested directly. Behaviors are sometimes described as automatically reinforced when they persist across many contexts independent of socially mediated consequences. This type of reinforcement is certainly a plausible explanation for behaviors that may be self-stimulatory or stereotypical.

Although environmental variables have been less dominant, functional assessment researchers have increasingly examined the importance of environmental variables that occur or are present prior to a behavior of interest (e.g., O'Reilly, Edrisinha, Sigafoos, Lancioni, & Andrews, 2006). These variables have included discriminative stimuli and establishing operations. Discriminative stimuli change behavior because they have been associated with the availability of reinforcement. For example, cursing has led to teacher inattention from some teachers but not from others. If attention is reinforcing, then one would expect that cursing would increase in the presence of the teachers who have attended to it. Establishing operations change the effectiveness of a consequence and evoke behaviors that have led to that reinforcer in the past (Michael, 1982). For example, deprivation is generally described as an establishing operation: A period of independent work might make attention more reinforcing and a period of fasting would likely make food more reinforcing.

Although an FBA can potentially assess any type of behavior–environment relationship, the balance of this chapter focuses primarily on the identification of the consequences that reinforce challenging behavior. Identification of these relationships has a far more thoroughly developed research base and has an extensive literature that demonstrates the treatment utility of assessment of the relationships.

Indirect Assessments

Functional assessment tools vary from those that are easily implemented but have the weakest evidence for treatment utility, to those that are exceedingly complex but have a well-developed literature to support their utility. All functional assessments are likely to begin with an interview. Interviews are useful for establishing rapport, identifying initial treatment targets, establishing collaborative roles, and setting goals. Although a number of guides to interviewing for functional assessment with supporting materials have been produced (e.g., O'Neill et al., 1997; Witt et al., 2000), no definitive source has emerged that is broadly accepted as the standard approach to interviewing. Aside from the general organizational features that are necessary for a consultative interview (see Bergan & Kratochwill, 1990), functional assessment interviews typically will focus on the situations in which the behavior occurs and those in which it does not, how often the behavior occurs, and what the typical consequences of the behavior are. The answers to these questions can be used to guide the selection of subsequent assessment occasions and procedures. How a functional assessment is developed should be strongly influenced by the frequency, contextual specificity, and nature of the target behavior.

In addition to interviews, some practitioners use rating scales for a structured format in which to obtain caregiver reports regarding behavior and consequences. Two commonly cited rating scales are the Motivational Assessment Scale (Durand & Crimmins, 1988) and the Questions About Behavioral Function (Paclawskyj, Matson, Rush, Smalls, & Vollmer, 2000). The outcome of a review of the research literature examining indirect functional measures, including interviews, appears to be largely dependent upon the standard that is used. As Sturmey (1996) noted, researchers generally have produced evidence for agreement between indirect measures and more labor-intensive direct measures. However, replication by researchers other than the instrument developers has frequently been absent or has not been confirmatory (Sturmey). Additionally, a number of methodological concerns such as the source of information regarding the child not being blind to more detailed assessment results have been raised in reviewing the literature regarding indirect assessment (Floyd, Phaneuf, & Wilczynski, 2005).

It seems reasonable to conclude that indirect measures may often be effective in pointing professionals toward hypotheses that will frequently be correct. However, given the modest number of hypotheses commonly examined (escape vs. attention being predominant), it is also plausible that a considerable number of agreements would occur by chance. If the standard applied to the literature is that indirect assessments should help focus, frame, or guide direct functional assessments, then the literature is relatively encouraging. However, if the standard applied to the literature is that indirect assessments should replace direct assessments, no measure has yet emerged that has a sufficiently large and compelling research base to support that it meets this standard. One further rational point is worth considering. It may be the case that indirect assessments will not be able to identify behavioral function reliably because teachers, students, and parents simply do not have the requisite information. No matter how carefully the questions may be posed, informants cannot provide information they do not have.

Descriptive Assessments

Descriptive assessments involve the observation of the target behavior as it naturally occurs in the relevant environments. A wide array of observational methods potentially can be used, but the selection of the observational method in education most often will be guided by the frequency of the target behavior and the environments in which the behavior occurs. For behaviors that occur at moderate to high rates, direct observation by a consultant typically will be necessary. In these instances, it will be unlikely that teachers can both teach and record the occurrence of the behavior. In contrast, low-rate behaviors usually will call for some form of participant recording that is completed by someone who is customarily in the natural environment. If the behavior only occurs once every other day, it may not be possible for a consultant to observe long enough to see even a single instance of the behavior. The following section briefly presents three observational strategies that can contribute to functional assessment; it begins with the simplest observation strategies that generally would be implemented by care providers and progresses to more complex strategies that generally would be implemented by a dedicated observer.

Perhaps the simplest recording method is the scatter plot. In a scatter plot, the day is broken up into meaningful units and the observer, who is often someone already present in the environment, records how often the target behavior occurs within each time block. Examples of recording forms may be found by searching "scatter plot," "behavior recording form," and similar search terms online and may also be found in various published guides (e.g., Witt et al., 2000). The meaningful time blocks are broken up by major activities in the school day. Disruptive behavior has been shown to be much more prevalent during language arts and social studies than at any other time during the day. This might reasonably raise the question of how the assignments and instruction during those two time periods is different from other times during the day when the behavior does not occur. Symons, McDonald, and Wehby (1998) provided a readily accessible example of using scatter plot data as part of a functional assessment.

Antecedent–behavior–consequence (A-B-C) recording has a long tradition of use within behavior analytic assessment (Bijou, Peterson, & Ault, 1968). Its goal is to identify patterns that may suggest function. For example, if acting-out behavior commonly follows handwriting demands and the student is usually sent to the principal's office, resulting in termination of the demand, it is plausible to conjecture that acting out is maintained by escape from handwriting demands. In A-B-C recording, the observer uses narrative recording to note the antecedents that preceded behaviors of interest, what the specific behavior that occurred was, and what consequence followed the behavior. Typically, a natural member of the environment will complete the form if the behavior occurs infrequently (e.g., once or twice per day), but the

A-B-C may be completed by an independent observer. For low-frequency behavior, the recording demands tend to be low, and the amount of time necessary for a consultant to be present to see the behavior may be impractical. In contrast, if the behavior occurs frequently (e.g., several times per hour), the recording demands of completing the A-B-C are likely to be incompatible with other responsibilities such as teaching. For those behaviors, a dedicated observer typically will be needed. A variety of recording formats are available in published resources and can also be found by searching "A-B-C recording form" through Internet search engines.

A third observational strategy is continuous observation and recording. This typically would be accomplished in either a narrative-recording format or an interval-recording procedure. Although narrative recordings can be very helpful when making initial observations with little background information about the case, they generally are regarded as a suboptimal approach because their extensive writing demands can cause the observer to miss important events, and they do not provide for an objective mathematical summary of the data (Witt et al., 2000). Interval recording usually is accomplished by dividing time into discrete blocks and then recording the occurrence of specific behaviors and environmental events within those time blocks using strategies such as partial- or whole-interval recording. Space limitations preclude an extensive discussion of the design of interval-based recording schemes. Interested readers might choose to consult Sulzer-Azaroff and Mayer (1991).

The goal of interval-based observation and recording within a functional assessment is to identify patterns that may suggest function (Lerman & Iwata, 1993). For example, examination of the record may reveal that self-injury is commonly preceded by the student not having teacher attention and is consistently followed by attention. This would suggest that attention may play a role in maintaining self-injury. However, it is important to recognize that any patterns observed in observational data are correlational. It is possible that the connection between attention and self-injury is not functional and that some more intermittent consequence is actually maintaining the behavior. Even more problematic for many observational assessments is the reality that one behavior commonly has many consequences; it often is difficult to sort out which ones might be important and which ones are coincidental. Lerman and Iwata (1993) provided a more detailed discussion of issues in the calculation of relationships between behavior and environmental events and the interpretation of those data.

Functional Analyses and Observational Test Conditions

The gold standard in functional assessment is the functional analysis. A functional analysis is a form of assessment in which a series of test conditions is arranged in which the effects of specific environmental events such as contingencies on the occurrence of behavior are observed. For example, in a functional analysis, the effect of attention and escape from demands on aggressive behavior can be directly observed because the consequences are controlled by the assessment team. These conditions are arranged within a single-subject experimental design so that evidence can be extracted that has strong evidence for internal validity, which permits strong conclusions to be drawn (Iwata et al., 1994). There are hundreds of published studies describing functional analyses (Hanley et al., 2003). Although published functional analysis studies have covered a range of behaviors, settings, and individuals, they are heavily disproportionate in their representation of children with developmental disabilities in hospitals, schools, and institutions. Within the context of schools, functional analyses typically have focused on one of two populations: young students or students with developmental disabilities (e.g., Noell, VanDerHeyden, Gatti, & Whitmarsh, 2001; Umbreit et al., 2006). Research with older students who are nearly typically developing is clearly underdeveloped. Functional analysis results typically are analyzed by graphing data from each of the conditions and identifying the condition(s) in which target behaviors are elevated.

Functional analyses have been conducted both in classrooms and in stand-alone assessment contexts. The tradeoffs between the two contexts present rather striking contrasts. In-class functional analyses are complicated to arrange and manage, but their results are more likely to generalize because they are occurring in the relevant environment. In contrast, functional analyses conducted in dedicated assessment environments may be easier to arrange and/or control but run the risk of generalizing poorly to the target environment (Noell et al., 2001). Implementing one or more brief test conditions in which the effects of controlled environmental conditions can be observed without a full functional analysis may be a practical alternative thereto. The practicality and relevance of full functional analyses in school contexts for the diverse range of populations and concerns confronted by educators have been questioned previously (Gresham et al., 2004). As a practical matter, it may not be possible or relevant to conduct a functional analysis of drug use at school by adolescents. However, it is also the case that for students with developmental disabilities and for younger students who are more nearly typically developing, published models are available describing in-class functional analyses that have been useful and may be practical in some contexts.

LINKING ASSESSMENT DATA TO TREATMENT PLANS IN FUNCTIONAL BEHAVIORAL ASSESSMENT

Although functional assessment has a number of potential uses as a research tool, its primary application in schools has been as an assessment to guide intervention design. An increasingly diverse array of interventions developed from functional analyses has been studied. These have included skill-teaching strategies, changing antecedents, modification of consequences, and combinations of these elements. Function-based treatments predominantly have been based on a few intuitive principles. First, perhaps the most intuitive and most widely studied treatment has been functional extinction (Mazaleski, Iwata, Vollmer, Zarcone, & Smith, 1993). The key and logical element of functional extinction is to block access to the consequence that has been maintaining the challenging behavior. If challenging behavior has served an escape function, escape is blocked. If challenging behavior was reinforced by attention, then attention is withheld when challenging behavior occurs.

A second and similarly intuitive intervention approach is to provide the consequence that has reinforced the problem behavior contingent on the occurrence of a desirable behavior and to place the challenging behavior on extinction (Carr & Durand, 1985). This strategy is described as differential reinforcement of an alternative behavior. It has the desirable property of both reducing the problem behavior and teaching the student a socially acceptable alternative that will still lead to reinforcement. One of the widely researched strategies based on these principles has been described as functional communication training (FCT; Carr & Durand, 1985). In FCT the person is taught a communicative behavior that will permit him or her to ask for a target reinforcer such as a break or attention.

A third intervention option incorporates elements of environmental enrichment and extinction. The procedure has been described as noncontingent reinforcement (NCR; Vollmer, Iwata, Zarcone, Smith, & Mazaleski, 1993). In NCR the relevant reinforcer is provided on a fixed time schedule. For example, a teacher might stop and attend to a student on a fixed time schedule such as once every 5 minutes (NCR—5 minutes). If the schedule is frequent enough, NCR is likely to be very successful in reducing challenging behavior. An individual who has frequent free access to something is unlikely to engage in effortful behavior to get what he or she already has. After the target behavior is reduced, typically the goal is to thin the schedule of the NCR procedure to a manageable one.

SUMMARY

Functional assessment grew out of applied behavior analysis. It was developed to provide a systematic means to isolate the environmental contingencies that maintain significant problem behaviors. Functional assessment is based on several core assumptions. First, environments strongly influence individual behavior. Second, the particular way environments influence individuals is idiographic. Third, despite this idiographic expression, there are general principles that underlie person–environment–behavior relationships that can guide assessment and intervention. Fourth, changing environments is a powerful means of changing behavior. A collection of assessment technologies that can assist in the development of functional hypotheses linking environments and behavior has been derived from these basic principles. These include indirect measures, interviews and rating scales, descriptive measures, observation in the natural environment, and functional analyses. These assessment tools vary considerably in the degree to which they provide a strong basis for hypotheses, are adaptable to diverse concerns, and are practical across diverse contexts. The dominant and intuitive treatment strategies derived from functional assessment have involved withholding access to the consequence that has maintained problem behavior, arranging for that consequence to reinforce a desirable behavior, and arranging the environment so that consequence is likely to lose its reinforcing effect. One of the substantial challenges confronting educators in evaluating this relatively mature assessment and treatment technology is evaluating when it is needed and what intensity of assessment is practical and appropriate to the individual, the environment, and the behavioral concern.

REFERENCES

Baer, D. M., Wolf, M. M., & Risley, T. R. (1968). Some current dimensions of applied behavior analysis. *Journal of Applied Behavior Analysis, 1*, 91–97.

Bergan, J. R., & Kratochwill, T. R. (1990). *Behavioral consultation and therapy*. New York: Plenum Press.

Bijou, S. W., Peterson, R. F., & Ault, M. H. (1968). A method to integrate descriptive and experimental field studies at the level of data and empirical concepts. *Journal of Applied Behavior Analysis, 1*, 175–191.

Broussard, C. D., & Northup, J. (1995). An approach to functional assessment and analysis of disruptive behavior in regular education classrooms. *School Psychology Quarterly, 10*, 151–164.

Burke, M. D., Hagan-Burke, S., & Sugai, G. (2003). The efficacy of function-based interventions for students with learning disabilities who exhibit escape-maintained problem behaviors: Preliminary results from a single-case experiment. *Learning Disability Quarterly, 26*, 15–25.

Carr, E. G., & Durand, V. M. (1985). Reducing behavior problems through functional communication training. *Journal of Applied Behavior Analysis, 18*, 111–126.

Cooper, J. O., Heron, T. E., & Heward, W. L. (2007). *Applied behavior analysis* (2nd ed.). Upper Saddle River, NJ: Pearson Education.

Durand, V. M., & Crimmins, D. B. (1988). Identifying the variables maintaining self-injurious behavior. *Journal of Autism and Developmental Disorders, 18*, 99–117.

Ebanks, M. E., & Fisher, W. W. (2003). Altering the timing of academic prompts to treat destructive behavior maintained by escape. *Journal of Applied Behavior Analysis, 36,* 355–359.

Education of the Handicapped Act Amendments of 1990, Pub. L. No. 101-476, 104 Stat. 1103. (1990).

Floyd, R. G., Phaneuf, R. L., & Wilczynski, S. W. (2005). Measurement properties of indirect assessment methods for functional behavioral assessment: A review of research. *School Psychology Review, 34,* 58–73.

Ghiselli, E. E., Campbell, J. P., & Zedeck, S. (1981). *Measurement theory for the behavioral sciences.* San Francisco: W. H. Freeman.

Gresham, F. M., McIntyre, L. L., Olson-Tinker, H., Dolstra, L., McLaughlin, V., & Van, M. (2004). Relevance of functional behavioral assessment research for school-based interventions and positive behavioral support. *Research in Developmental Disabilities, 25,* 19–37.

Hanley, G. P., Iwata, B. A., & McCord, B. E. (2003). Functional analysis of problem behavior: A review. *Journal of Applied Behavior Analysis, 36,* 147–185.

Humphreys, L. G. (1992). Commentary: What both critics and users of ability tests need to know. *Psychological Science, 3,* 271–274.

Individuals with Disabilities Education Improvement Act. 2004. Pub. L. No. 108-446, 118 Stat. 2647. Retrieved June 17, 2007, from http://idea.ed.gov

Ingram, K., Lewis-Palmer, T., & Sugai, G. (2005). Function-based intervention planning: Comparing the effectiveness of FBA function-based and non-function-based intervention plans. *Journal of Positive Behavior Interventions, 7,* 224–236.

Iwata, B. A., Dorsey, M., Silfer, K., Bauman, K., & Richman, G. (1994). Toward a functional analysis of self-injury. *Journal of Applied Behavior Analysis, 27,* 197–209.

Iwata, B. A., Wallace, M. D., Kahng, S., Lindberg, J. S., Roscoe, E. M., Conners, J., et al. (2000). Skill acquisition in the implementation of functional analysis methodology. *Journal of Applied Behavior Analysis, 33,* 181–194.

Johnston, J. M., & Pennypacker, H. S. (1980). *Strategies and tactics of human behavioral research.* Hillsdale, NJ: Erlbaum.

Kinch, C., Lewis-Palmer, T., Hagan-Burke, S., & Sugai, G. (2001). A comparison of teacher and student functional behavior assessment interview information from low-risk and high-risk classrooms. *Education and Treatment of Children, 24,* 480–494.

Lerman, D. C., & Iwata, B. A. (1993). Descriptive and experimental analyses of variables maintaining self-injurious behavior. *Journal of Applied Behavior Analysis, 26,* 293–319.

Lowe, P. A. (2007). Assessment of the psychometric characteristics of the Adult Manifest Anxiety Scale–Adult Version (AMAS-A) scores with adults. *Individual Differences Research, 5,* 86–105.

Marcus, B. A., Vollmer, T. R., Swanson, V., Roane, H. R., & Ringdahl, J. E. (2001). An experimental analysis of aggression. *Behavior Modification, 25,* 189–213.

Mazaleski, J. L., Iwata, B. A., Vollmer, T. R., Zarcone, J. R., & Smith, R. G. (1993). Analysis of the reinforcement and extinction components in DRO contingencies with self-injury. *Journal of Applied Behavior Analysis, 26,* 143–156.

McComas, J., Hoch, H., Paone, D., & Elroy, D. (2000). Escape behavior during academic tasks: A preliminary analysis of idiosyncratic establishing conditions. *Journal of Applied Behavior Analysis, 33,* 479–493.

Michael, J. (1982). Distinguishing between discriminative and motivational functions of stimuli. *Journal of the Experimental Analysis of Behavior, 37,* 149–155.

Noell, G. H., VanDerHeyden, A. M., Gatti, S. L., & Whitmarsh, E. L. (2001). Functional assessment of the effects of escape and attention on students' compliance during instruction. *School Psychology Quarterly, 16,* 253–269.

O'Neill, R., Horner, R., Albin, R., Sprague, R., Storey, K., & Newton, J. (1997). Functional assessment of problem behavior: A practical assessment guide (2nd ed.). Pacific Grove, CA: Brooks/Cole.

O'Reilly, M. F. (1995). Functional analysis and treatment of escape-maintained aggression correlated with sleep deprivation. *Journal of Applied Behavior Analysis, 28,* 225–226.

O'Reilly, M. F., Edrisinha, C., Sigafoos, J., Lancioni, G., & Andrews, A. (2006). Isolating the evocative and abative effects of an establishing operation on challenging behavior. *Behavioral Interventions, 21,* 195–204.

Paclawskyj, T. R., Matson, J. L., Rush, K. S., Smalls, Y., & Vollmer, T. R. (2000). Questions About Behavioral Function (QABF): A behavior checklist for functional assessment of aberrant behavior. *Research in Developmental Disabilities, 21,* 223–229.

Sasso, G. M., Conroy, M. A., Peck Stitcher, J., & Fox, J. J. (2001). Slowing down the bandwagon: The misapplication of functional assessment for students with emotional or behavioral disorders. *Behavioral Disorders, 26,* 282–296.

Sturmey, P. (1996). *Functional analysis in clinical psychology.* New York: Wiley.

Sulzer-Azaroff, B., & Mayer, G. R. (1991). *Behavior analysis for lasting change.* New York: Holt, Rinehart, & Winston.

Swanson, H. L., & Hoskyn, M. (1998). Experimental intervention research on students with learning disabilities: A meta-analysis of treatment outcomes. *Review of Educational Research, 68,* 277–321.

Symons, F. J., McDonald, L. M., & Wehby, J. H. (1998). Functional assessment and teacher collected data. *Education & Treatment of Children, 21,* 135–159.

Umbreit, J., Ferro, J., Liaupsin, C. J., & Lane, K. L. (2006). *Functional behavioral assessment and function-based intervention: An effective, practical approach.* Upper Saddle River, NJ: Pearson Education.

Vollmer, T. R., Iwata, B. A., Zarcone, J. R., Smith, R. G., & Mazaleski, J. L. (1993). The role of attention in the treatment of attention-maintained self-injurious behavior: Noncontingent reinforcement and differential reinforcement of other behavior. *Journal of Applied Behavior Analysis, 26,* 9–21.

Watson, T. S., & Steege, M. W. (2003). *Conducting school-based functional behavioral assessments: A practitioner's guide*. New York: Guilford.

Weiss, B., & Weisz, J. R. (1995). Relative effectiveness of behavioral versus nonbehavioral child psychotherapy. *Journal of Consulting and Clinical Psychology, 63*, 317–320.

Witt, J. C., Daly, E., & Noell, G. H. (2000). *Functional assessments: A step-by-step guide to solving academic and behavior problems*. Longmont, CO: Sopris West.

4

THE IMPORTANCE OF TREATMENT INTEGRITY IN SCHOOL-BASED BEHAVIORAL INTERVENTION

BRIAN K. MARTENS AND LAURA LEE McINTYRE

School-based behavioral interventions reduce problem behavior and increase desired behavior by changing the conditions surrounding their occurrence. These conditions often involve reinforcing consequences in the form of adult or peer attention, access to desired items and activities, or breaks from work, as well as antecedents that signal when behavior will be reinforced such as proximity to a peer or the presence of a good behavior chart. Because they manipulate the antecedents and consequences of problem behavior, behavioral interventions are implemented in settings in which such behavior occurs and that frequently involve direct care providers as primary treatment agents (e.g., Lerman, Vorndran, Addison, & Kuhn, 2004).

When assuming the role of treatment agent, direct care providers are expected to change their behavior in line with agreed-on intervention plans for at least part of the school day. Doing so means learning the steps of a treatment protocol and implementing these steps during each intervention episode (Lentz & Daly, 1996). For example, a typical reinforcement program such as a point system or token economy requires a teacher to perform seven steps each time it is implemented. The teacher must (a) have certain items present (e.g., charts, tokens), (b) provide an explanation to the child (e.g., "You can earn a point for every five problems you complete correctly"), (c) administer key antecedents (e.g., hand out assignments), (d) observe child behavior (e.g., score problems correct), (e) give points when earned, (f) allow the child to exchange points for backup reinforcers, and (g) record and chart child behavior. Not only must these steps be performed correctly and in sequence, but the teacher must also conduct enough intervention episodes (e.g., one a day for 6 weeks) to evaluate their effects on child behavior (Martens & DiGennaro, 2008). Whenever direct care providers are trained to implement treatment in the natural environment, treatment integrity becomes an important issue.

Treatment integrity refers to the degree to which an intervention is implemented accurately, consistently, or as planned (McIntyre, Gresham, DiGennaro, & Reed, 2007; Noell et al., 2000; Peterson, Homer, & Wonderlich, 1982; Yeaton & Sechrest, 1981). Yeaton and Sechrest suggested that treatment integrity is closely related to treatment strength or the extent to which a treatment, when implemented, contains those ingredients expected to produce the intended effects. Because behavioral interventions require adults to say, do, or even not do certain things at certain times in their interactions with children, changes in child behavior (i.e., the intended effects) will depend in large part on the nature and timing of adult behavior (i.e., the active treatment ingredients). If, for example, a teacher delays allowing a child to exchange points earned for desired back-up reinforcers until the next day, treatment strength will likely be reduced. Worse yet, if the teacher never awards points for problems completed, the active treatment ingredient of positive reinforcement will be lost altogether.

In general, three dimensions of treatment integrity have been examined in the literature, depending on the type of intervention being implemented. First, for procedures that require caregivers to implement each of several different steps once in sequence, integrity has been measured as the percentage of correct steps. Research by Noell and his colleagues (e.g., Noell, Witt, Gilbertson, Ranier, & Freeland, 1997; Noell et al., 2005) examined the effects of different training and follow-up strategies on the accuracy with which teachers implemented a reinforcement program similar to the one described above. Their intervention protocols contained up to 13 steps, with the completion of each step designed to produce a permanent product (e.g., grade written on a worksheet). These permanent products were collected at the end of each day and used to compute the percentage of correctly implemented steps in the treatment protocol.

Second, for procedures that require caregivers to make relatively simple responses (e.g., give praise or repeat a command) to each occurrence of some target child behavior, the percentage of behaviors consequated has been used as a measure of treatment integrity (e.g., Wickstrom, Jones, LaFleur, & Witt, 1998; Wilder, Atwell, & Wine, 2006). The notion here is that consequence-based treatments will be stronger if caregivers provide the consequences after every occurrence of the target behavior. Along these lines, Wickstrom et al. (1998) evaluated the effects of collaborative versus prescriptive consultation on the integrity with which teachers implemented versions of either a point-chart system to increase desired behavior or a response-cost procedure to decrease problem behavior. As one measure of treatment integrity, the researchers calculated the percentage of child target behavior occurrences that were followed by the programmed teacher consequence (i.e., give a point or remove a slip). Wilder et al. (2006) examined the effects of three different levels of treatment integrity on compliance to adult requests by two preschool children. Similar to Wickstrom et al. (1998), 100% integrity was defined as implementation of a three-step prompting procedure every time a child did not comply, 50% integrity as implementation every other time a child did not comply, and 0% integrity as no implementation of the procedure.

Third, for interventions that require adults to reinforce desired behavior and ignore problem behavior (i.e., differential reinforcement), treatment integrity has been measured as the degree of contingent application. Responding to children's behavior contingently means that a caregiver response (e.g., attention) is more likely to occur when the child engages in desired rather than problem behavior. This is important because children often learn what to say and do on the basis of the consequences of their actions (Martens & Witt, 2004). A considerable amount of research has shown that if desired consequences occur more often for undesired behavior, then such behavior will increase (Hanley, Iwata, & McCord, 2003). Conversely, the goal of differential reinforcement is to provide reinforcing consequences every time desired behavior occurs but never for problem behavior. Treatment strength is reduced when caregivers either miss opportunities to reinforce desired behavior or unwittingly reinforce occurrences of problem behavior (Martens, DiGennaro, Reed, Szczech, & Rosenthal, 2008). For example, Vollmer, Roane, Ringdahl, and Marcus (1999) examined the effects of a differential reinforcement procedure that was implemented with varying levels of integrity on severe problem behavior by three children with mental retardation. Full integrity was defined as every instance of desired alternative behavior being reinforced but no instances of problem behavior being reinforced (i.e., a 100/0% schedule). Four different partial integrity schedules were also evaluated on the basis of these same percentages and included 0/100%, 25/75%, 50/50%, and 75/25%.

RELATIONSHIP BETWEEN TREATMENT ACCEPTABILITY, INTEGRITY, AND OUTCOME

Wolf (1978) argued that demonstrations of treatment effectiveness alone may be inadequate to promote the adoption of behavioral interventions in applied settings such as homes, schools, and residential facilities. Rather, the extent to which caregivers in these settings are willing to use, or even be consumers of, behavioral interventions is also related to judgments of *social validity*, defined as the significance of treatment goals, the appropriateness of treatment procedures, and the importance of treatment effects.

An important dimension of social validity in Wolf's (1978) model is the extent to which a treatment is acceptable to its participants (Martens, Witt, Elliott, & Darveaux, 1985). Kazdin (1980) defined acceptability as perceptions of whether treatment is fair, reasonable or intrusive, appropriate for a given problem, and consistent with notions of what treatment should be. It makes intuitive sense that if caregivers like an intervention procedure, they may be more committed to implementing that procedure correctly and consistently over time (i.e., with integrity). Higher levels of implementation integrity are expected to result in better treatment outcomes that, in turn, are expected to positively influence judgments of acceptability. In fact, this logic formed the basis of several conceptual models proposed in the 1980s linking treatment acceptability, integrity, and outcome (Elliott, 1988).

Early acceptability research examined the influence of teacher, child, and treatment variables on consumer judgments of acceptability (e.g., Kazdin, 1980; Witt, Martens, & Elliott, 1984). In general, treatments were judged to be more acceptable if they involved some form of reinforcement rather than punishment, were applied to more severe child problems, were described in understandable terms, were accompanied by information supporting their effectiveness, and were efficient in terms of time and effort required for implementation (Elliott, 1988; Sterling-Turner & Watson, 2002). By characterizing acceptability as an important outcome variable, this line of research suggested how the social validity of behavioral interventions might be increased. Subsequent research in this area has focused on acceptability as a predictor variable by examining its relationship to implementation integrity and treatment outcome. Reimers, Wacker, Cooper, and DeRaad (1992) had parents rate behavioral intervention plans that had been suggested to them by clinic personnel in terms of acceptability, use, and effectiveness at 1-, 3-, and 6-month follow-ups. Results suggested that parent ratings of acceptability had a weak positive correlation with self-reported use during the same interval (mean $r = .22$) but a strong positive correlation with self-reported effectiveness (mean $r = .80$). Sterling-Turner and Watson (2002) had undergraduate students rate the acceptability of a behavioral treatment package for habit disorders both before and after using the procedure, trained them to implement the procedure, and observed them implementing the procedure with a confederate to measure treatment integrity. Correlations between implementation integrity and both pre- and posttreatment ratings of acceptability were nonsignificant ($r = .001$ and $.13$, respectively).

Although findings such as these suggest a generally weak relationship between acceptability ratings and implementation integrity, there appears to be a strong link between implementation integrity and treatment outcome. In both Vollmer et al. (1999) and Wilder et al. (2006), implementation at full or 100% integrity produced the greatest improvements in child behavior, partial integrity produced some improvements, and zero integrity produced either no improvements or caused behavior to worsen. DiGennaro, Martens, and Kleinmann (2007) found that the integrity with which special education teachers implemented a differential reinforcement procedure had a strong, negative correlation with problem child behavior (mean $r = -.63$) for all but one teacher–child dyad. After reviewing 181 school-based behavioral intervention studies published from 1980 to 1990, Gresham, Gansle, Noell, and Cohen (1993) concluded that overall implementation integrity was significantly correlated (mean $r = .55$) with measures of desired treatment outcome.

IMPORTANCE OF TREATMENT INTEGRITY IN PRACTICE

School-based behavioral interventions are more sophisticated now than ever before, given federal mandates for prereferral intervention, documentation of students' response to intervention, and intervention plans based on functional behavior assessments (Individuals With Disabilities Education Improvement Act [IDEA], 2004). Furthermore, federal legislation for both general and special education stipulates that evidence-based interventions be used to support students (IDEA; U.S. Department of Education, 2002). "Evidence-based" means that interventions are published in the research literature and have documented efficacy. Many preservice teachers are not exposed to evidence-based interventions in their teacher preparation programs (Begeny & Martens, 2006); thus, a certain amount of on-the-job training is required to ready teachers and support staff to implement evidence-based interventions.

School psychologists or other professionals are often called on to consult with teachers and school-based intervention teams (Erchul & Martens, 2002). Out of necessity for implementing evidence-based interventions, consultants have begun to take a more directive or prescriptive approach to working with teachers and students (Martens & DiGennaro, 2008; Watson & Robinson, 1996). This may involve training teachers or other caregivers to collect or analyze baseline data, implement multistep interventions, and monitor student progress (e.g., Sterling-Turner, Watson, & Moore, 2002). Given the added demands that such training places on teachers and other caregivers, it is not surprising that the risk of implementation inaccuracies is great (DiGennaro, Martens, & McIntyre, 2005).

In an era in which educational accountability is stressed, it is no longer acceptable for consultants to train teachers to implement interventions and then hope that these interventions are implemented accurately and consistently. This "consult and hope" approach does not yield sustained behavior change on the part of caregivers functioning as intervention agents (Witt, Noell, LaFleur, & Mortenson, 1997). A growing body of evidence suggests that teachers who are trained to accurately implement interventions typically do not maintain their accuracy without ongoing monitoring, corrective feedback, and reinforcement (e.g., DiGennaro et al., 2005; Noell et al., 2000). Thus, monitoring treatment integrity becomes an important aspect of school-based behavioral interventions.

If treatment integrity is not measured, it becomes difficult for consultants and other members of school-based intervention teams to draw conclusions about the efficacy of school-based behavioral interventions. For example, if treatment integrity is not measured and interventions do not result in anticipated student progress, it is impossible to know whether the intervention "failure" was due to poor treatment integrity or an ineffective intervention (Gresham, 1989). Having treatment integrity data allows interventionists to make informed decisions about student responsiveness to intervention. Indeed, federal law now mandates that intervention integrity be monitored when documenting students' responsiveness to interventions, especially when using these data to make decisions about special education eligibility (IDEA, 2004).

IMPORTANCE OF TREATMENT INTEGRITY IN RESEARCH

From a pragmatic perspective, monitoring and measuring treatment integrity is important in school-based practice; however, it is also important in research. Although it has been argued that reporting treatment integrity in published studies is important (e.g., Gresham, Gansle, & Noell, 1993), a perusal of the literature demonstrates that treatment integrity is often a neglected variable in most published school-based behavioral intervention studies. Published studies almost always include estimates of reliability for the dependent variable (i.e., the behavior targeted in the intervention) but are less likely to include similar estimates of reliability for the independent variable (i.e., the intervention; Gresham, Gansle, Noell, et al., 1993; McIntyre et al., 2007; Peterson et al., 1982). McIntyre et al. (2007), for example, reviewed school-based intervention studies published in the *Journal of Applied Behavior Analysis* (*JABA*) between 1991 and 2005. Of the 152 studies included in the review, only 30.3% included treatment integrity data. This figure is only slightly higher than the 20% figure Gresham, Gansle, and Noell (1993) reported in their review of child-based studies published in *JABA* between 1980 and 1990. Although McIntyre et al.'s more recent review presents a somewhat more optimistic picture of treatment integrity reporting trends, there remains a "curious double standard" (p. 478) when it comes to reporting reliability of dependent and independent variables (Peterson et al.,

1982). That is, reporting reliability on dependent measures is overly empha-sized in the published literature, with little regard for reporting the reliability of the independent variable manipulations.

Regularly including treatment integrity data in published studies of school-based behavioral interventions is important for several reasons. In-cluding treatment integrity data in published studies allows researchers and practitioners alike to consider all of the evidence when drawing conclusions regarding study results. A research study is said to have *internal validity* if "it produces a single, unambiguous explanation for the relationship between two variables" (Gravetter & Forzano, 2006, p. 140). Campbell and Stanley (1963) posited that experiments must have internal validity for the results to be interpretable. If treatments are implemented with integrity, the evidence is stronger for concluding that changes in the dependent variable (i.e., target behavior) were due to manipulations of the independent variable (i.e., the intervention) and nothing else.

Including treatment integrity data in published studies also allows for greater *external validity* or the generalizability of results across treatment agents, settings, investigators, materials, and so forth. According to Gravetter and Forzano (2006), external validity "concerns the extent to which the results obtained in a research study hold true outside the constraints of the study" (p. 140) and is closely related to replication. Replication allows for verifica-tion of research findings and is an important component in developing the "evidence" for mandated evidence-based interventions. Without a large body of published school-based behavioral interventions, it becomes challenging for practitioners to implement evidenced-based interventions that the No Child Left Behind Act of 2001 (U.S. Department of Education, 2002) and IDEA (2004) stipulate.

In addition to being important for school-based practice and research, specifying a plan for measuring treatment integrity is now a requirement to obtain funding from certain federal granting agencies. For example, researchers who submit single-case experimental-design grant applications to the U.S. Department of Education's Institute of Education Sciences (IES) now must describe "how treatment fidelity will be measured, frequency of assessments, and what degree of variation in treatment fidelity will be accepted over the course of the study" (IES, 2006, p. 50).

The inclusion of treatment integrity measures in intervention studies has been a topic of discussion within Division 16 (School Psychology) of the Ameri-can Psychological Association. In 2002, a special issue of the *School Psychology Quarterly* was devoted to evidence-based interventions in School Psychology and included a detailed plan for evaluating published studies in terms of their methodological rigor. A number of criteria for evaluating studies were described in this special issue. Shernoff, Kratochwill, and Stoiber (2002), for example, discussed evaluating single participant research designs, commonly used in school-based behavioral interventions. Shernoff et al. explained that reviewers consider the degree to which an intervention was implemented as intended. Although there may be slight variations in implementation, data on program fidelity are critical to determine if the intervention was responsible for the positive outcomes reported by the researchers. (p. 413)

Although including treatment integrity data collection in all school-based behavioral interventions and published research studies would be ideal, logistical factors may limit collecting and/or reporting integrity data in research and practice. For example, there may be a shortage of staff available to collect integrity data in schools, they may have limited expertise, and they may have insufficient knowledge surrounding the importance of including such data collection. Likewise, there are numerous barriers that may interfere with reporting treatment integrity in published studies. Some researchers, journal editors, or reviewers may (falsely) believe that large intervention effects are sufficient for demonstrating that an intervention was implemented as intended. Practically speaking, some journals may have space limitations that preclude providing a description of treatment integrity data collection and integrity results.

Beyond these logistical concerns are empirical questions that have yet to be adequately addressed in the literature. For example, more research is necessary to identify optimal and acceptable levels of treatment integrity for school-based interventions. Although generally recognized as important, treatment integrity research is sparse (e.g., McIntyre et al., 2007). Few published studies have analyzed various levels of intervention accuracy on child behavior (e.g., Vollmer et al., 1999; Wilder et al., 2006). This is an area of research with many important practical implications for conducting school-based behavioral intervention.

BEST PRACTICES IN IMPLEMENTATION SUPPORT

As early as 1982, Happe found that approximately 80% of teachers with whom school psychologists consulted concerning the use of school-based interventions agreed verbally to implement the plan, but only half carried the plan through to conclusion. Noell et al. (1997) monitored the number of intervention steps completed by three teachers each day after the procedure was explained and necessary materials were provided. All of the teachers implemented 100% of the treatment steps initially, but within 2 weeks this level had dropped to 0% for two teachers and 40% for the third teacher. Others have found similar drops in the percentage of treatment steps completed even after teachers have received direct instruction, modeling, and coaching during actual classroom implementation (e.g., DiGennaro et al., 2005; Witt et al., 1997). Mounting evidence in this area clearly suggests that in the absence of ongoing support and feedback, teachers are unlikely to implement behavioral intervention plans with integrity over time.

Promoting Implementation Integrity Through Performance Feedback

One way to promote high levels of implementation integrity by teachers is to provide them with performance feedback concerning the extent to which they are using a plan correctly. Noell and his colleagues (1997) conducted a series of investigations examining teachers' treatment integrity after initial training and following exposure to a performance feedback package (e.g., Mortenson & Witt, 1998; Noell et al., 1997; Witt et al., 1997). Each of the studies used a similar sequence of consultation activities and method for monitoring teacher implementation. The intervention plan was first described to the teacher, materials needed to implement the plan were provided, and use of the plan was modeled by the consultant who coached the teacher through implementation during one classroom session. After this initial training, the teacher implemented the plan independently, received a performance feedback package, and again implemented the plan independently. The performance feedback package typically consisted of graphs depicting levels of student behavior and teacher implementation (i.e., percentage of steps completed), discussion of implementation errors, and praise for implementing the intervention as planned.

A consistent pattern of findings emerged across the studies. Although teachers initially implemented all intervention steps, implementation dropped considerably within several weeks. Implementation levels increased dramatically with introduction of performance feedback, but maintenance after feedback ended was variable. More recent studies in this area have shown performance feedback to be superior at maintaining implementation integrity when compared with brief follow-up meetings or attempts to enhance teachers' commitment to agreed-on plans (Noell et al., 2000, 2005).

Promoting Implementation Integrity Through Reinforcement

When used with teachers, one component of performance feedback is for consultants to praise teachers for high levels of implementation integrity (e.g., Noell et al., 1997). Along these lines, several authors have suggested that teachers' implementation behavior may be affected by simple contingencies of reinforcement in much the same way as student behavior is affected by reinforcement (Lentz & Daly, 1996; Martens & DiGennaro, 2008). DiGennaro et al. (2005) examined this issue by evaluating the extent to which daily performance feedback, practice, and the opportunity to avoid meetings with a consultant influenced the treatment integrity of four teachers and reduced their students' problem behavior. Teachers were trained initially in how to implement an intervention in their classroom using procedures similar to those by Noell et al. (1997). After being observed implementing the intervention on their own, teachers were given daily written feedback about their implementation accuracy (i.e., performance feedback). Teachers were also able to avoid meeting with a consultant for directed rehearsal (i.e., to practice each missed step three times) by demonstrating 100% integrity, thereby establishing a negative reinforcement contingency for correct implementation. Results showed that integrity increased to 100% for all teachers following implementation of the performance feedback/negative reinforcement package. Integrity was maintained at high levels when the package was faded to once a week and then once every 2 weeks. Similar results were obtained with special education teachers who also judged the performance feedback/negative reinforcement package to be an acceptable way of supporting their implementation efforts (DiGennaro et al., 2007).

CONCLUSIONS

Treatment integrity refers to the degree to which an intervention is implemented accurately, consistently, or as planned. Measuring and monitoring treatment integrity in school-based behavioral interventions is especially important because school-based interventions often ask direct care providers (e.g., teachers) to change their behavior to evoke change in student behavior. In so doing, direct care providers must learn treatment protocols and implement multistep interventions. Knowing the extent to which interventions are implemented accurately aids school teams in the decision-making process and is essential in documenting student responsiveness to intervention under IDEA (2004). Evidence suggests that teachers and other direct care providers do not implement interventions as intended unless they receive training, ongoing monitoring, performance feedback, and reinforcement (e.g., DiGennaro et al., 2005; Noell et al., 2000). Thus, best practices in implementing school-based behavioral interventions should incorporate data collection and analysis of treatment integrity, as well as a plan to provide teachers with feedback and reinforcement surrounding intervention implementation. If treatment integrity is not considered when evaluating the effectiveness of school-based interventions, incorrect decisions could be made, costing schools valuable time and resources.

REFERENCES

Begeny, J. C., & Martens, B. K. (2006). Assessing pre-service teachers' training in empirically-validated behavioral instruction practices. *School Psychology Quarterly, 21,* 262–285.

Campbell, D. T., & Stanley, J. (1963). *Experimental and quasi-experimental designs for research*. Boston: Houghton-Mifflin.

DiGennaro, F. D., Martens, B. K., & Kleinmann, A. E. (2007). A comparison of performance feedback procedures on teachers' implementation integrity and students' inappropriate behavior in special education classrooms. *Journal of Applied Behavior Analysis, 40,* 447–461.

DiGennaro, F. D., Martens, B. K., & McIntyre, L. L. (2005). Increasing treatment integrity through negative reinforcement: Effects on teacher and student behavior. *School Psychology Review, 34,* 220–231.

Elliott, S. N. (1988). Acceptability of behavioral treatments in educational settings. In J. C. Witt, S. N. Elliott, & F. M. Gresham (Eds.), *Handbook of behavior therapy in education* (pp. 121–150). New York: Plenum.

Erchul, W. P., & Martens, B. K. (2002). *School consultation: Conceptual and empirical bases of practice* (2nd ed.). New York: Kluwer Academic/Plenum.

Gravetter, F. J., & Forzano, L. B. (2006). *Research methods for the behavioral sciences* (2nd ed.). Belmont, CA: Wadsworth/Thomson Learning.

Gresham, F. M. (1989). Assessment of treatment integrity in school consultation and preferral intervention. *School Psychology Review, 18,* 37–50.

Gresham, F. M., Gansle, K., & Noell, G. H. (1993). Treatment integrity in applied behavior analysis with children. *Journal of Applied Behavior Analysis, 26,* 257–263.

Gresham, F. M., Gansle, K., Noell, G. H., & Cohen, S. (1993). Treatment integrity of school-based behavioral intervention studies: 1980–1990. *School Psychology Review, 22,* 254–272.

Hanley, G. P., Iwata, B. A., & McCord, B. E. (2003). Functional analysis of problem behavior: A review. *Journal of Applied Behavior Analysis, 36,* 147–185.

Happe, D. (1982). Behavioral intervention: It doesn't do any good in your briefcase. In J. Grimes (Ed.), *Psychological approaches to problems of children and adolescents* (pp. 15–41). Des Moines: Iowa Department of Public Instruction.

Individuals With Disabilities Education Improvement Act. (2004). Pub. L. No. 108-446, 118 Stat. 2647. Retrieved June 17, 2007, from http://idea.ed.gov

Institute of Education Sciences. (2006). *Special education research grants 2007 request for applications*. Retrieved August 29, 2006, from http://ies.ed.gov/ncser/pdf/2007324.pdf

Kazdin, A. E. (1980). Acceptability of alternative treatments for deviant child behavior. *Journal of Applied Behavior Analysis, 13,* 259–273.

Lentz, F. E., & Daly, E. J. (1996). Is the behavior of academic change agents controlled metaphysically? An analysis of the behavior of those who change behavior. *School Psychology Quarterly, 11,* 337–352.

Lerman, D. C., Vorndran, C. M., Addison, L., & Kuhn, S. C. (2004). Preparing teachers in evidence-based practices for young children with autism. *School Psychology Review, 33,* 510–526.

Martens, B. K., & DiGennaro, F. D. (2008). Behavioral consultation. In W. P. Erchul & S. M. Sheridan (Eds.), *Handbook of research in school consultation* (pp. 147–170). New York: Lawrence Erlbaum.

Martens, B. K., DiGennaro, F. D., Reed, D. D., Szczech, F. M., & Rosenthal, B. D. (2008). Contingency space analysis: An alternative method for identifying contingent relations from observational data. *Journal of Applied Behavior Analysis, 41*, 69–81.

Martens, B. K., & Witt, J. C. (2004). Competence, persistence, and success: The positive psychology of behavioral skill instruction. *Psychology in the Schools, 41*, 19–30.

Martens, B. K., Witt, J. C., Elliott, S. N., & Darveaux, D. X. (1985). Teacher judgments concerning the acceptability of school-based interventions. *Professional Psychology: Research and Practice, 16*, 191–198.

McIntyre, L. L., Gresham, F. J., DiGennaro, F. D., & Reed, D. D. (2007). Treatment integrity of school-based interventions with children in the *Journal of Applied Behavior Analysis* studies from 1991–2005. *Journal of Applied Behavior Analysis, 40*, 659–762.

Mortenson, B. P., & Witt, J. C. (1998). The use of weekly performance feedback to increase teacher implementation of a prereferral academic intervention. *School Psychology Review, 27*, 613–627.

Noell, G. H., Witt, J. C., Gilbertson, D. N., Ranier, D. D., & Freeland, J. T. (1997). Increasing teacher intervention implementation in general education settings through consultation and performance feedback. *School Psychology Quarterly, 12*, 77–88.

Noell, G. H., Witt, J. C., LaFleur, L. H., Mortenson, B. P., Ranier, D. D., & LeVelle, J. (2000). Increasing intervention implementation in general education following consultation: A comparison of two follow-up strategies. *Journal of Applied Behavior Analysis, 33*, 271–284.

Noell, G. H., Witt, J. C., Slider, N. J., Connell, J. E., Gatti, S. L., Williams, K. L., et al. (2005). Treatment implementation following behavioral consultation in schools: A comparison of three follow-up strategies. *School Psychology Review, 34*, 87–106.

Peterson, L., Homer, A., & Wonderlich, S. (1982). The integrity of independent variables in behavior analysis. *Journal of Applied Behavior Analysis, 15*, 477–492.

Reimers, T. M., Wacker, D. P., Cooper, L. J., & DeRaad, A. O. (1992). Acceptability of behavioral treatments for children: Analog and naturalistic evaluations by parents. *School Psychology Review, 21*, 628–643.

Shernoff, E. S., Kratochwill, T. R., & Stoiber, K. C. (2002). Evidence-based interventions in school psychology: An illustration of task force coding criteria using single-participant research design. *School Psychology Quarterly, 17*, 390–422.

Sterling-Turner, H. E., & Watson, T. S. (2002). An analog investigation of the relationship between treatment acceptability and treatment integrity. *Journal of Behavioral Education, 11*, 39–50.

Sterling-Turner, H. E., Watson, T. S., & Moore, J. W. (2002). The effects of direct training and treatment integrity on treatment outcomes in school consultation. *School Psychology Quarterly, 17,* 47–77.

U.S. Department of Education. (2002). No Child Left Behind Act of 2001. Pub. L. No. 107-110, 115 Stat. 1425. Retrieved June 17, 2007, from http://www.ed.gov/policy/elsec/leg/esea02/index.html

Vollmer, T. R., Roane, H. S., Ringdahl, J. E., & Marcus, B. A. (1999). Evaluating treatment challenges with differential reinforcement of alternative behavior. *Journal of Applied Behavior Analysis, 32,* 9–23.

Watson, T. S., & Robinson, R. L. (1996). Direct behavioral consultation: An alternative to traditional behavioral consultation. *School Psychology Quarterly, 11,* 267–278.

Wickstrom, K. R., Jones, K. M., LaFleur, L. H., & Witt, J. C. (1998). An analysis of treatment integrity in school-based behavioral consultation. *School Psychology Quarterly, 13,* 141–154.

Wilder, D. A., Atwell, J., & Wine, B. (2006). The effects of varying levels of treatment integrity on child compliance during treatment with a three-step prompting procedure. *Journal of Applied Behavior Analysis, 39,* 369–373.

Witt, J. C., Martens, B. K., & Elliott, S. N. (1984). Factors affecting teachers' judgments of the acceptability of behavioral interventions: Time involvement, behavior problem severity, and type of intervention. *Behavior Therapy, 15,* 204–209.

Witt, J. C., Noell, G. H., La Fleur, L. H., & Mortenson, B. P. (1997). Teacher use of interventions in general education: Measurement and analysis of the independent variable. *Journal of Applied Behavior Analysis, 30,* 693–696.

Wolf, M. M. (1978). Social validity: The case for subjective measurement or how applied behavior analysis is finding its heart. *Journal of Applied Behavior Analysis, 11,* 203–214.

Yeaton, W. H., & Sechrest, L. (1981). Critical dimensions in the choice and maintenance of successful treatments: Strength, integrity, and effectiveness. *Journal of Consulting and Clinical Psychology, 49,* 156–167.

5

THE TRUE EFFECTS OF EXTRINSIC REINFORCEMENT ON "INTRINSIC" MOTIVATION

ANGELEQUE AKIN-LITTLE AND STEVEN G. LITTLE

The use of rewards and/or reinforcement is common in schools. Teachers frequently use some sort of reward system for academic output and/or appropriate behavior (e.g., stickers given for completed classwork, pizza coupons given for reading books, tokens given for appropriate classroom behavior), and decades of empirical research support the efficacy of reinforcement-based procedures in the classroom (e.g., Ayllon & Azrin, 1968; Barrish, Saunders, & Wolf, 1969; Birnbrauer, Wolf, Kidder, & Tague, 1965; Brondolo, Baruch, Conway, & Marsh, 1994; Buisson, Murdock, Reynolds, & Cronin, 1995; Cavalier, Ferretti, & Hodges, 1997; Mann-Feder & Varda, 1996; O'Leary & Drabman, 1971; Swiezy, Matson, & Box, 1992).

However, there has also been concern on the part of some educators and psychologists over the use of reward contingency systems in classrooms (Deci, Koestner, & Ryan, 1999a, 1999b, 2001; Kohn, 1993, 1996). The perceived problem is the belief that extrinsic reinforcers may have a detrimental effect on a student's intrinsic motivation to perform a task once the reinforcer for that task is withdrawn. These writers posit that if reinforcement is utilized, an individual's perceptions of competence and self-determination will lessen, thereby decreasing, possibly forever, that individual's intrinsic motivation to perform the task. Teachers and teacher education students are frequently told that the use of extrinsic reinforcement kills creativity (Tegano, Moran, & Sawyers, 1991). Further, many teacher education programs emphasize intuition and insight in order to facilitate learning. In the resulting teaching practices (e.g., discovery learning, constructivism), the teacher does not impart knowledge; rather the focus is on teacher arrangement of the environment in order to help students "discover" knowledge in the absence of external reinforcement. This pedagogical instruction is in direct conflict with the available data that supports the use of external reinforcers in the classroom and the efficacy of direct instruction (Alberto & Troutman, 2006).

In 1994, Cameron and Pierce conducted a meta-analysis on the effect of external reinforcement on intrinsic motivation, and it generated intense debate on this topic (Cameron & Pierce, 1996; Kohn, 1996; Lepper, 1998; Lepper, Keavney, & Drake, 1996; Ryan & Deci, 1996). Subsequently, two additional meta-analytic studies were conducted (Cameron, Banko, & Pierce, 2001; Deci et al., 1999a) with results being contradictory. Cameron and Pierce (1994) and Cameron et al. (2001) found no detrimental effect or detrimental effects only under certain proscribed conditions, whereas Deci et al. (1999a) found negative effect. Further, others have attempted to provide illumination for contradictory findings by examining findings of the detrimental effect from a more behavioral, scientific perspective (Akin-Little, Eckert, Lovett, & Little, 2004; Akin-Little & Little, 2004; Carton, 1996; Dickinson, 1989; Flora, 1990; Mintz, 2003). This chapter aims to synthesize research in the areas of extrinsic and intrinsic motivation to give readers a background from which they can effectively work with teachers and parents to implement behavioral interventions. Although this chapter has more of a research focus than other chapters in the book, we feel it is important for practitioners to have a conceptual foundation in this area.

DEFINITIONS OF INTRINSIC AND EXTRINSIC MOTIVATION

Deci and Ryan (1985) defined an intrinsically motivated behavior as one for which there exists no recognizable reward except the activity itself (e.g., reading). That is, behavior that cannot be attributed to external controls is usually attributed to intrinsic motivation. However, according to Flora (1990), no behavior occurs without an identifying external circumstance:

> A complete scientific explanation of behavior does not require reference to constructs which are, in principle, unobservable . . . . A complete scientific account for any behavior of any organism may be obtained with a complete description of the functional interdependency of the behavior-environment interaction. (p. 323)

Many behavioral researchers (e.g., Dickinson, 1989) have criticized continued attempts to identify the construct of intrinsic motivation, suggesting that such efforts impede the goal of the scientific study of behavior. Creating internal constructs, which depend on inferences in their explanations, may obstruct the discovery of the true function of behavior through more scientific, measurable, and observable means.

In general, if the dichotomy between intrinsic and extrinsic motivation is accepted, intrinsic motivation is assumed to be of greater value (Fair & Silvestri, 1992). This belief is due in large part to the Western conceptualization of the human as autonomous and individualistic. In this view, humans are driven toward self-actualization and any occurrence that impinges on self-determination causes dissonance. Further, the use of extrinsic reinforcement is seen as controlling and/or limiting self-discovery, creativity, and the capacity for humans to reach fulfillment (Eisenberger, Pierce, & Cameron, 1999). It is interesting that when this tenet is examined in relationship to the use of punishment, punishment is perceived as less of a threat to autonomy because humans may choose how to behave in order to avoid punishment (Maag, 1996).

It is not surprising that a debate has resulted surrounding the intrinsic/extrinsic distinction. Several critics (e.g., Guzzo, 1979; Scott, 1975) have produced data that illuminate the problems associated with identifying intrinsically motivated behaviors. Other theories have been proposed that purport to explain behavior that appears to occur in the absence of any extrinsic motivation. However, these behaviors may, in fact, be due to anticipated future benefits (Bandura, 1977) or intermittent reinforcement (Dickinson, 1989). Zimmerman (1985) stated that cognitive definitions of intrinsic motivation are definitions "by default" (p. 118). That is, behavior that cannot be attributed to external controls is usually attributed to intrinsic motivation.

According to Deci and Ryan's (1985) definition, intrinsic motivation is evidenced when people participate in an activity because of the internal enjoyment of the activity and not because of any perceived extrinsic reward. Intrinsic motivation enables people to feel competent and self-determining. Intrinsically motivated behavior is said to result in creativity, flexibility, and spontaneity. In contrast, extrinsically motivated actions are characterized by pressure and tension and are believed to result in low self-esteem and anxiety. Distinctions between extrinsic and intrinsic consequences from a more behavioral perspective can be found in writings by Horcones (1987) and Mawhinney, Dickinson, and Taylor (1989). Horcones stated that intrinsic consequences occur in the absence of programming by others. They are natural and automatic responses inevitably produced by the structural characteristics of the physical environment in which humans exist. Extrinsic consequences, conversely, are those that occur in addition to any intrinsic consequences and are most often programmed by others (i.e., the social environment, researchers, teacher, applied behavior analysts). On the basis of this differentiation, Mawhinney et al. (1989) subsequently defined intrinsic and extrinsic motivation in the following manner: "Intrinsically controlled behavior consists of behavior controlled by unprogrammed consequences while extrinsically controlled behavior consists of behavior controlled by programmed consequences" (p. 111).

THEORIES AND INVESTIGATIONS OF REINFORCER/REWARD EFFECTS

Theories and investigations of reinforcer/reward effects have generally fallen into two general categories: cognitive and behavioral. Cognitive theories include cognitive evaluation theory and the overjustification hypothesis. Behavioral investigations have generally tried to explain the same phenomena via various aspects of behavioral theory (e.g., behavioral contrast, discriminative stimuli, etc.).

Cognitive Evaluation Theory

Deci and Ryan's (1985) cognitive evaluation theory is based on the assumption that self-determination and competence are innate human needs. Cognitive evaluation theory states that events facilitate or hinder feelings of competence and self-determination depending on their perceived informational, controlling, or amotivational significance. Deci and Ryan divided rewards into two categories: task-contingent rewards and quality-dependent rewards. Task-contingent rewards are given for participation in an activity, solving a problem, or completing a task. Quality-dependent rewards involve the "quality of one's performance relative to some normative information or standard" (Deci & Ryan, 1985, p. 74). Task-contingent rewards are hypothesized to detrimentally affect intrinsic motivation by decreasing self-determination (i.e., reward is viewed as a controlling event attempting to determine behavior thereby decreasing self-determination and, consequently, intrinsic motivation). Quality-dependent rewards are also believed to act to decrease intrinsic motivation by reducing one's feelings of self-determination. However, quality-dependent rewards also serve to increase feelings of competence, according to Deci and Ryan (i.e., reward is viewed as an informational event indicating skill at a certain task, leading to an increase in feelings of competence, which serves to increase intrinsic motivation). Therefore, it is never clear whether the decremental effect to self-determination or the incremental effect to competence will be stronger when examining quality-dependent rewards. Thus, for Deci and Ryan, quality-dependent rewards may not decrease intrinsic motivation. The detrimental effect of greatest concern then is in circumstances involving task-completion rewards.

Eisenberger and Cameron (1996) further divided task-completion rewards into the subcategories of performance-independent rewards that individuals receive simply for participation in an activity and completion-independent rewards given when an individual has finished a task or activity. Cognitive evaluation theory would suggest that an individual's intrinsic motivation would be most detrimentally affected upon reception of tangible, anticipated rewards. Additionally, according to this theory, verbal rewards may be informational and therefore increase intrinsic motivation. Events may also be perceived as amotivational, indicating an individual's lack of skill that reduces his or her cognitions of competence and, subsequently, intrinsic motivation.

In 1988, Rummel and Feinberg conducted a meta-analysis assessing cognitive evaluation theory. They concluded that controlling, extrinsic rewards do have a damaging effect on intrinsic motivation, providing support for the theory. Basic problems with cognitive evaluation theory, however, were also identified. First, faulty reasoning was used because rewards were identified as either controlling, informational, or amotivational after the performance had been measured. Second, feelings of competence and self-determination, central to the theory as agents for change in intrinsic motivation, are not measurable. The assumption is made that changes are occurring because changes in behavior are observed. The constructs of self-determination, competence, and even intrinsic motivation are inferred from the very behavior they supposedly cause (Cameron & Pierce, 1994). The theory contains no explanation for why the disquiet associated with a decrease in self-determination would reduce intrinsic motivation. As Eisenberger and Cameron (1996) wrote, "based on the theory's premise, one could alternatively argue that reduced self-determination would, for example, reduce preference for the reward or instigate anger at the person delivering the reward" (p. 1156).

Results of a meta-analysis performed by Cameron and Pierce (1994) partly serve to refute cognitive evaluation theory. Deci and Ryan (1985) stressed the importance of measurements of attitude because they theorized that interest, enjoyment, and satisfaction are central emotions to intrinsic motivation. How a person feels about an activity is reflected behaviorally as time spent on task. The results of the Cameron and Pierce meta-analysis, however, suggest that reward (and subsequent withdrawal) tends not to affect attitude. They further found that attitude seems to be affected positively when verbal rewards are used, and when rewards are contingent on a precise level of achievement.

Other researchers (Cameron & Pierce, 1994; Eisenberger & Cameron, 1996; Eisenberger et al., 1999) have suggested that cognitive evaluation theory is not a useful or viable theory and that any decrements in behavior are better explained through learned helplessness or general interest theory. In learned helplessness, the decrement in intrinsic motivation is said to be due to the single reward delivery paradigm used by most studies in this area. General interest theory suggests that intrinsic motivation is driven by more than just self-determination and competence needs. Eisenberger et al. (1999) proposed that rewards must be examined for both content and context of tasks. Rewards that communicate task performance can satisfy needs, wants, and desires, which can increase intrinsic motivation, whereas rewards that convey that the task is extraneous to needs, wants, and desires may serve to decrease intrinsic motivation. The symbolic function of rewards is then what is important along with personality and cultural influences.

Overjustification Hypothesis

Lepper, Greene, and Nisbett (1973), divided preschool children into three groups: expected reward, unexpected reward, and no reward. Children in the first group were promised and received a good-player award contingent upon their drawing with magic markers. Children in the second group received an award but were not promised it beforehand, and children in the third group did not expect or receive an award. In subsequent free-play sessions, children from the expected-reward group were observed to spend less time drawing than the other two groups.

In an attempt to explain their results, Lepper et al. (1973) offered the overjustification hypothesis. According to this hypothesis, if a person is already performing an activity and receiving no extrinsic reward for that performance, introduction of an extrinsic reward will decrease intrinsic interest or motivation. This occurs because the person's performance is now overjustified, resulting in the person's perception that his or her level of intrinsic motivation to perform the activity is less than it was initially. According to this theory, the person subsequently performs the activity less once the reinforcement is removed (Lepper, 1983; Williams, 1980).

Lepper et al.'s (1973) results have been replicated (e.g., Deci & Ryan, 1985; Greene & Lepper, 1974; Morgan, 1984); however, research with more school-like tasks and older students suggested that an undermining effect of reward does not occur if the students are told they have achieved a preset standard and the task is at a challenging level for them (Pittman, Boggiano, & Ruble, 1983). The use of rewards has actually been shown to increase intrinsic motivation by studies in which rewards were administered contingent upon performance (e.g., Lepper, 1983), rewards provided information about the students' competence (e.g., Lepper & Gilovich, 1981; Rosenfield, Folger, & Adelman, 1980), and rewards were given to students not optimally motivated toward desirable educational goals (Morgan, 1984). Moreover, researchers have consistently found that verbal rewards tend to increase intrinsic motivation, whereas tangible rewards may decrease intrinsic motivation (Cameron & Pierce, 1994). Additionally, reductions of intrinsic motivation have not been found with traditionally behavioral studies utilizing a single-subject, repeated-measures design (Akin-Little & Little, 2004; Cameron & Pierce, 1994; McGinnis, 1996; Mintz, 2003).

Behavioral Investigations

Flora (1990) wrote that "psychology is supposedly the study of individual behavior, not the study of groups means" (p. 338). This statement succinctly illustrates the importance of within-subject designs in behavioral research. Behaviorally oriented researchers assert that cognitive researchers studying the effects of extrinsic reward using between-groups designs have used measurement phases that are too short to detect temporal trends or transition states (Cameron & Pierce, 1994). Within-subject designs, however, measure behavior over a number of sessions, thereby alleviating this shortcoming. Unlike between-groups paradigms, the within-subject design takes measurements of time on task over a number of sessions for each phase. After baseline (B) data are collected, reinforcement is introduced and measurements are again repeatedly taken. Finally, reinforcement is withdrawn (i.e., Baseline II [B II]), and measurements of time on task are taken again. Time on task is taken as a measurement of intrinsic motivation and the difference in time on task between pre- and postreinforcement (i.e., B I and B II) is cataloged as intrinsic motivation in which differences are attributed to external reinforcement. Behavioral investigations have also traditionally included a follow-up phase during which measures of behavior are taken 2 to 3 weeks after the conclusion of the experiment in order to assess trends and temporal states. Behavioral researchers have further stated that cognitivists fail to make any distinction between rewards and reinforcers. They posit that these two words cannot be used synonymously. A reinforcer is an event that increases the frequency of the target behavior it follows, and a reward is a pleasant occurrence that has not been shown to necessarily strengthen behavior (Cameron & Pierce, 1994). Behaviorists' use of within-subject repeated measures designs allows determination of whether a reward is actually a reinforcer for a particular subject. Compared with the large number of group studies examining this supposed event, very few studies examine the effects of extrinsic reinforcement from a behavioral standpoint (Akin-Little & Little, 2004; Davidson & Bucher, 1978; Feingold & Mahoney, 1975; Mawhinney et al., 1989; Mintz, 2003; Vasta, Andrews, McLaughlin, Stirpe, & Comfort, 1978; Vasta & Stirpe, 1979).

Akin-Little and Little (2004) attempted to examine the possible overjustification effects of the implementation of token economy for appropriate behavior. Although exhibiting appropriate behavior in a classroom setting may not be seen as intrinsically motivated behavior, many reward contingency systems are used to increase compliant behavior. No previous study used appropriate classroom behavior as the dependent variable, although classroom management and student behavior is a major concern of many classroom teachers. The subjects in this study were elementary school students chosen by their teacher as high in compliant behavior to classroom rules. The token system was implemented in an actual classroom setting. Subjects' behavior was analyzed after a B I, reward procedure, B II, and follow-up period. No overjustification effect was found for any of the students (i.e., no student's behavior dropped below B I in either the B II or follow-up phase).

Mintz (2003) used a multielement, multiple baseline across participant design with three children to test the overjustification effect on behaviors for which each child demonstrated a preference in the absence of external reinforcement. The purpose of the study was to examine the effect of expected and unexpected reinforcers on behavior that met the definition for intrinsically motivated behavior (i.e., one for which there exists no recognizable reward except the activity itself). Results provided no support for the overjustification effect. In fact, an additive effect was found; that is, after reinforcement was removed responding remained stable and at a higher level than was observed during baseline.

Flora and Flora (1999) evaluated the effects of extrinsic reinforcement for reading during childhood on reported reading habits of college students. Specifically, they investigated the effects of participation in a particular reading program and parental reinforcement for reading on reading habits of college students. Results indicated that being reinforced with money or pizza neither increased nor decreased the amount of reading; nor did it influence participants' self-reported intrinsic motivation for reading. These results provide no support for the hypothesis that extrinsic rewards for reading undermine intrinsic interest in reading. Rather, it appears that extrinsic rewards set the conditions for continued interest in reading.

BEHAVIORAL CRITICISMS OF COGNITIVE RESEARCH

The neglect of the behavioral literature and principles in the majority of past studies on intrinsic motivation has served to encourage cognitive researchers to develop their own theories and explanations (McGinnis, 1996). Behavioral explanations for intrinsically motivated behavior, such as anticipated future benefits (Bandura, 1977), intermittent reinforcement (Dickinson, 1989), competing response theory (Reiss & Sushinsky, 1975), behavioral contrast (Bates, 1979; Feingold & Mahoney, 1975), and the presence of discriminative stimuli (Flora, 1990), have been ignored.

Reiss and Sushinsky (1975) were especially critical of the overjustification hypothesis, stating that the theory is too vague to be useful for scientific purposes and competing response theory more adequately accounts for any obtained decrements in intrinsic motivation. Competing response theory suggests that a student's intrinsic motivation may decrease because of other stimuli present in the environment. Students respond to these stimuli, which results in a decrease of their response to the targeted activity before termination of contingencies occurs. Bates (1979) offered behavioral contrast as an additional explanation for decrements in intrinsic motivation. In this paradigm, two behaviors are reinforced on different schedules. One behavior is then extinguished. This produces an increase in response of the other behavior. The classic example is of the pigeons pecking at different colors. When the reinforcer for pecking at one color is withheld, the pecking at the remaining color increases in rate and intensity. Finally, Flora (1990) discussed the possibility of discriminative stimuli as an explanation. According to this account, behaviors occur in an environmental context. Instead of examining an unobservable construct such as intrinsic motivation, Flora suggested it is more useful to determine the discriminative stimulus and the reinforcers in the environment that maintain a functional relationship. These factors, Flora proposed, maintain behavior rate and occurrence.

Additionally, Dickinson (1989) proposed that decrements in intrinsic motivation may occur if the activity is one that subjects find boring or uninteresting, rewards are given for activities culturally praised as intrinsically motivated behaviors (e.g., artistic or creative activities), or rewards become aversive stimuli. In the first instance, motivation is decreased because satiation is reached through repeated exposure to sensory reinforcement. In the second illustration, decrement is explained through an examination of cultural norms. People are often praised if they engage in certain activities that supposedly offer specific intrinsic rewards (e.g., painting, dancing). If an individual is then extrinsically rewarded for this activity, the person may experience a decrease in praise. If praise is reinforcing for that person, he or she may engage in the activity less often because the activity is now differentially correlated with the loss of praise. In the third example, the subjects may not participate in the activity because they are angry with the experimenter for withholding the reward, they fail to meet the performance standards, or they are offered rewards for engaging in nonpreferred activities and/or threatened with punishment for noncompliance (Dickinson, 1989).

Eisenberger and Cameron (1996) also presented an interpretation of the specified conditions under which rewards may decrease intrinsic motivation. They stated that individuals who receive performance-independent rewards may perceive that they have no control over the reward. This perception may lead to a decrease in performance that may be misinterpreted as a decrease in intrinsic motivation. We suggest that the intrinsic interest decrement may be better explained by learned helplessness that asserts that "uncontrollable aversive stimulation results in generalized motivational deficits" (Eisenberger & Cameron, p. 1156). The learned helplessness theory predicts a decrease in intrinsic motivation for performance-independent rewards. However, unlike cognitive evaluation theory, no prediction of a decrement is suggested following task-completion rewards.

Carton (1996) examined the social cognitivist assertion that praise appears to increase intrinsic motivation whereas the delivery of tangible rewards appears to decrease intrinsic motivation. These assumptions are based on cognitive evaluation theory (Deci & Ryan, 1985). However, as Carton further stated, operant psychologists' reviews of the literature on the effects of rewards on intrinsic motivation (e.g., Dickinson, 1989; Flora, 1990; Scott, 1975) reach vastly different conclusions than those conducted by psychologists with decidedly cognitive viewpoints. Important points raised by operant psychologists include the finding that many social cognitivists have presumed that reinforcement decreases intrinsic motivation when in fact the rewards utilized in these particular studies often did not show a clear increase in response rate. Thus, by definition, these presumed rewards were not reinforcement. Furthermore, cognitive studies did not assess response rates for stability, behavioral observations included in most of these studies were often relatively brief, and these studies rarely included follow-up observations. Carton eloquently stated that a review of the literature found little support for examples of a decrease in intrinsic motivation on the basis of the cognitive evaluation theory and revealed three confounding effects: (a) temporal contiguity, (b) the number of reward administrations, and (c) discriminative stimuli associated with reward availability.

Carton (1996) also discussed the effects of temporal contiguity. Temporal contiguity refers to the amount of time between the occurrence of the target behavior and the delivery of the consequence. In an examination of the literature, Carton found time differences between the delivery of tangible rewards and verbal rewards (i.e., praise) in many studies. Most of the verbal rewards were delivered immediately after the target behavior occurred, thereby increasing the likelihood that behavior would be repeated. In contrast, tangible rewards were often delivered days or weeks after the treatment setting, virtually ensuring a decrease in the occurrence of the target behavior. Carton's finding that researchers in those studies have consistently found decreases in intrinsic motivation following the administration of tangible rewards and increases in intrinsic motivation following the administration of verbal rewards then is not surprising.

Cameron and Pierce's (1994) meta-analytic findings that reinforcement did not harm intrinsic motivation have been criticized by researchers who stated that their methodology and, consequently, the conclusions drawn were flawed (Kohn, 1996; Lepper et al., 1996). Kohn argued that Cameron and Pierce ignored important findings that suggested that the reception of tangible rewards is associated with less voluntary time on task as contrasted with the no-reward condition. Kohn further stated that Cameron and Pierce's methodology was flawed. He suggested that it was inappropriate to detect an overall effect by combining results from studies in which informational praise was delivered (i.e., no detrimental effects on intrinsic motivation expected) with studies in which praise was delivered that might be construed as manipulative (i.e., detrimental effects on intrinsic motivation expected). Further, Kohn pointed out that, in his view, the more common type of praise in a classroom is the latter, and, therefore, studies that utilized manipulative praise should be examined separately. Lepper et al. (1996) labeled Cameron and Pierce's (1994) meta-analysis overly simplistic and of little theoretical value. Similar to Kohn (1996), Lepper et al. wrote that the 1994 meta-analysis should not have focused on an overall effect because rewards have a variety of effects dependent on the nature of the activities, the manner in which the rewards are administered, and the situation surrounding administration. For example, the reception of a tangible reward would be expected to decrease intrinsic motivation, whereas the reception of a verbal reward (i.e., social reinforcement) would be expected to maintain or increase intrinsic motivation.

Cameron and Pierce (1996) responded to these criticisms by first stating that investigating the overall effect of extrinsic rewards is necessary for practical and theoretical reasons. From a practical standpoint, it is clear that many parents, educators, and administrators have embraced Kohn's (1993) view that overall, incentive systems are damaging. Many classroom teachers, however, still wish to adopt an incentive program. These teachers are, therefore, interested in whether or not, overall, rewards would disrupt intrinsic motivation for completing work or attaining a specified level of performance. The overall effect of reward, then, is critical (Cameron & Pierce, 1996). Theoretically, many academic journals and textbooks point to the overall detrimental effects of rewards or reinforcement. Consequently, many parents, teachers, and others are loath to use any reinforcement procedure under any conditions. It is necessary then, according to Cameron and Pierce, to analyze the overall effect of rewards because many writers are criticizing the use of incentive programs in educational settings. These criticisms are based on research findings that some interpret as indicating an overall negative effect. Cameron and Pierce concluded their response by stating that their meta-analysis was the most thorough to date on this topic and compared favorably with Tang and Hall's (1995) analysis that included 50 studies, Wiersma's (1992) analysis that contained 20 studies, and Rummel and Feinberg's (1988) analysis that comprised 45 studies. Each of these analyses discovered overall that extrinsic rewards had detrimental effects on intrinsic motivation. These findings were in direct contrast to the conclusions of Cameron and Pierce, who stated emphatically that their results, from an analysis of over 100, illustrated that rewards can be used to maintain or even enhance intrinsic motivation. More important, the conditions under which detrimental effects to intrinsic motivation are exhibited occur under highly circumscribed conditions, situations that are easily avoided by the proper use of token reinforcement programs.

In response to Cameron and Pierce's (1994) meta-analytic findings, Deci et al. (1999a) conducted a separate meta-analysis in part to refute the previous findings. They included 128 studies and arranged the analysis to provide a test of cognitive evaluation theory. Deci and colleagues did find support for cognitive evaluation theory and substantial undermining effects following the use of external rewards. They specifically examined verbal rewards (termed *positive feedback*) separately from tangible rewards. The tangible rewards were further divided into the categories of unexpected and expected. The expected-reward category included the divisions of task noncontingent (rewards given not for engaging in the task specifically but for participation in the experiment), engagement contingent (rewards given for participation in the task), completion contingent (rewards given for completion of the task), and performance contingent (rewards given only for performing the task well, or surpassing a previously set standard). A decrement in intrinsic motivation, measured by time on task for 101 of the studies and self-report of interest for 84 of the studies, was found in every category except verbal rewards and unexpected rewards. It is interesting that Deci et al. divided the verbal reward studies into the categories of college-age and children. Although verbal rewards enhanced the intrinsic motivation of college students (i.e., significant increase), the delivery of verbal rewards did not enhance children's intrinsic motivation. Deci et al. also discussed the importance of the interpersonal context in the delivery of verbal reward (i.e., rewards delivered in a controlling manner will tend to decrease intrinsic motivation, whereas rewards delivered in a noncontrolling manner will tend to increase feelings of competence and, hence, intrinsic motivation).

On the basis of the finding that children exhibited less enhancement from verbal rewards than college students, Deci et al. (1999a) suggested that this finding has important implications for the use of verbal praise in the classroom, writing that "verbal rewards are less likely to have a positive effect for children . . . [they] can even have a negative effect on intrinsic motivation" (p. 9). That is a misleading assumption. The importance (Maag & Katsiyannis, 1999) and effectiveness of teacher attention, particularly in the form of verbal praise, have been documented (Drevno et al., 1994; Parrish, Cataldo, Kolko, Neef, & Engel, 1986; Valcante, Roberson, Reid, & Wolking, 1989). The assertion that verbal praise should not be utilized in a classroom setting is in direct opposition to the available data.

Cameron et al. (2001) completed the most recent meta-analysis and found, in general, that rewards do not decrease intrinsic motivation. Their sample included 145 studies and similar categorizations to Deci et al. (1999a). Although the sample was not homogeneous, an overall effect size was calculated. Cameron (2001) stated this overall effect is important as educators and other school personnel often report that all rewards are harmful to motivation. Contrary to Deci et al., Cameron et al. included the categories of high and low initial interest. Notably, they found that reward can enhance time on task and intrinsic motivation. This is in accordance with Bandura's (1986) finding that most activities have little initial interest for people but that engagement in the activity may increase interest. This has important implications for schools because many children do not find academic tasks initially appealing. The reward, then, may be used to increase students' time on task and intrinsic motivation for a task. Cameron et al. (2001) did not find decremental effects with the use of verbal praise for either children or college students. Instead, they found a significant increase.

In terms of tangible reward, no detrimental effect was found for unexpected rewards or for rewards that are closely tied to specific standards of performance and to success. Detrimental effect was found when rewards were not explicitly connected to the task and signified failure. This last finding is also important to educators who may be attempting to use reinforcement to increase either social or academic behavior. Often, teachers will set the goals for a student too high. Behavioral principles state that it is important to shape behavior, reinforcing the child's current competencies and giving the child a chance for success.

It is also important to remember that neither of these meta-analyses examined the results of more behavioral studies (e.g., Feingold & Mahoney, 1975). No study to date utilizing single-case design (e.g., Akin-Little & Little, 2004; Mintz, 2003) has found any detrimental effects with the use of reinforcement contingencies (Akin-Little et al., 2004). This is significant, as those studies tend to more typically mimic the use of reward contingencies in classrooms. Perhaps if more behaviorally oriented studies were conducted, there would be no detection of the supposed detrimental effects of the reward on any task or behavior.

BEST PRACTICES IN THE USE OF REINFORCEMENT PROCEDURES IN THE CLASSROOM

In 1991, the National Education Association published a document titled *How to Kill Creativity* (Tegano et al., 1991) that stated the following:

> The expectation of reward can actually undermine intrinsic motivation and creativity of performance . . . . A wide variety of rewards have now been tested, and everything from good-player awards to marshmallows produces the expected decrements in intrinsic motivation and creativity of performance. . . . [making] them [students] much less likely to take risks or to approach a task with a playful or experimental attitude. (p. 119)

However, a review of several educational psychology books (e.g., Slavin, 2006; Woolfolk, 2007) revealed a more balanced view of the effects of rewards by including the findings of Cameron and Pierce (1994), along with Deci and

Ryan (1985) and Lepper et al. (1973). This is an encouraging sign because many of the findings in this area support the effectiveness of reinforcement procedures in the classroom, and many researchers have criticized the literature on supposed damaging effects (e.g., Bandura, 1986; Bates, 1979; Dickinson, 1989; Flora, 1990; Morgan, 1984).

Additionally, any detrimental effects of the use of extrinsic reinforcement can be easily avoided. Rewards should not be presented for mere participation in a task without regard for completion or quality. Decrements have also been found in the social cognitive literature when rewards are presented on a single occasion. This is not the most common method used in classrooms. In general, reward contingencies used in schools are presented repeatedly with appropriate thinning of schedules utilized when behavior change has occurred. Psychologists are advised to heed this advice when consulting and planning with teachers on the use of reinforcers in the school setting.

Teachers continually request training in behavior and classroom management (Maag, 1999). The irony is that techniques that aid teachers in improving their management skills have existed since Skinner's (1953) seminal work on the principles of operant conditioning. Techniques based on the use of extrinsic reinforcers (i.e., positive reinforcement) work in the classroom. These include verbal praise, token economies, group contingencies, and contracts (Little & Akin-Little, 2003). The question, then, is why teacher education programs are not incorporating these principles into their curriculum. Why is there such resistance to the data? Axelrod (1996) suggested that some causes for the lack of both professional and popular acceptance (Kohn, 1993) may be that the use of positive reinforcement consumes too much time, attempts to eliminate human choice, and offers little compensation for educational personnel for using these procedures. This is a somewhat discouraging view, and one can only hope that future and current teachers and educational personnel make evidence-based decisions when choosing interventions for children and youth.

Bribery is defined in the dictionary as an inducement to engage in illegal or inappropriate behavior. When education personnel, including school psychologists, extol the use of extrinsic reinforcement in the classroom, the motive is clearly not to "bribe" children and youth, but to increase appropriate academic and social behavior. The goal is obviously not to decrease intrinsic motivation, although it is unclear that the construct exists or is useful in the science of psychology. It is apparent through an examination of the data that any decrease occurs only under specifically circumscribed conditions, conditions that are easily avoidable. Best practice suggests that children and youth deserve interventions based on sound, empirical findings. The positive effect of the use of reinforcers in the classroom is one such conclusion.

REFERENCES

Akin-Little, K. A., Eckert, T. L., Lovett, B. J., & Little, S. G. (2004). Extrinsic reinforcement in the classroom: Bribery or best practice? *School Psychology Review*, *33*, 344–362.

Akin-Little, K. A., & Little, S. G. (2004). Re-examining the overjustification effect: A case study. *Journal of Behavioral Education*, *13*, 179–192.

Alberto, P. A., & Troutman, A. C. (2006). *Applied behavior analysis for teachers* (7th ed.). Upper Saddle River, NJ: Prentice Hall.

Axelrod, S. (1996). What's wrong with behavior analysis? *Journal of Behavioral Education*, *6*, 247–256.

Ayllon, T., & Azrin, N. (1968). *The token economy: A motivational system for therapy and rehabilitation*. New York: Appleton-Century-Crofts.

Bandura, A. (1977). *Social learning theory*. Englewood Cliffs, NJ: Prentice Hall.

Bandura, A. (1986). *Social foundations of thought and action: A social cognitive theory*. Englewood Cliffs, NJ: Prentice Hall.

Barrish, H. H., Saunders, M., & Wolf, M. M. (1969). Good behavior game: Effects of individual contingencies for group consequences on disruptive behavior in a classroom. *Journal of Applied Behavior Analysis*, *2*, 119–124.

Bates, J. A. (1979). Extrinsic reward and intrinsic motivation: A review with implications for the classroom. *Review of Educational Research*, *49*, 557–576.

Birnbrauer, J. S., Wolf, M. M., Kidder, J. D., & Tague, C. E. (1965). Classroom behavior of retarded pupils with token reinforcement. *Journal of Experimental Child Psychology*, *2*, 219–235.

Brondolo, E., Baruch, C., Conway, E., & Marsh, L. (1994). Aggression among inner-city and minority youth: A biopsychosocial model for school-based evaluation and treatment. *Journal of Social Distress and the Homeless*, *3*, 53–80.

Buisson, G. J., Murdock, J. Y., Reynolds, K. E., & Cronin, M. E. (1995). Effect of tokens on response latency of students with hearing impairments in a resource room. *Education and Treatment of Children*, *18*, 408–421.

Cameron, J., Banko, K. M., & Pierce, W. D. (2001). Pervasive negative effects of rewards on intrinsic motivation: The myth continues. *The Behavior Analyst*, *24*, 1–44.

Cameron, J., & Pierce, W. D. (1994). Reinforcement, reward, and intrinsic motivation: A meta-analysis. *Review of Educational Research*, *64*, 363–423.

Cameron, J., & Pierce, W. D. (1996). The debate about rewards and intrinsic motivation: Protests and accusations do not alter the results. *Review of Educational Research*, *66*, 39–51.

Carton, J. S. (1996). The differential effects of tangible rewards and praise on intrinsic motivation: A comparison of cognitive evaluation theory and operant theory. *The Behavior Analyst*, *19*, 237–255.

Cavalier, A. R., Ferretti, R. P., & Hodges, A. E. (1997). Self-management within a classroom token economy for students with learning disabilities. *Research in Developmental Disabilities, 18,* 167–178.

Davidson, P., & Bucher, B. (1978). Intrinsic interest and extrinsic reward: The effects of a continuing token program on continuing nonconstrained preference. *Behavior Therapy, 9,* 222–234.

Deci, E. L., Koestner, R., & Ryan, R. M. (1999a). A meta-analytic review of experiments examining the effects of extrinsic rewards on intrinsic motivation. *Psychological Bulletin, 125,* 627–668.

Deci, E. L., Koestner, R., & Ryan, R. M. (1999b). The undermining effect is a reality after all-extrinsic rewards, task interest, and self-determination. Reply to Eisenberger, Pierce, and Cameron (1999) and Lepper, Henderlong, and Gingras (1999). *Psychological Bulletin, 125,* 692–700.

Deci, E. L., Koestner, R., & Ryan, R. M. (2001). Extrinsic rewards and intrinsic motivation in education: Reconsidered once again. *Review of Educational Research, 71,* 1–27.

Deci, E. L., & Ryan, R. (1985). *Intrinsic motivation and self-determination in human behavior.* New York: Plenum.

Dickinson, A. M. (1989). The detrimental effects of extrinsic reinforcement on "intrinsic motivation." *The Behavior Analyst, 12,* 1–15.

Drevno, G., Kimball, J., Possi, M., Heward, W., Gardner, R., & Barbetta, P. (1994). Effects of active student response during error correction on the acquisition, maintenance, and generalization of science vocabulary by elementary students: A systematic replication. *Journal of Applied Behavior Analysis, 27,* 179–180.

Eisenberger, R., & Cameron, J. (1996). Detrimental effects of reward: Reality or myth? *American Psychologist, 51,* 1153–1166.

Eisenberger, R., Pierce, W. D., & Cameron, J. (1999). Effects of reward on intrinsic motivation: Negative, neutral, and positive. *Psychological Bulletin, 125,* 677–691.

Fair, E. M., & Silvestri, L. (1992). Effects of reward, competition and outcome on intrinsic motivation. *Journal of Instructional Psychology, 19,* 3–8.

Feingold, B. D., & Mahoney, M. J. (1975). Reinforcement effects on intrinsic interest: Undermining the overjustification hypothesis. *Behavior Therapy, 6,* 367–377.

Flora, S. R. (1990). Undermining intrinsic interest from the standpoint of a behaviorist. *The Psychological Record, 40,* 323–346.

Flora, S. R., & Flora, D. B. (1999). Effects of extrinsic reinforcement for reading during childhood on reported reading habits of college students. *Psychological Record, 49,* 3–14.

Greene, D., & Lepper, M. R. (1974). Effects of extrinsic rewards on children's subsequent intrinsic interest. *Child Development, 45,* 1141–1145.

Guzzo, R. A. (1979). Types of rewards, cognitions and work motivation. *Academy of Management Journal, 22,* 75–86.

Horcones, C. (1987). The concept of consequences in the analysis of behavior. *The Behavior Analyst, 10,* 291–294.

Kohn, A. (1993). *Punished by rewards: The trouble with gold stars, incentive plans, A's, praise, and other bribes.* Boston: Houghton Mifflin.

Kohn, A. (1996). By all available means: Cameron and Pierce's defense of extrinsic motivators. *Review of Educational Research, 66,* 1–3.

Lepper, M. R. (1983). Extrinsic reward and intrinsic motivation: Implications for the classroom. In J. M. Levine & M. C. Wang (Eds.), *Teacher and student perceptions: Implications for learning* (pp. 281–317). Hillsdale, NJ: Erlbaum.

Lepper, M. R. (1998). A whole much less than the sum of its parts. *American Psychologist, 53,* 675–676.

Lepper, M. R., & Gilovich, T. (1981). The multiple functions of reward: A social developmental perspective. In S. S. Brehm, S. Kassin, & F. X. Gibbons (Eds.), *Developmental social psychology* (pp. 5–31). New York: Oxford University Press.

Lepper, M. R., Greene, D., & Nisbett, R. E. (1973). Undermining children's intrinsic interest with extrinsic reward: A test of the "overjustification" hypothesis. *Journal of Personality and Social Psychology, 28,* 129–137.

Lepper, M. R., Keavney, M., & Drake, M. (1996). Intrinsic motivation and extrinsic rewards: A commentary on Cameron and Pierce's meta-analysis. *Review of Educational Research, 66,* 5–32.

Little, S. G., & Akin-Little, K. A. (2003). Classroom management. In W. O'Donohue, J. Fisher, & S. Hayes (Eds.), *Empirically supported techniques of cognitive behavioral therapy: A step-by-step guide for clinicians* (pp. 65–70). New York: Wiley.

Maag, J. W. (1996). *Parenting without punishment.* Philadelphia: Charles Press.

Maag, J. W. (1999). *Behavior management: From the theoretical implications to practical applications.* San Diego, CA: Singular.

Maag, J. W., & Katsiyannis, A. (1999). Teacher preparation in E/BD: A national survey. *Behavioral Disorders, 24,* 189–196.

Mann-Feder, V., & Varda, R. (1996). Adolescents in therapeutic committees. *Adolescence, 31,* 17–28.

Mawhinney, T. C., Dickinson, A. M., & Taylor, L. A., III. (1989). The use of concurrent schedules to evaluate the effects of extrinsic rewards on "intrinsic motivation." *Journal of Organizational Behavior Management, 10,* 109–129.

McGinnis, J. C. (1996). *On intrinsic motivation: A proposal for and validation of a unique dependent measure.* Unpublished master's thesis, University of Southern Mississippi, Hattiesburg.

Mintz, C. M. (2003). *A behavior analytic evaluation of the overjustification effect as it relates to education.* Unpublished doctoral dissertation, University of Nevada, Reno.

Morgan, M. (1984). Reward-induced decrements and increments in intrinsic motivation. *Review of Educational Research, 54,* 5–30.

O'Leary, K. D., & Drabman, R. (1971). Token reinforcement programs in the classroom: A review. *Psychological Bulletin, 75,* 379–398.

Parrish, J., Cataldo, M., Kolko, D., Neef, N., & Engel, A. (1986). Experimental analysis of response covariation among compliant and inappropriate behavior. *Journal of Applied Behavior Analysis, 19*, 241–254.

Pittman, T. S., Boggiano, A. K., & Ruble, D. N. (1983). Intrinsic and extrinsic motivational orientations: Limiting conditions on the undermining and enhancing effects of reward on intrinsic motivation. In J. M. Levine & M. C. Wang (Eds.), *Teacher and student perceptions: Implications for learning* (pp. 319–340). Hillsdale, NJ: Erlbaum.

Reiss, S., & Sushinsky, L. W. (1975). Overjustification, competing, responses, and the acquisition of intrinsic interest. *Journal of Personality and Social Psychology, 30*, 1116–1125.

Rosenfield, D., Folger, R., & Adelman, H. F. (1980). When rewards reflect competence: A qualification of the overjustification effect. *Journal of Personality and Social Psychology, 39*, 368–376.

Ryan, R. M., & Deci, E. L. (1996). When paradigms clash: Comments on Cameron and Pierce's claim that rewards do not undermine intrinsic motivation. *Review of Educational Research, 66*, 33–38.

Rummel, A., & Feinberg, R. (1988). Cognitive evaluation theory: A meta-analysis review of the literature. *Social Behavior and Personality, 16*, 147–164.

Scott, W. E., Jr. (1975). The effects of extrinsic rewards on "intrinsic motivation." *Organizational Behavior and Human Performance, 25*, 311–335.

Skinner, B. F. (1953). *Science and human behavior.* New York: Macmillan.

Slavin, R. E. (2006). *Educational psychology: Theory and practice* (8th ed.). Boston: Allyn & Bacon.

Swiezy, N. B., Matson, J. L., & Box, P. (1992). The good behavior game: A token reinforcement system for preschoolers. *Child and Family Behavior Therapy, 14*, 21–32.

Tang, S., & Hall, V. (1995). The overjustification effect: A meta-analysis. *Applied Cognitive Psychology, 9*, 365–404.

Tegano, D. W., Moran, D. J., III, & Sawyers, J. K. (1991). *Creativity in early childhood classrooms.* Washington, DC: National Education Association.

Valcante, G., Roberson, W., Reid, W., & Wolking, W. (1989). Effects of wait-time and intertrial interval durations on learning by children with multiple handicaps. *Journal of Applied Behavior Analysis, 13*, 43–55.

Vasta, R., Andrews, D. E., McLaughlin, A. M., Stirpe, L. A., & Comfort, C. (1978). Reinforcement effects on intrinsic interest: A classroom analog. *Journal of School Psychology, 16*, 161–166.

Vasta, R., & Stirpe, L. A. (1979). Reinforcement effects on three measures of children's interest in math. *Behavior Modification, 3*, 223–244.

Wiersma, U. J. (1992). The effects of extrinsic rewards in intrinsic motivation: A meta-analysis. *Journal of Occupational and Organizational Psychology, 65*, 101–114.

Williams, B. W. (1980). Reinforcement, behavior constraint, and the overjustification effect. *Journal of Personality and Social Psychology, 39*, 599–614.

Woolfolk, A. E. (2007). *Educational psychology* (10th ed.). Boston: Allyn & Bacon.

Zimmerman, B. J. (1985). The development of "intrinsic" motivation: A social learning analysis. *Annals of Child Development, 2,* 117–160.

II

SYSTEMATIC APPROACHES TO PREVENTION AND INTERVENTION

6

AN INTRODUCTION TO COGNITIVE BEHAVIOR THERAPIES

RAYMOND DIGIUSEPPE

The way children and adolescents behave in school has much to do with their cognitive schema; that is, their estimation of self-worth and attitudes about other people's motivations. Clinical problems such as depression and anxiety also impact school behavior. This chapter aims to give readers a survey view of cognitive behavior therapy (CBT) and how it has been and could be applied to school-based behavior interventions.

HISTORY OF COGNITIVE BEHAVIOR THERAPY

Since the beginning of Western Civilization, philosophers have been concerned with the relationship between what people think and how they feel. Thinkers such as Aristotle, Plato, and Seneca identified beliefs, ideas, and attitudes that lead to emotional disturbance. They also identified thoughts, attitudes, and beliefs that could help people lead productive, happy lives. The rhetorical debate to convince people to give up the former and believe the latter took up a large part of their classic writings. This idea of helping people lead adjusted, productive lives by focusing on what they thought and believed seemed to have been lost in the initial approaches to psychotherapy.

Behavioral approaches to psychotherapy started a new scientifically based approach to the study of behavior change. Originally, behavior therapy and behavior modification defined themselves as clinical procedures on the basis of the laws of learning. Most of these laws of learning were based on the animal models of operant and classical conditioning. Behavioral theorists and clinicians attempted to avoid the unscientific nature of previous attempts at psychotherapy by studying only observable behavior. Because thoughts are not observable, the role of cognitions in behaviorism and behavior therapy generated considerable controversy in the early history of our field. Skinner originally thought of thoughts as covert verbal behavior that followed the same rules of learning as other behaviors. However, Ellis (1955) and Beck (1976) introduced "cognitive" approaches to therapy just as the new field of behavior therapy emerged. These cognitive therapists included many behavioral interventions into their practice and strove to have the same scientific values that behavior therapy advanced. From the beginning of behavior therapy, cognitive and behavioral approaches existed side by side. In fact, the first volume of the journal *Behavior Therapy* included an article by Beck (1970) on cognitive therapy.

CBT represents an integration of behavioral and cognitive interventions. The history of CBT can be traced to the first Cognitive Behavior Therapy Research conference, sponsored by Albert Ellis in 1977. This conference brought together the leading published authors in the field, including Ellis (1962); Beck (1976); Meichenbaum (1977); Mahoney (1976); and Spivack, Platt, and Shure (1976) as well as other individuals who had been developing interventions that involved cognitive procedure under a common orientation called cognitive-behavior therapy. This year also coincided with the publication of Meichenbaum's (1977) *Cognitive Behavior Modification*.

CBT emerged from two disparate traditions. The first tradition started in behavior therapy when therapists became disappointed that token economies had produced poor generalization across time and place (O'Leary & Drabman, 1971). Behaviorists could not always provide the reinforcement for the adaptive behavior. Even for areas such as assertiveness training, which involved rehearsing a client's new adaptive skill, most authors advise that therapists should plan generalization across situations rather than assume that it will occur automatically (Alberti & Emmons, 2008; Duckworth & Mercer, 2006). The exigencies of life presented clients with so many variations on the type of problematic situations that it was impossible to rehearse an adaptive response for all the events that could cue maladaptive behavior. Behavior therapists wanted to teach a skill that people could use to cue the desired behaviors and to self-reinforce for their occurrence. This would require some language-based rule to generate coping behaviors that would work across a wide variety of situations. The initial CBT interventions involved teaching people self-control skills focused on responding to situations outside of the therapy sessions (Kanfer & Goldstein, 1975).

They second tradition came from Ellis (1962), Beck (1976), and Spivack et al. (1976). These individuals received their initial training in psychoanalytic approaches and became dissatisfied with the length of treatment. The scientific and clinical failure to confirm unconscious processes led these therapists to focus on clients' present and conscious thoughts. They each incorporated directive techniques into their practices and created a number of the CBT interventions used today. Although the nature of cognition and its role in guiding behavior is still unclear and still intensely studied, the role of cognitive interventions has been mostly welcomed into behavior therapy, forming the most popular theoretical orientation among psychologists. In this chapter, I attempt to identify the major cognitive interventions. However, CBT is a hyphenated moniker. All advocates of cognitive interventions integrate them with the behavioral interventions identified in the other chapters of this book.

ASSUMPTIONS ABOUT EMOTIONS, THOUGHTS, AND BEHAVIOR CHANGE

All forms of CBT assert that a person's present conscious thoughts, images, perceptions, schema, predictions, and appraisals mediate human emotion and behavior. This statement does not imply that behavior cannot be mediated by purely conditional influences. A model of CBT proposed by Power and Dalgliseh (1999) suggests that different pathways to emotion may exist for conditioning-based learning and cognitions. The focus of cognitive therapies is on conscious cognitions. The field does not deny that some cognitions or information processing might be unconscious. However, most CBT practitioners believe that unconscious thoughts can easily become conscious. Bringing unconscious thoughts into consciousness does not change them but allows the therapist and client to begin the change.

CBT focuses less on the unconscious motivational intent of a person's actions than traditional psychotherapy and focuses on information processing rather than motivation (Ingram, 1984). Therapists learn how clients construe their world, what types of information they perceive, and what aspects of a situation they fail to understand and process. Regardless of how emotional disturbance is learned, CBT approaches posit that therapists focus on the cognitive structures and behaviors that maintain the disturbance. Focusing on the direct change of the thoughts associated with disturbed emotions and dysfunctional behaviors is one effective way of changing emotion and behavior. Clients can learn new cognitions through active learning of new ideas (Mahoney, 1991).

Two controversies surrounding the nature of cognitions have persisted throughout the history of CBT. The first controversy concerns whether cognitions cause emotional disturbance. Initially, modern cognitive theorists proposed that dysfunctional, illogical, or irrational beliefs cause disturbed emotions (David, Freeman, & DiGiuseppe, in press). The causal link between thoughts and emotions remains unproven and is still an intense area of research today. Beck (2005) and Ellis (2005) evolved the position that thoughts, emotions, and behaviors are interwoven aspects of the human experience. Thoughts, emotions, and behaviors are hopelessly interconnected and separated only in the mind of theorists. People cannot change one of these without changing the others. Cognition restructuring is an accessible intervention when emotions are intense. People are reluctant to engage in direct behavioral change assignments such as exposure when the emotional reactions are strong and painful. The choice of cognitive interventions does not require proof that dysfunctional cognitions cause the clinical symptoms. It only requires that they co-occur and that the emotions change in response to cognitive interventions. Medical treatments may work directly on the emotional sites of the brain but bring about changes in thoughts and behavior. Cognitive interventions will result in the same effects. The proof concerning ultimate causation remains elusive.

For example, a child with social anxiety may benefit from direct exposure trials to social situations. However, he or she may refrain from participating in the exposure assignments because the thought of the exposure arouses the irrational thoughts and intense fear. This social anxiety may have resulted from early conditioning experiences or previous learning of thought patterns. The clinician may never know. A cognitive intervention aimed at these thoughts could help reduce the thoughts and lower emotional arousal. This allows the child or adolescent to have sufficient control over his or her emotions as he or she attempts the exposure assignment. The exposure assignments further change the thoughts and reduce the emotions. The cognitions associated with social anxiety may not have caused the problem; however, they may be a practical area for initial interventions. Thus, the ultimate causal connection is not important for the therapy to work.

Cognitive interventions rest on views concerning how people change their thinking. The second controversy is whether insight into incorrect ideas causes behavior change or whether a process of thought rehearsal is necessary for change to occur. Psychotherapists have long thought that insight and understanding are the primary mechanisms of change in psychotherapy. In traditional psychotherapy models, change occurs because of insight (Prochaska & DiClemente, 2005). This is the "aha!" that people experience when they understand or discover that their old ideas are incorrect. Once people conclude that existing ideas are incorrect and that they need to replace them with new ones, what happens to their old ideas? The replacement of old ideas with new ones has received considerable attention in psychology and goes back to a debate between proponents of the theories of Descartes and Spinoza (Gilbert, 1991). Descartes believed that once a person understood or believed a new idea, he or she gave up the old idea. Thus, the transition from old to new thoughts was discrete. Understanding or insight was the mechanism for this change. This model of change forms the foundation for most forms of psychotherapy.

Spinoza maintained that when people learn new ideas, a memory trace of the old idea always remains. He proposed that people just learn new ideas over old ones. Thus, a situation or cue elicits a cognitive reaction or thought. When we convince ourselves that an idea is wrong, we rehearse a new, alternative thought. Whenever a person confronts the original cue for the old thought, he or she will briefly experience the old idea followed by the new idea. Rehearsal or practice strengthens the connection between the old idea and the new idea. With rehearsal, people lessen the time that they experience the old idea and increase the strength of the new thought until the old thoughts no longer reach awareness. After sufficient rehearsal, this connection may occur so quickly that people barely experience the old idea at all: They go from the original stimulus to the new idea (Mahoney, 1991). Under stress, however, people sometimes revert to experiencing the old idea when the stimulus occurs. Under these situations, people need to work hard to challenge the old idea and activate the new idea.

Research in human learning supports Spinoza's view that rehearsal is important rather than Descartes's reliance on insight (Gilbert, 1991). Because many mental health professions associate the term *cognitive* with insight or understanding, they assume that it would be sufficient that their clients understand that their negative automatic thoughts or irrational beliefs are wrong. However, cognitive psychotherapies rely more on rehearsal to help people internalize new, adaptive cognitions than they rely on insight. In this way, one sees the ideas presented originally by Skinner (1957) and Hayes (2004) that verbal behavior and thoughts follow the same laws of learning as muscular responses.

Cognitions that guide behaviors are strengthened by rehearsal more than insight or understanding. Practicing the thoughts that will guide adaptive behavior or repeatedly challenging negative dysfunctional thoughts and replacing them with rational ones is the hallmark of CBT. For some people this representation of CBT is less philosophical and represents the behavioral legacy of CBT. School psychologists should not assume that a child's understanding of why a thought is dysfunctional will lead to change. Rehearsal is still necessary regardless of the insight, verbal intelligence, or maturity of the child.

DEVELOPMENTAL MODELS OF BEHAVIOR CHANGE

CBT interventions are sometimes divided into two types of theories. First are the cognitive deficit models. These theories assert that normal development involves the acquisition of certain cognitive processes that guide coping. Well-adjusted children develop some cognitive processes and structures that mediate or guide their adaptive behavior when they encounter stressful situations. Such models posit that children and adolescents with emotional and behavioral problems fail to develop these adaptive cognitive processes. Cognitive deficit model interventions originally appeared for children with externalizing disorders. They include the social problem-solving model (SPS) and self-instructional training (SIT; Kendall, 2002).

The second model focuses on changing dysfunctional thoughts and beliefs. This dysfunctional cognitions model includes Ellis's (1962) rational emotive behavior therapy (REBT) and Beck's (1976) cognitive therapy (CT). These therapies were designed mostly with adults who suffered with internalizing disorders and were then adapted for work with children.

Social Problem Solving

The first cognitive deficit model, the SPS model, rests on the assumption that people will inevitably face social conflicts. The successful resolution of social conflicts requires some problem-solving skills. Social problem-solving skills are learned from modeling and direct instruction. The successful resolution of social conflicts involves first recognizing that a problem or conflict exists. Next, the child would generate all the possible alternative solutions to the problem. This ability is termed *alternative solution thinking*. Then, the child would image the consequences that each solution might produce. After reviewing the solutions and the consequences, the child would pick a solution. Children who generate the more alternative solutions usually have the best adjustment. The generation of these thoughts, not the recognition of them, is the skill associated with adjustment.

Because SPS interventions were originally used with young aggressive children (Spivack et al., 1976), the teaching of consequential thinking might inhibit or interfere with the teaching of alternative solution thinking. Suppose a child generates a list of alternative responses to frustrating social events that include aggressive responses. The therapist faces a dilemma. Should he or she, on the one hand, point out the negative consequences of aggression and squelch that type of response? On the other hand, should he or she allow the child to keep generating alternatives and review the consequences of each response when the child completes the generation of solutions? That is, does one stop aggression first or the generation process? Most experts in problem solving consider it better to promote generation and review the consequences for all of the responses together when the generation of alternatives is completed (Nezu, personal communication, 2008).

Once a person chooses which solution to implement, or strategy to solve a conflict, he or she needs to work out the details. This is referred to as means-ends thinking and involves alternative solution thinking and consequential thinking on a microlevel (D'Zurilla & Nezu, 2006). Suppose a child wants to make friends with another child in his class. He can wait until the other child speaks to him, wait for another child he knows to speak to the child and then begin to talk to both children, or he can go up to the child and start a conversation. Suppose our hypothetical child decides that the first two strategies are inefficient because they rely on someone else's behavior. The chances of success are too low. The third solution seems better. Now when he thinks about going up to the child and starting a conversation, he needs to decide what to say. Therefore, he again generates solutions. He might think, "I could ask about the New York Mets' game last night," "I could ask about the lunch room food that is notoriously bad," or "I could ask him about the new bike I saw him riding." He thinks the child will be more interested in talking about his new bike, so he chooses that opening comment. In this way, means-ends thinking is a downward extension of the first two strategies.

Social problem-solving skills can be measured validly in preschool children to adults. A long history of research indicates that disturbed groups score lower on social problem-solving skills than normal comparison groups. Social problem-solving skills are analogous to the steps people would use to solve problems having to do with inanimate objects. However, these two sets of skills correlate very little. In addition, social problem-solving skills correlate very poorly with intelligence. Thus, intelligence and active thinking about the nonsocial world do not seem to relate to how someone uses the same skills when people are involved. A transfer of learning from the inanimate world to the social world does not automatically take place. Although self-report assessment scales of social problem-solving skills exist for adults, most researchers measure these skills in youth with performance-based measures (see examples by Fenstermacher, Olympia, & Sheridan, 2006; Nock & Mendes, 2008). Reliable and valid self-report measures for youth that can be used in professional practice have not yet been developed. Presently, practitioners must rely on interview strategies to assess them.

Social problem-solving intervention manuals have been tested for people across a wide range of ages, from preschoolers through adults, and across a wide range of behavior problems, from aggression to depression. These skills can be taught in individual, small group sessions, or in the classroom. Elisa and Butler's (2005) book represents an excellent example of a treatment manual for school-age children. Research has supported their efficacy as interventions (Sukhodolsky, Golub, Stone, & Orban, 2005) and as primary prevention programs (Daunic, Smith, Brank, & Penfield, 2006) for treating anger (Sukhodolsky et al., 2005), aggression (Daunic et al., 2006), or general emotional reactions (Kraag, Zeegers, Kok, Hosman, Abu-Sadd, 2006). The SPS model represents one of the most researched areas in CBT and would be a good first-line intervention for most problems that school psychologists encounter.

Self-Instructional Training

Meichenbaum (1977, 1993) developed SIT for treating people with schizophrenia. He quickly applied this procedure to children with impulsivity problems. Meichenbaum based his therapeutic intervention on the Soviet developmental psychologist Vygotsky's (1962) model of sequential-verbal cognitive processing. Vygotsky pondered the problem of whether language was necessary for thought. He concluded that it was not. People and animals could think without language. However, he demonstrated that language did facilitate sequential thought. The dominant hemisphere of the brain controls both language and sequential reasoning. Vygotsky observed that children learned to use language to guide complex behaviors that required the sequencing of many responses. He noticed that learning to guide behavior by language followed a sequence. First, children learned to encode the complex, sequential task in language. Then, they spoke the words aloud as they performed the behavior. Then, they lowered their voice and spoke in a whisper to guide the behavior. Finally, children reported using subvocal speech to guide their behavior.

Meichenbaum (1977, 1993) noticed that most people talked to themselves. Subvocal speech was a common experience when people were trying to perform complex new tasks. Many people who behaved dysfunctionally had little, if any, internal language to guide their responses. When faced with desires to approach or avoid a stimulus, they acted immediately with little or no conscious processing. When they encountered problems, they often had what Meichenbaum termed the *internal dialogue*. That is, conflicting ideas compete for space in one's consciousness. At the time, talking to oneself was a colloquial sign of insanity. Meichenbaum argued that conventional wisdom was wrong. Those who talked to themselves were the best adjusted.

Meichenbaum proposed a model of intervention based on Vygotsky's (1962) model of language and thought. Most adaptive behavior requires the sequencing of many small behaviors to produce a complex reaction. If a boy is insulted by a peer while walking down the school hallway and has the impulse to strike back in revenge, a complex set of responses is necessary to inhibit that response. People with behavioral problems often fail to use language to guide their behavior. This failure may occur for two reasons. First, they may have failed to learn to use language to guide their behavior at all. They do not think of their responses beforehand and set up statements to think while acting. Second, they have learned the process, but have a very limited repertoire of verbal responses to guide their behavior. They might not have learned to apply this skill or have language guiding responses for the dysfunctional behavior problem.

The steps of SIT reflect the stages that Vygotsky (1962) noticed children use to learn language mediation of behavior. First, the therapist and the client identify the problem and decide on an appropriate response. Although

Meichenbaum did not write much about SPS activities, it seems that SPS may be a good first step before SIT. The steps were encoded into language. The client is then presented with stimuli that will occur in the real world that will elicit either their old dysfunctional behavior or the new behavior that they have verbally encoded. At the presentation of the stimuli, the therapist models the rehearsal of the verbally encoded statements aloud. The clients then rehearse the same statements when prompted by the same stimuli. The therapist then models the same acts while lowering his or her voice. This is followed by rehearsal by the child. The therapist and the child gradually lower their voices until they rehearse the self-statements only in subvocal speech.

SIT is a very flexible intervention that has been used across all ages and with a wide variety of problems from impulsive classroom behavior and aggression to anxiety, depression, and pain management. Research in this intervention has tapered off considerably in the last decade since claims that the intervention failed to produce sustained improvements (see Diaz & Berk, 1999, for a review). However, SIT has been used successfully as part of a multicomponent treatment for attention-deficit/hyperactivity disorder (ADHD; Nolan & Carr, 2000) and as a multicomponent treatment for aggressive children with ADHD (Miranda & Presentacion, 2000). It is often used with mentally retarded individuals when other cognitive interventions are not appropriate.

The disruptive, dysfunctional cognitions models focus on the role of beliefs and thoughts in triggering disturbed emotions. These models have emerged from research in the psychology of emotions that emphasizes the role of thoughts and appraisals on emotions. The basic premise is that emotional disturbance results from the presence of dysfunctional, incorrect, or irrational thoughts. The two most prominent therapies under this heading are REBT (Ellis, 1962, 2005) and CT (Beck, 1976, 2005).

Rational Emotive Behavior Therapy and Self-Esteem

Ellis relied on his earlier readings in classical philosophy to guide his clinical practice. He often quoted the philosopher Epictetus, who said, "People are not disturbed by things, but by the views they take of them." Ellis (1962, 2005) maintained that all serious emotional disturbance was caused (or strongly influenced) by thoughts and beliefs. Ellis eventually came to believe that the core cognition that caused disturbance was demandingness. In our language, these thoughts take the form of sentences starting with "I must," "You must," "It must," "I have to," "You have to," "It has to," "I've got to," "I need," and "I should." Ellis contrasts demands with desires or preferences. He asserts that people become disturbed when they believe that what they desire must be reality.

In Ellis's model, demands represent rigid, absolutistic schemas of the world—not any aspect of the world, but the presence of what one desires. As

Piaget noted, when reality differs from people's schema, they use the cognitive processes of accommodation or assimilation to resolve the inconsistency. When people accommodate, they include the new information that conflicts with their schema and change their schema to fit this new information. When people assimilate, they fail to change their schema and persist in trying to make reality fit what they believe. When people demand that reality comply with their preference, they predict that their desires will be present even if they have much empirical evidence that they are not. Desires or wants never cause disturbance according to REBT; rather, people's rigid demands that reality must include what they desire causes disturbance.

Demands lead to other psychological derivative beliefs that Ellis believes also drive disturbance. These include catastrophizing ("It's horrible, terrible, and awful"); feelings of intolerance of frustration ("I can't stand it"); and global ratings of the self or others ("I'm no good, rotten, bad, and worthless"). Inability to tolerate frustration has been associated with school-related problems, such as poor grades and disruptive school behavior (Ellis & Bernard, 2006).

REBT posits a unique position on self-esteem. This theory holds that humans all have equal worth. The belief that one is a bad or worthless person is indefensible and leads to depression, shame, guilt, and anxiety. REBT maintains that the solution to such problem is not to build self-esteem. The belief that one is a good person because one does well at certain acts provides short-lived adjustment. High self-esteem helps people feel better until they fail, perform poorly, or encounter others who outperform them. Unconditional self-acceptance will result in more lasting mental health. Thus, REBT teaches people to monitor their behaviors to perform as well as they can but not to evaluate their worth on such performance. REBT proposes that people accept that one is a complex person who does well on some tasks and poorly on others and that such performance is unrelated to one's worth as a person. REBT proposes that emotional adjustment is related to such abstract philosophical ideas. A 30-year-long research tradition demonstrates that children as young as 8 years can understand and benefit from these ideas (Ellis & Bernard, 2006).

In the process of REBT, therapist tasks include (a) identifying the client's maladaptive cognitions (the demands and the derivatives); (b) actively and persuasively challenging the client's maladaptive/irrational cognitions; (c) helping the client formulate alternative adaptive/rational beliefs to replace her or his maladaptive or irrational beliefs; (d) providing the client practice in actively challenging his or her maladaptive cognitions and rehearsing the new alternative adaptive/rational beliefs; and (e) collaborating with the client to design homework that helps her or him identify, evaluate and/or challenge, and replace maladaptive cognitions and behave in ways inconsistent with the disturbance.

Ellis and Bernard (2006) and DiGiuseppe (2007) have identified REBT applications to help children, adolescents, and their parents with a wide range of problems. REBT treatment protocols exist for individual and group therapy sessions and classroom lessons to improve a variety of clinical problems. They also exist as primary prevention programs and as a model for school consultation with parents and teachers who have any emotional difficulties that interfere with their functioning. School psychologists can also use REBT to work with children whose anxiety, depression, or anger interferes with their functioning. A recent major review of REBT with school-age children documented its effectiveness with children and adolescents (Esposito, 2008).

Cognitive Therapy

Beck (1976, 2005) developed CT at about the same time that Ellis was developing REBT, and the two corresponded frequently. Beck was attempting to test the psychodynamic theory of depression. The psychodynamic theory stated that depression was anger turned inward. Beck's research failed to find evidence for this. Instead, he found that patients with depression had conscious thoughts that popped into their heads. These "automatic thoughts" usually were negative distortions of reality and focused in what Beck labeled the *cognitive triad*. That is, the world is bad, the future is bleak, and I am responsible and condemnable for this state of affairs. Beck noticed that the negative automatic thoughts usually contained certain types of errors. The common cognitive distortions that occur in depressive automatic thoughts are as follows:

- *All-or-nothing thinking:* People restrict possibilities and options of what they can think of only two choices—yes or no (all or nothing).
- *Overgeneralization:* People view a single, negative event as a continuing and never-ending pattern of defeat.
- *Negative mental filter:* People dwell mostly on the negatives and generally ignore the positives.
- *Discounting the positives:* People insist that their achievements or positive efforts do not count.
- *Jumping to conclusions:* People think instinctively without reflecting on the truth of their thoughts.
- *Mind reading:* People assume that others are reacting negatively to them without any objective evidence.
- *Fortune-telling:* People predict that things will turn out badly without any objective evidence.
- *Magnification or minimization:* People blow things out of proportion or minimize their importance.

- *Emotional reasoning:* People base their reasoning upon their feelings (e.g., "I feel like a loser, so I must be one").
- "Mustabatory thinking" or "shoulding all over yourself": People believe things must be a certain way with "musts," "shoulds," "oughts," and "have to's."
- *Labeling:* Instead of saying "I made a mistake," a person thinks, "I'm an idiot" or "I'm a loser."
- *Personalization:* People blame themselves for something for which they were not entirely responsible.

Beck later noticed that the negatively distorted automatic thoughts seemed to relate to more enduring, nonconscious, underlying schema that clients had developed in their lives. He defined an underlying schema as a broad, pervasive theme or pattern of thought comprising memories, bodily sensations, emotions, and cognitions. Schemas could include representations of oneself or one's relationships with others. Schemas are developed during childhood or adolescence and elaborated throughout one's lifetime. They represent dysfunctional ideas to a significant degree. Some examples of dysfunctional schemas would be the following:

- Dependent personalities might think: I am too weak to do things alone; I must depend on others.
- Those in enmeshment families might think: I must not act on my own; I must consider what others want.
- Depressive personalities might think: I am defective; there is something wrong with me.

The primary intervention in CT is challenging the negative automatic thoughts and underlying schema. Beck (2005) identified a strategy, which he termed *collaborative empiricism*. The therapist and the client work together at identifying what data would be relevant to test the veracity of the thought and how to collect the data. Once ideas are challenged, the client and therapist work to develop more rational replacement beliefs. Initially, CT spent most of the time in therapy focusing on the negative automatic thoughts and then moved to the underlying schema. In recent years, cognitive therapists work at challenging the underlying schema more in earlier sessions than in the past.

Homework is an important component of CT. Clients are encouraged to keep logs of their negative thoughts, challenge their thoughts, rehearse new rational alternatives, and act against their thoughts and emotions. Depressed patients engage in pleasure activities and record their successes. Anxious patients work at confronting their fears. Thus, from its beginnings, CT has been an integrative form of CBT. CT has been shown to be an effective intervention for child and adolescent anxiety, depression, and a number of other common problems that school psychologists encounter (Reinecke, Datillio, & Freeman, 2003).

The Third Wave

Recently, a third wave of behavior therapy has emerged that also focuses on cognitions, thoughts, and attitudes. This approach is best presented by Hayes's (2004) acceptance and commitment therapy (ACT). On the basis of a Skinnerian approach to verbal behavior and cognition, Hayes proposes that it is important to change the functional relationship between a client's thoughts and his or her emotions and behavior rather than to change the thoughts. Certain thoughts and cognitions may have become responses that precede dysfunctional behavior. Learning to disconnect this relationship and helping the client not react with dysfunctional behavior to the thoughts is the task of ACT. The client accepts that he or she has the thoughts, does not dwell on them or try to change them, and attempts to act in a way to achieve his or her goals. This model differs from REBT and CT by avoiding challenging negative automatic thoughts, irrational beliefs, or underlying schema. Instead, clients are persuaded to let the thoughts persist and change their reactions to them. They learn that the thought cannot trigger the emotional reaction but can lead to a new action. Although this approach represents a promising development, very limited clinical applications and no research has appeared that uses this model with children and adolescents (Murrell, Coyne, & Wilson, 2005).

CONCLUSIONS

All models of CBT propose an integrative form of psychotherapy. These approaches are integrative in three ways. First, CBT always incorporates the common factors that appear to contribute to all forms of effective psychotherapy. These include an emotionally charged, confiding relationship with a helper; a healing setting with the expectation of professional assistance; a plausible explanation for symptoms, and treatment; a ritual that requires active participation of therapist and client (Wampold, 2001). Second, CBT always includes both cognitive and behavioral interventions. Cognitive interventions help increase children's or adolescent's motivation for change and help them identify and control the emotions and thoughts that lead to disturbed behavior. These activities prepare the child or adolescent for actual behavior change. The rehearsal and reinforcement of the actual behaviors is a crucial part of treatment.

Much debate has ensued in CBT on the relative contribution of the cognitive components of these treatments to their effectiveness. Such component analysis research is helpful in identifying the most effective intervention. However, a CBT perspective usually supports the use of multiple interventions. The major theories of CBT previously outlined represent the original models and their application. However, practitioners usually use elements of all of these models. A good example of this inclusiveness is the Penn Resiliency Project, a school-based depression prevention program for high school students (Gillham et al., 2007). This well-researched program includes aspects of CT, REBT, SPS, and some additional behavioral components. An inclusive model of CBT would include a functional analysis of the symptoms that identifies the antecedents and consequences of target behaviors plus an assessment of the thoughts that contribute to dysfunctional emotions and behaviors. This would identify how the thoughts, attitudes, and beliefs relate to a child's or adolescent's emotional and behavioral problems. Interventions from any or all of the models could be used to identify the mediating cognitions that are present in the individual case. In addition, elements of good psychotherapy practice would be included by focusing on relational elements such as a good therapeutic alliance, empathy, collaboration, and unconditional positive regard (Wampold, 2001).

REFERENCES

Alberti, R., & Emmons, M. (2008). *Your perfect right: Assertiveness and equality in your life and relationships*. Atascedero, CA: Impact Publishers.

Beck, A. T. (1970). Cognitive therapy: Nature and relation to behavior therapy. *Behavior Therapy, 1*, 184–200.

Beck, A. T. (1976). *Cognitive therapy and the emotional disorders*. New York: International Universities Press.

Beck, A. T. (2005). The current state of cognitive therapy: A 40-year retrospective. *Archives of General Psychiatry, 62*(9), 953–959.

Braswell, L., & Kendall, P. (2002). Cognitive-behavior therapy with youth. In K. Dobson (Eds.), *Handbook of cognitive-behavior therapies* (2nd ed., pp 246–294). New York: Guilford.

Daunic, A., Smith, S. W., Brank, E. M., & Penfield, R. D. (2006). Classroom-based cognitive–behavioral intervention to prevent aggression: Efficacy and social validity. *Journal of School Psychology, 44*(2), 123–139.

David, D., Freeman, A., DiGiuseppe, R. (in press). Rational and irrational beliefs: Implications for psychotherapy. In D. David & G. Eifort (Eds.), *Rational and irrational beliefs in human functioning and disturbances: Implication for research, theory, and practice*. New York: Oxford University Press.

Diaz, R. M., & Berk, L. E. (1999). A Vygotskian critique of self-instructional training. In P. Lloyd & C. Fernyhough (Eds.), *Lev Vygotsky: Critical assessment* (Vol. IV, pp. 221–252). Florence, KY: Taylor & Frances/Routledge.

DiGiuseppe, R. (2007). Rational emotive behavioral approaches. In H. T. Prout & D. T. Brown (Eds.), *Counseling and psychotherapy with children and adolescents: Theory and practice for school and clinical settings* (4th ed., pp. 279–331). Hoboken, NJ: Wiley.

Duckworth, M. P., & Mercer, V. (2006). Assertiveness Training. In J. E. Fisher & W. T. O'Donohue (Eds.), *Practitioner's guide to evidence-based psychotherapy* (pp. 80–92). New York: Springer Science + Business Media.

D'Zurilla, T., & Nezu, A. M. (2006). *Problem-solving therapy: A positive approach to clinical intervention* (3rd ed.). New York: Springer Publishing Co.

Elisa, M., & Butler, L. B. (2005). *Social decision making/social problem solving for middle school students: Skills and activities for academic, social, and emotional success.* Champaign, IL: Research Press.

Ellis, A. (1955). New approaches to psychotherapy techniques. *Journal of Clinical Psychology, 11,* 207–260.

Ellis, A. (1962). *Reason and emotion in psychotherapy.* New York: Citadel Press.

Ellis, A. (2005). Rational emotive behavior therapy. In R. Corsini & D. Wedding (Eds.), *Current psychotherapies* (7th ed., pp. 166–201). Belmont, CA: Brooks/Cole.

Ellis, A., & Bernard, M. E. (2006). (Eds.). *Rational emotive behavioral approaches to childhood disorders.* New York: Springer.

Esposito, M. (2008). *The efficacy of rational emotive behavior therapy with children and adolescents: A meta-analysis.* Poster session presented at the annual convention of the American Psychological Association, Boston, MA.

Fenstermacher, K., Olympia, D., & Sheridan, S. M. (2006). Effectiveness of a computer-facilitated interactive social skills training program for boys with attention deficit hyperactivity disorder. *School Psychology Quarterly, 21,* 197–224.

Gilbert, D. T. (1991). How mental systems believe. *American Psychologist, 46,* 107–119.

Gillham, J., Reivich, K., J., Freres, D., Chaplin, T., Shaffe, A., Samuels, B., et al. (2007). School-based prevention of depressive symptoms: A randomized controlled study of the effectiveness and specificity of the Penn resiliency program. *Journal of Consulting and Clinical Psychology, 75,* 9–19.

Hayes, S. C. (2004). Acceptance and commitment therapy, relational frame theory, and the third wave of behavioral and cognitive therapies. *Behavior Therapy, 35,* 639–665.

Ingram, R. E. (1984). Information processing and feedback: Effects of mood and information favorability on the cognitive processing of personally relevant information. *Cognitive Therapy and Research, 8,* 371–386.

Kanfer, F. H., & Goldstein, A. P. (1975). *Helping people change: A textbook of methods.* Oxford, England: Pergamon Press.

Kraag, G., Zeegers, M. P., Kok, G., Hosman, C., & Abu-Sadd, H. H. (2006). School programs targeting stress management in children and adolescents. *Journal of School Psychology, 44,* 449–471.

Mahoney, M. (1976). *Cognition and behavior modification.* Cambridge, MA: Ballinger.

Mahoney, M. (1991). *Human change processes: The scientific foundations of psychotherapy.* New York: Basic Books.

Meichenbaum, D. (1977). *Cognitive behavior modification: An integrative approach.* New York: Plenum.

Meichenbaum, D. (1993). Changing conceptions of cognitive behavior modification: Retrospect and prospect. *Journal of Consulting and Clinical Psychology, 61,* 202–204.

Miranda, A., & Presentacion, M. J. (2000). Efficacy of cognitive-behavioral therapy in the treatment of children with ADHD, with and without aggression. *Psychology in the Schools, 37,* 169–182.

Murrell, A. R., Coyne, L. W., & Wilson, K. G. (2005). ACT with children, adolescents, and their parents. In S. C. Hayes & K. D. Strosahl (Eds.), *A practical guide to acceptance and commitment therapy* (pp. 249–273). New York: Springer Science.

Nock, M. K., & Mendes, W. B. (2008). Physiological arousal, distress tolerance, and social problem solving deficits among adolescent self-injurers. *Journal of Consulting and Clinical Psychology, 76,* 28–38.

Nolan, M., & Carr, A. (2000). *What works with children and adolescents: A critical review of psychological interventions with children, adolescents, and their families.* Florence, KY: Taylor & Frances/Routledge.

O'Leary, K. D., & Drabman, R. (1971). Token reinforcement programs in the classroom: A review. *Psychological Bulletin, 75,* 379–398.

Power, M. J., & Dalgleish, T. (1999). Two routes to emotion: Some implications of multi-level theories of emotion for therapeutic practice. *Behavioural and Cognitive Psychotherapy, 27,* 129–141.

Prochaska, J. O., & DiClemente, C. C. (2005). The transtheoretical approach. In J. Norcross & M. Goldfried (Eds.), *Handbook of psychotherapy integration* (2nd ed., pp. 147–171). New York: Oxford University Press.

Reinecke, M. A., Datillio, F. M., & Freeman, A. (2003). (Eds.). *Cognitive therapy with children and adolescents: A case book for clinical practice* (2nd ed.). New York: Guilford.

Skinner, B. F. (1957). *A functional analysis of verbal behavior.* East Norwalk, CT: Appleton-Century-Crofts.

Spivack, G., Platt, J., & Shure, M. (1976). *The social problem solving approach to adjustment.* San Francisco: Jossey-Bass.

Sukhodolsky, D., Golub, A., Stone, E., & Orban, L. (2005). Dismantling anger control training for children: A randomized pilot study of social problem solving versus social skills training components. *Behavior Therapy, 36,* 15–23.

Wampold, B. (2001). *The great psychotherapy debate: Models, methods and findings.* Mahwah, NJ: Erlbaum.

Vygotsky, L. S. (1962). *Thought and language.* Oxford, England: Wiley.

7

IMPROVING CHILDREN'S FLUENCY IN READING, MATHEMATICS, SPELLING, AND WRITING: A REVIEW OF EVIDENCE-BASED ACADEMIC INTERVENTIONS

TANYA L. ECKERT, ROBIN M. CODDING, ADREA J. TRUCKENMILLER,
AND JENNIFER L. RHEINHEIMER

Many children enrolled in American public schools are unable to read, write, and compute. The latest reports from the National Assessment of Educational Progress reveal that 68% of fourth- and 70% of eighth-grade students could not read at the proficient level (Lee, Grigg, & Donahue, 2007). In the area of writing, 72% of fourth- and 69% of eighth-grade students could not write at the proficient level (Persky, Daane, & Jin, 2003). In the area of mathematics, 62% of fourth- and 69% of eighth-grade students could not demonstrate proficiency at the basic level (Lee, Grigg, & Dion, 2007). In response to these achievement results, reports by the National Research Council (Kilpatrick & Swafford, 2002; Snow, Burns, & Griffin, 1998), the National Council of Teachers of Mathematics (NCTM; 2000), and the National Commission on Writing (2003) recommended identifying effective instructional procedures that can be applied in classrooms with vigorous effects. These recommendations are consistent with federal efforts to improve standards for identifying effective practices and advancing knowledge of evidence-based interventions for children (Eckert, 2005). These proposals emphasize the need for empirically supported instructional practices that have been field-tested in classrooms.

Empirically supported practice, including interventions that demonstrate efficacy in randomized controlled trials as well as utility in clinical applications, has become a central theme in psychology (American Psychological Association Presidential Task Force on Evidence-Based Practice, 2006; Kratochwill & Shernoff, 2004). The importance of school psychology practice focusing on empirically supported practices was recognized as one of the broad themes identified in the 2002 Multisite Conference on the Future of School Psychology (Dawson et al., 2004). To date, a number of empirically supported instructional practices have been demonstrated to improve the reading skills of children. These practices include explicit instruction in decoding, word recognition, fluency, and reading comprehension. Similar advances have been made in the content area of mathematics, including instructional practices focusing on fluency and problem solving. In the area of writing, a number of instructional techniques have been empirically examined, including handwriting and spelling instruction, fluency-based interventions incorporating feedback, and strategy instruction. Many of these interventions are consistent with national initiatives to provide children with instruction in reading, mathematics, and writing (Oxaal, 2005).

Given the importance of improving children's educational outcomes, it is essential that school professionals are informed of instructional strategies supported by scientific evidence. Specifically, instructional techniques that are based on behavioral principles have led to a number of empirically supported interventions to improve children's academic skills (Martens, Daly, Begeny, & VanDerHeyden, in press). In this chapter, we review interventions that can be used to improve children's academic skill development and achievement. We begin by reviewing empirically supported interventions to improve children's reading skills. Next, we discuss interventions to improve children's mathematics skills. Finally, we examine interventions to improve children's written expression and spelling skills.

READING INTERVENTION:
EMPIRICALLY SUPPORTED PRACTICES

A number of empirically supported instructional practices have been demonstrated to improve the reading skills of children (National Reading Panel, 2000). Additional practices have been recently examined that involve highly structured and explicit instruction in decoding, word recognition, fluency, and reading comprehension as well as incorporate peer-assisted learning strategies (Fuchs & Fuchs, 2005; Williams, 2005). These instructional practices are reviewed across three essential areas of reading: emergent reading, reading fluency, and reading comprehension in the following sections.

Improving Children's Emergent Reading Skills

Early reading instruction efforts have been directed toward improving young children's phonemic awareness skills (i.e., concentrate on and manipulate phonemes in spoken words). In a meta-analysis of the effects of phonemic awareness instruction on young children's reading skills, Ehri et al. (2001) concluded that phonemic instruction resulted in statistically significant improvements in children's phonemic awareness ($d = .86$), reading ($d = .53$), and spelling ($d = .59$) skills. Characteristics that enhanced outcomes included teaching children to manipulate phonemes with letters, providing instruction on one or two types of phonemes, and teaching children in small groups.

In addition to focusing on phonemic awareness skills, instructional practices for young children have also focused on phonics (i.e., emphasizing the letter-sound correspondences in reading and spelling). The National Reading Panel (National Institute of Child Health and Human Development [NICHHD], 2000), in its meta-analysis of systematic phonics instructional methods, concluded that a moderate effect was observed ($d = .41$) in improving children's word reading, spelling, and text processing. When phonics instruction was provided early (i.e., kindergarten or first grade) and continued for 2 years or more, the effects were moderate to strong (range, $d = .43$–.54). Although these results suggest that systematic phonics instruction is beneficial for elementary-aged students, significantly larger effect sizes were observed for children enrolled in kindergarten and first grade ($d = .55$) than for children enrolled in second through sixth grade ($d = .27$). Furthermore, the impact of systematic phonics instruction was significantly lower among children with disabilities ($d = .32$) and children experiencing reading difficulties ($d = .15$).

Improving Children's Reading Fluency

Despite the importance of early literacy skills (i.e., phonological awareness, vocabulary knowledge), it is important for children to read connected text with sufficient accuracy and speed that is prerequisite for comprehension (Chard, Vaughn, & Tyler, 2002). As a result, increasingly more attention is being focused on reading fluency. The National Reading Panel (NICHHD, 2000), in their meta-analysis of fluency-based interventions, concluded that guided oral reading procedures were moderately effective ($d = .41$) in improving children's oral reading fluency and overall reading achievement. This repeated readings practice, within the context of a school reading program, provides children with multiple exposures to the same words, resulting in greater fluency on the practiced passage. Improvements in reading fluency have been observed for children in kindergarten through fifth grade, with teachers, parents, or peers implementing the procedure. A recent meta-analysis (Morgan & Sideridis, 2006) reported that variations of repeated readings that included motivational components (e.g., goal setting, performance feedback) were significantly more effective than variations of repeated readings that did not include these components. Specifically, when the practice of repeated readings was combined with goal-setting interventions, strong, immediate effects were observed (i.e., intercept effects) as well as moderate improvements over time (i.e., slope effects).

Improving Children's Reading Comprehension

Reading comprehension is often considered the critical component of reading (Durkin, 1993). The National Reading Panel (NICHHD, 2000) reviewed the empirical literature on reading comprehension instruction. Although a meta-analysis could not be conducted, conclusions were made regarding instructional techniques with sufficient empirical support. The seven types of instruction that were found to improve children's reading comprehension were (a) comprehension monitoring, (b) cooperative learning, (c) use of graphic and semantic organizers, (d) question answering, (e) question generation, (f) story structure, and (g) summarization. The authors of this report further concluded that although each type of instruction was found to be effective in isolation, stronger outcomes were typically observed when two or more strategies were combined and implemented as part of a multiple-strategy method.

MATHEMATICS INTERVENTIONS: EMPIRICALLY SUPPORTED PRACTICES

Attention to the identification and evaluation of effective mathematics instructional interventions has increased, particularly as mathematics education in the United States has been criticized as inappropriately emphasizing a breadth of topics without adequate depth (Schmidt, McKnight, & Raizen, 1997). The following section describes strategies that current research has suggested may be effective for improving mathematics performance.

Improving Children's Basic Computational Skills

Primarily, mathematics intervention research has focused on investigating effective strategies for improving basic computational skills. This was highlighted in a meta-analysis conducted by Kroesbergen and Van Luit (2003) in which 51% of the intervention studies (N = 58) focused on basic facts compared with 28% for problem solving. Moreover, the highest effect sizes were obtained for interventions that focused on basic facts. The reason for this emphasis may be that acquisition of and fluency with mathematics operations are important for the development of more advanced mathematics skills (Mercer & Miller, 1992; Shapiro, 2004). In fact, the relevance of computational fluency was recently promoted by NCTM (2006) in its publication of curriculum focus points.

Three reviews have attempted to synthesize the research on effective computational intervention components (Baker, Gersten, & Lee, 2002; Kroesbergen & Van Luit, 2003; Panahon, Codding, Hilt-Panahon, & Benson, 2007). The findings from these analyses presented some commonalties in recommended instructional approaches as well as some inconsistencies. In their meta-analysis, Kroesbergen and Van Luit (2003) summarized the research studies (N = 31) according to three general approaches to instruction. The authors found that direct instruction was more effective than mediated instruction or self-instruction for improving mathematics facts. It is interesting that this meta-analysis suggested that peer tutoring was less effective than other methods for improving basic computation. In a second meta-analysis (N = 15) examining specific instructional components, Baker et al. (2002) found moderate effect sizes for peer tutoring (d = .62) and providing performance feedback to students (d = .57). A more recent review, extending the work of Baker and colleagues, found large effects for cover-copy-compare, self-instruction, and self-monitoring (Panahon et al., 2007). For peer tutoring, effect sizes ranged from negligible to large, with the mean yielding a large effect size. These specific instructional components and interventions are described in more detail in the following sections.

Direct Instruction

This method of instruction refers generally to lessons delivered to small groups that are fast-paced, well-sequenced, and focused (Swanson & Sasche-Lee, 2000). Instruction and academic tasks are commonly divided into small, sequential steps to ensure skill mastery. Students are provided with frequent opportunities to respond and receive feedback regarding those responses. Opportunities to practice on previously learned skills are incorporated to help to prevent skill loss once a unit has been completed (Goldman, 1989).

Mediated Instruction

Guided experience and scaffolding are utilized in mediated or assisted instruction. Teachers model task performance at a more advanced level than students can perform independently. Specific strategies include coaching, fading, questioning, and explanation. This differs from direct or self-instruction because learning begins with the students' representation of a task rather than with immediate presentation and training in the expert model (for more details, see Goldman, 1989).

Self-Instruction

Two components of self-management include self-instruction and self-monitoring. Self-instruction strategies often incorporate verbal prompts that are used to remind students of the steps required to solve problems. Teachers often provide modeling-in-context to help students acquire the prompt sequences (Goldman, 1989). Guidelines for training often incorporate the following five steps: (a) the teacher solves the problem using self-instructions while the student observes, (b) the student performs the task while the teacher provides the self-instructions, (c) the student solves the problem using the verbal prompts with the teacher's support, (d) the student independently uses the verbal prompts to solve the problem, and (e) the student uses private speech to represent the verbal prompts and solves the problem (Meichenbaum & Goodman, 1971).

Performance Feedback

Performance feedback interventions can be described as procedures that provide information to students regarding their specific performance on an academic activity (Shapiro, 2004) and have been shown to be effective in a number of academic domains (see Eckert et al., 2006, for a review). Performance feedback can be provided by teachers as well as by computers and often includes goal setting. For example, students might be provided with the number of correct problems they performed previously as well as the number they should try to complete in a specified amount of time (Baker et al., 2002). Including the time, or rate, with which students accurately complete problems is important, as it helps build fluency.

Cover-Copy-Compare

Cover-copy-compare is a self-managed intervention that provides a series of learning trials within a short period of time through the use of five steps: (a) look at the mathematics problem with the answer, (b) cover the mathematics problem with the answer, (c) record the answer, (d) uncover the mathematics problem with the answer, and (e) compare the answer (Skinner, McLaughlin, & Logan, 1997). Repeated learning trials promote mathematics accuracy by providing students with practice of accurate responses.

Peer Tutoring

It is possible that the mixed results obtained in the aforementioned reviews were related to the type of peer tutoring provided (e.g., cross age, same age, cooperative learning) or to other moderating variables such as grade level, type of evaluation procedures, or amount and type of training provided to teachers and students. A broader term that encompasses dyadic peer tutoring and small-group cooperative learning interventions is *peer-assisted learning*. A recent meta-analysis of 81 peer-assisted learning studies found a significant, albeit small, effect size ($n = 33, d = .22$) for mathematics (Rohrbeck, Ginsburg-Block, Fantuzzo, & Miller, 2003). These authors also found several moderating variables. That is, peer-assisted interventions that included interdependent reward contingencies and individualized evaluation procedures and that provided students with opportunities for self-management (e.g., goal setting, reward selection and administration) had greater outcomes. The authors also found that peer-assisted interventions seemed to be particularly effective for students in lower elementary grades (1–3), attending urban schools, and from diverse ethnic backgrounds. Specific review of the same- and cross-age tutoring literature found that both types are useful for increasing mathematics achievement, and students serving as both a tutor and tutee may yield larger academic gains than students serving in either role in isolation (Robinson, Schofield, & Steers-Wentzell, 2007).

Improving Children's Problem-Solving Skills

As previously noted, less research has examined the instructional components effective for improving general or problem-solving mathematics skills. Of those techniques examined, four interventions have received the most attention: (a) peer tutoring, (b) computer-assisted instruction (i.e., use tutorials or videodisc programs such as Math Blaster [Eckert & Davidson, 1987]), (c) representation techniques (i.e., solving word problems by interpreting information from the problem by diagramming; using manipulatives, mapping, or schemas; or using linguistic training), and (d) strategy instruction (i.e., using explicit [e.g., direct instruction] and/or cognitive and metacognitive [e.g., self-regulation, self-instruction, self-questioning] problem-solving procedures as well as paraphrasing, visualizing, hypothesizing, and estimating the answer).

Findings from two reviews introduced earlier (Baker et al., 2002; Kroesbergen & Van Luit, 2003) and a third review (Xin & Jitendra, 1999) are described here to illustrate the effectiveness of these strategies. Kroesbergen and Van Luit (2003) found that peer tutoring and computer-assisted instruction were less effective than other methods, such as direct instruction. Baker et al. (2002) found similar findings. A small effect ($d = 0.29$) was yielded for peer-tutoring, a moderate effect ($d = 0.58$) for explicit instruction (which included direct instruction), and no effect for representation techniques. Xin and Jitendra (1999) provided the most comprehensive examination of word-problem solving interventions ($N = 25$). Large effects were found for computer-assisted instruction and representation techniques, and moderate effects were found for strategy instruction. Evidence of maintenance and generalization of these effects to other tasks and settings was found for strategy instruction (i.e., moderate to large effect sizes). Computer-assisted instruction seemed to promote maintenance but was less effective at promoting generalization. The authors also found that length of treatment, instructional grouping, and word-problem task mediated treatment outcomes. That is, better outcomes were associated with treatment that was provided individually, lasted more than 1 month, and addressed simple one-step problems.

WRITING INTERVENTIONS: EMPIRICALLY SUPPORTED PRACTICE

Fewer interventions have been empirically examined in the content area of writing than in the areas of reading and mathematics. The National Center on Accelerated Student Learning conducted a multisite evaluation of the efficacy of two groups of writing interventions (Oxaal, 2005). Although the results provided empirical support for the interventions used, they also supported the need for additional research to "identify powerful instructional techniques that are effective with good, average, and struggling writers" (Graham & Harris, 2005, p. 32). The following sections review writing instructional strategies, including handwriting instruction, performance feedback, and strategy instruction, which have some empirical support for improving children's writing skills.

Developmentally Based Handwriting and Extended Text Interventions

Berninger and colleagues (2006) developed a two-tier model of intervention that is developmentally driven. The first tier focuses on handwriting and orthographic skills during kindergarten through second grade. Proficiency in these skills is required to facilitate children's success in the upper elementary grades, when writing instruction begins to emphasize more complex composition skills. Berninger et al. (2006) found that adding direct instruction in both orthographic skills and motor exercises to regular handwriting instruction yielded significant increases in growth over time for letter-naming, copying, and letter-writing automaticity.

The second tier begins in third grade, utilizes more intensive intervention, and involves the development and accommodation of writing skills for broader applications. Intervention at this level includes sharing stories in small groups and providing direct instruction on the use of graphic organizers, text generation, and revising written work. This tier of intervention significantly increased performance on fourth-grade, high-stakes testing.

Strategy Instruction

Strategy instruction is the most well-developed and empirically supported writing intervention, although it also requires the most time to implement. Strategy instruction includes three components: (a) an adult or peer explicitly teaches/models the strategy, (b) instruction spans at least 3 days, and (c) students gradually progress toward independent use of the strategy (Graham, 2006). Strategy instruction—in particular, self-regulated strategy instruction (Graham & Harris, 1996)—is a versatile intervention yielding large effects sizes (Graham, 2006). In a meta-analysis, Graham (2006) found large effects for strategy instruction (d = 0.89) as well as for self-regulated strategy instruction (d = 1.57). Students who benefited from strategy instruction maintained these effects 1 month later and generalized the strategies to narrative and expository composition formats.

Performance Feedback

Performance feedback is a fairly unobtrusive and less intensive intervention that can be incorporated within the context of classroom instruction. In the context of writing, performance-feedback interventions provide quantitative information on students' written composition in response to a story prompt. Recent research has suggested that individualized performance feedback in writing can improve children's writing fluency (d = .76; Eckert et al., 2007). Additionally, Van Houten (1980) identified several intervention components (e.g., explicit timing, praise, public posting) that can increase the effectiveness of performance feedback.

SPELLING INTERVENTIONS: EMPIRICALLY SUPPORTED PRACTICES

As with the content areas of reading, mathematics, and writing, teachers are concerned with students' accuracy and fluency in spelling. Within a classroom, spelling instruction is either embedded in reading and writing instruction or directly taught using textbooks that emphasize phonology, morphology, and syntactic rules (Okyere & Heron, 1991). In a chapter reviewing best practices in spelling and handwriting, Schlagal (2007) emphasized that although many students succeed in spelling without direct instruction, some students experience difficulties. Specifically, these students may demonstrate short-term gains in their spelling performance; however, deficits are observed in their long-term retention and mastery of previously instructed skills. As a result, these students may benefit from individualized spelling interventions.

Okyere and Heron (1991) detailed various approaches to individualized spelling interventions that differ according to the severity of the spelling difficulty, the amount of time required to implement the intervention, and the instructional type (i.e., teacher directed, peer/tutor mediated, or semi-independent). The most frequently highlighted spelling interventions in-

clude (a) modeling, (b) time delay, (c) error drill, (d) interspersing procedures, (e) instructional ratios, (f) high-p sequencing, (g) cover-copy-
compare methods, and (h) performance feedback and self-correction procedures (Cates et al., 2003; Okyere & Heron, 1991; Ross & Stevens, 2003).
However, the most researched and seemingly effective practices for students
experiencing spelling difficulties include self-correction with performance
feedback and cover-copy-compare interventions.

Self-Correction Interventions

Self-correction interventions with performance feedback require a
teacher-directed or student-mediated approach to instruction. Spelling words
are read to the student, and the student responds by attempting to spell the
dictated words. The teacher or tutor provides feedback on the student's performance by identifying specific spelling mistakes (i.e., omissions, repetitions,
and transpositions). Then, the student self-corrects the errors. For the intervention to be most effective, students should self-correct until achieving three
consecutive trials with no errors. In an analysis of past research, Okyere and
Heron (1991) concluded that students with learning disabilities participating in self-correction procedures that utilize opportunities to respond and
performance feedback performed better (86.2% accuracy at postassessment)
than did students with learning disabilities receiving traditional spelling practices (65.6% accuracy at postassessment). Furthermore, students receiving
self-correction interventions demonstrated greater maintenance (59% retention accuracy) and generalization (59% transfer accuracy) of their spelling skills in comparison with students receiving traditional spelling practices
(51% retention accuracy, 41% transfer accuracy).

Cover-Copy-Compare Interventions

Cover-copy-compare interventions are similar to self-correction strategies in that they are based on opportunities to respond and performance feedback. However, unlike self-correction interventions, cover-copy-compare
methods may be more functional for a teacher to incorporate into a student's
independent learning plan. Cover-copy-compare interventions afford a semi-
independent learning approach and involve five steps in which the student
(a) reviews the targeted spelling word, (b) covers the word, (c) writes the
word, (d) uncovers the original word, and (e) compares the written response
to the correct word (Skinner et al., 1997). If the response is accurate, the
student moves on to the next spelling word. However, if the student replies
incorrectly, the cover-copy-compare procedure is repeated. Skinner and colleagues (1997) argued that cover-copy-compare interventions allow students
to rapidly complete several learning trials in a short period of time, allowing
them to build accuracy, fluency, and maintenance in spelling. Furthermore,

cover-copy-compare interventions can be combined with other reinforcement interventions (e.g., beat-your-score contingency) to further improve students' spelling fluency.

In a qualitative review of cover-copy-compare interventions, Skinner et al. (1997) concluded that there is substantial empirical support for their use with general education students (elementary and secondary levels) and special education students (i.e., students with learning disabilities and students with behavior disorders). In a comparative study of cover-copy-compare procedures, Nies and Belfiore (2006) found that students with learning disabilities receiving the cover-copy-compare intervention gained more spelling words (7.3 spelling words per week) than when a copy-only intervention was implemented (3.7 spelling words per week). Furthermore, when the students were assessed for maintenance, a substantially higher retention rate was observed for students receiving the cover-copy-compare intervention (95%) than for students receiving the copy-only intervention (64%).

SUMMARY

Given that many children experience academic difficulties in reading, mathematics, written expression, and spelling, it is imperative that school professionals intervene. The instructional strategies reviewed in this chapter should provide school professionals with effective techniques to positively impact children's learning experiences and educational outcomes. Furthermore, many of these academic interventions are feasible to use with general and special education children at the elementary and middle school levels.

REFERENCES

American Psychological Association Presidential Task Force on Evidence-Based Practice. (2006). Evidence-based practice in psychology. *American Psychologist, 61*, 271–285.

Baker, S., Gersten, R., & Lee, D. (2002). A synthesis of empirical research on teaching mathematics to low-achieving students. *The Elementary School Journal, 103*, 51–73.

Berninger, V. W., Rutberg, J. E., Abbott, R. D., Garcia, N., Anderson-Youngstrom, M., Brooks, A., et al. (2006). Tier 1 and tier 2 early intervention for handwriting and composing. *Journal of School Psychology, 44*, 3–30.

Cates, G. L., Skinner, C. H., Watson, T. S., Meadows, T. J., Weaver, A., & Jackson, B. (2003). Instructional effectiveness and instructional efficiency as considerations for data-based decision making: An evaluation of interspersing procedures. *School Psychology Review, 32*, 601–616.

Chard, D. J., Vaughn, S., & Tyler, B. J. (2002). A synthesis of research on effective interventions for building reading fluency with elementary students with learning disabilities. *Journal of Learning Disabilities, 35*, 386–406.

Dawson, M., Cummings, J. A., Harrison, P. L., Short, R. J., Gorin, S., & Palomares, R. (2004). The 2002 multisite conference on the future of school psychology: Next steps. *School Psychology Review, 33*, 115–125. (Published concurrently in *School Psychology Quarterly, 2003, 18,* 497–509)

Durkin, D. (1993). *Teaching them to read* (6th ed.). Boston: Allyn & Bacon.

Eckert, T. L. (2005). Improving children's educational outcomes by advancing assessment and intervention practices: An overview of the special series. *School Psychology Review, 34,* 4–8.

Eckert, R., & Davidson, J. (1987). Math blaster plus [Computer Software]. Torrance, CA: Davidson & Associates.

Eckert, T. L., Lovett, B. J., Rosenthal, B. D., Jiao, J., Ricci, L. J., & Truckenmiller, A. J. (2006). Classwide instructional feedback: Improving children's academic skill development. In S. Randall (Ed.), *Learning disabilities: New research* (pp. 271–285). Hauppauge, NY: Nova Science.

Eckert, T. L., Ricci, L. J., Truckenmiller, A. J., Rosenthal, B. D., Doyle, N. M., Rheinheimer, J. L, et al. (2007, March). *Using classwide performance feedback to improve elementary-aged children's written compositions.* Poster session presented at the annual convention of the National Association of School Psychologists, New York, NY.

Ehri, L. C., Nunes, S. R., Willows, D. M., Schuster, B., Yaghoub-Zadeh, Z., & Shanahan, T. (2001). Phonemic awareness instruction helps children learn to read: Evidence from the National Reading Panel's meta-analysis. *Reading Research Quarterly, 36,* 250–287.

Fuchs, D., & Fuchs, L. S. (2005). Peer-assisted learning strategies: Promoting word recognition, fluency, and reading comprehension in young children. *The Journal of Special Education, 39,* 34–44.

Goldman, S. R. (1989). Strategy instruction in mathematics. *Learning Disability Quarterly, 12,* 43–55.

Graham, S. (2006). Strategy instruction and the teaching of writing: A meta-analysis. In C. A. MacArthur, S. Graham, & J. Fitzgerald (Eds.), *Handbook of writing research* (pp. 187–207). New York: Guilford.

Graham, S., & Harris, K. (1996). Self-regulation and strategy instruction for students who find writing and learning challenging. In M. Levy and S. Ransdell (Eds.), *The science of writing: Theories, methods, individual differences, and applications* (pp. 347–360). Hillsdale, NJ: Erlbaum.

Graham, S., & Harris, K. R. (2005). Improving the writing performance of young struggling writers: Theoretical and programmic research from the Center on Accelerated Student Learning. *The Journal of Special Education, 39,* 19–33.

Kilpatrick, J., & Swafford, J. (Eds.). (2002). *Helping children learn mathematics.* Washington, DC: National Academy Press.

Kratochwill, T. R., & Shernoff, E. S. (2004). Evidence-based practice: Promoting evidence-based interventions in school psychology. *School Psychology Review, 33,* 34–48. (Also published in *School Psychology Quarterly, 2003, 18,* 389–408)

Kroesbergen, E. H., & Van Luit, J. E. H. (2003). Mathematics interventions for children with special education needs. A meta-analysis. *Remedial and Special Education, 24*, 97–114.

Lee, J., Grigg, W., & Dion, G. (2007). *The nation's report card: Mathematics 2007* (NCES 2007-494). Washington, DC: National Center for Education Statistics, Institute of Education Sciences, U.S. Department of Education.

Lee, J., Grigg, W., & Donahue, P. (2007). *The nation's report card: Reading 2007* (NCES 2007-496). Washington, DC: National Center for Education Statistics, Institute of Education Sciences, U.S. Department of Education.

Martens, B. K., Daly III, E. J., Begeny, J. C., & VanDerHeyden, A. (in press). Behavioral approaches to education. In W. Fisher, C. Piazza, & H. Roane (Eds.), *Handbook of applied behavior analysis*. New York: Guilford.

Meichenbaum, D. H., & Goodman, J. (1971). Training impulsive children to talk to themselves: A means of developing self-control. *Journal of Abnormal Psychology, 7*, 117–126.

Mercer, C. D., & Miller, S. P. (1992). Teaching students with learning problems in mathematics to acquire, understand, and apply basic math facts. *Remedial and Special Education, 13*, 19–35.

Morgan, P. L., & Sideridis, G. D. (2006). Contrasting the effectiveness of fluency interventions for students with or at risk for learning disabilities: A multilevel random coefficient modeling meta-analysis. *Learning Disabilities Research, 21*, 191–210.

National Commission on Writing. (2003). *The neglected "R."* Princeton, NJ: College Entrance Examination Board.

National Council of Teachers of Mathematics. (2000). *Principles and standards for school mathematics*. Reston, VA: National Council of Teachers of Mathematics.

National Council of Teachers of Mathematics. (2006). *Curriculum focal points for mathematics in prekindergarten through grade 8*. Retrieved July 26, 2007, from http://www.nctmmedia.org/cfp/full_document.pdf

National Institute of Child Health and Human Development. (2000). *Report of the National Reading Panel. Teaching children to read: An evidence-based assessment of the scientific literature on reading and its implications for reading instruction: Reports of the subgroups* (NIH Publication No. 00-4754). Washington, DC: U.S. Government Printing Office.

National Reading Panel. (2000). *Teaching children to read: An evidence-based assessment of the scientific research literature on reading and its implication for reading instruction*. Washington, DC: National Institute of Child Health and Human Development and U.S. Department of Education.

Nies, K. A., & Belfiore, P. J. (2006). Enhancing spelling performance in students with learning disabilities. *Journal of Behavioral Education, 15*, 162–169.

Okyere, B. A., & Heron, T. E. (1991). Use of self-correction to improve spelling in regular education classrooms. In G. Stoner, M. R. Shinn, & H. M. Walker (Eds.), *Interventions for achievement and behavior problems* (pp. 399–413). Silver Spring, MD: The National Association of School Psychologists.

Oxaal, I. (2005). Accelerating student learning in kindergarten through grade 3: Five years of OSEP-sponsored intervention research. *The Journal of Special Education, 39,* 2–5.

Panahon, C., Codding, R. S., Hilt-Panahon, A., & Benson, J. (2007, March). Individualized mathematics interventions: A review of what works? In A. Hilt-Panahon (Chair), *Addressing mathematics problems through school-based interventions: What works?* Symposium presented at the meeting of the National Association of School Psychologists, New York, NY.

Persky, H. R., Daane, M. C., & Jin, Y. (2003). *The nation's report card: Writing 2002* (NCES 2003-529). Washington, DC: National Center for Education Statistics, Institute of Education Sciences, U.S. Department of Education.

Robinson, D. R., Schofield, J. W., & Steers-Wentzell, K. L. (2007). Peer and cross-age tutoring in math: Outcomes and their design implications. *Educational Psychology Review, 17,* 327–362.

Rohrbeck, C. A., Ginsburg-Block, M. D., Fantuzzo, J. W., & Miller, T. R. (2003). Peer-assisted learning intervention with elementary school students. A meta-analytic review. *Journal of Educational Psychology, 95,* 240–257.

Ross, A. H., & Stevens, K. B. (2003). Teaching spelling of social studies convent vocabulary prior to using the vocabulary in inclusive learning environments: An examination of constant time delay, observational learning, and instructive feedback. *Journal of Behavioral Education, 12,* 287–309.

Schlagal, B. (2007). Best practices in spelling and handwriting. In S. Graham, C. A. MacArthur, & J. Fitzgerald (Eds.), *Best practices in writing instruction* (pp. 179–200). New York: Guilford.

Schmidt, W. H., McKnight, C. C., & Raizen, S. A. (1997). *A splintered vision: An investigation of U.S. science and mathematics education.* Dordrecht, the Netherlands: Kluwer Academic.

Shapiro, E. S. (2004). *Academic skills problems: Direct assessment and intervention* (3rd ed.). New York: Guilford.

Skinner, C. H., McLaughlin, T. F., & Logan, P. (1997). Cover, copy, and compare: A self-managed academic intervention effective across skills, students, and settings. *Journal of Behavioral Education, 7,* 295–306.

Snow, C. E., Burns, M. S., & Griffin, P. (Eds.). (1998). *Preventing reading difficulties in young children.* Washington, DC: National Academy Press.

Swanson, L., & Sachse-Lee, C. (2000). A meta-analysis of single-subject-design intervention research of students with LD. *Journal of learning Disabilities, 33,* 114–136.

Van Houten, R. (1980). *Learning through feedback: A systematic approach for improving academic performance.* New York: Human Sciences Press.

Williams, J. P. (2005). Instruction in reading comprehension for primary-grade students: A focus on text structure. *The Journal of Special Education, 39,* 6–18.

Xin, Y. P., & Jitendra, A. K. (1999). The effects of instruction in solving mathematical word problems for students with learning problems: A meta-analysis. *The Journal of Special Education, 32,* 207–225.

8

SCHOOL-WIDE POSITIVE BEHAVIOR SUPPORT: A SYSTEMS-LEVEL APPLICATION OF BEHAVIORAL PRINCIPLES

BRANDI SIMONSEN AND GEORGE SUGAI

School-wide positive behavior support (SWPBS) is a proactive, positive, and systemic approach to effect meaningful educational and behavioral change. Positive behavior support (PBS) was first introduced into federal legislation in 1997 with the amendments to the Individuals With Disabilities Education Act (IDEA), which was an important legislative act that reinforced the importance of a behavioral approach to meeting the needs of individuals with disabilities and significant problem behaviors (Carr et al., 2002). As authorized under IDEA, the Office of Special Education Programs (OSEP) established the National Technical Center on Positive Behavior Interventions and Support (OSEP Center on PBIS). The IDEA amendments refer to

Preparation of this manuscript was supported in part by a grant from the Office of Special Education Programs, U.S. Department of Education, Center on Positive Behavioral Interventions and Support (H326S980003; http://www.pbis.org). Opinions expressed herein are those of the authors and do not necessarily reflect the position of the U.S. Department of Education, and such endorsements should not be inferred. For more information, contact Brandi Simonsen (brandi.simonsen@uconn.edu).

PBS in the context of individual students with disabilities and mandate services for students whose behaviors interfere with their ability to benefit from education. The PBIS Center expanded the focus of PBS implementation to school-, district-, and state-level systems. Over the last decade, researchers, practitioners, and policymakers have demonstrated increasing interest in SWPBS. For example, U.S. Senate and House representatives have introduced amendments to the Elementary and Secondary Education Act of 1965 that would allow state and local educational agencies and schools to make greater use of early intervening services, particularly school-wide positive behavior supports (Positive Behavior for Effective Schools Act, 2007). Functionally, these amendments would incorporate SWPBS language into the reauthorization of the No Child Left Behind Act of 2001 (2002).

SWPBS has received a great deal of attention and is built upon a long and rich history of applied behavioral theory, research, and practice. In this chapter, we elucidate the behavioral roots of SWPBS; specifically, we (a) present an overview of SWPBS; (b) introduce and define key behavioral principles that underlie SWPBS; and (c) illustrate how the behavioral principles are implemented with all (school-wide), some (targeted group), and individual students.

OVERVIEW OF SWPBS

The features, practices, and processes of SWPBS have been described in detail (Lewis & Sugai, 1999; OSEP Center on PBIS, 2004; Safran & Oswald, 2003; Sugai et al., 2000). In this section, we provide a brief overview of SWPBS: (a) three tiers of support, (b) critical elements, and (c) implementation.

Three Tiers of Support

SWPBS interventions are organized into a three-tiered framework of prevention (OSEP Center on PBIS, 2004; Walker et al., 1996) that provides logic for organizing the outcomes, data management, practices, and systems along a continuum of support for all students. *Primary* (universal) tier support is available to all students across all school environments (i.e., classroom and nonclassroom settings). Establishing and teaching positively stated expectations, increasing active supervision, and developing a school-wide reinforcement system are typical examples of primary support that enable most students to be successful. For example, preliminary descriptive data (collected across 1,010 elementary, 312 middle/junior, and 104 high schools implementing SWPBS) suggested that when primary support is in place, approximately 84% of students will receive one or fewer office discipline referrals for major rule violations during a school year (Horner, 2007).

For students who do not respond to primary support, *secondary* (targeted group) tier support is implemented. Secondary support is characterized by systematically increasing the prompts, instructions, monitoring, and reinforcement available for appropriate behavior. Of the 16% of students who do not respond to primary support, schools can expect that approximately 11% will require and receive secondary support (Horner, 2007). Finally, *tertiary* (individual) tier support is designed to meet the needs of students who do not respond to the first two layers of support (approximately 5%). Individualized, high-intensity, function-based, and positive behavior intervention plans; person-centered planning; and services identified and coordinated through wrap-around process are elements of tertiary support.

Critical Elements of SWPBS

Schools implementing SWPBS identify relevant outcomes, use data to guide the selection and implementation of evidence-based practices, and establish systems to sustain implementation and evaluation activities. The interrelationship among these four critical elements of SWPBS (outcomes, data, practices, and systems) is described in the following sections.

Outcomes are observable and measurable goals that are locally determined; based on and validated by collection and analysis of local data; considerate of cultural and regional demographics and customs; related to state, district, and federal priorities; and feasible within the allocated time frame. *Data* are collected to determine the present level of performance (i.e., baseline) of all, some, or individual students at the primary, secondary, and tertiary levels, respectively. Thus, data are used to (a) prioritize need areas; (b) select outcomes that are observable, measurable, and specific; and (c) evaluate progress toward outcomes. Data also guide the selection of practices across the three levels of intervention. Given the importance of data for decision making and evaluation, SWPBS schools capitalize on data sources that are readily available (e.g., extant data) and invest in a data management system that allows efficient input and creates flexible and meaningful visual displays (e.g., graphs or tables) to facilitate decision making (e.g., Simonsen & Sugai, 2007).

Systems are the organizational and process structures and activities designed to support staff and ensure sustained implementation of SWPBS. One of the key structures within SWPBS is teaming. In particular, teams are formed at the state, district, and school level to oversee and guide implementation of primary, secondary, and tertiary supports. For example, the school-level team includes (a) a school administrator, who ensures that the team is given priority, status, and resources; and (b) a select group of staff members who are chosen to be representative of the grade levels, disciplines, and types of staff within the school. For each team, members meet regularly, have clearly defined roles and responsibilities, and are held accountable by a documented action plan. In addition, school staff members engage in professional development and staff reinforcement activities that are designed to initiate, maintain, and increase implementation of practices. In sum, systems-level activities focus on the needs and supports of those staff members who are responsible for accurately and consistently implementing effective practices to achieve SWPBS outcomes.

Practices, then, are the interventions selected, developed, and implemented to support students. Social skills instruction and contingency management (e.g., systematic reinforcement) are typical components of most SWPBS interventions. Selected practices should be preventative, evidence-based, indicated by data, aligned with identified outcomes, clearly supported by systems, and positive. In addition, these practices are adapted to accommodate the unique characteristics (e.g., language, culture, ethnicity, family) of students who are intended to benefit from and staff members who are responsible for their implementation. Positive practices are designed to teach (establish stimulus control) and increase (reinforce), rather than decrease (punish), behavior.

Implementation of SWPBS

As of 2007, over 6,000 schools across more than 40 states and 3 countries have received training and technical assistance in implementing SWPBS from the OSEP Center on PBIS; many more schools and districts that have not been supported by the Center are estimated to have adopted SWPBS practices and processes. Typical training and technical assistance activities span 3 or more years and are designed to promote the careful adoption, accurate and sustained implementation, and controlled expansion or scaling of the full continuum of SWPBS support. Across these years, school teams are guided through a series of capacity building stages: (a) meet readiness requirements, (b) participate in intensive team and school-wide systems development, (c) develop and implement with fidelity primary practices and support systems, (d) develop and implement with fidelity secondary and tertiary practices and support systems, and (e) participate in regular "booster" professional development events for sustaining and enhancing implementation efforts and outcomes.

Prior to receiving training or assistance, schools are required to meet certain readiness requirements, which typically include formal commitments and agreements from 80% of the school staff, active involvement of a school administrator, district-level support and priority, a 3- to 4-year commitment, efficient data management system, established school-level team, and coaching or facilitation support. After readiness requirements are met, school-level teams participate in approximately 6 days of training spread across the initial planning year. During the course of the training, the team members identify the outcomes, data, systems, and practices that will be involved in their implementation of SWPBS. Then, the team members build an action plan detailing how they will (a) share information gained during the training with the entire school staff, (b) perform the tasks required to ensure a successful rollout of the primary system (e.g., establishing a small number of positively stated rules, designing student and staff reinforcement systems) during the upcoming year, and (c) monitor progress toward identified outcomes. The "coach" or facilitator serves as a follow-up link or prompt between training events and team implementation of action plan activities.

After completing the initial planning year, team members facilitate a rollout or formal introduction by all staff members of primary support within their school. During the initial implementation year, school teams continue to participate in training activities (approximately 3 days across the year) and receive support through coaching networks. Activities emphasize, for example, data-based enhancements of practices, school-wide fidelity and fluency of implementation, and acknowledgements for data-based demonstrations of success and progress. In subsequent years, teams continue to receive training and technical assistance to sustain their implementation of primary systems and establish secondary- and tertiary-level systems. In addition, various states have established advanced professional development activities to promote further professional growth. These activities may be available to schools across all stages of implementation but are specifically designed to support schools that have been implementing for 4 or more years. Examples of implementation across various states and for additional information on SWPBS are available at the website of the OSEP Center on PBIS (http://www.pbis.org).

Across all levels of training, school teams are presented with user-friendly and applied information that is directly based on early behavioral theory (i.e., the work of B. F. Skinner), years of applied behavior analytic research and practice (e.g., studies published in the *Journal of Applied Behavior Analysis* and *Journal of Positive Behavioral Interventions*), and other applications of behavioral theory (e.g., organizational behavior, industrial-organizational psychology). Therefore, to understand SWPBS, the basic tenets and principles of behavioral theory also must be acknowledged, understood, and given priority.

KEY BEHAVIORAL PRINCIPLES THAT UNDERLIE SWPBS

Behaviorism is the theory and applied behavior analysis is the applied science that underlies SWPBS. In this section, we describe the behavioral principles that serve as the foundation and guidelines for the development and implementation of the practices and systems of SWPBS: (a) basic tenets of behavioral theory and (b) behavioral principles in the context of the three-term contingency.

Basic Tenets of Behavioral Theory

Behaviorism is a theory-based and empirical approach to studying behavior (e.g., Alberto & Troutman, 2006; Cooper, Heron, & Heward, 2007). Unlike other fields of study within psychology, behaviorism does not focus on mental and emotional states that cannot be directly observed; instead, observable and measurable events are used to more objectively predict, explain, and modify behavior (e.g., Skinner, 1953). Early behaviorism emphasized experimental work designed to describe, understand, and confirm the principles and mechanisms that could be used to expand the theory, explain observed behavioral phenomena, and refine interventions and treatments for individuals with behavioral problems.

From this early work, researchers and practitioners developed awareness that behavioral theory had applications to problems being experienced by humans in everyday life (e.g., mental retardation, emotional disturbance, mental health, juvenile delinquency) and an extension of behaviorism emerged: applied behavior analysis (ABA). In a seminal article published in the first volume of the *Journal of Applied Behavior Analysis*, Baer, Wolf, and Risley (1968) defined ABA as a science that addresses real (applied) behavior problems (e.g., decreasing aggressive behavior of an individual), in a systematic and objective manner, by (a) applying conceptually sound behavioral interventions and (b) analyzing the effect of those interventions on the target behaviors of an individual to ensure that a meaningful, socially significant, and enduring behavior change occurs.

From ABA, we have learned that all behaviors (desired and undesired) are learned by and functional (i.e., operate on and are responsive to the environment) for an individual (Baer et al., 1968; Cooper et al., 2007). The basic unit of analysis for describing, understanding, and affecting occurrences of behavior is the three-term contingency, which is characterized as an antecedent–behavior–consequence (ABC) sequence (e.g., Alberto & Troutman, 2006).

Behavioral Principles in the Context of the Three-Term Contingency

The ABC or three-term contingency demonstrates that behavior does not occur in a vacuum or independent of environmental factors. Specifically, behavioral occurrences are described as being "occasioned" and maintained by environmental events; that is, the presence (or absence) of specific antecedent stimuli (e.g., conditions, activities, objects, events) sets the occasion or opportunity for specific consequence conditions (i.e., punishment or reinforcement) if a specific behavior is emitted (or not) in the presence of the antecedent stimuli.

The development, implementation, and evaluation of behavioral intervention are guided by the three-term contingency. Interventions are designed to (a) change antecedent stimuli such that they trigger (occasion) desired (appropriate) behaviors and do not trigger undesired (problem) behaviors, (b) teach appropriate behavior(s) that more efficiently and effectively lead to reinforcement than problem behavior, and (c) modify consequence stimuli such that emission of appropriate behaviors are more likely to result in reinforcement and inappropriate behaviors are less likely. In the following subsections, we discuss the specific principles and procedures used to modify the antecedents, behaviors, and consequences.

Strategies to Modify Antecedent Stimuli

In each ABC sequence, a specific antecedent (discriminative stimulus or S^D) triggers or occasions a particular behavior, or response. The S^D is described as "signaling" an increased likelihood of a particular consequence (reinforcement) if the behavior is emitted in the presence of that S^D and of a different consequence (neutral or punishment) if the behavior is emitted in the absence of the same S^D. In more applied or lay terms, individuals learn that if "A" is present and they do "B," then "C" will follow.

Therefore, to effect a desired change in behavior, antecedent stimuli should be modified in two key ways. First, the presentation or availability of antecedent stimuli that occasion desired behavior should be increased or enhanced. For example, if teacher attention is a desired (positively reinforcing) consequence and if a student has received teacher attention for engaging in appropriate behavior in the past, then the presence of a teacher is more likely to occasion appropriate student behavior. So, to occasion more desired student behavior, an intervention plan would include manipulations that increase teacher presence, for example, closer and more frequent teacher proximity, increased teacher initiated interactions, or more teacher-directed instruction. Another way to enhance an antecedent stimulus is to add prompts to the environment that draw students' attention to the S^D and remind them of the desired behavior, for example, teacher statements (e.g., "I like talking with *respectful* students"), posted rule-reminders (e.g., "Raise your hand before answering or asking"), or modeling gestures (e.g., teacher raised hand while asking a question).

Second, the stimuli that trigger or occasion undesired behavior should be eliminated or modified; that is, remove or alter stimuli that typically signal reinforcing consequences for displays of undesired behavior. For example, if slowdowns and collisions in a particular crowded stairway occasion verbal and physical aggression (e.g., maintained by peer attention), then modifying antecedent stimuli might include instituting a staggered hallway dismissal to reduce crowding, or adding "stay to the right" arrows on the floor to decrease collisions.

By altering antecedent stimuli, the objective is to increase the likelihood of appropriate behavior and prevent (decrease the likelihood of) problem behavior. For antecedent strategies to be effective, individuals must

(a) already have the behavior in their behavioral learning history and (b) have been trained to perform the behavior under the specific antecedent conditions. Thus, antecedent strategies are only useful when an individual has learned how and when (i.e., stimulus control) to emit and not emit the behavior.

Strategies to Teach Behavior

When a behavior is not already within an individual's repertoire or when a behavior has not been learned under the desired conditions, stimulus control must be established, that is, the behavior must be taught. Whether learning an academic or a behavior skill, teaching is about establishing lasting behavior change through four phases of learning: (a) acquisition—accurate (> 90% correct) responding, (b) fluency—accurate responding at acceptable rates, (c) maintenance—accurate responding at acceptable rates over time, and (d) generalization—accurate and adapted responding at acceptable rates over time and under a variety of stimulus conditions. When an individual has not emitted accurate displays of a behavior under desired instructional stimulus conditions, the focus of instruction is on skill acquisition. This phase emphasizes stimulus control, which is established by (a) providing reinforcement contingent on accurate displays of a target behavior in the presence of specific antecedent conditions (discriminative stimuli) and (b) withholding reinforcement for displays of the target behavior when the specific antecedent conditions are not present or for displays of other behaviors in the presence of the specific antecedent conditions. Stimulus control is evident when the desired response occurs more often (or exclusively) in the presence of the S^D than in its absence.

To facilitate skill acquisition, an explicit and systematic instructional approach is adopted: define, model, assess, and reinforce. With academic skills, like reading, math, and social studies, this "direct instruction" approach (Engelmann & Carnine, 1982; Kameenui & Simmons, 1990) is characterized as a "model-lead-test" (or "I do, we do, you do") approach. A similar approach is adopted for teaching social behaviors or skills. For example, *shaping* (i.e., differentially reinforcing successive approximations of a desired behavior) is used to teach simple (single-step) behaviors and *chaining* (i.e., breaking a task down into component parts and reinforcing the learner for completing more and more steps in succession) is used to teach complex (multistep) behaviors (e.g., Alberto & Troutman, 2006).

After the skill has been acquired, the focus of instruction moves toward increasing the fluency with which the behavior is performed. High levels of accuracy are maintained, and reinforcement is provided systematically and contingently as more acceptable rates or consistency of performance is acquired. Again, shaping is emphasized along with repeated practice.

In the maintenance phase, skill practice is continued; however, schedules of reinforcement are leaned or thinned to approximate what might be available in the natural or noninstructional environment. The goal is to establish maintained rates of responding by shifting control from instructional to naturally occurring prompts and consequences. If expected schedules of reinforcement are not available to maintain behavioral occurrences, self-management strategies can be taught (e.g., self-manipulation of antecedent and consequence events) to provide what is needed.

Ultimately, teaching is not successful if the newly acquired skill is not used and maintained in noninstructional settings and conditions in which the skill has not been taught and practiced. To program for generalized responding, instruction shifts to teaching with a full range of examples and nonexamples (i.e., antecedent and consequence conditions) such that a "general case," rule, or concept is established (Horner, Bellamy, & Colvin, 1984). As in maintenance, the instruction continues to emphasize approximating consequence conditions that characterize the natural or generalization settings, but increased attention is placed on teaching a representative sample of the stimulus conditions that exist outside the instructional context.

In sum, when an individual does not know how to perform a behavior, the focus of instruction is on skill acquisition (teaching the B part of the ABC chain). Once an individual emits the behavior accurately, the focus of instruction is on building the AB portion of the chain, or establishing stimulus control. When an individual knows how and when to perform a desired behavior but does not perform it with the expected frequency, rate, or intensity, instructional focus shifts to modifications of consequences, or the C part of the three-term contingency.

Strategies to Modify Consequences

In behavioral theory, consequence manipulations may have one of three associated effects on a behavior: (a) none—consequence manipulation is associated with no predictable effect on occurrence of behavior in future; (b) increase—manipulation of consequence stimuli is associated with an increased likelihood that a behavior will occur in the future (reinforcement); and (c) decrease—consequence manipulation is associated with a decrease in likelihood that a behavior will occur in the future (punishment). In general, two types of manipulations are considered: (a) give or present (positive) and (b) remove or take (negative). Thus, four types of consequences can be characterized by two manipulations (positive or negative) and two effects (increase or decrease) on the future probability of behavior.

Positive reinforcement describes a condition in which a consequence stimulus is presented contingent upon emission of a behavior and is associated with an increase in probability of future behavior occurrences. For example, a student is working quietly on a sheet of math problems and the teacher gives verbal praise (e.g., "I like how you are working quietly"). If the student is more likely to work quietly in the future, then the contingent presentation of verbal praise is positive reinforcement.

Negative reinforcement describes a condition in which a stimulus is removed contingent on emission of a behavior and is associated with an increase in probability of future behavior occurrences. For example, because another student is working slowly on her math problems, the teacher "nags" at the student to work faster, stop talking, and keep her eyes on her own work. The student works faster to reduce the amount of teaching nagging. If the student is more likely to work quietly and faster in the future, then the contingent removal of teacher nagging is negative reinforcement.

Positive punishment is used to describe a condition in which a stimulus is added contingently on the emission of a behavior and is associated with a decrease in the likelihood of future occurrences of the behavior. For example, a child throws blocks and the caregiver gives a reprimand (e.g., "No. We do not throw blocks."). If future occurrences of block throwing decrease, then positive punishment describes the situation.

Negative punishment describes a condition in which a stimulus is removed contingent on emission of a behavior and is associated with a decrease in the future probability of that behavior being emitted. For example, a different child is throwing blocks and the caregiver takes the blocks away. If future occurrences of block throwing decrease, negative punishment is used to describe the situation. Caution should be taken whenever punishment procedures are used. The literature is replete with considerations when using punishment-based interventions, for example, (a) always include and emphasize strategies that are based on positive reinforcement, (b) never use punishment-only procedures, (c) use effective punishment procedures and fade their use as quickly as possible, (d) plan for side effects (e.g., aggression, escape, withdrawal), (e) monitor fidelity of implementation and behavior effects continuously, (f) use the most effective and least aversive, (g) do no harm, and (h) emphasize teaching of prosocial alternative behaviors (Alberto & Troutman, 2006; Cooper et al., 2007).

Extinction is a variation of negative punishment, and is a condition in which reinforcing consequences that have been shown to maintain a behavior are withheld or removed contingent on a behavior occurrence and are associated with a decrease in future occurrences of that behavior. Extinction procedures can be difficult to implement in an applied setting because (a) all reinforcement must be identified and withheld consistently and completely upon emission of the targeted response and (b) temporary increases in the frequency, rate, or intensity of the response (extinction burst) can be experienced before decreases are observed. For example, a student repeatedly talks out during teacher-directed instruction. In the past, the teacher has responded to these talk-outs by giving immediate attention (e.g., called on the student, redirected the student to another task, asked the student to wait and try again later). Realizing that talking out has been positively reinforced by teacher attention, the teacher decides to implement an extinction procedure. Specifically, the teacher decides to withhold attention each time the student talks out. Initially, the student talks out more frequently in a louder tone of voice (extinction burst). If the teacher consistently and contingently withholds attention every time the student talks out, then that behavior will eventually decrease in frequency.

Like any reduction procedure, extinction always should be combined with constructive strategies that teach and strengthen occurrences of appropriate alternative behaviors (e.g., raise hand for 5 seconds, and if necessary try again later). Combinations of positive reinforcement and extinction (differential reinforcement) can take a variety of forms (e.g., differential reinforcement of an alternative behavior). For example, the teacher may remove attention each time a talk-out occurs but immediately present attention each time the student seeks teacher attention appropriately (e.g., raises hand, approaches teacher's desk appropriately).

These basic consequence procedures can be used to manipulate environmental stimuli to increase occurrences of desired, or decrease occurrences of undesired, behavior in the future. In a school setting, students often have stimuli presented (e.g., praise, tokens, points, grades, items, activities) or removed (e.g., homework pass) in an effort to increase desired behavior. Similarly, students often have stimuli presented (e.g., office discipline referrals, verbal reprimands) or removed (e.g., detention from fun activities, recess taken away) in an effort to decrease undesired behaviors. Regardless of intent, school staff can use observations of student behavior to determine if they are actually reinforcing desired behavior and punishing or extinguishing undesired behavior. For example, a principal may assign (give) a student in-school suspension for engaging in disruptive behavior, thinking that positive punishment is being applied. However, if disruptive behavior continues or increases, the principal's consequence procedure is more likely to be positive (presentation of adult attention) or negative (removal from an aversive classroom environment) reinforcement.

BEHAVIORAL PRINCIPLES APPLIED THROUGHOUT TIERS OF SWPBS

Most ABA applications have involved individuals who present behavioral challenges (behavior deficits and/or excesses) and require individualized behavior intervention plans. ABA principles and interventions can be extended easily to organizations like classrooms and schools. The behavior of the individual remains a primary consideration; however, applications are extended to groups of individuals in a consistent and efficient manner. In particular, the three-term contingency remains central to SWPBS applications, and behavioral principles (e.g., reinforcement, stimulus control, punishment) guide the development, implementation, and evaluation of SWPBS.

SWPBS is the systems-level approach that organizes the application of basic behavioral principles in the previously described three-tiered continuum of behavior support: primary tier for all students, secondary tier for smaller groups of individuals whose behaviors are not responsive to primary tier interventions, and tertiary tier for individual students whose behaviors are not responsive to primary and secondary tier interventions. Across each intervention tier, school staff members implement strategies that involve modifying antecedent and consequence conditions and teaching of prosocial behaviors. The ultimate goals are to redesign teaching and learning environments to (a) eliminate triggering antecedent stimuli and maintaining reinforcing stimuli for undesirable behaviors, (b) establish strong stimulus control for (i.e., teach) prosocial desirable behaviors, and (c) increase availability and presentation of triggering antecedent stimuli and maintaining (reinforcing) consequence stimuli for desirable behavior. Examples of SWPBS practices and interventions across the three-tiered continuum of support are described in the following sections.

SWPBS Primary Tier Intervention

At the primary tier, interventions are implemented by all staff members for all students across all classroom and school settings. Changes are made to the larger environmental conditions to occasion (antecedent strategies) and reinforce (consequence strategies) desired, rule-following behaviors. In particular, schools implementing SWPBS emphasize systematically teaching rule-following behaviors within each school routine and setting. For example, visual prompts (e.g., posters, pictures) are added to key settings (e.g., classroom, cafeteria, hallway, playground, and common areas). A small set of general school-wide behavioral expectations are established and taught. Often, schools approach this practice by building a school-wide rule matrix that highlights specific behavior examples that are relevant to each school setting and general school-wide expectation. Sound teaching and behavioral principles are applied by emphasizing context (e.g., hallway, classroom, bus, hallways, cafeteria), specific behavioral examples that are linked to context (e.g., walk to the right in hallway, share equipment on playground, sit in your seat on the bus until you get to school, return your tray to the stack and litter to the trash can), and school-wide expectations (e.g., being responsible, being respectful, being safe, being a learner).

Primary tier SWPBS intervention also emphasizes the need to provide regular, contingent, and effective positive reinforcement. In many implementations, a token economy is established for all staff, students, and settings. Student displays of rule/expectation-following behaviors is followed by presentation of social and token reinforcers, which are linked to later social and back-up reinforcers. Individual students, whole classrooms, entire grade levels, and/or the whole student body can receive a positive reinforcer on the basis of cumulative performances. It also should be noted that school administrators and SWPBS leadership team members also provide positive reinforcers for staff members who accurately adhere to teaching and intervention protocols.

In addition, primary tier SWPBS includes a continuum of consequences for rule violations. This continuum begins with the least intrusive/aversive for minor rule violations (e.g., extinction, reminder and reteaching, differential reinforcement, conference) and progresses to more intrusive/aversive strategies for moderate (e.g., brief verbal reprimands, response costs, short timeouts) and severe (e.g., in-school detention, out-of-school detention) violations. It is important to note that behavior-reduction procedures are not repeatedly intensive for students whose behaviors do not decrease. Instead, decision rules are applied to determine when the next intervention tier should be considered (i.e., responsiveness-to-intervention).

SWPBS Secondary Tier Interventions

At the secondary tier, interventions are focused on increasing structure and prompting, intensifying instruction, increasing the frequency and intensity of reinforcement, or some combination of all of the above (Crone, Horner, & Hawken, 2004). Typically, schools will adopt one or two standardized behavioral intervention to be implemented at the secondary level (e.g., targeted social skills instruction or check-in/check-out). The logic is that students whose behaviors are unresponsive to primary tier interventions (school-wide) require more intensive and specialized behavioral strategies; however, the same basic intervention can be applied to all students in a similar or group-based manner, making implementation more efficient, relevant, and cost-effective than attempting more costly and complicated individualized programming for each student. In general, secondary tier interventions are characterized as having (a) regular and frequent daily behavior assessments (self or other), (b) direct alignment with the school-wide behavioral expectations, (c) regular and frequent daily positive reinforcement for displays of appropriate behavioral expectations, (d) group-based contingencies that involve positive reinforcers for whole classrooms on the basis of individual student/group performance, (e) behavior reporting to and positive reinforcement opportunities by parents, and (f) routine progress review and intervention adjustments on the basis of student responsiveness.

SWPBS Tertiary Tier Interventions

At the tertiary level, individualized interventions are developed for each student on the basis of student-specific information. These students are identified for tertiary tier interventions because their behaviors are unresponsive to interventions at the primary and secondary tiers. At the crux of this intervention tier is a function-based approach to behavioral assessment and behavior-support planning (Crone & Horner, 2003; Sugai, Lewis-Palmer, & Hagan-Burke, 1999–2000). Specifically, a functional behavioral assessment is conducted to identify typical antecedent and consequence conditions that occasion and maintain, respectively, undesired behavior. In other words, the assessment data identify the "function" or type of reinforcement that maintains the undesired behavior (positive vs. negative reinforcement). This information is used to guide the development of a positive behavior intervention plan that specifies (a) changes to the antecedent conditions, (b) strategies for teaching replacement behaviors that are more efficient and effective than the problem behavior at meeting the same function, (c) strategies for providing function-based reinforcement contingent on displays of the replacement behavior (i.e., the identified positive or negative reinforcement currently maintaining the undesired behavior), (d) strategies for reinforcing successive approximations of the ultimate desired behavior (i.e., the expected behavior for the identified antecedent conditions, which may not meet the same function as the undesired behavior), and (e) strategies for preventing reinforcement of the undesired behavior (i.e., put the undesired behavior on extinction).

Behavior-support planning at the tertiary level requires individuals with specialized behavioral competence who can work as a team to develop comprehensive, positive, thorough, and effective assessment-/function-based behavior intervention plans. The need for this level of specialized support is evidenced by the student's behavior being relatively unresponsive to intervention attempts at the primary and secondary tiers.

SUMMARY

SWPBS has gained popularity as a school-wide intervention approach; it is based on a rich tradition of basic and applied research and practice that is ground in sound behavioral theory and applied behavior analysis. SWPBS is a system-wide intervention approach focused on helping schools adopt, learn, organize, and implement evidence-based behavioral interventions with fidelity and durability. Specifically, schools implement a continuum of behavior support that comprises primary tier support for all students across all settings, secondary tier support for a targeted group of students who display at-risk behavior and require additional support to be successful, and tertiary tier support for individual students who display high-risk behavior and require individualized support to be successful.

In addition to these practices, schools implementing SWPBS identify relevant outcomes, collect data to measure progress and guide intervention decisions, and establish systems to ensure sustained implementation of adopted practices. SWPBS is not a new approach but instead is the demonstrated application and extension of sound behavioral theory, principles, and practices that had beginnings at the individual level in noneducation-related settings. Unlike traditional behavioral approaches that focus on supporting individuals who present significant problem behavior repertoires, SWPBS addresses the needs of all students by emphasizing prevention (Biglan, 1995): (a) preventing the development or acquisition of problem behavior; (b) preventing the occurrence and intensifying of existing problem behavior; (c) teaching prosocial behavior that is more efficient, effective, and relevant than problem behavior; and (d) redesigning teaching and learning environments that promote more prosocial behavior.

REFERENCES

Alberto, P. A., & Troutman, A. C. (2006). *Applied behavior analysis for teachers* (7th ed.). Upper Saddle River, NJ: Pearson.

Baer, D. M., Wolf, M. M., & Risley, T. R. (1968). Some current dimensions of applied behavior analysis. *Journal of Applied Behavior Analysis, 1*, 91–97.

Biglan, A. (1995). Translating what we know about the context of antisocial behavior in to a lower prevalence of such behavior. *Journal of Applied Behavior Analysis, 28*, 479–492.

Carr, E. G., Dunlap, G., Horner, R. H., Koegel, R. L., Turnbull, A. P., & Sailor, W. (2002). Positive behavior support: Evolution of an applied science. *Journal of Positive Behavior Interventions, 4*, 4–16.

Cooper, J. O., Heron, T. E., & Heward, W. L. (2007). *Applied behavior analysis* (2nd ed.). Upper Saddle River, NJ: Prentice Hall.

Crone, D. A., & Horner, R. H. (2003). *Building positive behavior support systems in schools: Functional behavioral assessment.* New York: Guilford.

Crone, D. A., Horner, R. H., & Hawken, L. S. (2004). *Responding to problem behavior in schools: The behavior education program.* New York: Guilford.

Engelmann, S., & Carnine, D. (1982). *Theory of instruction: Principles and applications.* New York: Irvington.

Horner, R. (2007). *Discipline prevention data.* Eugene, OR: Office of Special Education Programs Center on Positive Behavior Interventions and Supports, University of Oregon.

Horner, R. H., Bellamy, G. T., & Colvin, G. T. (1984). Responding in the presence of nontrained stimuli: Implications of generalization error patterns. *Journal of the Association of the Severely Handicapped, 9*, 287–295.

Individuals With Disabilities Education Act (IDEA) Amendments of 1997, Pub. L. No. 105-17, 111 Stat. 37 (1997).

Kameenui, E. J., & Simmons, D. C. (1990). *Designing instructional strategies: The prevention of academic learning problems.* Columbus, OH: Merrill.

Lewis, T. J., & Sugai, G. (1999). Effective behavior support: A systems approach to proactive school-wide management. *Focus on Exceptional Children, 31*(6), 1–24.

No Child Left Behind Act of 2001, Pub. L. No. 107-110, 115 Stat. 1425 (2002).

Office of Special Education Programs Center on Positive Behavioral Interventions and Supports. (2004). *School-wide positive behavior support: Implementers' blueprint and self-assessment.* Eugene: University of Oregon.

Positive Behavior for Effective Schools Act, H.R. 3407, 110th Cong. (2007).

Safran, S. P., & Oswald, K. (2003). Positive behavior supports: Can schools reshape disciplinary practices? *Exceptional Children, 69,* 361–373.

Simonsen, B., & Sugai, G. (2007). Using school-wide data systems to make decisions efficiently and effectively. *School Psychology Forum, 1*(2), 46–58.

Skinner, B. F. (1953). *Science of human behavior.* New York: Macmillan.

Sugai, G., Horner, R. H., Dunlap, G. Hieneman, M., Lewis, T. J., Nelson, C. M., et al. (2000). Applying positive behavioral support and functional behavioral assessment in schools. *Journal of Positive Behavior Interventions, 2,* 131–143.

Sugai, G., Lewis-Palmer, T., & Hagan-Burke, S. (1999–2000). Overview of the functional behavioral assessment process. *Exceptionality, 8,* 149–160.

Walker, H. M., Horner, R. H., Sugai, G., Bullis, M., Sprague, J. R., Bricker, D., et al. (1996). Integrated approaches to preventing antisocial behavior patterns among school-age children and youth. *Journal of Emotional and Behavioral Disorders, 4,* 194–209.

9

PROACTIVE INSTRUCTIONAL STRATEGIES FOR CLASSROOM MANAGEMENT

JOSEPH H. WEHBY AND KATHLEEN LYNNE LANE

Today's educators are under tremendous pressure to meet calls for academic excellence (e.g., No Child Left Behind Act of 2001, 2002) while serving an increasingly diverse student population that is inclusive of students with learning and behavioral challenges (Fuchs & Fuchs, 1994; Lane & Wehby, 2002). Whereas some students come to school "ready to learn" as evidenced by having the necessary prerequisite academic skills and behavior patterns that facilitate instruction (e.g., compliance, appropriate use of wait time), others do not. Some students come ill-prepared, demonstrating limited prerequisite skills and aversive behavior patterns (e.g., noncompliance, verbal and physical aggression) that make it difficult for students to participate in instructional activities and impede teachers' ability to teach (Walker, Irvin, Noell, & Singer, 1992). Decades of research have determined that academic performance and behavioral performance are not separate, mutually exclusive entities (Hinshaw, 1992; Kern & Clemens, 2007). Yet, the exact nature of the relationship between academic and behavioral performance is not entirely clear (Lane, 2004).

Fortunately, many schools have addressed this relationship between learning and behavioral performance patterns as they have move forward with the design, implementation, and evaluation of positive behavior support systems (see chap. 8, this volume) to create host environments to facilitate positive learning environments (Sugai & Horner, 2002). At the base of three-tiered models of support are school-wide, primary prevention efforts that contain clearly defined behavioral expectations for all common areas students in the building (e.g., classrooms, hallways, cafeterias). By establishing common expectations that are practiced and reinforced, the playing field is leveled for all students (Lane, Robertson, & Graham-Bailey, 2006). All students are aware of the expectations; however, they may still not choose to adhere to the established behavior expectations. Consequently, it is imperative that teachers have well-developed classroom management skills to (a) prevent problem behaviors from occurring and (b) respond to existing instances of problem behaviors in a manner that facilitates instruction.

Volumes have been written about how classroom structure influences students' behavior and participation in a range of instructional activities (e.g., Cipani, 2008; Evertson & Weinstein, 2006; Kerr & Nelson, 2002). *Classroom structure* refers to the manner in which the classroom is organized and includes features such as (a) physical arrangement, (b) operating procedures, and (c) teacher expectations. For example, in terms of physical arrangement, it is important that the physical arrangement of the classroom supports the wide range of functions and operations (e.g., independent seat work, cooperative group work, transitions, material storage) that occur in a given classroom. In brief, the main goal of establishing classroom structure is to ensure that classroom events are as predictable as possible (Paine, Radicchi, Rosellini, Deutchman, & Darch, 1983; Walker, Ramsey, & Gresham, 2004). This is particularly important for students with and at risk of emotional or behavioral disorders, who often come from home environments that are characterized by limited predictability, poor supervision, and limited involvement (Reid & Patterson, 1991). If the classroom environment is predictable, teacher expectations are understood and consistently reinforced, and the instructional tasks are appropriate to the students' developmental and instructional level, then students are better able to participate in instruction and problem behaviors are less likely to occur than in classrooms that lack these features (Lane, Pierson, & Givner, 2004; Lane, Wehby, & Cooley, 2006; Walker et al., 2004).

Another body of literature documents the impact of teacher–student interactions on instruction (Carr, Taylor, & Robinson, 1991; Wehby, Symons, Canale, & Go, 1998). In brief, results of these studies suggest that teacher behavior influences student behavior and student behavior influences teacher behavior. For example, Carr et al. (1991) reported that academic instruction was less in-depth and at an easier level for students with a history of problem behavior when compared with students without behavior problems in the same classroom. Similarly, Wehby et al. (1998) reported that the percentage of time teachers spent providing academic instruction was significantly lower for those students identified as having high levels of aggressive behavior. In terms of classroom management, these findings suggest that one method of preventing students from exhibiting behaviors that impede instruction is to provide teachers with evidence-based strategies that can be embedded within academic instruction to prevent misbehavior from occurring.

In this chapter, we do not attempt to reiterate the well-established literature on classroom structure (such a review may be found in Evertson & Weinstein, 2006). Instead, we introduce four proactive strategies teachers can implement during academic instruction to facilitate appropriate decorum and help a classroom run smoothly. Each strategy is an antecedent-based approach to preventing problems from occurring. Whereas consequent-based interventions require the problem behavior to occur before invoking the strategy (e.g., verbal redirect, time-out), antecedent-based approaches can be introduced without waiting for the problems to occur. The most common strategies include (a) proximity, (b) high rates of opportunities to respond, (c) high-probability requests (behavioral momentum), and (d) choice making. In the sections that follow, we define each of these strategies and document the effects of these interventions when used with students with or at risk for learning and behavior problems. While research has focused mostly on elementary school students, these techniques, with some possible modifications, should be appropriate for all grade levels and students in regular and special education classes. Finally, we conclude with a brief summary and discussion of the educational implications associated with employing antecedent-based, teacher-focused strategies for preventing problems from occurring.

PROXIMITY

In a review of classroom management strategies, Shores, Gunter, and Jack (1993) reported that movement of a teacher in a classroom may be one of the most effective means of managing student behavior. That is, teachers' physical proximity to a student or group of students has been known to curtail disruptive behavior and refocus a student to the instructional task at hand. This well-known, low-profile technique for managing classroom behavior is referred to as *proximity control.*

The mechanisms that allow proximity control to be such an effective tool are not clearly understood. It has been suggested that close physical proximity between a teacher and a student functions as an external model or prompt that allows a student to better control his or her behavior (Estcheidt, Stainback, & Stainback, 1984), whereas others have suggested that it allows for higher quality interactions between students and teachers (Shores et al.,

1993). Although the reasons for its effectiveness are unclear, it is one of the most recommended strategies for controlling classroom behavior.

Proximity control is one of the easiest management tools to implement and can be conducted in a variety of ways (Glass, Christiansen, & Christiansen, 1982). Many teachers often seat a student who is likely to be disruptive at a desk closest to the teacher's primary instructional area to better manage behavior. Others may patrol a classroom, which allows for more fluid proximity control and permits a teacher to move toward a problem area before behavior becomes too disruptive (Fifer, 1986). Unfortunately, despite the ease of implementation and the low cost of this procedure, it has been reported that proximity control is not used on a frequent basis and that it is not unusual to observe the adults in some classrooms remaining stationary for entire academic periods (Gunter, Shores, Jack, Rasmussen, & Flowers, 1995).

Although proximity control is frequently recommended to teachers for managing problem behavior, there is limited research in this area. However, research that has been conducted has resulted in several recommendations to increase the efficacy of the procedure. For example, most research has suggested that effective proximity control is maintained when a teacher is within approximately 3 feet of the disruptive student (Estcheidt et al., 1984; Van Houten, Nau, MacKenzie-Keating, Sameoto, & Colavecchia, 1982). In addition, when delivering behavioral feedback using proximity control, interactions with students are more effective if they are relatively brief (Van Houten et al.). Again, it appears that close proximity increases the effectiveness of behavioral feedback given by the teacher, resulting in minimum need for extended interactions that may often lead to prolonged episodes of off-task behavior (Wehby, Symons, & Shores, 1995).

One added benefit of proximity control is the reported impact it has on other students seated near the targeted student. Several studies have reported that the behavior of nontargeted adjacent students improved when a teacher moved within close proximity to manage the behavior of another student (Broden, Bruce, Mitchell, Carter, & Hall, 1970; Okovita & Bucher, 1976). The exact mechanism for improved behavior is not known, although Gunter et al. (1995) speculated that it may be a result of the feedback (positive or negative) given to the target student. Regardless of the reason, it appears that proximity control can be a powerful tool to effect change for a group of students rather than just an individual student.

Teachers can use a number of methods to monitor their proximity habits. Videotapes of instructional activities can be recorded and reviewed to determine whether proximity patterns are distributed in such a manner that a teacher is maneuvering throughout a classroom, coming within close proximity of all students during a portion of an instructional period. Similarly, teachers can ask other teachers or support staff to observe their classrooms and give feedback on monitoring patterns. Finally, physical reminders (e.g., charts, posters) can be placed throughout the classroom reminding a teacher to be mobile during instructional periods.

It is important to keep in mind that proximity control may be implemented by other school personnel as well. For those settings in which educational assistants are present, incorporating active mobility as a part of their daily responsibilities can also be used to increase the use of proximity control. Although not formally studied, Gunter et al. (1995) and others (e.g., Giangreco, Edelman, Luiselli, & MacFarland, 1997) have observed that classroom assistants tend to spend the majority of their time in one location, either with a specific student or at a desk. Having both support staff and teachers use proximity control may result in greater coverage of the entire classroom during academic activities.

In summary, proximity control is one of the simplest, low-cost methods for managing behavior in classrooms. Yet, it may also be underused by teachers and support staff. Evaluating proximity patterns on an ongoing basis should lead to more consistent use of this method, resulting in fewer instances of misbehavior during instructional periods.

HIGH RATE OF OPPORTUNITIES TO RESPOND

As mentioned in the introduction to this chapter, there seems to be a strong connection between academic interactions and problem behavior in classrooms. That is, classrooms with higher rates of academic instruction tend to be those with the lowest level of problem behavior (Gunter & Denny, 1998). Unfortunately, it has been well documented that students exhibiting problem behavior often receive the lowest amount of instruction. Carr et al. (1991) reported that in comparison with their classmates, students showing problem behavior received fewer teacher-directed instructional commands. Similarly, Wehby et al. (1998) reported that students identified as high aggressors were likely to receive less than half of the instruction provided to low aggressors in the same classroom. Given the inverse relation between instruction and problem behavior, researchers have recently targeted increased academic instruction as a means to improve the levels of appropriate behavior in classrooms. More specifically, research has focused on improving the rate at which students are given opportunities to respond (OTR) to instruction as a method to not only improve academic achievement but also minimize the opportunities that students have to engage in acting-out behavior (Deno, 1998; Gunter & Denny, 1998; Sutherland, Adler, & Gunter, 2003).

In a review of the literature on the relationship between OTR and problem behavior, Sutherland and Wehby (2001) identified six studies that examined the impact of increasing OTR on a variety of misbehavior that occurs in classrooms. For example, West and Sloane (1986) manipulated high and low presentation rates (OTR) to five students with emotional and behavioral disorders and found that increased OTR resulted in lower levels of disruptive behavior as well as increased academic responding by the participants. In an earlier study, Carnine (1976) demonstrated that higher rates of OTR resulted in increased classroom participation and lower levels of off-task behavior. The results of these and other studies suggest that one simple method of improving the management of classrooms is to incorporate higher levels of active responding by students, which, by default, should lead to fewer opportunities for students to engage in inappropriate behavior.

It is important to note that increased OTR should occur within the context of effective instructional practices inclusive of adequate amounts of instructional talk, prompts for correct responding, sufficient wait time for students to respond, and positive feedback or praise for correct responding (Stichter, Lewis, Richter, Johnson, & Bradley, 2006). Instructional talk should make up approximately 50% of an academic activity and should include relevant information, demonstrations, and guided practice. Prompts or requests for information from students (i.e., OTR) should occur within and following periods of teacher instruction at a rate of approximately three to four requests per minute (Sutherland et al., 2003). Following OTR, students should be given adequate time to respond to the prompt. Although the amount of wait time may vary dependent upon the type of response being requested, a minimum of 3 minutes should be allocated before repeating the prompt or initiating an error correction procedure (cf. Stichter et al., 2006). Finally, correct responses should be contingently praised throughout the instructional sequence to provide students with necessary feedback that would potentially reward appropriate classroom behavior.

Although the effectiveness of the above sequence is established, this sequence occurs at less than optimal levels when students are engaged in disruptive classroom behavior. Research on teacher instruction toward students who engage in high levels of problem behavior has suggested that these students often disrupt the flow of instruction in classrooms. These disruptions, over time, may shape teachers away from the necessary amount and sequence of academic instruction and OTR that are needed to maintain classroom order (Wehby, Lane, & Falk, 2003; Wehby et al., 1998). Thus, teachers may require additional supports to assist them in maintaining high levels of instruction across a school day.

Several methods of support may be incorporated by teachers to help them maintain effective instructional practices and high levels of OTR. For example, self-evaluation and feedback have proven to be effective methods of increasing the use of targeted instructional behaviors (Hoover & Carroll, 1987; Kilbourn, 1991; Sutherland et al., 2003; Sutherland & Wehby, 2001; Sutherland, Wehby, & Copeland, 2000). In some of these studies, existing levels of OTR were recorded via direct observation and shared with teachers. Teachers used this information to set goals for desired levels of OTR during a specified period of time (e.g., 15 minutes). Teachers were trained on how to audiotape their instructional language using a microcassette recorder and specific coding procedures. Each day, teachers listened to a 5-minute taped sample of one of their lessons and coded occurrences of OTR accordingly. They then multiplied the total number of occurrences by 3 to get a rate of OTR per 15 minutes and graphed their progress toward their goal. This relatively simple method of self-evaluation resulted in both increased levels of OTR as well as increased academic responding by students and lower levels of disruptive behavior. Similarly, peer feedback would work with a second adult in the classroom recording OTR during an instructional period and providing feedback to a teacher on whether or not adequate levels were observed.

In summary, effective interventions for improved classroom management should begin with instructional practices by teachers. It appears that increasing rates of OTR is an effective means of achieving this goal. By incorporating relatively straightforward evaluation procedures, teachers should be able to monitor the frequency of their instructional practices that should result in an overall improvement in appropriate classroom behavior.

HIGH-PROBABILITY REQUESTS: BEHAVIORAL MOMENTUM

In relation to OTR, requests or commands given by teachers can be placed into two broad categories: those that are likely to be complied with by a student (high-probability requests) and those requests that have a history of noncompliance (low-probability requests). Recently, a strategy termed *high-probability request sequencing* (high-p requests) has been demonstrated to be effective at increased responding to requests that have been associated with student noncompliance. In brief, this technique consists of providing a series of high-probability requests prior to the delivery of a low-probability request. The principle behind this strategy has been referred to as *behavioral momentum* (Mace & Belfiore, 1990; Nevin, Mandell, & Atak, 1983) and is discussed in greater detail in chapter 11 of this volume. In practice, the goal is to establish a compliant environment with the sequence of high-probability requests, which increase the likelihood that when the low-probability or less preferred request is made, the student continues to engage in compliant behavior. High-probability request sequencing has been implemented to increase compliance with simple behavioral requests (Davis, Brady, Williams, & Hamilton, 1992; Ducharme & Worling, 1994), improve compliance to transition demands (Ardoin, Martens, & Wolfe, 1999), and comply with requests to engage in appropriate social behavior such as sharing (Davis et al., 1992; Davis & Reichle, 1996). In addition, this strategy has been found to decrease the amount of time it takes to initiate independent seat work (Wehby & Hollahan, 2000).

Use of high-probability request sequencing requires the identification of a number of simple requests to which the student has a history of complying (e.g., 80%–100% of the time). High-probability requests can be identified either through direct observation or through teacher interview. During implementation of the procedures, three to five of these high-probability requests are delivered immediately prior to the delivery of the request associated with some form of noncompliance (low-probability request). A teacher would deliver each high-probability request, which, if followed by compliance, would be followed by some type of brief praise or positive feedback. Following the delivery of praise for compliance to the final high-probability request, the low-probability request would be delivered. On the basis of the research in this area, compliance and subsequent reinforcement with the first three requests increase the probability of compliance with the target low-probability request.

As noted previously, this procedure has been successful in improving compliance to low-probability requests across a number of domains. For example, Ardoin et al. (1999) reported the impact of high-probability request sequencing on student compliance during transitions in a second-grade classroom. Three typically developing students served as the participants in the study, and 12 high-probability requests were identified and confirmed using direct observation. The transition activity consisted of five distinct requests, each identified as having a low probability for compliance. During intervention, the teacher delivered the high-probability request procedures prior to each low-probability command. Results indicated that for two of the three participants, the procedure resulted in increased compliance to the low-probability requests and the overall latency of the transition period decreased for these students.

In a similar study, Wehby and Hollahan (2000) used the high-probability procedure to address compliance with the completion of a math worksheet during an independent activity. The participant was a 13-year-old girl with a learning disability who had a history of refusing to complete her independent practice math assignments. A list of high-probability requests, related to completion of the worksheet, was identified through direct observation. These requests consisted of basic commands such as writing her name on the assignment, taking out her pencil, or circling certain problems. The low-probability request was for her to begin the worksheet. Implementation of the high-probability sequence resulted in a significant decrease in the time to begin the task from a mean of approximately 11 minutes to less than 30 seconds. In addition, slight increases in overall engagement during the independent activity were also noted. Additional studies in this area have also shown impressive improvements in compliant behavior across a range of tasks.

Research has revealed several variables that influence the effectiveness of this intervention: (a) the low-probability request needs to be delivered within 5 seconds of the last high-probability request (Mace et al., 1988) and (b) the high-probability requests need to be varied and randomized (Davis & Reichle, 1996). In addition, it is important to identify high-probability requests that have an established history and that can easily be embedded within the context of an activity. Using the information from the previous section on OTR, it seems reasonable that combining these two strategies would allow the teacher to increase OTR while interspersing the high-probability request sequence during a variety of classroom academic activities, thus resulting in a powerful tool for addressing misbehavior in classrooms.

In summary, high-probability request sequencing is an effective strategy for addressing specific areas in which noncompliance is likely to occur. Other than identification of the high-probability requests, it requires little modification of existing instructional approaches. Used in combination with some of the other strategies presented in this chapter, high-probability sequencing should significantly improve overall levels of active engagement in classrooms.

CHOICE MAKING

Choice making is another teacher-led strategy that has resulted in improved academic and task performance (e.g., Dunlap, Kern-Dunlap, Clarke, & Robbins, 1991; Parsons, Reid, Reynolds, & Bumgarner, 1990), social relatedness (e.g., Koegel, Dyer, & Bell, 1987), and decreased disruption (e.g., Dyer, Dunlap, & Winterling, 1990). In addition, choice-making skills and opportunities have also become a focal point of interventions aimed at promoting self-determination skills (Algozzine, Browder, Karvonen, Test, & Wood, 2001; Carter, Lane, Pierson, & Stang, 2007), consistent with positive behavior support efforts (see chap. 8, this volume).

In brief, choice-making interventions focus on decreasing the aversive nature of a given task by incorporating student-identified preferred activities or stimuli into the existing instructional tasks (Dunlap et al., 1994). Interventions incorporating choice-making opportunities into instruction have several benefits. First, choice-making interventions allow students to exert more control in their daily lives, producing a positive impact on the lives of students with exceptionalities beyond the potentially reinforcing value of expressing a preference (Kern et al., 1998; Romaniuk & Miltenberger, 2001; Shogren, Faggella-Luby, Bae, & Wehmeyer, 2004). Second, choice-making interventions involve antecedent-based techniques that do not require the problem behavior to occur as in consequent-based interventions. Third, in addition to reducing undesirable behaviors, choice-making interventions are an efficient, effective method of improving task engagement and accuracy amongst students with learning and behavioral concerns (Cole, Davenport, Bambara, & Ager, 1997; Cosden, Gannon, & Haring, 1995; Dunlap et al., 1994; Jolivette, Wehby, Canale, & Massey, 2001; Kern et al., 1998).

Dunlap et al. (1991) demonstrated the efficacy of choice making with a 12-year-old girl receiving services in a self-contained classroom for students with severe emotional disturbances. In this study, the participant completed four assignments (math, science, social studies, and handwriting) in two conditions: no choice and choice. In the no-choice condition, the teacher randomly selected the order in which the four tasks were completed. In the choice condition, the students selected the order of completion. Results indicated substantially higher levels of academic engagement and reduction of disruption during the choice condition relative to the no-choice condition.

These findings were confirmed in a similar study with three male elementary students with emotional and behavioral disorders also receiving services in a self-contained classroom (Jolivette et al., 2001). In this study, the content area was mathematics. Students participated in two conditions: choice (students selected the order in which worksheets were completed) and no choice (the teacher selected order of completion). Consistent with Dunlap et al. (1991), task engagement was higher in the choice condition, with students attempting more math problems.

Similar interventions have also demonstrated positive outcomes, with a range of students exhibiting a variety of behaviors. For example, choice-making improved the task accuracy and task completion of middle school boys with severe behavior problems living in residential settings (Cosden et al., 1995), decreased aggression and disruption exhibited by students with developmental disabilities (Dyer et al., 1990), and increased correct responding and task completion as well as decreased disruption for students with autism (Moes, 1998).

In fact, in a meta-analysis of single-subject research studies using choice making as an intervention for problem behavior, Shogren et al. (2004) identified 13 studies that met inclusion criteria. These 13 studies involved 30 participants, with results suggesting that providing participants with choices yielded clinically significant reductions in the number of occurrences of problem behaviors. Specifically, findings revealed that choice-making interventions were effective in reducing undesirable behaviors and sustaining the effects as evidenced by "treatment levels below the lowest baseline data point 65.7% of the time, and 42.3% of the treatment points after the first zero point remained a zero level" (Shogren et al., p. 233).

Although it appears clear that choice making is an effective, efficient intervention for decreasing undesirable behaviors and increasing desirable behaviors, the process by which this occurs is debated (Kern, Mantegna, Vorndran, Bailin, & Hilt, 2001). Some researchers contend that the effectiveness of the intervention is due to the reinforcing value of the selection, whereas others suggest that choice, in and of itself, is the reason for the positive outcomes. Results of a study examining the mechanisms accounting for the influence of choice on behavior suggested that choice making itself appeared to be reinforcing (Kern et al., 2001). However, additional inquiry is needed in this area before drawing definitive conclusions regarding the mechanisms underlying the effectiveness of choice-making interventions.

In sum, choice making is an effective, inexpensive, antecedent-based intervention that has yielded positive outcomes for a range of students. In addition, choice making has the potential to improve students' overall self-determination skills and, ultimately, quality and control in one's life (Shogren et al., 2004).

SUMMARY AND EDUCATIONAL IMPLICATIONS

In an effort to serve an increasingly diverse student body, it is important that today's educators be prepared to deliver appropriate curricula using sound instructional procedures. Given that teachers' behavior influences students' academic and behavioral performance (Carr et al., 1991; Lane & Wehby, 2002; Wehby et al., 1998), it is particularly important for teachers to acquire the strategies necessary to facilitate instruction and prevent disruptive behavior. Many schools have recognized this relationship between learning and behavioral performance and have consequently developed multitiered models of positive behavior supports to (a) prevent problems from occurring by explicitly teaching desired behavioral expectations and (b) respond to problem behaviors that do occur (Lane, 2007; Sugai & Horner, 2002).

In this chapter, we reviewed four teacher-directed, antecedent-based approaches for managing student behavior consistent with the focus on positive behavior supports. The specific strategies included proximity, OTR, high-probability requests, and choice making. As previously discussed, these strategies can be embedded during instruction to (a) facilitate the learning process and (b) minimize problem behaviors from disrupting the educational environment. Because of space considerations, we will not reiterate the definitions and outcomes associated with each strategy.

However, we would like to conclude by stating that it is imperative that teachers be well prepared to manage the wide range of learners they will encounter in general and special education settings. Too often teachers leave the field of education early not because they feel ill-equipped to teach but because they report feeling less than capable in terms of classroom management skills. Attrition rates are particularly high in the field of special education (Billingsley, 1993), with rates of 10% during the first 6 years of teaching (Singer, 1993). To encourage teacher retention and promote positive student outcomes, we encourage teacher preparation programs to focus on a ranges of strategies such as those discussed in this chapter.

REFERENCES

Algozzine, B., Browder, D., Karvonen, M., Test, D. W., & Wood, W. M. (2001). Effects of interventions to promote self-determination for individuals with disabilities. *Review of Educational Research, 71*, 219–277.

Ardoin, S. P., Martens, B. K., & Wolfe, L. A. (1999). Using high probability instructional sequences with fading to increase student compliance during transitions. *Journal of Applied Behavior Analysis, 32*, 339–351.

Billingsley, B. S. (1993). Teacher retention and attrition in special and general education: A critical review of the literature. *The Journal of Special Education, 27*, 137–174.

Broden, M., Bruce, C., Mitchell, M. A., Carter, V., & Hall, R. V. (1970). Effects of teacher attention on attending behavior of two boys at adjacent desks. *Journal of Applied Behavioral Analysis, 3*, 205–211.

Carnine, D. W. (1976). Effects of two teacher-presentation rates on off-task behavior, answering correctly, and participation. *Journal of Applied Behavior Analysis, 9*, 199– 206.

Carter, E. W., Lane, K. L., Pierson, M. R., & Stang, K. K. (2007). *Promoting self-determination for transition-age youth: Views of high school general and special educators.* Manuscript submitted for publication.

Carr, E. G., Taylor, J. C., & Robinson, S. (1991). The effects of severe behavior problems in children on the teaching behavior of adults. *Journal of Applied Behavior Analysis, 9*, 199–206.

Cipani, E. (2008). *Classroom management for all teachers: Plans for evidence-based practice* (3rd ed.). Columbus, OH: Merrill Prentice Hall.

Cole, C. L., Davenport, T. A., Bambara, L. M., & Ager, C. L. (1997). Effects of choice and task preference on the work performance of students with behavior problems. *Behavioral Disorders, 22*, 65–74.

Cosden, M., Gannon, C., & Haring, T. G. (1995). Teacher-control versus student-control over choice of task and reinforcement for students with severe behavior problems. *Journal of Behavioral Education, 5*, 11–27.

Davis, C. A., Brady, M. P., Williams, R. E., & Hamilton, R. (1992). Effects of high-probability requests on the acquisition and generalization of responses to requests in young children and behavior disorders. *Journal of Applied Behavior Analysis, 25*, 905– 916.

Davis, C. A., & Reichle, J. (1996). Variant and invariant high-probability requests: Increasing appropriate behaviors in children with emotional-behavioral disorders. *Journal of Applied Behavior Analysis, 29*, 471–481.

Deno, S. L. (1998). Academic progress as incompatible behavior: Curriculum based measurement (CBM) as intervention. *Beyond Behavior, 9*(3), 12–17.

Ducharme, J., & Worling, D. (1994). Behavioral momentum and stimulus fading in the acquisition and maintenance of child compliance in the home. *Journal of Applied Behavior Analysis, 27*, 639–647.

Dunlap, G., dePerczel, M., Clarke, S., Wilson, D., Wright, S., White, R., et al. (1994). Choice making to promote adaptive behavior for students with emotional and behavioral challenges. *Journal of Applied Behavior Analysis, 27*, 505–518.

Dunlap, G., Kern-Dunlap, L., Clarke, S., & Robbins, F. R. (1991). Functional assessment, curricular revision, and severe behavior problems. *Journal of Applied Behavior Analysis, 24*, 387–397.

Dyer, K., Dunlap, G., & Winterling, V. (1990). Effects of choice making on the serious problem behaviors of students with severe handicaps. *Journal of Applied Behavior Analysis, 23*, 515–524.

Estcheidt, D., Stainback, S., & Stainback, W. (1984). The effectiveness of teacher proximity as an initial technique of helping pupils control their behavior. *The Pointer, 28*, 33–35.

Evertson, C. M., & Weinstein, C. S. (2006). *Handbook of classroom management: Research, practice, and contemporary issues.* Mahwah, NJ: Erlbaum.

Fifer, F. L. (1986). Effective classroom management. *Academic Therapy, 21*, 401–410.

Fuchs, D., & Fuchs, L. S. (1994). Inclusive schools movement and the radicalization of special education reform. *Exceptional Children, 60*, 294–309.

Giangreco, M. F., Edelman, S. W., Luiselli, T. E., & MacFarland, S. Z. C. (1997). Helping or hovering? Effects of instructional assistant proximity on students with disabilities. *Exceptional Children, 64*, 7–18.

Glass, R. M., Christiansen, J., & Christiansen, J. L. (1982). *Teaching exceptional students in the regular classroom.* Boston: Little, Brown and Company.

Gunter, P. L., & Denny, R. K. (1998). Trends and issues in research regarding academic instruction of students with emotional and behavioral disorders. *Behavioral Disorders, 24*, 44–50.

Gunter, P. L., Shores, R. E., Jack, S. L., Rasmussen, S. K., & Flowers, J. (1995). On the MOVE: Using teaching/student proximity to improve students' behavior. *Teaching Exceptional Students, 28*, 12–14.

Hinshaw, S. P. (1992). Externalizing behavior problems and academic underachievement in childhood and adolescence: Causal relationships and underlying mechanisms. *Psychological Bulletin, 111*, 127–155.

Hoover, N. L., & Carroll, R. G. (1987). Self-assessment of classroom instruction: An effective approach to inservice education. *Teaching and Teacher Education, 3*, 179–191.

Jolivette, K., Wehby, J. H., Canale, J., & Massey, N. G. (2001). Effects of choice making opportunities on the behavior of students with emotional and behavioral disorders. *Behavioral Disorders, 26*, 131–145.

Kern, L., & Clemens, N. H. (2007). Antecedent strategies to promote appropriate classroom behavior. *Psychology in the Schools, 44*, 65–75.

Kern, L., Mantegna, M. E., Vorndran, C. M., Bailin, D., & Hilt, A. (2001). Choice of task sequence to reduce problem behaviors. *Journal of Positive Behavior Intervention, 3*, 3–10.

Kern, L., Vorddran, C. M., Hilt, A., Ringdahl, J. E., Adelman, B. E., & Dunlap, G. (1998). Choice as an intervention to improve behavior: A review of the literature. *Journal of Behavioral Education, 8*, 151–169.

Kerr, M. M., & Nelson, C. M. (2002). *Strategies for addressing behavior problems in the classroom* (5th ed.). Columbus, OH: Merrill Prentice Hall.

Kilbourn, B. (1991). Self-monitoring in teaching. *American Educational Research Journal, 28*, 721–736.

Koegel, R. L., Dyer, K., & Bell, L. (1987). The influence of child-preferred activities on autistic children's social behavior. *Journal of Applied Behavior Analysis, 20*, 243–252.

Lane, K. L. (2004). Academic instruction and tutoring interventions for students with emotional/behavioral disorders: 1990 to present (pp. 462–486). In R. B. Rutherford, M. M. Quinn, & S. R. Mathur (Eds.), *Handbook of research in emotional and behavioral disorders*. New York: Guilford.

Lane, K. L. (2007). Identifying and supporting students at risk for emotional and behavioral disorders within multi-level models: Data driven approaches to conducting secondary interventions with an academic emphasis. *Education and Treatment of Children, 30*(4), 135–164.

Lane, K. L., Pierson, M., & Givner, C. C. (2004). Secondary teachers' views on social competence: Skills essential for success. *Journal of Special Education, 38*, 174–186.

Lane, K. L., Robertson, E. J., & Graham-Bailey, M. A. L. (2006). An examination of school-wide interventions with primary level efforts conducted in secondary schools: Methodological considerations. In T. E. Scruggs & M. A. Mastropieri (Eds.), *Applications of research methodology: Advances in learning and behavioral disabilities* (Vol. 19). Oxford, England: Elsevier.

Lane, K. L., & Wehby, J. (2002). Addressing antisocial behavior in the schools: A call for action. *Academic Exchange Quarterly, 6*, 4–9.

Lane, K. L., Wehby, J. H., & Cooley, C. (2006). Teacher expectations of student's classroom behavior across the grade span: Which social skills are necessary for success? *Exceptional Children, 72*, 153–167.

Mace, F. C., & Belfiore, P. (1990). Behavioral Momentum in the treatment of escape-motivated stereotypy. *Journal of Applied Behavior Analysis, 23*, 507–514.

Mace, F. C., Hock, M. L., Lalli, J. S., West, B. J., Belfiore, P., Pinters, E., et al. (1988). Behavioral momentum in the treatment of noncompliance. *Journal of Applied Behavior Analysis, 21*, 123–141.

Moes, D. R. (1998). Intergrating choice-making opportunities within teacher-assigned academic tasks to facilitate the performance of children with autism. *Journal of the Association for Persons with Severe Handicaps, 10*, 183–193.

Nevin, J. A., Mandell, C., & Atak, J. R. (1983). The analysis of behavioral momentum. *Journal of the Experimental Analysis of Behavior, 39*, 49–59.

No Child Left Behind Act of 2001, Pub. L. No. 107–110, 115 Stat. 1425 (2002).

Okovita, H. W., & Bucher, B. (1976). Attending behavior of children near a child who is reinforced for attending. *Psychology in the Schools, 13*, 205–211.

Paine, S. C., Radicchi, J., Rosellini, L. C., Deutchman, L., & Darch, C. B. (1983). *Structuring your classroom for academic success*. Champaign, IL: Research Press.

Parsons, M. B., Reid, D. H., Reynolds, J., & Bumgarner, M. (1990). Effects of chosen versus assigned jobs on the work performance of persons with severe handicaps. *Journal of Applied Behavior Analysis, 23*, 253–258.

Reid, J., & Patterson, G. R. (1991). Early prevention and intervention with conduct problems: A social interactional model for the integration of research and practice. In G. Stoner, M. Shinn, & H. M. Walker (Eds.), *Interventions for achievement and behavior problems* (pp. 715–740). Silver Spring, MD: Nation Association of School Psychologists.

Romaniuk, C., & Miltenberger, R. G. (2001). The influence of preference and choice of activity on problem behavior. *Journal of Positive Behavior Interventions, 3,* 152–159.

Shogren, K. A., Faggella-Luby, M. N., Bae, S. J., & Wehmeyer, M. L. (2004). The effect of choice-making as an intervention for problem behavior for problem behavior: A meta-analysis. *Journal of Positive Behavior Interventions, 6,* 228–237.

Shores, R. E., Gunter, P. L., & Jack, S. L. (1993). Classroom management strategies: Are they setting events for coercion? *Behavioral Disorders, 18,* 92–102.

Singer, J. D. (1993). Are special educators' career paths special? Results from a 13-year longitudinal study. *Exceptional Children, 59,* 262–279.

Stichter, J. P., Lewis, T. J., Richter, M., Johnson, N. W., & Bradley, L. (2006). Assessing antecedent variables: The effects of instructional variables on student outcomes through in-service and peer coaching professional development models. *Education and Treatment of Children, 29,* 665–692.

Sugai, G., & Horner, R. (2002). The evolution of discipline practices: School-wide positive behavior supports. *Child and Family Behavior Therapy, 24,* 23–50.

Sutherland, K. S., Adler, N., & Gunter, P. L. (2003). The effect of varying rates of opportunities to respond to academic requests on the classroom behavior of students with EBD. *Journal of Emotional and Behavioral Disorders, 11,* 239–248.

Sutherland, K. S., & Wehby, J. H. (2001). Exploring the relation between increased opportunities to respond to academic requests and the academic and behavioral outcomes of students with emotional and behavioral disorders: A review. *Remedial and Special Education, 35,* 161–171.

Sutherland, K. S., Wehby, J. H., & Copeland, S. R. (2000). Effect of varying rates of behavior-specific praise on the on-task behavior of students with EBD. *Journal of Emotional and Behavioral Disorders, 8,* 2–8.

Van Houten, R., Nau, P. A., Mackenzie-Keating, S. E., Sameoto, D., & Colavecchia, B. (1982). An analysis of some variables influencing the effectives of reprimands. *Journal of Applied Behavior Analysis, 15,* 65–83.

Walker, H. M., Irvin, I. K., Noell, J., & Singer, G. H. S. (1992). A construct score approach to the assessment of social competence: Rationale, technological considerations, and anticipated outcomes. *Behavior Modification, 16,* 448–474.

Walker, H. M., Ramsey, E., & Gresham, F. M. (2004). *Antisocial behavior in school: Evidence-based practices.* Belmont, CA: Wadsworth.

Wehby, J. H., & Hollahan, M. S. (2000). Effects of high probability requests on the latency to initiate academic tasks. *Journal of Applied Behavior Analysis, 33,* 259–262.

Wehby, J. H., Lane, K. L., & Falk, K. B. (2003). Academic instruction for students with emotional and behavioral disorders. *Journal of Emotional and Behavioral Disorders, 11,* 194–197.

Wehby, J. H., Symons, F. J., Canale, J. A., & Go, F. J. (1998). Teaching practices in classrooms for students with emotional and behavioral disorders: Discrepancies between recommendations and observations. *Behavioral Disorders, 24*, 51–56.

Wehby, J. H., Symons, F. J., & Shores, R. E. (1995). A descriptive analysis of aggressive behavior in the classrooms for children with emotional and behavioral disorders. *Behavioral Disorders, 20*, 87–105.

West, R. P., & Sloane, H. N. (1986). Teacher presentation rate and point delivery rate: Effect on classroom disruption, performance accuracy, and response rate. *Behavior Modification, 10*, 267–286.

10

APPLYING GROUP-ORIENTED
CONTINGENCIES IN THE CLASSROOM

CHRISTOPHER H. SKINNER, AMY L. SKINNER, AND BOBBIE BURTON

Classrooms are complex environments, and students can choose to engage in a variety of behaviors, including desired academic and social behaviors, and undesired disruptive and passive (e.g., staring out the window) behaviors. Contingencies applied to student behavior in classroom environments have been shown to impact students' allocation of time to these competing behaviors (e.g., Heering & Wilder, 2006). These contingencies include individual and group-oriented contingencies. In this chapter, contingency components are described, strengths and weakness of different types of contingencies are analyzed, and recommendations for classroom applications of group-oriented contingencies are provided.

CONTINGENCY COMPONENTS

Contingencies describe an if–then environment-behavior relationship. *If*, under certain environmental conditions (antecedent conditions or stimuli), the student exhibits a behavior (target behavior) to criterion (goal), *then* the environment (e.g., a teacher, peer, computer) will respond with another stimuli (consequent stimuli). For example, when given a math assignment containing 20 items (antecedent stimulus), if a student completes 18 or more items accurately within 20 minutes (target behavior and criterion), then the student will receive a letter grade of A (consequence). It is likely that there are other consequences associated with this behavior. When the student finishes the assignment before the allotted time, he or she may be allowed to choose to engage in a higher probability behavior (reading a novel) without the possibility of punishment. The student's parents may praise his or her academic performance, and the student may receive a high report card grade that is based partially on this assignment (Skinner, Williams, & Neddenriep, 2004).

The previous example can be used to analyze contingency components. Contingencies typically contain two types of stimuli, antecedent and consequent stimuli. In our example, the obvious antecedent stimuli are the math assignment and the teacher's directions to complete the assignment. Other antecedent stimuli include the classroom setting, teacher presence, and classmates who become quiet and begin working on the assignment. Additionally, there are both immediate and delayed consequent stimuli delivered contingent on the student's behavior. The opportunity to engage in a higher probability behavior (read the novel) after completing the assignment may serve as immediate reinforcement. The letter grade that is received the next day, after the teacher scores the assignment, may serve as a delayed reinforcer. The A in mathematics the student receives on his or her quarterly report (i.e., report card) and the praise from parents for making the A also may reinforce this behavior.

Although both antecedent and consequent stimuli influence student behavior, the contingent relationship between these stimuli and the student behavior is critical and typically includes a target behavior and criteria. In our example, the target behavior is working on the math problems, and consequences are delivered on the basis of several criteria. The opportunity to read a novel is delivered contingent upon finishing the assignment before the allotted 20 minutes. If this were the only reinforcement available, the student could quickly write down any answer, regardless of accuracy, so that more time would be available for engaging in the preferred behavior. However, because the delayed reinforcement (e.g., assignment grades, report card grade, praise from parents) is delivered contingent upon completion and accuracy, the student is more likely to attempt to complete the problems accurately.

Schedules of consequences and the target students are also contingency components. With respect to schedules, parental praise for earning an A is not going to occur consistently. Thus, the consequences are delivered intermittently on the basis of a variable schedule. Finally, the student(s) who receives access to consequent stimuli contingent upon the target behavior meeting or exceeding a criterion serves as one basis for discriminating contingencies.

INDIVIDUAL CONTINGENCIES

Contingency contracts are good examples of individual contingencies. These contracts describe in writing an if–then relationship indicating the target student, the student's behavior, and the criterion needed for the student to receive access to a consequence. In most instances, contracts describe individual contingencies because the consequence is delivered only to the target student, and the student's success with meeting the criteria is based solely on his or her performance (Hall & Hall, 1998).

The primary advantage of individual contingencies is that all aspects of the contingency can be tailored to meet idiosyncratic needs, preferences, and skills. Thus, for John the contingency may target reduced levels of fighting, but for Jane the contingency may target increasing assignment completion. The criterion may vary across students. Thus, Cindy may be required to complete all assignments at 90% accuracy or higher each day. However, for Carl the criteria may be adjusted to provide more time to complete the work (i.e., 90% accuracy or higher and the assignment can be completed for homework). The antecedent also can vary so that Craig must complete fourth-grade level assignments, but Billy is required to complete second-grade level assignments. The ability to manipulate the target behaviors and criteria across students in a classroom allows educators to address individual student needs and skill development levels. Additionally, within students educators can alter the target behaviors and criteria as students' needs change and skills develop. For example, John may initially receive access to consequences contingent on improvements in staying in his seat. After John's in-seat behavior improves, the contingency can be altered so that reinforcement is delivered contingent on staying in his seat and completing more of his academic assignments.

It has been said that one man's meat is another man's poison. The value of consequences (e.g., reinforcers) often is based on an individual's idiosyncratic learning history (ontogeny). Thus, for one student a consequence may serve as a high-quality reinforcer, but the same consequence may serve as a low-quality reinforcer for another student and as a punisher for a third student. The ability to select reinforcers on the basis of idiosyncratic preferences enhances the probability that contingencies will be effective.

INDEPENDENT GROUP-ORIENTED CONTINGENCIES

With independent group-oriented contingencies, the term *group-oriented* refers to each contingency component (i.e., antecedent, target behavior, criteria, and consequence) being held constant across all students in a group (i.e., classroom, school). *Independent* refers to access to the consequence being delivered to each student after their own behavior (independently) meets the criteria (Litow & Pumroy, 1975; Skinner et al., 2004). Given the numerous advantages associated with individual contingencies, many may be surprised to learn that educators and others (e.g., the U.S. legal system) rely on independent group-oriented contingencies. Typically, grades are delivered using independent group-oriented contingencies. Other examples of independent group-oriented contingencies include requirements for promotion to the next grade level, prerequisite requirements to take advanced-level courses, and requirements for awards such as honor role. Most classroom and school discipline procedures are independent group-oriented contingencies. For example, a school or entire county could attempt to establish a policy in which any student caught bringing firearms to school would be suspended for a year. Teachers may establish rules and consequences (punishment) for breaking classroom rules.

There are several reasons why educators use independent group-oriented contingencies. Because the target behavior, criterion, and consequences are the same for all students (group characteristic), and each student's access to consequences is contingent on his or her own behavior (independent characteristic), educators, administrators, parents, and students rate them as fair (Skinner, Skinner, Skinner, & Cashwell, 1999). When all contingency components (i.e., target students, antecedents, target behaviors and criteria, consequences) are held constant, it is often easier and more efficient for educators to implement contingency procedures with integrity (consistency).

When rewards are offered contingent on specific behaviors, the effectiveness of those rewards is dependent on several factors, including reward quality, rate, and immediacy, and the time and effort to complete the target behavior to criterion (Neef, Shade, & Miller, 1994). Because all contingency components are held constant across each student, the effectiveness of independent group-oriented contingencies will vary across students and within students. For example, consider Martha Math, who has strong math skills but weak reading skills. A contingency may be established in which children who perform at 90% or higher on their homework receive a letter grade of A. Assuming an A serves as a moderate reinforcer for Martha, this contingency may increase the probability that Martha does her math homework but not her reading homework. One reason is because the math takes little effort, and thus the reinforcement is powerful enough to warrant such effort. The time required to complete the work also influences the contingency. Martha may need only 15 minutes to complete her math, but the reading may require 60 minutes. Thus, the rate of reinforcement (i.e., one letter grade A per 15 minutes for math vs. one letter grade A for 60 minutes for reading) is stronger for the math than reading (Skinner, Pappas, & Davis, 2005).

There are social side effects associated with these independent group-oriented contingencies. When the contingency is held constant across students and consequences are public, students acquire information about their classmates' performance by observing who receives access to rewards. For example, if students are required to perform at 80% or higher to gain access to a consequence, then peers know that those who did not get the consequence performed poorly on the academic task (Cashwell, Skinner, Dunn, & Lewis, 1998).

INTERDEPENDENT GROUP-ORIENTED CONTINGENCIES

With interdependent group-oriented contingencies, all members of the group (e.g., class, school) receive access to a consequence on the basis of some aspect of the group's behavior meeting a group-oriented criterion (Litow & Pumroy, 1975; Skinner et al., 2004). Thus, all members of a class may receive a pizza if the class averages 90% on an exam or sells 200 raffle tickets. Such contingencies are said to be interdependent because each student's access to consequences is not merely dependent on their own behavior but also on his or her peers' behavior.

Because all or none of the group receives access to consequences, interdependent group-oriented contingencies often are easier to manage (i.e., easier to deliver rewards to all than to some and not others). When all or none receive access, teachers may not have to be as concerned with students who did not earn tangible rewards gaining access to them by purchasing them on their own, stealing them from peers, or classmates sharing. Finally, using such contingencies allows educators to use inexpensive activity rewards that are often difficult to deliver to some and not others (i.e., difficult to apply individual or independent group-oriented contingencies). For example, the class may earn listening to music during independent seat work or extra recess. In addition to these procedural advantages associated with reinforcement delivery, interdependent group-oriented contingencies may cause peers to encourage each other's desired target behaviors. Finally, when all or none receive access to consequences, students are not provided information regarding their peers' performance, and all students, as opposed to only a portion, are able to celebrate successes (Skinner et al., 2005).

Despite these advantages, interdependent group-oriented contingencies rarely are part of educational contingencies primarily because they are not "fair." Specific concerns involve students who performed/behaved poorly gaining access to rewards, and those who performed/behaved appropriately being punished for their peers' behavior. Additionally, students may threaten or aggress against those who caused the group to lose access to rewards or be punished. These negative side effects are more likely to occur with public behaviors or when public feedback is provided that allows students to identify those who behaved in such a manner to cause the group to lose access to rewards. Another concern with these contingencies is that all students receive access to the same consequence. If a consequence is desired by most of the group but aversive to a small number of students, those students may sabotage the contingency so that they can avoid the aversive consequence (Skinner, Cashwell, & Dunn, 1996). These saboteurs are actually merely responding to a contingency known as negative reinforcement (e.g., avoid aversive consequence by engaging in inappropriate behaviors).

DEPENDENT GROUP-ORIENTED CONTINGENCIES

A dependent group-oriented contingency is applied when all or none of a group (group-oriented aspect) receives access to consequences contingent upon the behavior of one (dependent aspect) or just several students. Procedurally, dependent group-oriented contingencies have many advantages. With respect to consequences, the all-or-none aspect reduces the probability of reinforcement stealing, sharing, or belittling weakening the contingency and allows educators to use activity rewards that are often resource efficient but difficult to deliver to some and not others. An additional procedural advantage is related to determining if the target student met the criterion. With dependent group-oriented contingencies, educators only have to evaluate one or a few students' performance(s) to determine whether the group gains access to the consequence (Gresham & Gresham, 1982; Heering & Wilder, 2006).

Despite these procedural advantages, several undesirable outcomes may occur with such contingencies. Dependent group-oriented contingencies may place a tremendous amount of pressure on the target student. When the target student earns the reward for the group, peers may praise the student. However, when the student fails to earn a reward for the group, the group may punish him or her. Second, such contingencies often cause peers to monitor and evaluate the target student's behavior. Thus, these contingencies may draw additional peer attention to a student's different, undesirable, or underdeveloped social and/or academic skills. When those target behaviors are academic, peers may help the target student succeed. This help may be appropriate or inappropriate. For example, suppose the entire class receives access to a reward contingent on Steve scoring 80% or higher in spelling. To help Steve succeed, classmates may (a) practice spelling words with him while on the bus to school, (b) threaten him with aversive consequence if he does not make 80% or higher on the test, and/or (c) teach Steve how to cheat on the spelling test. Disruptive inappropriate social behaviors are public (i.e., if they disrupt others they must be public) and often controlled with punishment. Therefore, peers may be more likely to threaten target students when dependent group-oriented contingencies target decreasing disruptive behaviors (Pigott & Heggie, 1985).

CLASSROOM APPLICATIONS: DOS AND DON'TS

As educators attempt to apply group-oriented contingencies, they may occasion both desired and undesired changes in student behavior. In this section, we summarize some strategies and procedures designed to increase the probability of the group-oriented contingency effecting target behaviors and increasing other desired behaviors in the classroom, while reducing the probability of negative side effects.

No Punishing Consequences

Do not use interdependent or dependent group-oriented contingencies with punishment and/or high-stakes consequences when access to consequence is based partially on a peer's behavior. Students who are punished on the basis of their peer's behaviors may be placed in a situation in which they have little or no control over whether they are punished. This model may cause a plethora of side effects, including learned helplessness and/or avoiding the environment in which they are punished on the basis of another's behavior (Repp & Singh, 1990). Additionally, students may try to control peers' behavior, and this can result in peers threatening and aggressing against each other.

Pitfalls of Academic Grades as Consequences

Although some forms of cooperative learning encourage delivering academic credit (grades) on the basis of peers' performance (Lew, Mesch, Johnson, & Johnson, 1986; Slavin, 1991), there are several reasons to avoid doing this. First, grades are more than consequences; they also are symbols or ratings that provide information regarding a student's level of achievement or learning. This information is used to make various educational decisions. For example, if a student who learns little receives a letter grade of A because the rest of his or her group learned much, that student may be placed in advanced courses. Unfortunately, this student may lack the prerequisite skills to succeed in those courses. Another concern is related to other contingencies linked to grades. For example, admission to college or access to scholarships may be contingent on grades. Thus, students who learn much but receive weaker grades because of their group's performance may suffer some very high stakes consequences.

Allow Choice, Random Selection, or Exchangeable Rewards

Some consequences are reinforcing to some students but not others. Thus, when attempting to construct a group-oriented contingency in which all students can or do receive access to the same consequence, educators may have difficulty developing consequences that are reinforcing to all students and have sufficient strength to cause students to choose to engage in high-effort behaviors. When using independent group-oriented reinforcement, one solution is to allow students to choose their rewards. Almost all token economies use such procedures and are designed to allow students to earn more powerful rewards for stronger performance. Another solution is to allow students to randomly select rewards.

Random selection of rewards is particularly useful when implementing interdependent and dependent group-oriented rewards (Kelshaw, Sterling-Turner, Henry, & Skinner, 2000). Thus, when the entire group earns a reward, the teacher could merely pull a slip of paper out of a container. The slip of paper indicates the consequence the group earned. This procedure is valuable for several reasons. First, as long as there is a powerful reward for each student in the reward pool, but not necessarily the same reward, each student may be highly motivated to "do their best" (Popkin & Skinner, 2003). Additionally, when using random selection, educators are using variable schedules of reinforcement (variable quality). Variable schedules have been shown to be more effective than fixed schedules for maintaining behavior (Skinner et al., 2004).

To randomly select rewards, educators need a pool of rewards. The easiest way to develop the pool may be to ask the students. Educators should provide students with guidelines for their suggestions including rewards that (a) are free or inexpensive, (b) most students like, (c) are legal and moral, and (d) are easy to deliver. Educators may want to provide examples of acceptable rewards and include tangibles, activities, exchangeables, recognition, and embarrassing behaviors. Although students and educators have little trouble generating tangible reinforcers, one of the biggest procedural advantages of interdependent and dependent group-oriented contingencies is that resource efficient (free) activity rewards can be used. Such activities can include playing a game (e.g., silent ball), extra time for recess, and even going on a field trip. One particularly powerful reinforcer we used was for the class to be able to listen to music during independent seatwork. Of course, we then had to select the music, but that was easy, as we just randomly selected from a pool of tapes/CDs that students brought to school (Skinner et al., 2004).

Exchangeable rewards are often easy to add when teachers have a token economy in place. Thus, when an interdependent or dependent group goal is met, all students could earn 1, 5, or even 50 extra tokens. Although U.S. currency is a practical exchangeable, we do not recommend giving the student money because many parents want to monitor their children's money supply and purchases. Recognition often is a powerful reinforcer. For example, sending a note home that informs each student's parents how well the group did can serve as a powerful reinforcer that may occasion more reinforcement delivery at home. Finally, embarrassing behaviors can serve as strong reinforcers (Skinner et al., 1999). The first author once had to sing the students a song. Although this would surely be a punisher to most, for these students this appeared to be a potent reinforcer.

Students provide suggestions, but teachers decide which suggestions go into the rewards pool. If a suggestion box is used to solicit possible group rewards, educators should not read these suggestions in front of the class because many inappropriate suggestions can cause teachers to laugh. Instead, educators should read suggestions when students are not observing (they may want to share some with fellow teachers who also need a good laugh) and then announce only appropriate suggestions when they are added to the pool of potential rewards. Once drawn, some consequences can and should be added back to the pool while others should be discarded.

Incidental Target Behaviors

One of the primary advantages to having a pool of group rewards available is that teachers can react to unplanned events by reinforcing the group. For example, suppose a student who is not very popular observes a small child fall and begin crying on the playground. This unpopular student helps the small child up and calms him down. The teacher who observed this behavior may reward the unpopular student (individual reward); however, this is unlikely to cause a reaction from peers. Alternatively, the teacher could announce this event at the end of the day and randomly select a group reward. By rewarding the group contingent on this unpopular student's behavior, the teacher may increase the probability of peers praising this unpopular student and increase the probability of all students engaging in similar behaviors in the future.

Social Target Behaviors

While we discourage delivering any type of punishment to the entire group on the basis of inappropriate behaviors of peers, interdependent and even dependent group-oriented contingencies can be delivered contingent on desired behavior. For example, researchers taught students to do the opposite of tattling by teaching them to report instances of classmates engaging in incidental prosocial behaviors ("tootles"). The entire class then earned a group reward when they reached a total number of tootles (cumulative criteria). Thus, students were encouraged to engage in prosocial behaviors and report each others' prosocial, as opposed to antisocial, behaviors (Cashwell, Skinner, & Smith, 2001; Skinner, Cashwell, & Skinner, 2000).

Academic Target Behaviors

Although grades should not be delivered on the basis of peers' performance, we want to encourage educators to supplement grades (independent group-oriented contingencies) with interdependent and even dependent group-oriented contingencies. In fact, such contingencies may prove extremely valuable in motivating those who require much effort to perform well. Again consider Martha Math, the student with strong math but weak reading skills. The typical reinforcement for math (e.g., grades, gold stars, praise) may be sufficient to cause her to put the time and effort into her math assignments but insufficient to cause her to allocate the larger amount of time and effort required to earn the same rewards for reading. However, for Martha to develop her reading skills, it is essential that she put forth this effort (Skinner et al., 2004).

Several researchers have shown how interdependent group-oriented contingencies can be layered on top of independent group-oriented contingencies and enhance students' performance and learning. For example, Sharp and Skinner (2004) increased the number of books read and performance on comprehension tests by supplementing an independent group-oriented contingency with a dependent group-oriented contingency. Specifically, when students earned a small toy for passing an exam (independent group-oriented contingency), over a 3-week period only three exams were passed. However, when interdependent group-oriented contingencies were added, all students began passing these exams and the class average increased more than 350%.

Varying Criteria Across Students

When using independent group-oriented contingencies, educators who make exceptions (i.e., reduce the criteria for a particular student or provide an easier but more appropriate assignment for a particular student) often face complaints from peers (e.g., "it's not fair"). However, with interdependent group-oriented contingencies, all students benefit when classmates succeed. Thus, educators who are required by law (special education teachers) to vary target behaviors across students are likely to find interdependent group-oriented contingencies highly acceptable to students. For example, Popkin and Skinner (2003) implemented interdependent group contingencies in a self-contained classroom for students with emotional/behavioral disorders targeting spelling, math, and language arts. Each student was placed in a different level of the curriculum and had different tasks each day. Thus, on any given day one student may have been doing very advanced academic work (e.g., taking a prealgebra exam) and a peer may have been doing basic but appropriate math work for his or her skill development level. The student with the higher-level material did not complain about the classmate having easier work because if that classmate succeeded, the student with higher-level material was more likely to be reinforced.

Random Selection of Group Criteria

Although considerable work has established the effectiveness of group contingencies, there is no science that allows one to set the most appropriate criteria for an individual student, let alone a group of students. For example, Campbell and Skinner (2004) wanted to decrease room-to-room transition time in a second-grade classroom. Baseline data showed an average transition time of approximately 300 seconds. Because the class moved through the hallway as a group, an interdependent group-oriented contingency appeared to be the most obvious contingency to apply. However, the researchers did not know how to set the criteria. While some have suggested setting small improvement (e.g., 10%) and then gradually altering the requirements (shaping), the researchers randomly selected both the criteria and the specific transition (e.g., to recess, back from recess, to lunch, back from lunch). Thus, whereas the group knew the goal (reduced transition time), they did not know which specific transition would serve as the criterion or what the specific criteria was. The group's average transition times immediately decreased more than 400%.

Random Selection of Target Students

Although dependent group-oriented contingencies can put much pressure on target students and draw classmate's attention to target students' underdeveloped skills or inappropriate target behaviors, randomly selecting target students reduces these side effects (Gresham & Gresham, 1982). For example, Heering and Wilder (2006) rewarded the entire class contingent on a few students' behavior. Specifically, the teacher collected on-task data on students on a row-by-row basis. The teacher then rewarded the entire class on the basis of the performance of a specific row. However, the class did not know which students' (i.e., row) performance was targeted. Thus, all students were potentially targeted. In these situations it is acceptable for the teacher to announce the randomly selected students (row) who earned to reward for the class. However, if the group did not earn the reward, the teacher should not reveal which randomly selected group failed to meet the target criterion, as peers may aggress against this group (Pigott & Heggie, 1985).

MAINTAINING DESIRED BEHAVIORS

One concern with reinforcement is maintenance after reinforcement is withdrawn. We have already discussed how randomly selecting rewards may enhance maintenance because the schedule is variable. Other researchers have faded reinforcement by altering the group criteria for earning reinforcement. For example, as students demonstrated proficiency in tootling (students reporting of classmates' incidental prosocial, as opposed to antisocial, behaviors), Skinner et al. (2000) increased the number of tootles required for the class to earn the group reward. Others have delivered letters on the basis of the group meeting a criterion. These letters spelled out the reward

(Yarbrough, Skinner, Lee, & Lemmons, 2004). Thus, initially the group may earn a party (five letters), then recess (six letters), then popcorn (seven letters). When randomly selected criteria are used, educators can alter the criteria pool to enhance requirements as students' behavior improves (Skinner et al., 2004).

Finally, educators can add target behaviors. For example, Popkin and Skinner (2003) began their interdependent group-oriented contingency targeting spelling and randomly selected the criterion (class average percentage correct) each day. After several weeks, the teacher randomly selected the criteria and the target behavior (spelling or math). After another several weeks, language arts was added. Thus, in the beginning the group was working hard on spelling to earn the group reward. However, by the end they were working on all three curricular areas to earn the same reward. Thus, students were putting forth more effort to earn the same rewards, a method of fading that enhances and maintains more behaviors without removing pleasant stimuli (rewards).

CONCLUSION: FAIRNESS AND PHILOSOPHY

Educators may not feel comfortable when a student works hard, does well, but does not earn a group reward because of his or her peers' behavior. It is important for educators to continue to implement other contingencies (e.g., independent group-oriented contingencies) designed to reinforce this student's behavior (grades, praise, and gold stars), because interdependent and dependent group-oriented contingencies are designed to supplement, not replace, the other contingencies. When Christopher H. Skinner added interdependent group-oriented rewards to the classroom, he dealt with complaints from students who did well but did not get access to the group reward by simply offering to withdraw the program. No students took him up on it.

A related concern with interdependent and dependent group-oriented rewards is that some students who did not earn rewards get them anyway. We have no answer to this limitation except to offer the alternative. Some students go to school every day with dread, hoping to avoid negative events. These students have little hope of earning rewards because the criteria and target behaviors are set the same for everyone, but perhaps too high for these students. By adding these group-oriented rewards, these students who have given up may now go to school thinking: I am going to do my best, and something wonderful could happen today—my group could earn a reward.

REFERENCES

Campbell, S., & Skinner, C. H. (2004).Combining explicit timing with interdependent group contingency program to decrease transition times: An investigation of the timely transitions game. *Journal of Applied School Psychology, 20*(2), 11–28.

Cashwell, C. S., Skinner, C. H., Dunn, M., & Lewis, J. C. (1998). Group reward programs: A humanistic approach. *The Journal of Humanistic Education and Development, 37,* 47–53.

Cashwell, T. C., Skinner, C. H., & Smith, E. S. (2001). Increasing second-grade students' reports of peers' prosocial behaviors via direct instruction, group reinforcement, and progress feedback: A replication and extensions. *Education and Treatment of Children, 24,* 161–175.

Gresham, F. M., & Gresham, G. N. (1982). Interdependent, dependent, and independent group contingencies for controlling disruptive behavior. *Journal of Special Education, 16,* 101–110.

Hall, R. V., & Hall, M. L. (1998). *How to negotiate a behavioral contract* (2nd ed.). Austin, TX: Pro-Ed.

Heering, P. W., & Wilder, D. A. (2006). The use of dependent group contingencies to increase on-task behavior in two general education classrooms. *Education and Treatment of Children, 29,* 459–467.

Kelshaw, K., Sterling-Turner, H. E., Henry, J., & Skinner, C. H. (2000). Randomized interdependent group contingencies: Group reinforcement with a twist. *Psychology in the Schools, 37,* 523–533.

Lew, M., Mesch, D., Johnson, D. W., & Johnson, R. (1986). Components of cooperative learning: Effects of collaborative skills and academic group contingencies on achievement and mainstreaming. *Contemporary Educational Psychology, 11,* 229–239.

Litow, L., & Pumroy, D. K. (1975). A brief review of classroom group-oriented contingencies. *Journal of Applied Behavior Analysis, 8,* 341–347.

Neef, N. A., Shade, D., & Miller, M. S. (1994). Assessing influential dimensions of reinforcers on choice in students with serious emotional disturbance. *Journal of Applied Behavior Analysis, 27,* 575–583.

Pigott, H. E., & Heggie, D. L. (1985). Interpreting the conflicting results of individual versus group contingencies in classrooms: The targeted behavior as a mediating variable. *Child and Family Behavioral Therapy, 7,* 1–15.

Popkin, J., & Skinner, C. H. (2003). Enhancing academic performance in a classroom serving students with serious emotional disturbance: Interdependent group contingencies with randomly selected components. *School Psychology Review, 32,* 271–284.

Repp, A. C., & Singh, N. N. (1990). *Perspectives on the use of nonaversive and aversive interventions for persons with developmental disabilities.* Sycamore, IL: Sycamore.

Sharp, S., & Skinner, C. H. (2004). Using interdependent group contingencies with randomly selected criteria and paired reading to enhance class-wide reading performance. *Journal of Applied School Psychology, 20*(2), 29–46.

Skinner, C. H., Cashwell, C., & Dunn, M. (1996). Independent and interdependent group contingencies: Smoothing the rough waters. *Special Services in the Schools, 12,* 61–78.

Skinner, C. H., Cashwell, T. H., & Skinner, A. L. (2000). Increasing tootling: The effects of a peer monitored interdependent group contingencies on students' reports of peers' prosocial behaviors. *Psychology in the Schools, 37*, 263–270.

Skinner, C. H., Pappas, D. N., & Davis, K. A. (2005). Enhancing academic engagement: Providing opportunities for responding and influencing students to choose to respond. *Psychology in the Schools, 42*, 389–403.

Skinner, C. H., Skinner, C. F., Skinner, A. L., & Cashwell, T. C. (1999). Using interdependent contingencies with groups of students: Why the principal kissed a pig at assembly. *Educational Administration Quarterly, 35*, 806–820.

Skinner, C. H., Williams, R. L., & Neddenriep, C. E. (2004). Using interdependent group-oriented reinforcement to enhance academic performance in general education classrooms. *School Psychology Review, 33*, 384–397.

Slavin, R. E. (1991). Cooperative learning and group contingencies. *Journal of Behavioral Education, 1*, 105–116.

Yarbrough, J. L., Skinner, C. H., Lee, Y. J., & Lemmons, C. (2004). Decreasing transition times in a second grade classroom: Scientific support for the timely transitions game. *Journal of Applied School Psychology, 20*(2), 85–108.

11

CLASSROOM APPLICATION OF REDUCTIVE PROCEDURES: A POSITIVE APPROACH

STEVEN G. LITTLE, ANGELEQUE AKIN-LITTLE, AND CLAYTON R. COOK

Reductive procedures entail the use of behavioral approaches in an attempt to reduce the frequency of undesirable behaviors (Lentz, 1989) and include reinforcement-based techniques as well as punishment. In schools, reducing the incidence of disruptive and other problem behavior is of great concern to teachers (Stephenson, Linfoot, & Martin, 2000), and punishment procedures are fairly widely practiced (Hyman & Snook, 1999). Although some research (e.g., Pfiffner, Rosen, & O'Leary, 1985) has suggested that a classroom can be managed using only positive consequences, other research has indicated that the addition of negative consequences may be necessary to reduce inappropriate behavior and initially maintain appropriate behavior at acceptable levels (Walker, Ramsey, & Gresham, 2004). It is therefore the intent of this chapter to present an overview of empirically supported and socially valid procedures to reduce the incidence of problem behavior in the classroom and summarize supplemental positive approaches to compliment and build on these reductive procedures.

Specifically, this chapter has three major objectives: (a) to discuss the concept of behavioral momentum and relate Newton's second law of motion to behavioral functioning; (b) to summarize the most recent research on reductive procedures, particularly time-out; and (c) to provide school personnel with evidence-based approaches to the use of reductive procedures that emphasize the positive, proper, and proactive aspects.

BEHAVIORAL MOMENTUM AND
NEWTON'S SECOND LAW OF MOTION

The concept of behavioral momentum provides a structure to understand the effective use of reductive procedures. Nevin (2002) drew on physics in explaining the metaphor of behavioral momentum. Applications of this theory have been used to explain reinforcer rates in individuals with developmental disabilities (Dube, MacIlvane, Mazzitelli, & McNamara, 2003); academic achievement for students with behavior disorders (Belfiore, Lee, Scheeler, & Klein, 2002); behavior of children with conduct disorder (Strand, 2000); transferring stimulus control when working with a student with autism (Ray, Skinner, & Watson, 1999); conceptualization of behavior disorders (Gresham, 1991); and even men's college basketball (Roane, Kelley, Trosclair, & Hauer, 2004). Specifically, in physics a moving body possesses both mass and velocity, with the velocity of the object remaining constant under constant conditions. To change the velocity of the object, it is necessary to exert an external force in inverse proportion to its mass. In terms of student inappropriate behavior, the baseline level of that behavior is considered to be the initial velocity and the resistance to change of that response rate is its mass; that is, the lesser the change in response rate as a function of intervention, the greater the behavioral mass and the greater the strength of the intervention needed to produce change in behavior. The goal of intervention is believed to be not just a function of decreasing the momentum of the undesirable behavior but also a function of increasing the momentum of the alternate, more desirable behavior.

Gresham (2004) drew on the metaphor of behavioral momentum in discussing factors related to resistance to intervention. These factors include (a) severity of behavior (initial velocity), which is related to the amount of reinforcement the behavior is receiving prior to intervention; (b) chronicity of behavior; and (c) generalization of behavior change (i.e., the problem of behavior change not generalizing outside of the intervention environment). Generalization is a problem when the intervention focuses primarily on reducing the momentum of the undesirable behavior and not on attempting to increase the momentum of an alternative, more positive behavior. Indeed, it is unethical to leave a behavioral vacuum by focusing only on the reduction of the problematic behavior; appropriate behavior must also be taught. Gresham's factors also include (a) tolerance of behavior, arguing that the more the behavior disrupts others, the more likely people in the environment will take steps to reduce its occurrence; and (b) treatment strength. In general, all other things being equal, the greater the momentum of the problem behavior, the stronger the treatments will have to be to increase the likelihood of producing behavior change in the desirable direction.

For the purpose of this chapter, we also draw on another analogy to physics that relates to the concept of behavioral momentum and helps to conceptualize patterns of disruptive behavior in the classroom. Newton's second law of motion states that the net force acting on an object equals the product of the mass and the acceleration of the object. In other words, force is believed to equal mass times acceleration ($F = MA$). We can conceptualize force as analogous to the magnitude of the behavior and mass, as in behavioral momentum theory, the behavior's resistance to change. What behavioral momentum theory fails to clearly articulate is the acceleration of the behavior. In studies investigating the behavioral concept of chaining (Dinsmoor, 1998), when a behavioral sequence leads to a reinforcer, each response in the sequence acts as a conditioned reinforcer for the preceding response. We know that if a behavior (positive or negative) is occurring on a regular basis in the classroom, it is leading to some form of reinforcement for that student. If we can identify the steps in the chain leading to the undesirable behavior, we can disrupt the acceleration and therefore the force of the behavior. The new conceptualization of time-out, as discussed later in this chapter, relies heavily on this concept.

REDUCTIVE PROCEDURES AND REINFORCEMENT

The use of punishment procedures, although widely practiced, is in itself not sufficient to improve a student's behavior (Kazdin, 2001). In addition, punishment procedures may lead to undesirable associations with the punishing agent (teacher or parent), the environment in which the punishment occurs (e.g., classroom), or appropriate behaviors that may be temporally related to the undesirable behavior (e.g., classwork, homework). This has led many people to recommend the use of reinforcement-based procedures as one method to reduce the incidence of undesirable behavior (Alberto & Troutman, 2006). It has also been recommended that the use of pretreatment functional analysis can increase the likelihood of the use of reinforcement-based procedures by developing an understanding of the factors maintaining the inappropriate behavior (Wilder, Harris, Reagan, & Rasey, 2007). The four levels of reductive procedures to be discussed include (a) differential reinforcement of low rates of behavior, (b) differential reinforcement of other behavior, (c) differential reinforcement of incompatible behavior, and

(d) differential reinforcement of alternative behavior (see Lentz, 1989, for a more in-depth discussion of these procedures).

Differential Reinforcement of Low Rates of Behavior

Under the differential reinforcement of low rates of behavior (DRL) schedule, reinforcement is contingent on a response being emitted fewer than a predetermined number of times after a specified minimum time period has elapsed. DRL has been demonstrated to be effective in reducing problem behavior, but it requires continuous effort by the teacher (Lentz, 1989), and its utility in the classroom may be limited. This may explain why there are few recent examples of the use of DRL in an educational context. Eccles and Pitchford (1997) used DRL with noncompliance in a multielement plan with a 6-year-old boy with severe behavior problems and noted sufficient improvement in 12 weeks. The only other school-based study published after 1995 is an application of DRL targeting a 13-year-old girl with a psychogenic cough (Watson & Heindl, 1996).

Differential Reinforcement of Other Behavior

Differential reinforcement of other behavior (DRO) is the most researched differential reinforcement procedure and sometimes referred to as differential reinforcement of zero responding. With DRO, reinforcement occurs following a specified period of time in which there are no occurrences of the target behavior. When using a DRO schedule, it is best to start off with a relatively short time period determined on the basis of baseline rate of behavior and then gradually increase the interval required to earn reinforcement until the behavior is occurring rarely if at all and the reinforcement given is minimal.

DRO can be either whole interval or momentary. In whole interval DRO (wDRO), the target behavior must not be exhibited during the entire interval. In momentary DRO (mDRO), behavior is sampled at the specific moment the interval ends and reinforcement is given if the target behavior is not evident at that time. Conyers, Miltenberger, Romaniuk, Kopp, and Himle (2003) found wDRO with edible reinforcement to be more effective in reducing mild disruptive behavior in a preschool classroom than mDRO or wDRO with token reinforcers. In addition, DRO procedures have been found to be effective in eliminating body rocking in an autistic boy (Shabani, Wilder, & Flood, 2001), and in reducing disruptive behavior (e.g., Conyers et al., 2003), aggression (Hegel & Ferguson, 2000), and a variety of self-injurious behaviors (Lindberg, Iwata, Kahng, & DeLeon, 1999). Perhaps most encouraging are the enhanced effects found when combining DRO procedures with extinction (Neidert, Iwata, & Dozier, 2005; Wilder, Chen, Atwell, Pritchard, & Weinstein, 2006).

Differential Reinforcement of Incompatible Behavior and Differential Reinforcement of Alternative Behavior

Differential reinforcement of incompatible behavior (DRI) involves reinforcing a response that is opposite, or incompatible, with the target behavior. For example, sitting and standing cannot occur at the same time. Differential reinforcement of alternative behavior (DRA), on the other hand, involves reinforcing a positive behavior that is not necessarily incompatible with the target behavior. We have combined our discussion of these schedules as research based on functional analyses has found that DRA is more effective when using a replacement behavior that is functionally equivalent rather than just incompatible (Vollmer & Iwata, 1992).

DRA schedules also appear to have the greatest applicability in the classroom of all the differential reinforcement schedules. The primary purpose of students being in schools is the acquisition of academic competencies. If teachers are concerned about student disruptive and inattentive behavior, the most logical alternative behavior to reinforce would be academic performance. This is particularly true if the function of a student's inappropriate behavior is to garner teacher attention. The logical way to proceed with intervention would be structured ignoring (extinction) of the student's inappropriate behavior with attention (praise) being provided for appropriate academic behaviors. Reinforcement of academic behavior has been consistently demonstrated to contribute to increases in on-task behavior and decreases in disruptive behavior (Lentz, 1989). Although reinforcement of academic behavior has demonstrated efficacy, teacher attention for appropriate academic behaviors may be even more effective, and it is relatively easy for teachers to implement (Maag, 2001). DRA has also been found to be effective in improving self-control (Vollmer, Borrero, Lalli, & Daniel, 1999), avoidance responding in a child who stutters (Woods, Fuqua, & Waltz, 1997), and destructive behavior in a child with autism (Piazza, Moes, & Fisher, 1996). However, there are treatment challenges that are unique to DRA that need to be considered (Vollmer, Roane, Ringdahl, & Marcus, 1999). For example, if the implementer is not paying close attention, he or she could potentially provide reinforcement to the student even though there were some occurrences of the problem behavior. Or, the implementer could withhold reinforcement even though there were some occurrences of the alternative behavior. The point being made here is that DRA can be a powerful intervention if implemented consistently and accurately.

Extinction

Extinction has been defined as "a procedure in which the reinforcer is no longer delivered for a previously reinforced response that results in a decrease in the probability or likelihood of a response" (Kazdin, 2001, p. 454).

It is important to recognize that although extinction may be an effective procedure to reduce or eliminate the incidence of maladaptive behaviors, it does not aid in the development of appropriate prosocial behaviors. The most effective use of extinction is in combination with one of the differential reinforcement procedures described above, particularly DRA or DRI (Kazdin, 2001).

Research suggests that treatment with operant extinction may result in adverse side effects (Lerman, Iwata, & Wallace, 1999). Foremost is the extinction burst, an increase in the frequency of the target behavior at the beginning of the extinction period. Lerman and Iwata (1995) found that an extinction burst occurred in approximately one third of the cases when extinction was the sole intervention. When combined with other treatment components such as differential reinforcement, the incidence of an extinction burst can be reduced substantially. It is important, however, if implementing an extinction procedure with teachers or parents, that they be apprised of the possibility of an extinction burst and advised that this is a temporary phenomenon.

In the schools extinction is used primarily to decrease the frequency of behaviors maintained by teacher attention, but it is also important to consider extinction when behaviors are controlled by negative reinforcement (i.e., escape or avoidance). For example, in the classroom a child may become disruptive to escape a specific activity (e.g., math assignment) or an aversive environment (e.g., the classroom itself). If the student is not allowed to escape or avoid, one would expect the incidence of the disruptive behavior to eventually decrease. This should be particularly effective if combined with reinforcement for appropriate academic activities and performance. To use extinction effectively, it is important to understand the function that behavior performs (Gresham, Watson, & Skinner, 2001). Once the function of a behavior is identified, it is much easier to design an intervention to reduce the problem behavior and increase positive behavior (Witt, Daly, & Noell, 2000). Extinction has been used to decrease many maladaptive behaviors, including disruptive/aggressive behavior (Richman, Wacker, Asmus, Casey, & Andelmann, 1999), nonstudy behaviors (Hall, Lund, & Jackson, 1968), and obscene language (Salend & Meddaugh, 1985).

PUNISHMENT

The use of the term *punishment* can be controversial, especially in the context of public education (e.g., Hyman & Snook, 1999). For example, a Google search using the key words *school punishment* yielded more than 9 million hits. A review of the first five sites indicated all contained arguments, both pro and con, on the use of punishment in schools. The definition of punishment is simply a stimulus that (a) is administered as a consequence of a response and (b) reduces the future probability of that response (Dinsmoor, 1998). Maag (2001) believed that educators may adopt the use of punishment because it is easy to administer and works quickly to suppress behavior, and because encouragement of punishment (i.e., discipline) is part of our cultural ethos. It is important that psychologists working in the schools recognize these issues when suggesting behavioral interventions to teachers. It is also important to recognize that some educators may evidence disdain for reinforcement-based techniques (Axelrod, 1996). Therefore, if punishment is the initial recommendation, it may strengthen the teacher's existing bias in favor of punishment and lower the acceptability of reinforcement-based procedure. Also, it is important to understand each student for whom punishment will be used, because in some cases the intention to punish a behavior results in the behavior being inadvertently reinforced (e.g., removal of student from class for disruptive behaviors when the function of the problem behavior was to avoid doing academic work). Although the following punishment procedures are offered, we recommend that they be used sparingly and only in the context of a more comprehensive behavior management program that includes positive reinforcement.

Response Cost

Response cost, defined as a procedure for "reducing inappropriate behavior through withdrawal of specific amounts of reinforcer contingent upon the behavior's occurrence" (Alberto & Troutman, 2006, p. 422), is a versatile procedure with few negative side effects. It is particularly adaptable to a token reinforcement system in which students can earn token reinforcers for appropriate behaviors and lose tokens for misbehavior. Kazdin (2001) noted that token systems have been applied advantageously in settings such as group homes, psychiatric facilities, and schools. In a review of 25 years of token economy research, Glynn (1990) wrote that "token economies are among the most well-validated and effective behavioral treatments" (p. 383) for everything from severe psychiatric disorders to regular education classrooms. Kazdin (2001) emphasized the utility of a response cost procedure within a token economy by stating that "response cost, when in the form of loss of tokens (a generalized conditioned reinforcer), is likely to be more effective than loss of any particular activity or other single reinforcer that serves as one of the backup reinforcers that can be purchased by tokens" (p. 217).

Response cost procedures can also be implemented without a token economy system being in place in the classroom. A teacher who "fines" a child with the loss of free time or recess would be an example of a response cost procedure. Alberto and Troutman (2006) offered a guide to setting up a response cost procedure in the classroom. They recommend asking (a) Have reinforcement-based procedures been considered first?, (b) Does the student have access to a pool of reinforcers from which to deduct payment?, (c) Are there clear rules for appropriate behavior and are the penalties for violation of these rules clear?, (d) Has the magnitude of the penalty relative to the infraction been considered?, (e) Is there a way in which the student can earn back the reinforcer?, and (f) Is there adequate reinforcement available to the student? If these conditions are met, then a response cost procedure may be appropriate. Some of the behaviors in which response cost procedures have been shown to be effective include dropping to the floor (Hagopian, van Stone, & Crockett, 2003), off-task behavior (Pelios, MacDuff, & Axelrod, 2003), classroom disruptive behavior (McGoey & DuPaul, 2000; Musser, Bray, Kehle, & Jenson, 2001), and accuracy on an arithmetic task (Carlson, Mann, & Alexander, 2000).

Overcorrection

Overcorrection involves penalizing an undesirable behavior by having the student perform some other behavior (Kazdin, 2001). Alberto and Troutman (2006) described two types of overcorrection. Restitutional overcorrection consists of correcting the environmental effect of the student's misbehavior, not only to its original condition but to a better condition. For example, if a student is caught writing on his or her desk, the teacher may require the child to erase/clean not only this writing, but also all writing on the desk. This can be a particularly effective form of punishment for vandalism, littering, or other behavior that has a clear environmental outcome. Although meeting the definition of punishment because of its ability to reduce behavior, MacKenzie-Keating and McDonald (1990) argued that it differs from punishment in its social validity and educative value. They proposed that the term *overcorrection* be eliminated and that the term *restitution training* would be more appropriate. Regardless of the terminology used, restitutional overcorrection has been demonstrated to be effective in reducing a wide variety of behaviors (Alberto & Troutman, 2006).

Positive-practice overcorrection is cited much more frequently in the psychological literature and consists of repeatedly practicing the appropriate behavior, sometimes in an exaggerated or overly correct form. It has been found to be effective in reducing the incidence of a variety of behaviors including pica (Myles, Simpson, & Hirsch, 1997) and bruxism (Watson, 1993). Although not technically reductive in nature, it has also been used successfully with a variety of academic behaviors, such as mathematics fluency (Rhymer, Dittmer, Skinner, & Jackson, 2000) and oral reading (Singh & Singh, 1986).

TIME-OUT

Time-out is one of the most popular and possibly most misunderstood forms of behavior management used in the classroom, and there is little question concerning its efficacy (Sterling-Turner & Watson, 1999). Griffin (1998) found that special education teachers depended heavily on time-out. Other studies have found that 88% of special education teachers (Ruhl, 1985) and 85% of school psychologists (Shapiro & Lentz, 1985) used time-out procedures. Time-out has been found to be an effective procedure with many different behaviors, populations, and environments (Costenbader & Reading-Brown, 1995; Jenson, Sloane, & Young, 1988; Kazdin, 2001; Sterling-Turner & Watson, 1999; Yell, 1994). In spite of its effectiveness and popularity, "teachers probably use time-out ineffectively as often as effectively" (Goldstein, 1995, p. 249).

Research on time-out is based on the two general categories into which time-out is usually divided: exclusionary and nonexclusionary. Exclusionary (isolation) time-out involves removing the individual from the environment in which reinforcement is occurring and is the most frequently used and cited time-out procedure (Costenbader & Reading-Brown, 1995). Nonexclusionary time-out involves withholding reinforcement from the child without removing him or her from the classroom. The biggest difference between the two is that exclusionary time-out attempts to remove the child from all forms of reinforcement contingent on the undesired behavior and nonexclusionary time-out usually involves the removal of social reinforcement from a specific behavior that has previously been reinforced.

Although time-out has been used effectively in the classroom for a variety of problem behaviors, a number of barriers to effective implementation are present (Martens, Witt, Daly, & Vollmer, 1999). One such barrier is teachers' understanding of time-out and their history of success with the procedure. Data from a survey that questioned regular education teachers' understanding and use of time-out (Little, 1997) indicated that although the vast majority of respondents reported having used time-out in their classroom (91.1%) and found time-out to be an acceptable behavior management procedure (85.7%), a significant number of teachers had little understanding of the type of behaviors for which time-out was most appropriate or what constituted time-out. The work of Noell and Witt (1998) and Martens et al. (1999) indicates that it is best to approach implementation of time-out in the classroom with the assumption that implementation skills must be systematically taught to the teacher (see Sterling-Turner & Watson, 1999, for specific suggestions).

A New Conceptualization of Time-Out

A slightly different way to conceptualize time-out may have greater utility in the classroom. Most of the research on time-out has conceptualized the process as a punishment procedure (i.e., the removal of the individual from access to positive reinforcement for a specific period of time). This presents methodological as well as ethical concerns. An alternative conceptualization to the use of time-out in the classroom may help facilitate teachers' understanding of time-out and improve treatment integrity in situations in which it is implemented. It may be best to conceptualize time-out not as punishment but as an impediment to behavioral momentum and acceleration. A chain represents a series of responses that tend to be performed in a particular order. In the behavioral literature, this has usually been discussed in the context of training a new response (Alberto & Troutman, 2006). However, just as a new response can be taught by building sequences of behaviors (chaining), existing responses can be reduced in frequency by interfering with the sequence. It seems unlikely that the student's behavior of concern manifests itself initially in the manner in which the teacher attends. It is more likely that other, less obtrusive, behaviors appear, and when they do not attract the teacher's attention, they serve as the trigger for the next, more obtrusive, behavior in the sequence. It is possible that there are many steps in the behavioral sequence before the behavior reaches the level to which the teacher attends.

Take the example of a student who exhibits disruptive behavior. A functional assessment has determined that this behavior is maintained through teacher and peer attention. It is entirely possible that the behavior of concern is at the end of a behavioral chain. If we can identify the antecedents to the disruptive behavior in the chaining sequence, we may be able to stop the behavior from accelerating, thus effectively eliminating the force of the behavior. Using the $F = MA$ analogy from physics, we can attempt to reduce the acceleration of the behavior to close to zero. We have therefore effectively eliminated the force (i.e., magnitude) of that behavior, at least at that particular time. If, over time, we have interrupted the chain sufficiently, the reinforcement that occurs at the end of the chain will no longer be associated with the behaviors at the beginning of the chain. We may then have effectively extinguished the problem behavior. The focus is then on reinforcing a functionally equivalent behavior (e.g., on-task, academic behaviors) so that the probability of the inappropriate behavior returning is minimal. We have, in effect, decreased the behavioral momentum of the disruptive behavior and increased the momentum of appropriate classroom behavior. We know that short duration time-out can be effective (Kazdin, 2001; Marlow, Tingstom, Olmi, & Edwards, 1997), but additional research is necessary to fully understand the mechanisms by which it is effective.

POSITIVE, PROPER, AND PROACTIVE INTERVENTIONS

Resistance to the use of operant procedures to change behavior has come from a variety of sources, and some individuals have been particularly harsh in their criticism of the use of positive reinforcement (e.g., Kohn, 1993; see Akin-Little, Eckert, Lovett, & Little, 2004, for a discussion).

Because of the inherent ethical and methodological problems with punishment and the apparent acceptability of punishment procedures among educators, the use of punishment and alternative reductive procedures must be carefully considered before making recommendations to teachers. We therefore recommend considering the following three words in designing interventions to reduce the occurrence of maladaptive behavior: positive, proper, and proactive.

Positive

The focus should always be on positive aspects of student behavior and on strengthening those behaviors. There is little doubt that positive reinforcement-based procedures have been proven efficacious in increasing and maintaining appropriate academic and social behaviors as well as contributing to the reduction of maladaptive behaviors. We should also be guided by the principle of least restrictive alternative in which positive approaches should receive first consideration. It seems clear that, when given alternatives for the reduction of maladaptive behavior, ethical, research-based psychologists should consider positive interventions first.

Proper

Proper refers to interventions that are both research based and socially valid. Although the methods we use have gone through changes over the years, one thing has remained invariant: Scientific validation of our techniques is essential. In fact, this could be seen as the defining characteristic of behavioral approaches. We cannot assume that a technique is effective just because it is widely used or sounds good. We must have data that support the efficacy of the procedure. Nevertheless, this does not guarantee the effectiveness of an intervention. Even a well-designed, empirically supported plan will not be effective if it is not implemented with integrity.

Proactive

If we can prevent the occurrence of behavior problems, we have no need to even worry about reductive procedures. It is also easier to prevent behavior problems than deal with them reactively (Maag, 2001). This leads us to a discussion of our last consideration, being proactive. One alternative to traditional use of reductive procedures and other disciplinary techniques is the use of positive behavioral supports (PBS; Safran & Oswald, 2003). PBS interventions are designed to prevent problem behaviors by providing environmental modifications before problems escalate, while concurrently teaching appropriate alternatives (Bambara & Kern, 2005). In fact, PBS has been incorporated into federal legislation governing special education practice.

Specifically, the law reads that an individualized education plan team shall "consider, when appropriate, strategies, including positive behavioral interventions, strategies, and supports to address that behavior" (Individuals with Disabilities Education Improvement Act Amendments of 2004, 20 U.S.C. § 1414 (d)(3)(B)(i), 2004). Educators are required to write a behavior intervention plan that includes PBS strategies and interventions (a) when a student's behavior is impeding learning and/or (b) prior or subsequent to the student being removed from his or her educational placement in excess of 10 days.

It is also important that consultation with teachers not always be in response to a specific child with a specific problem behavior. Changing teachers' approach to classroom management and reinforcing positive, preventive teacher behaviors should be an aspect of all school psychologists' routines. Maag (2001) offered five easy to implement recommendations for teachers.

1. *Catch students being good.* Teachers and parents too often focus on the negative aspects of student behavior. Jenson, Olympia, Farley, and Clark (2004) call the classroom a "sea of negativism" (p. 69) and report that teachers are more likely to attend to students' inappropriate behaviors than to respond to positive behaviors using praise and other positive techniques. It is important for teachers to attend to and reinforce appropriate social and academic behavior, especially with students with existing behavior problems.

2. *Think small.* Shaping is an important concept to convey to teachers. A student who is having difficulty behaving in a manner consistent with the rules and expectations in the classroom is unlikely to change his or her behavior rapidly. Shaping involves the reinforcement of successive approximations of the desired behavior. Teachers need to focus on and be willing to recognize small improvements in behavior because that is the only way they will arrive at large-scale behavior change.

3. *Have a group management plan.* It is easier to manage specific students with behavior problems when the entire class is well-behaved (Maag, 2001). One way to increase the likelihood of a well-behaved class is through the use of a class-wide behavior management plan. Kehle, Bray, Theodore, Jenson, and Clark (2000) and DeMartini-Scully, Bray, and Kehle (2000) offered a multicomponent intervention that could be adaptable to an entire class. Using a contingency contract, their intervention comprises precision requests, antecedent strategies, positive reinforcement, and response cost. They report that this intervention has been successful with both regular and special education students.

4. *Prevent behavior problems.* Teachers should be encouraged to take steps to insure a positive class climate. Maag (2001) suggested this can be accomplished by (a) establishing classroom rules and reinforcing students for obeying the rules, (b) having students academically engaged at least 70% of the day, (c) not letting children with challenging behaviors sit next to one another, and (d) having teachers move around the room as much as possible to monitor student behavior and reinforce appropriate behavior.

5. *Use peer influence favorably.* Peers, through their smiles, comments, gestures, etc., have a tremendous influence on classroom behavior. Attempts at eliminating these behaviors through punishment are unlikely to be effective, so teachers should be encouraged to use these behaviors to their advantage. One way to effectively use peer influence is through the use of group contingencies (see Skinner, Williams, & Neddenriep, 2004).

SUMMARY

Punishment procedures may be the intervention of choice for a majority of teachers (Maag, 2001). Chances are they are using punishment strategies on a daily basis and may not even realize their reliance on such tactics. It has been pointed out that reinforcement-based approaches may be seen negatively by teachers (Axelrod, 1996). There is, however, an extensive body of research which supports the efficacy for these procedures in the reduction of problem behavior and the increase in appropriate behavior in a wide variety of contexts, including schools. This is not to say that techniques involving the use of punishment should never be considered. There are times when the rapid suppression of behavior is important and punishment may be the most appropriate technique in that situation. We have attempted to conceptualize a new approach to the use of time out which may be a valuable tool when considering the use of this reductive procedure. As school psychologists we must recognize, however, that if we are to assist teachers and school administrators in developing positive learning environments for students we must first focus on positive approaches.

REFERENCES

Akin-Little, K. A., Eckert, T. L., Lovett, B. J., & Little, S. G. (2004). Extrinsic reinforcement in the classroom: Bribery or best practice? *School Psychology Review*, *33*, 344–362.

Alberto, P. A., & Troutman, A. C. (2006). *Applied behavior analysis for teachers* (7th ed.). Upper Saddle River, NJ: Pearson Prentice Hall.

Axelrod, S. (1996). What's wrong with behavior analysis? *Journal of Behavioral Education, 6,* 247–256.

Bambara, L. M., & Kern, L. (2005). *Individualized supports for students with problem behaviors: Designing positive behavior support plans.* New York: Guilford.

Belfiore, P. J., Lee, D. L., Scheeler, C., & Klein, D. (2002). Implications of behavioral momentum and academic achievement for students with behavior disorders: Theory, application, and practice. *Psychology in the Schools, 39,* 171–179.

Carlson, C. L., Mann, M., & Alexander, D. K. (2000). Effects of reward and response cost on the performance and motivation of children with ADHD. *Cognitive Therapy & Research, 24,* 87–98.

Costenbader, V., & Reading-Brown, M. (1995). Isolation timeout used with students with emotional disturbance. *Exceptional Children, 61,* 353–363.

Conyers, C., Miltenberger, R., Romaniuk, C., Kopp, B., & Himle, M. (2003). Evaluation of DRO schedules to reduce disruptive behavior in a preschool classroom. *Child & Family Behavior Therapy, 5,* 1–6.

DeMartini-Scully, D., Bray, M. A., & Kehle, T. J. (2000). A packaged intervention to reduce disruptive behaviors in general education students. *Psychology in the Schools, 37,* 149–156.

Dinsmoor, J. A. (1998). Punishment. In W. O'Donohue (Ed.), *Learning and behavior therapy* (pp. 188–204). Boston: Allyn and Bacon.

Dube, W. V., MacIlvane, W. J., Mazzitelli, K., & McNamara, B. (2003). Reinforcer rate effects and behavioral momentum in individuals with developmental disabilities. *American Journal on Mental Retardation, 108,* 134–143.

Eccles, C., & Pitchford, M. (1997). Understanding and helping a boy with problems: A functional approach to behavior problems. *Educational Psychology in Practice, 13,* 115–121.

Glynn, S. M. (1990). Token economy approaches for psychiatric patients: Progress and pitfalls over 25 years. *Behavior Modification, 14,* 383–407.

Goldstein, S. (1995). *Understanding and managing children's classroom behavior.* New York: Wiley-Interscience.

Gresham, F. M. (1991). Conceptualizing behavior disorders in terms of resistance to intervention. *School Psychology Review, 20,* 23–36.

Gresham, F. M. (2004). Response to intervention: An alternative means of identifying students as emotionally disturbed. *Education and Treatment of Children, 28,* 328–344.

Gresham, F. M., Watson, T. S., & Skinner, C. H. (2001). Functional behavioral assessment: Principles, procedures, and future directions. *School Psychology Review, 30,* 156–172.

Griffin, D. K. (1998). A survey of common behavioral procedures used by exceptional educational teachers in the greater Miami/Ft. Lauderdale, FL area public schools. *The Behavior Therapist, 21,* 163–165, 193.

Hagopian, L. P., van Stone, M., & Crockett, J. L. (2003). Establishing schedule control over dropping to the floor. *Behavioral Interventions, 18,* 291–297.

Hall, R. V., Lund, D., & Jackson, D. (1968). Effects of teacher attention on study behavior. *Journal of Applied Behavior Analysis, 1,* 1–12.

Hegel, M. T., & Ferguson, R. J. (2000). Differential reinforcement of other behavior (DRO) to reduce aggressive behavior following traumatic brain injury. *Behavior Modification, 24,* 94–101.

Hyman, I., & Snook, P. (1999). *Dangerous schools: What we can do about the physical and emotional abuse of our children.* San Francisco: Jossey-Bass.

Individuals With Disabilities Education Improvement Act Amendments of 2004, 20 U.S.C. § 1462(h) et seq.

Jenson, W. R., Olympia, D., Farley, M., & Clark, E. (2004). Positive psychology and externalizing students in a sea of negativity. *Psychology in the Schools, 41,* 67–79.

Jenson, W. R., Sloane, H. N., & Young, K. R. (1988). *Applied behavior analysis in education: A structured teaching approach.* Englewood Cliffs, NJ: Prentice Hall.

Kazdin, A. E. (2001). *Behavior modification in applied settings* (6th ed.). Belmont, CA: Wadsworth/Thomson Learning.

Kehle, T. J., Bray, M. A., Theodore, L. A., Jenson, W. R., & Clark, E. C. (2000). A multi-component intervention designed to reduce disruptive classroom behaviors. *Psychology in the Schools, 37,* 475–481.

Kohn, A. (1993). *Punished by rewards: The trouble with gold stars, incentive plans, A's, praise, and other bribes.* Boston: Houghton Mifflin.

Lentz, F. E. (1989). Reductive procedures. In J. C. Witt, S. N. Elliott, & F. M. Gresham (Eds.), *Handbook of behavior therapy in education* (pp. 439–468). New York: Plenum.

Lerman, D. C., & Iwata, B. A. (1995). Prevalence of the extinction burst and its attenuation during treatment. *Journal of Applied Behavior Analysis, 28,* 93–94.

Lindberg, J. S., Iwata, B. A., Kahng, S., & DeLeon, I. G. (1999). DRO contingencies: An analysis of variable-momentary schedules. *Journal of Applied Behavior Analysis, 32,* 123–136.

Lerman, D. C., Iwata, B. A., & Wallace, M. D. (1999). Side effects of extinction: Prevalence of bursting and aggression during the treatment of self-injurious behavior. *Journal of Applied Behavior Analysis, 32,* 1–8.

Little, S. G. (1997, April). Teacher's use, understanding, and acceptability of time-out. In S. G. Little (Chair), *Behavioral school psychology: Time-out revisited.* Symposium conducted at the annual meeting of the National Association of School Psychologists, Anaheim, CA.

Maag, J. W. (2001). Rewarded by punishment: Reflections on the disuse of positive reinforcement in schools. *Exceptional Children, 67,* 173–186.

MacKenzie-Keating, S. E., & McDonald, L. (1990). Overcorrection: Reviewed, revisited and revised. *Behavior Analyst, 13,* 39–48.

Marlow, A. G., Tingstom, D. H., Olmi, D. J., & Edwards, R. P. (1997). The effects of classroom-based time-in/time-out on compliance rates in children with speech/language disabilities. *Child & Family Behavior Therapy, 19,* 1–15.

Martens, B. K., Witt, J. C., Daly, E. J., & Vollmer, T. R. (1999). Behavior analysis: Theory and practice in educational settings. In C. R. Reynolds & T. B. Gutkin (Eds.), *The handbook of school psychology* (3rd ed., pp. 638–663). New York: Wiley.

McGoey, K. E., & DuPaul, G. J. (2000). Token reinforcement and response cost procedures: Reducing the disruptive behavior of preschool children with attention-deficit/hyperactivity disorder. *School Psychology Quarterly, 15*, 330–343.

Musser, E. H., Bray, M. A., Kehle, T. J., & Jenson, W. R. (2001). Reducing disruptive behaviors in students with serious emotional disturbance. *School Psychology Review, 30*, 294–304.

Myles, B. S., Simpson, R. L., & Hirsch, N. C. (1997). A review of literature on interventions to reduce pica in individuals with developmental disabilities. *Autism, 1*, 77–95.

Neidert, P. L., Iwata, B. A., & Dozier, C. L. (2005). Treatment of multiply controlled problem behavior with procedural variations of differential reinforcement. *Exceptionality, 13*, 45–53.

Nevin, J. A. (2002). Measuring behavioral momentum. *Behavioral Processes, 57*, 187–198.

Noell, G. H., & Witt, J. C. (1998). Toward a behavior analytic approach to consultation. In T. S. Watson & F. M. Gresham (Eds.), *Handbook of child behavior therapy* (pp. 41–57). New York: Plenum.

Pelios, L. V, MacDuff, G. S., & Axelrod, S. (2003). The effects of a treatment package in establishing independent academic work skills in children with autism. *Education & Treatment of Children, 26*, 1–21.

Pfiffner, L. J., Rosen, L. A., & O'Leary, S. G. (1985). The efficacy of an all positive approach to classroom management. *Journal of Applied Behavior Analysis, 18*, 257–261.

Piazza, C. C., Moes, D. R., & Fisher, W. W. (1996). Differential reinforcement of alternative behavior and demand fading in the treating fading in the treatment of escape-maintained destructive behavior. *Journal of Applied Behavior Analysis, 29*, 569–572.

Ray, K. P., Skinner, C. H., & Watson, T. S. (1999). Transferring stimulus control via momentum to increase compliance in a student with autism: A demonstration of collaborative consultation. *School Psychology Review, 28*, 622–628.

Rhymer, K. N., Dittmer, K. I., Skinner, C. H., & Jackson, B. (2000). Effectiveness of a multi-component treatment for improving mathematics fluency. *School Psychology Quarterly, 15*, 40–51.

Richman, D. M., Wacker, D. P., Asmus, J. M., Casey, S. D., & Andelmann, M. (1999). Further analysis of problem behavior in response class hierarchies. *Journal of Applied Behavior Analysis, 32*, 269–283.

Roane, H. S., Kelley, M. E., Trosclair, N. M., & Hauer, L. S. (2004). Behavioral momentum in sports: A partial replication with women's basketball. *Journal of Applied Behavior Analysis, 37*, 385–390.

Ruhl, K. (1985). Handling aggression: Fourteen models teachers use. *Pointer, 29*, 30–33.

Safran, S. P., & Oswald, K. (2003). Positive behavior supports: Can schools reshape disciplinary practices? *Exceptional Children, 69,* 361–373.

Salend, S. J., & Meddaugh, D. (1985). Using a peer-mediated extinction procedure to decrease obscene language. *Pointer, 30,* 8–11.

Shabani, D. B., Wilder, D. A., & Flood, W. A. (2001). Reducing stereotypic behavior through discrimination training, differential reinforcement of other behavior, and self monitoring. *Behavioral Interventions, 16,* 279–286.

Shapiro, E. S., & Lentz, F. E. (1985). A survey of school psychologists' use of behavior modification procedures. *Journal of School Psychology, 23,* 327–336.

Singh, N. N., & Singh, J. (1986). A behavioural remediation program for oral reading: Effects on errors and comprehension. *Educational Psychology, 6,* 105–114.

Skinner, C. H., Williams, R. L., & Neddenriep, C. E. (2004). The negative side effects of rewarding academic behavior: Problems revisited and resolved via randomizing interdependent group contingency components. *School Psychology Review, 33,* 384–397.

Sterling-Turner, H., & Watson, T. S. (1999). Consultant's guide for the use of time-out in the preschool and elementary classroom. *Psychology in the Schools, 36,* 135–148.

Strand, P. S. (2000). A modern behavioral perspective on child conduct disorder: Integrating behavioral momentum and matching theory. *Clinical Psychology Review, 20,* 593–615.

Stephenson, J., Linfoot, K., & Martin, A. (2000). Behaviours of concern to teachers in the early years of school. *International Journal of Disability, Development and Education, 47,* 225–235.

Vollmer, T. R., Borrero, J. C., Lalli, J. S., & Daniel, D. (1999). Evaluating self-control and impulsivity in children with severe behavior disorders. *Journal of Applied Behavior Analysis, 32,* 451–466.

Vollmer, T. R., & Iwata, B. A. (1992). Differential reinforcement as treatment for behavior disorders: Procedural and functional variations. *Research in Developmental Disabilities, 13,* 393–417.

Vollmer, T. R., Roane, H. S., Ringdahl, J. E., & Marcus, B. A. (1999). Evaluating treatment challenges with differential reinforcement of alternative behavior. *Journal of Applied Behavior Analysis, 32,* 9–23.

Walker, H. M., Ramsey, E., & Gresham, F. M. (2004). *Antisocial behavior in school: Evidence-based practices* (2nd ed.). Belmont, CA: Wadsworth/Thomson.

Watson, T. S. (1993). Effectiveness of arousal and arousal plus overcorrection to reduce nocturnal bruxism. *Journal of Behavior Therapy and Experimental Psychiatry, 24,* 181–185.

Watson, T. S., & Heindl, B. (1996). Behavioral case consultation with parents and teachers: An example using differential reinforcement to treat psychogenic cough. *Journal of School Psychology, 34,* 365–378.

Wilder, D. A., Chen, L., Atwell, J., Pritchard, J., & Weinstein, P. (2006). Brief functional analysis and treatment of tantrums associated with transitions in preschool children. *Journal of Applied Behavior Analysis, 39,* 103–107.

Wilder, D. A., Harris, C., Reagan, R., & Rasey, A. (2007). Functional analysis and treatment of noncompliance by preschool children. *Journal of Applied Behavior Analysis, 40,* 173–177.

Witt, J. C., Daly, E., & Noell, G. H. (2000). *Functional assessment: A step-by-step guide to solving academic and behavioral problems.* Longmont, CO: Sopris West.

Woods, D. W., Fuqua, R. W., & Waltz, T. J. (1997). Evaluation and elimination of an avoidance response in a child who stutters: A case study. *Journal of Fluency Disorders, 22,* 287–297.

Yell, M. L. (1994). Timeout and students with behavior disorders: A legal analysis. *Education and Treatment of Children, 17,* 293–301.

12

GENERALIZATION AND MAINTENANCE OF LEARNED POSITIVE BEHAVIOR

MARK W. STEEGE AND ERIN SULLIVAN

Learning one aspect of anything never means that you know the rest of it. Doing something skillfully now never means that you will always do it well . . . no one learns a generalized lesson unless a generalized lesson is taught. (Baer, 1981, pp. 1–2)

Within schools, the acquisition of academic and prosocial behaviors is of critical importance to educators, parents, and students. Indeed, the No Child Left Behind Act of 2001 (2002) and the Individuals With Disabilities Education Improvement Act (2004) reauthorization of 2006 both emphasize the use of evidence-based interventions to teach skills and to assess student progress (Brown-Chidsey & Steege, 2005). Although the measure of skill acquisition is one way of determining student progress, the generality of student behavior is of equal importance. This chapter includes definitions, descriptions, and procedures for promoting the generalization and maintenance of positive student behaviors.

Skill acquisition programs are designed to develop new behaviors or increase performance ability or frequency of the learned behavior. However, doing something well now does not mean that one will execute the behavior well in the future. Likewise, demonstrating a skill within one setting does not mean that it will occur in others; for example, in the case of a student who is learning daily living skills, learning to operate one vending machine does not guarantee that he or she will be able to navigate the operation of other vending machines. The process of exhibiting the same behavior across varying situations is referred to as generalization. The process of continued display of behavior over time is referred to as *maintenance*.

GENERALIZATION

If behavior change is to be truly worthwhile and effective, it must last and be useful to the individual in different settings and in various ways (Cooper, Heron, & Heward, 2007). A behavior change is said to have generality if it lasts over time, occurs in settings other then the one in which it was originally learned, and/or spreads to other related behaviors (Baer, Wolf, & Risley, 1968). Stokes and Baer (1977) use the term *generalization* to refer to the generality of behavior change, defining it as

> the occurrence of relevant behavior under different, non-training conditions (i.e., across subjects, settings, people, behaviors and/or time) without scheduling of the same events in those conditions. Thus, generalization may be claimed when no extra training manipulations are needed for extra training changes; or may be claimed when some extra manipulations are necessary, but their cost is clearly less than that of the direct intervention. Generalization will not be claimed when similar events are necessary for similar effects across conditions. (p. 350)

Two important concepts embedded within theories and models of generalization are *stimulus class* and *response class*. Stimulus class refers to a group of stimuli that occasion the same response. That is, we respond to members of the set in the same way. In everyday language, stimulus classes might be referred to as categories. For example, writing instruments such as ballpoint pens, felt-tip pens, pencils, and markers share similar stimulus features. As such, they are members of the same stimulus class. One method of promoting generalization involves teaching a response to occur across an array of stimulus conditions (e.g., teaching a child to say "Hi" to various teachers and familiar classmates; teaching a student to operate varying types of vending machines to get a snack). Response class refers to a group of behaviors that achieve the same reinforcing consequences. For example, greeting behaviors such as communicating "Hi," "Hello," "Whatzzup," and "Hey, dude" all result in social reinforcement and are considered members of the same response class. Reinforcing one of these greeting responses typically results in the increase of the other greetings.

There are three types of generalization: *temporal generalization, stimulus generalization,* and *response generalization*. The three types of generalization are described in the following section.

Temporal Generalization

Temporal generalization is the generality of behavior over time. This phenomenon is also referred to as maintenance and includes procedures to ensure that appropriate changes in behavior will last (Stokes & Osnes, 1988). When a person is learning a new behavior, a continuous schedule of reinforcement is typically used. This means that each time the desired behavior occurs, it is followed by some form of reinforcement. For example, when teaching a student to complete a daily journal entry, the teacher allows the student access to computer time following each successful entry. Once the student has achieved a steady state of responding, a shift to a schedule of reinforcement that is not continuous should be made to maintain the established behavior. Whereas previously the student earned computer time after each completed journal entry, the teacher would now thin the schedule of reinforcement so that only one out of every two or three (and eventually more) completed entries would result in the student's access to computer time. This shift to a delivery of reinforcement that is not continuous is referred to as *intermittent reinforcement*. The unpredictability of reinforcement inherent in intermittent schedules of reinforcement guards against satiation effects (i.e., decrease in response rates due to too much reinforcement) and increases resistance to extinction (i.e., persistence in responding during periods of nonreinforcement).

Stimulus Generalization

Stimulus generalization refers to the generalization or transfer of a response to situations other than those in which training takes place (i.e., settings, subjects, times, people, and behavior). Stimulus generalization occurs when responses that have been reinforced in the presence of a specific stimulus "generalize" to different but similar stimuli (Kazdin, 2001). Stimulus generalization is enhanced to the degree that the student experiences similar conditions. For example, an elementary student tells a "colorful" joke to a male classmate, who finds it rip-roaringly funny. He then tells the same joke to several other male classmates, who provide varying degrees of social reinforcement (e.g., laughter, smiles, groans). He then tells the same joke to first one and then several female classmates, who all laugh. The behavior of telling a joke has generalized across students who share similar stimulus features (e.g., size, age, grade level, school setting, gender).

Response Generalization

Another type of generalization involves responses rather than stimulus conditions. Response generalization refers to the changes in behaviors or responses other than those that have been trained or developed (Kazdin, 2001). In other words, the student performs a variety of similar functional responses in addition to the one trained. For example, a student who has been reinforced for turning in math assignments on time also begins turning in her history assignments on time. Or a student who has been trained to greet others by saying "Hello" begins using additional nontrained, but appropriate, greetings such as "Hi, how are you?" or "Hey, what's up?"

PROCEDURES FOR INCREASING GENERALIZATION

Generalization does not occur naturally; therefore, it is necessary to program for generalization. Stokes and Baer (1977), Miltenberger (2004), and Cooper et al. (2007) discussed a number of strategies that may be used to promote generalization of behaviors. These strategies are summarized in the following section.

Reinforcing Generalization

One way to increase occurrences of generalization is to simply reinforce it when it occurs. In other words, reinforce the behavior when it occurs outside of the training situation (Miltenberger, 2004). For example, consider the case of a young child with autism who has been taught, within the context of a cubicle within her classroom, to name objects (e.g., spoon, cup, fork, plate) via a massed practice discrete trial training procedure. Later, during lunch, the student spontaneously points to her plate and says "plate." The classroom teacher immediately provides verbal praise. This is an example of stimulus generalization across settings. In this example, the classroom teacher did not knowingly arrange the environment to increase the probability of a generalized response. However, in many cases generalized responding does not occur naturally, and one or several strategies may be used to increase the probability of generalization. These strategies are discussed in the following sections.

Sequential Modification

Sequential modification is a systematic approach to the process of generalization in which a student is exposed to the same contingencies across responses, subjects, settings, or instructors. Initially, a behavior is taught within a specific setting. Next, the target behavior is taught across all settings and situations in which it is expected to occur. For example, if a teaching strategy was used to increase social commenting behavior with a student with Asperger's syndrome during morning snack period, but this behavior did not transfer to the afternoon snack, the same teaching strategies would be employed during the afternoon snack period to increase social commenting behaviors. Suppose that social commenting behaviors did not generalize or only partially generalized to other times during the school day when this behavior was appropriate (e.g., lunch, homeroom, recess). In this case, sequentially offering the teaching strategies within each setting would be a strategy for increasing the generality of appropriate social behaviors.

Naturally Maintaining Contingencies of Reinforcement

When teaching behaviors, a good rule is to select behavior changes that will result in opportunities for naturally occurring reinforcement. Breaking this rule requires the interventionist to maintain and extend the behavior changes indefinitely (Baer, 1981). Allyon and Azrin (1968) developed what is known as the relevance of behavior rule. It states that only behaviors that will be maintained by the natural environment should be selected for modification in a behavior change program. This is important because in bringing behavior under the control of consequences that occur naturally in the environment, the transfer of responding increases. When using this strategy, it is important to identify conditions present in the natural environment that are likely to reinforce the target behavior. Therefore, it is important to consider the functionality and age-appropriateness of the target behavior. For example, a student who has recently moved to Maine from Somalia and who has very limited English proficiency is first taught social greetings within a small group setting with a plan for generalizing these behaviors to natural social situations (e.g., recess, lunch). Prior to instruction, her teachers observed and recorded the types of greetings exchanged by same-age classmates. This was done to ensure that the behaviors being taught would be consistent with the behavior of classmates and therefore would result in naturally occurring social reinforcement from peers, thus increasing the probability of generalization. In addition, the student's greeting behavior should be carefully monitored for consistency to ensure that it will come into contact with the natural contingencies of reinforcement.

Training Sufficient Exemplars

This strategy involves teaching enough examples so that target behaviors generalize to new situations. If the target behavior is to appear in a wide variety of settings and situations, teach the behavior under those varied conditions; if varying forms of the behavior are to be expected, then teach several examples to increase response generalization. If our teaching is to have true impact on the learner's lifestyle, he or she must be able to perform the target behavior with the precision required by the natural environment (Horner, Dunlap, & Koegel, 1988). By teaching the behavior within several stimulus conditions and by teaching multiple forms of the behavior, subsequent generalization within novel situations and environments is maximized. This strategy could be used during instructional programming to address a wide variety of behaviors, including age-appropriate functional life-skills. For example, Sprague and Horner (1984) described the use of general case programming in which multiple training examples are used to sample a range of relevant stimulus variations and responses. They facilitated the use of 10 vending machines with six students with developmental disabilities. In contrast to sequential modification, in which the students would be taught to use each of the 10 machines, with general case programming students were first taught to use 3 different vending machines (the general case training machines) within the high school. When asked to use the 10 nontraining vending machines, the students were able to operate the machines correctly. In a related study, Neef, Lensbower, Hockersmith, DePalma, and Gray (1990) trained one group of students to use only one washer and dryer, whereas they trained another group to use several washers and dryers. In follow-up, the group trained to use several machines was much more successful in operating a novel washer and dryer than the students who were taught to use only one washer and dryer.

Train Loosely

This strategy involves varying as many noncritical (functionally irrelevant) dimensions of the antecedent stimuli as possible during instruction and accepting a wide range of responses as correct in order to promote the transfer of skills to more variable conditions that would achieve the same reinforcing outcomes. Training "loosely" enhances the likelihood that variation of stimulus features will not override the critical stimulus features and therefore the desired function of the stimulus. Furthermore, widening the dimensions of training stimuli allows for a greater probability that at least some of those stimuli will be present in the generality setting. Some examples of stimulus features that could be loosened to promote generality include using two or more instructors; teaching in two or more places; teaching from a variety of positions; varying tone of voice; varying choice of words; varying people present; varying reinforcers; dressing differently; and varying light, decorations, furniture, location, and time of day. To illustrate, at the Margaret Murphy Center for Children, a preschool through Grade 12 special-purpose program serving children with developmental disabilities in Auburn, Maine, programming for generalization is an integral component of each student's education plan. Teachers are assigned to one student in the morning and another student in the afternoon. This means that each student will receive instruction from a minimum of two teachers each day. In addition, students' individual program plans are tailored to include a dynamic blend of instructional methods (e.g., discrete trial teaching, incidental teaching, task analysis, large and small group instruction) that include exposure to a wide range of stimulus conditions; varied instructional prompting strategies; and flexible schedules of reinforcement across school, community, and home settings.

Indiscriminable Contingencies

The clear, predictable, and immediate reinforcing consequences that are typically built into systematic instruction, although often necessary in the acquisition phase, may actually work against the goal of generalized responding (Cooper et al., 2007). Promoting generality of responding over time (i.e., temporal generalization) often involves using reinforcement contingencies in the training setting or situation that are unpredictable to the student and therefore more closely mirror the reinforcement contingencies that operate in the generality setting. Two specific strategies fall under this general method for promoting generalization of behavior: intermittent schedules of reinforcement and delayed reinforcement (Cooper et al., 2007). Intermittent schedules of reinforcement include variable ratio and variable interval schedules of reinforcement. With both of these schedules, the student is unable to predict when reinforcement will be delivered, thus resulting in sustained and durable responding. A variable ratio schedule of reinforcement is one in which reinforcement is delivered following a varying number of occurrences of the target behavior. A classic example of a variable ratio schedule of reinforcement is the playing of a slot machine. Monetary rewards are delivered with varying amounts and on a random schedule wherein the gambler may experience a "payout" after only a few pulls of a lever, or after dozens, perhaps hundreds. When using these types of reinforcement schedules, it is difficult for a student to discriminate antecedent and consequential contingencies operating at any particular moment, and generalized responding ensues.

A variable interval (VI) schedule of reinforcement is one in which reinforcement is provided following varying durations of the target behavior. For example, a student practicing the piano may receive social reinforcement (e.g., praise, smiles, applause) on the average every 5 minutes (VI 5) during her first year of instruction and every 30 minutes (VI 30) as she progresses. The VI 5 schedule, while averaging every 5 minutes, may include reinforcement following 1 minute, 3 minutes, 5 minutes, 7 minutes, and so on. Likewise, the VI 30 schedule, although averaging every 30 minutes, may include reinforcement following 10 minutes, 25 minutes, 30 minutes, 38 minutes, or 50 minutes.

In addition, delayed reinforcement on a variable interval schedule may involve praise from family members for the student when she practices diligently much later in the evening or perhaps the next day. For delayed reinforcement to have an effect on generalized outcomes, there must be a discernible relationship between the performance of the target behavior and the reward that is received later.

Program Common Stimuli

Another method of increasing generalization involves making sure that the training and anticipated generalization situations share similar stimulus features. This can be accomplished by incorporating stimuli from the training environment into the generalization situation. Making the training setting and generalization setting as similar as possible by including common stimuli increases the probability that behaviors learned in the teaching situation will transfer to the natural environment. For example, to teach children with autism to participate in dental examinations without problem behaviors, students at the Margaret Murphy Center for Children are taught the steps involved in routine dental care by replicating the dental environment and routines as much as possible. This project began by observing and recording the steps of a dental examination and identifying specific stimulus features of the dental environment (e.g., white gowns, masks, dental tools, reclining chair, background music, specific instructions used by the dentists and hygienist). Students were taught to follow and reinforced for completion of steps of a task analysis by teachers who replicated the dental visit in their dress, directions, and procedures. Upon completion of the training experience with no or very limited problem behaviors, students were taken to the dentist's office, where they proceeded to successfully participate in the dental examination.

Teaching Self-Control

Self-control refers to those behaviors that a student deliberately undertakes to achieve self-selected outcomes (Kazdin, 2001). Relative to generalization, the student is taught and reinforced for being the facilitator of generalized behavior. The logic of this method is that (a) the student is taught a target behavior, (b) the student is taught a strategy for transferring the behavior from one situation to another, and (c) the student uses this strategy within the novel situation to self-direct the occurrence of the target behavior. In short, the student has become the self-generated mediator of generalization (Miltenberger, 2004). Self-control includes strategies such as self-monitoring and self-reinforcement that are typically used to promote the generalization of student behaviors. Self-monitoring, or self-observation, consists of observing and recording specific target behaviors. By engaging in self-monitoring behaviors, desired behaviors are increased and problem behaviors decreased. Self-reinforcement involves the student self-administering reinforcement following the occurrence of the behavior targeted for generalization. As a strategy for promoting generalization, self-monitoring and self-reinforcement are typically used in concert to transfer the occurrence of a target behavior to anticipated generalization situations. For example, a high school student regularly discusses relevant topics at length when engaged in one-to-one discussions with his history teacher. However, the student rarely contributes to class discussion. To increase his participation in class discussion, the school psychologist helped the student develop a self-control procedure involving (a) a definition of contributing to class discussion, (b) identification of a goal to contribute to class discussion a minimum of five times per class period, (c) a chart for recording each occurrence of his contribution to class discussion, and (d) a reinforcement schedule and menu corresponding to his class participation. After only a few days of implementing this strategy, the student had increased his participation to class discussion to an average of six times per class session.

Blending Strategies

The aforementioned strategies for reinforcing generalization should not be viewed as mutually exclusive. That is, they can and often should be implemented concurrently. For example, consider a situation in which the target skill is to teach a student to make smoothies. Several strategies could be combined to teach the student to make a variety of smoothies across various settings. Programming for generalization could include training sufficient exemplars (i.e., different types of smoothies), training loosely (i.e., making smoothies in a kitchen at school, in a kitchen at home, and at a job site; making smoothies for morning, afternoon, and evening snacks), including various instructors (i.e., teachers, educational technicians, therapists, parents), and programming common stimuli (i.e., using the same type of blender and recipe cards across training sessions).

STRATEGIES FOR PLANNING, IMPLEMENTING, AND MONITORING GENERALIZATION

An all too familiar practice found within applied settings has been referred to as "train and hope" (Stokes & Baer, 1977). Within this model, students are taught behaviors with little regard or planning for generalized responding. In contrast to this train and hope practice, careful planning is a fundamental aspect of accomplishing generalized responding. If these goals are to be met with success, it is important to have a process for determining generality objectives; developing generalization strategies; and implementing, measuring, and monitoring generalization outcomes. Relative to the acquisition and generalization of target behaviors, the following five-stage problem-solving model is offered for consideration (Miltenberger, 2004; Steege & Brown-Chidsey, 2005).

Problem Identification

Generality planning begins with an emphasis on the student and the identification of specific skill or behaviors. This can be achieved by observing the student and his or her instructors and instructional setting and collaborating with the student's entire team (as well as the student if it is reasonable to do so) to outline critical concerns and desired outcomes. When making these determinations, the team should always consider the social significance of the target behavior. That is, if the generality outcomes are met with success, will the result be an improvement in the student's quality of life?

Problem Definition

Once the target behavior has been determined, an accurate and operational description should be created. Hawkins and Dobes (1977) described three characteristics of an accurate behavioral definition.

1. The definition should be objective, referring only to observable characteristics of the behavior (and environment, if needed) and translating any inferential terms (such as "expressing hostile feelings," "intended to help," "or "showing interest in") into more objective ones.
2. The definition should be clear, in that it should be readable and unambiguous so that experienced observers could read it and readily paraphrase it accurately.
3. The definition should be complete, delineating the "boundaries" of what is to be included as an instance of the response and what is to be excluded, thereby directing the observers in all situations that are likely to occur and leaving little to their judgment (p. 169).

Adhering to these criteria makes it possible to make reliable determinations about the relevance of the target behavior, which paves the way for the development of specific intervention plans. At this stage of the model, decisions should be made with regard to data collection. When making these decisions, consider which of the following—rate, accuracy, duration, latency, and magnitude of the response—are important. Once these determinations are made, accurate, reliable, and manageable data collection methods should be developed (Watson & Steege, 2003). By having a clear and precise definition of the skill or behavior that is to be taught, the data collected about that behavior are more likely to be accurate and useful (Brown-Chidsey & Steege, 2005). Once the target behavior has been defined, baseline data should be collected to determine the student's current level of performance of the target behavior, and potential threats and opportunities associated with desired student outcomes should be identified.

Designing Intervention Plans

At this point, the student's team should meet again to brainstorm and discuss various evidence-based intervention strategies for achieving the target behavior and for increasing the probability of generalized responding. Careful consideration should be given to all variables that could potentially influence desired outcomes. It is advisable to determine all settings and situations in which the student should be expected to emit the target behavior, potential desired and undesired variations of the target behavior, and key people in the generality setting. Next, determine the components of the target behavior that will be taught directly, and the settings and situations in which they will be taught. Making these determinations allows the team to make an informed decision about the most appropriate intervention strategy or combination of strategies. When designing the intervention plan, it is important that all members of the team feel that the decided-on strategies are acceptable and achievable. Agreement among team members increases the probability that the intervention will be implemented reliably and with treatment integrity.

Implementing the Intervention

It is critical that intervention strategies are used accurately and that student progress is carefully monitored. During the implementation phase, the behavior of both the interventionist and the student are observed and recorded. Interventionists are observed to document accurate implementation of the procedures (i.e., treatment integrity or treatment adherence). Observing and recording the student's acquisition and generality of target behaviors is an objective way of measuring student progress. If these data document that either (a) the intervention is not implemented as intended or (b) there has been little or no student progress, then strategic changes can be made to address areas of concern. Ongoing data collection and analysis are critical in determining treatment integrity and student progress. Steege, Brown-Chidsey, and Mace (2002) described several methods for documenting the effectiveness of interventions and generalized outcomes.

Defining the Solution

The solution to the "problem" is dependent on the needs and characteristics of the individual, the goals of intervention, and the contexts in which behaviors will ultimately be required. This involves analyzing progress monitoring data collected within the environments of ultimate concern. Relative to generalization, the problem is resolved when the student is consistently displaying targeted skills and behaviors within all relevant appropriate settings and situations.

SUMMARY

The ultimate success of any intervention is the degree to which it helps learners achieve generalized change in socially significant behaviors. Behavior change, no matter how important initially, is of limited value to the learner if it does not last over time, is not emitted in appropriate contexts, or occurs in restricted forms when varied or expanded topographies are appropriate (Cooper et al., 2007). Rather than allowing generalized responding to occur by chance, instructors can use a wide range of procedures and processes to promote generalization of desired behaviors. Well-designed and accurately implemented interventions increase the individual's repertoire of behaviors and their usefulness across and within a wide range of situations, resulting in an improved quality of life for the person served.

REFERENCES

Allyon, T., & Azrin, N. H. (1968). *The token economy: A motivational system for therapy and rehabilitation*. New York: Appleton-Century-Crofts.

Baer, D. M. (1981). *How to plan for generalization*. Lawrence, KS: H & H Enterprises.

Baer, D. M., Wolf, M. M., & Risley, T. R. (1968). Some current dimensions of applied behavior analysis. *Journal of Applied Behavior Analysis, 1,* 91–97.

Brown-Chidsey, R., & Steege, M. W. (2005). *Response to intervention*. New York: Guilford.

Cooper, J. O., Heron, T. E., & Heward, W. L (2007). *Applied Behavior Analysis* (2nd ed.). Upper Saddle River, NJ: Prentice Hall.

Hawkins, R. P., & Dobes, R. W. (1977). Behavioral definitions in applied behavior analysis: Explicit or implicit? In B. C. Etzel, J. M. LeBlanc, & D. M. Baer (Eds.), *New developments in behavioral research: Theory, mind, and application* (pp. 359–376). Upper Saddle River, NJ: Prentice Hall.

Horner, R. H., Dunlap, G., & Koegel, R. L. (1988). *Generalization and maintenance: Life-style changes in applied settings*. Baltimore: Paul H. Brooks.

Individuals with Disabilities Education Improvement Act (IDEA) of 2004. Pub. L. No. 108-446, 118 Stat. 2647.

Kazdin, A. E. (2001). *Behavior modification in applied settings* (6th ed.). Belmont, CA: Wadsworth.

Miltenberger, R. G. (2004). *Behavior modification: Principles and procedures* (2nd ed.). Belmont, CA: Wadsworth Thomson Learning.

Neef, N. A., Lensbower, J., Hockersmith, I., DePalma, V., & Gray, K. (1990). In vivo versus stimulation training: An interactional analysis of range and type of training exemplars. *Journal of Applied Behavior Analysis, 23,* 447–458.

No Child Left Behind Act of 2001, Pub. L. No. 107–110, 115 Stat. 1425 (2002).

Sprague, J. R., & Horner, R. H. (1984). The effects of single instance, multiple instance, and general case training on generalized vending machine use by moderately and severely handicapped students. *Journal of Applied Behavior Analysis, 17,* 273–278.

Steege, M. W., & Brown-Chidsey, R. (2005). Functional behavioral assessment: The cornerstone of effective problem solving. In R. Brown-Chidsey (Ed.), *Assessment for intervention: A problem solving approach* (pp. 131–154). New York: Guilford.

Steege, M. W., Brown-Chidsey, R., & Mace, F. C. (2002). Best practices in evaluating interventions. In A. Thomas & J. Grimes (Eds.), *Best practices in school psychology IV* (pp. 517–534). Washington, DC: National Association of School Psychologists.

Stokes, T. F., & Baer, D. M. (1977). An implicit technology of generalization. *Journal of Applied Behavior Analysis, 10,* 349–367.

Stokes, T. F., & Osnes, P. G. (1988). The developing applied technology of generalization and maintenance. In R. Horner, G. Dunlap, & R. L. Koegel (Eds.), *Generalization and maintenance: Life-style changes in applied settings* (pp. 5–19). Baltimore: Paul H. Brookes.

Watson, T. S., & Steege, M. W. (2003). *Conducting school-based functional behavior assessments: A practitioner's guide.* New York: Guilford.

III

SPECIFIC BEHAVIORAL
TECHNIQUES

13

USING RESPONSE TO INTERVENTION FOR IDENTIFICATION OF SPECIFIC LEARNING DISABILITIES

FRANK M. GRESHAM

The field of specific learning disabilities (SLD) cannot be characterized as one that has been built either on the strongest base of empirical support or on unanimity of professional agreement regarding etiology, identification practices, and remedial strategies. A pivotal issue that has always faced the field of SLD is the determination of which students need special education and related services, what types of services are needed, and with what intensity or strength such services should be delivered to effectively remediate academic difficulties of these students. At the heart of these issues lies a fundamental but critical question: Which children have an SLD and therefore are legally entitled to special education and related services, and which children do not have a disability? More specifically, to what extent, if at all, are low-achieving students who are given the SLD label different from low-achieving students who are not given that label? This has always been and continues to be more of a legal entitlement decision rather than a scientific question. The process by which public schools qualify and or disqualify students as having or not having a SLD is often confusing, logically inconsistent, unfair, and potentially biased (Bocian, Beebe, MacMillan, & Gresham, 1999).

The purpose of this chapter is to present an alternative approach to determining which students are and are not eligible for special education as SLD. This alternative approach is based on the concept of response to intervention (RTI), whereby students are exposed to multitiered interventions in general education settings to determine which students need what services delivered, with how much intensity and for how long (Gresham, 2002, 2006; National Association of State Directors of Special Education [NASDE], 2005). If the amount and costs of services exceed the scope and resources of general education, then the student may be deemed eligible to receive additional resources and supports, including special education and related services. RTI cannot be used exclusively as the single approach to determining which students are eligible for special education services. This chapter presents conceptual, methodological, technical, and logistical issues involved with implementing an RTI approach. Future directions for research and practice are also discussed.

DISENCHANTMENT WITH IQ–ACHIEVEMENT DISCREPANCY

Historically, a fundamental assumption in the identification of SLD is that presence of the IQ–achievement discrepancy is a valid marker for the presence of SLD. That is, students displaying unexpected and "severe" low achievement (discrepant underachievement) relative to their IQ are different in some ways compared with students not showing such discrepancies (nondiscrepant underachievers). The Isle of Wight studies can perhaps be viewed as the watershed event in canonizing the notion of IQ–achievement discrepancy in defining SLD and solidifying its subsequent use in determining SLD eligibility (Rutter & Yule, 1975). These studies defined two types of underachievement in reading: general reading backwardness (GRB) and specific reading retardation (SRR). GRB was defined as children having reading achievement scores that were consistent with their IQ (less than two standard errors of estimate predicted from their IQ score). SRR was characterized as deficient reading achievement that was equal or greater than two standard errors of estimate predicted from their IQ score. Thus, the GRB group was similar to what have been called "garden variety" low achievers (nondiscrepant low achievers), and the SRR group was similar to what we traditionally have called SLD (discrepant low achievers).

Rutter and Yule (1975) examined the distribution of predicted achievement scores and found an overrepresentation of children with GRB in the lower tail of the distribution of predicted reading scores, thereby representing a "hump." The Isle of Wight studies appeared to support the IQ–achievement discrepancy approach to defining reading disabilities and differentiating SRR (discrepant low achievers) from GRB (nondiscrepant low achievers) groups. It should be noted that the Isle of Wight studies focused exclusively on reading disabilities and did not investigate the validity of discrepancy notions in other academic areas (e.g., mathematics, written expression, oral expression, listening comprehension).

Several lines of converging evidence strongly suggest that IQ–achievement discrepancy is not a valid marker for the presence of SLD (Share, McGee, & Silva, 1989; Shaywitz, Fletcher, Holahan, & Shaywitz, 1992; Stanovich & Siegel, 1994; Vellutino, Scanlon, & Lyon, 2000; Vellutino et al., 1996). These lines of research tested directly the hypothesis that discrepant low achievers (SLD) were different from nondiscrepant low achievers (garden variety low achievers). Overall, these studies showed that discrepant and nondiscrepant low-achieving children did not differ on measures of reading achievement, response to instruction, cognitive abilities, phoneme awareness, short-term memory, visual processing, or word retrieval.

Furthermore, several meta-analyses have contrasted low achievers with SLD (discrepant) groups on a variety of measures (Fuchs, Fuchs, Mathes, Lipsey, & Roberts, 2002; Hoskyn & Swanson, 2000; Steubing et al., 2002). Hoskyn and Swanson (2000) reviewed 19 studies that contrasted low achievers and SLD groups. On the basis of 274 weighted effect sizes, these authors found small and few statistically significant differences between the two groups on measures of cognitive skills related to reading, such as pseudoword reading, real-word phonetic analysis, speech-related phonological processing, automaticity, and spelling. On the basis of a regression model analysis, these authors concluded that both low achievers and SLD groups share a general phonological deficit, a conclusion consistent with other findings in reading disability research (Perfetti, Beck, Bell, & Hughes, 1987; Stanovich & Siegel, 1994; Torgesen, 1999; Torgesen & Burgess, 1998; Torgesen, Burgess, & Rashotte, 1996).

More recently, Steubing et al. (2002) conducted a meta-analysis of 46 studies that investigated the validity of IQ–achievement discrepancy for children with learning disabilities LD in the domains of achievement, behavior, and cognitive skills. These studies contrasted low achievers and SLD groups and included most of the 19 studies reviewed by Hoskyn and Swanson (2000). Steubing et al. reported statistically insignificant effect size differences between low achievers and SLD groups in the domains of achievement and behavior and small differences in the cognitive domain. These authors concluded that defining SLD on the basis of IQ–achievement discrepancy has very little evidence for validity.

The IQ–achievement discrepancy approach to determining which children have or do not have SLD has numerous conceptual and measurement problems that seriously call into question its continued use in making eligibility determinations. At the heart of the criticism of discrepancy are the now well-established findings that discrepant and nondiscrepant low achievers are not meaningfully different in domains of achievement, behavior, and processes related to reading. Moreover, discrepant and nondiscrepant low achievers do not differ in their response to instruction, nor does the discrepancy approach inform instructional decisions (Gresham, 2002; Gresham & Witt, 1997; Vaughn & Fuchs, 2003; Vellutino et al., 2000).

An alternative to the discrepancy approach is known as RTI and is part of the reauthorization of the Individuals with Disabilities Education Improvement Act (IDEA) of 2004. The advantages and potential of this approach to defining SLD are discussed in the remainder of this chapter along with measurement issues, implementation challenges, and decision rules that must be resolved in the future. Before describing the RTI approach, a description and consideration of the role of processing in SLD determination is provided.

DISENCHANTMENT WITH PROCESSING AND SLD

IDEA (2004) states that an SLD is "a disorder in one or more of the basic psychological processes involving understanding or using language, spoken or written, that may manifest itself in an imperfect ability to listen, think, speak, read, write, spell, or do mathematical calculations." Some professionals take this description to mean that identifying processes and/or cognitive ability deficits is necessary to the identification of SLD, and in fact required by the law (Hale, Kaufman, Naglieri, & Kavale, 2006). There is nothing written in the law that necessarily requires the assessment and documentation of a processing disorder. In fact, one's ability to do this is hampered by a variety of measurement-related factors.

Nothing has changed in the statutory definition of SLD over the past 32 years. The statute has always used the language of processing as a conceptual or theoretical explanation of learning difficulties. There has never been a requirement in either the statute or the regulations that a so-called "processing disorder" be demonstrated. As we know, the conceptual definition of SLD was operationalized into IQ–achievement discrepancy with the 1977 regulations for P.L. 94-142 released by the U.S. Department of Education (USDOE; 1977). As such, we have a conceptual definition of SLD based on processing language and an operational definition of SLD based on discrepancy language ("severe discrepancy between achievement and intellectual ability"; USDOE, 1977, p. 65083).

The reason for this is based on the fact that, other than phonological processing, direct, reliable, and valid measures of processing were not and currently are not available. A more serious problem, however, is that there is not a single, randomized clinical trial using the Institute for Educational Sciences's (IES's) evidence-based standards that has related processing strengths to effective intervention outcomes. To be fair, IES's criteria for evidence-based standards have only recently been advanced; therefore, much of the existing research correlating processing strengths and academic performance was conducted before IES standards were developed. There are no experimental research studies showing a causal relationship between processing and academic performance. Some processing measures may moderate (correlate) academic performance, but they have not been demonstrated to mediate (cause) academic performance.

Many, if not most, proponents of processing often confuse correlation with causation (i.e., they confuse moderation with mediation; Hale et al., 2006; Kaufman & Kaufman, 2006; Naglieri & Das, 1997). A moderator variable is one that affects the direction or strength of the relationship between a predictor variable and a criterion variable. Thus, the impact of the predictor variable on the criterion varies with the level or value of the moderator. A mediator variable specifies how, or the mechanism by which, a given effect occurs. In other words, the predictor causes the mediator that, in turn, causes the criterion or outcome (see Baron & Kenny, 1986; Holmbeck, 1997).

Consider a simple example that assumes three variables: A: Predictor: Verbal Conceptualization or VC (WISC-IV); B: Moderator: Working Memory or WM (WISC-IV); C: Criterion: Reading Skill or RC. VC correlates with RC. WM correlates with RC. VC correlates with WM. We thus have three correlations (A:B; B:C; A:C). Poor readers have lower VC than average or good readers. Poor readers have lower WM scores than average or good readers. VC and WM deficits do not necessarily cause poor reading skills. Numerous studies have shown that groups of at-risk and SLD learners score lower on some processing measures. It does not necessarily follow that these processing deficits cause SLD. This would not be unlike saying low IQ causes mental retardation or high IQ causes giftedness.

Group mean differences on processing measures do not necessarily imply that these measures are diagnostically accurate in identifying SLD. This is an example of faulty reasoning based on the notion of inverse probabilities (Meehl & Rosen, 1955; Watkins, 2000). For example, the so-called ACID profile (low scores on Arithmetic, Coding, Information, and Digit Span) of the Wechsler scales is often considered a processing marker variable for SLD. Suppose a sample of SLD students is found to have low scores on ACID subtests (i.e., the probability of this profile is high given that the child is SLD). This, however, is not how a referral in schools or a clinic takes place. What we want to know is the probability a child is SLD given an ACID profile. Inverse probabilities of this nature systematically overestimate diagnostic accuracy (Meehl & Rosen, 1955).

RTI MODELS

Two basic approaches are used to deliver interventions in an RTI framework: (a) problem-solving approaches and (b) standard protocol approaches

(Fuchs, Mock, Morgan, & Young, 2003). Emerging models that combine these two approaches may be particularly promising in school settings (Barnett, Daly, Jones, & Lentz, 2004; VanDerHeyden, Witt, & Naquin, 2003).

Problem Solving

Problem solving derives from the behavioral consultation model first described by Bergan (1977) and later revised by Bergan and Kratochwill (1990). Problem solving takes place in four stages: (a) problem identification, (b) problem analysis, (c) plan implementation, and (d) plan evaluation. The goal of problem-solving consultation is to define the referral problem in specific, operational terms, to identify environmental conditions related to the referral problem, to design and implement an intervention plan with integrity, and to evaluate the effectiveness of the intervention (Bergan & Kratochwill, 1990).

There is a considerable research base showing that interventions developed within a problem-solving model can be implemented with integrity and doing so improves student outcomes. Noell et al. (2000), borrowing from the performance management literature for business and industry (Balcazar, Hopkins, & Suarez, 1985), demonstrated that teachers can reliably implement a variety of academic and behavioral interventions. Specifically, these researchers have shown that follow-up contact by a consultant that includes review of student progress and treatment implementation can lead to high levels of intervention implementation (see Mortenson & Witt, 1998; Noell, Duhon, Gatti, & Connell, 2002; Noell et al., 2000).

The above series of studies, along with an abundant literature in applied behavior analysis, strongly suggests that interventions developed in a problem-solving model can (a) be implemented with integrity but only with specific performance feedback from consultants, and (b) if implemented correctly, produce substantial changes in student behavior (Alberto & Troutman, 2003; Elliott, Witt, Kratochwill, & Stoiber, 2002). A fundamental and unresolved issue is the extent to which typical school personnel can or will achieve similar levels of integrity with implementation and student outcomes using problem-solving methods. It is clear that RTI delivered within a problem-solving model will bring more responsibility on the part of professionals such as school psychologists to increase the precision and intensity of intervention efforts.

Standard Protocol Approaches

Another approach to RTI is the use of empirically validated treatment protocols that can be implemented with students having academic difficulties in a given domain such as reading. Many students classified as SLD may fail to acquire basic academic skills not because of some mysterious, unobservable processing disorder but because they have not been given adequate opportunities to learn (Gresham, 2002). The current use of IQ–achievement discrepancy and processing assessment does not screen out those children whose reading difficulties might be due to either inadequate schooling or limited exposure to effective reading instruction (Clay, 1987; Vellutino et al., 1996). Vellutino et al. (1996) suggested that exposure to validated reading instruction for a period of time should be used as a "first cut diagnostic aid" (p. 601) in distinguishing between reading problems caused by cognitive deficits versus those caused by experiential deficits (i.e., poor reading instruction).

Vellutino et al.'s (1996) research is an exemplary illustration of the standard protocol approach in distinguishing between cognitive and experiential deficits for children with reading difficulties. These authors conducted a longitudinal study with 183 kindergarten children composed of poor readers ($n = 118$) and normal reader controls ($n = 65$). Poor readers were selected on the basis of scoring below the 15th percentile on measures of word identification or letter-sound correspondence using nonsense words. Selected children in the poor-reader group ($n = 74$) were given daily one-to-one tutoring (30 minutes per day) for a total of 15 weeks over 70 to 80 sessions (35 to 40 hours of tutoring). Vellutino et al. calculated growth curves for each child from kindergarten to second grade. Slopes from these analyses were rank-ordered and used to place children into one of four groups: very limited growth, limited growth, good growth, and very good growth. Approximately two thirds of children in the sample showed either very good growth or good growth, indicating that they had caught up with their peers who did not have reading difficulties. This would suggest that these children would have been "instructional casualties" because they would not otherwise have received sufficient reading instruction and/or other necessary preliteracy experiences. Other standard protocol approaches for reading have received empirical support (see Foorman, Francis, Fletcher, Schatschneider, & Mehta, 1998; Torgesen et al., 2001; Vaughn, Linan-Thompson, & Hickman, 2003).

Standard protocol approaches have convincing empirical evidence that they can be used effectively to remediate rather severe reading difficulties in most, but not all, poor readers. The primary advantage of the standard protocol approach compared with problem-solving approaches is that it may afford better quality control of instruction. Given that these protocols are scripted, they can be used to ensure the integrity of instruction. It should be noted, however, that standard protocols have been used almost exclusively by researchers and not by school practitioners (Fuchs et al., 2003). This research-to-practice gap represents a challenge in the area of RTI.

RTI AND SLD: A PROMISING ALTERNATIVE TO DISCREPANCY AND PROCESSING

With the passage of IDEA (2004), RTI is now approved as a viable alternative to IQ–achievement discrepancy and the determination of processing strengths and weaknesses in the identification of children as having SLD. The law now reads:

> Specific learning disabilities (A) General: Notwithstanding section 607 of this Act, or any other provision of law, when determining whether a child has a specific learning disability as defined under this Act, the LEA (Local Education Agency) shall not be required to take into consideration whether a child has a severe discrepancy between achievement and intellectual ability in oral expression, listening comprehension, reading recognition . . . (B) Additional Authority: In determining whether a child has a specific learning disability, a LEA *may use a process which determines if a child responds to a scientific, research based intervention* [italics added]. (p. 118, Stat. 2647)

Although the law does not specifically advocate RTI as a viable alternative to the IQ–achievement discrepancy approach, it does say that both approaches may be used. Clearly, the reauthorized version of IDEA does not require nor does it eliminate IQ–achievement discrepancy as a basis for identifying children as having SLD. Additionally, neither the law nor the attendant regulations have ever required or currently require the identification of processing strengths or weaknesses in identifying children as having SLD. Moreover, the law allows, but does not require, that school districts use a response-to-intervention approach in the identification of SLD.

The RTI concept is based on adequate or inadequate change in academic performance as a function of intervention (Gresham, 2002). In an RTI approach, eligibility determinations or diagnostic decisions are based on how children respond to evidence-based interventions implemented with integrity. RTI logic is used to select, change, or titrate interventions on the basis of how a child responds to the intervention. RTI assumes that if a child shows an inadequate response to the best intervention available, then that child can and should be eligible for additional assistance, including, but not limited to, special education and related services (Gresham, 2006).

The goal of all interventions is to reduce the discrepancy between current and desired levels of performance. In an RTI model, a problem is defined as a discrepancy between the child's current level of functioning and the desired level of functioning. The larger this discrepancy, the larger the problem and the more resistant that problem will be to intervention efforts (Gresham, 2006). RTI uses data-based decision making as the basis for changing the nature of an intervention. These changes might include increasing the nature, strength, intensity, duration, and/or frequency of a given intervention. RTI provides the opportunity for school personnel to function within an intervention framework rather than an overly constrictive psychometric eligibility approach that has virtually no evidence for treatment validity (Gresham, 2002; Reschly & Tilly, 1999).

At least four advantages emerge from using an RTI approach in the identification of SLD: (a) early identification of learning difficulties, (b) conceptualization of learning problems in terms of a risk model rather than a deficit model, (c) reduction of identification biases, and (d) an emphasis on student outcomes (Fletcher et al., 2002; Gresham, 2002, 2006; Vaughn & Fuchs, 2003). Each of these is discussed in the following sections.

Early Identification of Learning Difficulties

The most convincing reason for using an RTI approach is that it offers the opportunity of providing help to struggling children immediately rather than waiting for them to get further behind academically. The past and current use of IQ–achievement discrepancy to identify SLD has been termed a "wait-to-fail" approach because it requires that a child fail severely enough and long enough for the teacher to make a decision to refer and for a psychologist to provide assessment data demonstrating a severe discrepancy. The developmental odds of being classified as SLD increase dramatically from first to fourth grades. For example, between first and second grades, the SLD rate doubles, from second to third grades, the rate doubles again, and between third and fourth grades, the odds go up 150% (U.S. Department of Education, 2002). Thus, between first and fourth grades, the odds of being labeled SLD increase linearly by 450%. Discrepancy approaches penalize younger children and delay potentially effective intervention services because younger children are far less likely to demonstrate a severe discrepancy than older children (Fletcher et al., 2002).

An RTI approach to the identification of SLD can assist in closing the gap between identification and intervention (Vaughn & Fuchs, 2003). Students can be easily and efficiently screened for early academic difficulties and can be provided with effective early interventions to remediate academic difficulties (Gresham, 2002; Jenkins & O'Connor, 2002; NASDE, 2005). Without early intervention efforts, children's academic difficulties will become well-entrenched and more resistant to change. An RTI approach holds great promise for preventing more serious and debilitating academic difficulties.

Risk Versus Deficit Models

Historically, the field of SLD has operated under a deficit model in which underlying cognitive and processing deficits are identified, and specifically designed instructional strategies are recommended to remediate those deficits (Mann, 1979; Ysseldyke, 2001). Vaughn and Fuchs (2003) noted that the field of SLD has simply not been successful in reliably identifying underlying processing deficits and linking that assessment information to effective instructional strategies. Past and current approaches to SLD assessment rely heavily on aptitude × treatment interaction (ATI) logic in which instructional treatments are matched to putative aptitude strengths presumably to produce better outcomes. To date, no randomized clinical trial data support this practice. In fact, after 20 years of disappointing research, Cronbach (1975) abandoned ATI as a basis for applied psychology and recommended a process akin to what is now called problem solving and short-run empiricism (see Reschly & Tilly, 1999; Reschly & Ysseldyke, 2002).

RTI operates under a risk model that emphasizes early identification of learning difficulties. Under this model, all students are screened for potential learning difficulties, preferably early in their school careers (e.g., kindergarten to first grade). Those students identified as being at risk are given supplemental instruction, which has been shown to be an effective practice through research (i.e., evidence-based practice) to remediate these learning difficulties. The most important concept in any RTI model is the notion of matching the intensity of intervention to the severity and resistance of the problem to intervention efforts. This approach characterizes interventions that differ in terms of their nature, comprehensiveness, and intensity as well as the degree of unresponsiveness of the problem to those interventions (Gresham, 2006). RTI provides better opportunities to integrate services between general and special education (NASDE, 2005).

Reduction of Identification Biases

Special education eligibility in the public schools almost always begins with a general education teacher's decision to refer a child for special education consideration. The decision to refer a child for SLD assessment is almost always based on academic difficulties, particularly in reading (Bocian et al., 1999). The principle guiding teacher referral is one of relativity—that is, what is the child's academic performance relative to the model performance of the class or the gap between the referred child's academic performance level and that of other low-performing members of the class?

A teacher's decision to refer is influenced not only by academic deficiencies but also by other factors such as gender, socioeconomic status, or minority group membership (MacMillan & Siperstein, 2002; Reschly, 2002). Donovan and Cross (2002) argued that an RTI approach to the referral process has the potential of reducing and perhaps eliminating the disproportionate overrepresentation of certain minority groups in special education resulting from biases in the teacher referral process. Also, it is well established that there is a bias in overidentifying boys and underidentifying girls as SLD in reading by the classroom teacher in the referral process, despite virtually equal levels of reading difficulties in boys and girls (Shaywitz, Escobar, Shaywitz, Fletcher, & Makuch, 1992). The power of iterative problem-solving efforts implemented within an RTI model of identification has great potential to reduce disproportionate identification of academic difficulties by ethnicity and gender and is superior to other identification methods such as teacher referral (Donovan & Cross, 2002; Van DerHeyden et al., 2003).

Focus on Child Outcomes

RTI is based on the notion that measures and domains assessed should be determined by their relationships to child outcomes. Domains that are useful and appropriate should have an empirically established relationship to positive child outcomes, rather than simply predictions of failure. Reschly and Tilly (1999) argued that using assessment methods without such relationships do little to benefit children and often deflect attention away from measures and domains that can be used to predict positive outcomes. RTI stresses direct measurement of achievement and the instructional environment as core foci of a comprehensive evaluation of a child's academic difficulties. RTI emphasizes assessment of measurable and changeable aspects of academic performance and the instructional environment.

RTI assumes that a significant proportion of children who are or might be identified as SLD may be more accurately characterized as instructional causalities (Vaughn et al., 2003). Clay (1987) suggested that many children learn to be learning disabled because they are not exposed to early fundamental literacy skills in kindergarten and first grade. Many of these children are exposed to marginally effective general education reading curricula and instruction that either have not been scientifically validated or have been implemented with poor integrity (National Reading Panel, 2000).

In an RTI approach, prior and current instructional opportunities and application of evidence-based instructional strategies are analyzed. Instructional variables are assessed and include alterable factors such as opportunities to respond, time allocated for instruction, pacing of instruction, sequencing of examples and nonexamples of skills, and so forth (Denton, Vaughn, & Fletcher, 2003; National Reading Panel, 2000; Witt, Van DerHeyden, & Gilbertson, 2004). Treatment integrity is a fundamental component of any RTI model and must be directly measured over time to ensure that interventions are being implemented as planned or intended (Gresham, 1989).

SUMMARY

RTI is based on a child's inadequate responsiveness to evidence-based instruction rather than IQ–achievement discrepancy. The RTI approach is a viable alternative to identifying SLD in light of the myriad difficulties associated with discrepancy and processing approaches for eligibility determination. Part of the appeal of RTI is that it allows one to rule out inadequate instruction as a cause of insufficient academic achievement and allows for decision making within an ecologically valid setting (i.e., the general education classroom).

RTI requires the direct measurement of behavior, the instructional environment, and intervention outcomes rather than traditional indirect assessments that focus on within-child processing strengths and weaknesses. Some argue that cognitive ability must be part of a comprehensive evaluation, even within an RTI approach to identifying children with SLD (Hale et al., 2006). Only 1 of the 13 categories in IDEA would necessarily mandate an assessment of cognitive ability: mental retardation. If the referral concern is suspected mental retardation, then cognitive ability testing would be essential. Apart from this issue, three criteria should be used to decide whether any assessment procedure (including cognitive abilities) should be used: (a) Does the measure inform the selection of interventions?, (b) Can the measure be used to monitor progress?, and (c) Does the measure contribute to beneficial intervention outcomes? Cognitive ability measures at the present time meet none of these criteria and thus are superfluous in an RTI model (Gresham, 2002; Gresham & Witt, 1997; Vellutino et al., 2000).

Current evidence suggests that RTI can be implemented responsibly while the evidence base accumulates and that iterations and modifications are not only inevitable but also desirable. Although ultimately RTI is a process that is implemented by people who could use it effectively or ineffectively, the benefits of RTI far outweigh potential costs for children and will only facilitate refinements toward a model supported by converging sources of evidence. The changes and challenges presented by RTI necessarily will move the field away from exclusive reliance on eligibility determination into intervention-oriented practices of both general and special education.

REFERENCES

Alberto, P., & Troutman, A. (2003). *Applied behavior analysis for teachers* (6th ed.). Upper Saddle River, NJ: Merrill Prentice Hall.

Balcazar, F., Hopkins, B., & Suarez, Y. (1985). A critical objective review of performance feedback. *Journal of Organizational Behavioral Management, 7*, 65–89.

Barnett, D., Daly, E., Jones, K., & Lentz, F. E. (2004). Response to intervention: Empirically based special service decisions for increasing and decreasing intensity using single case designs. *Journal of Special Education, 38*, 66–79.

Baron, R. M., & Kenny, D. A. (1986). The moderator-mediator variable distinction in social psychology research: Conceptual, strategic, and statistical considerations. *Journal of Personality and Social Psychology, 51*, 1173–1182.

Bergan, J. (1977). *Behavioral consultation*. Columbus, OH: Merrill.

Bergan, J., & Kratochwill, T. (1990). *Behavioral consultation and therapy*. New York: Plenum.

Bocian, K., Beebe, M., MacMillan, D., & Gresham, F. M. (1999). Competing paradigms in learning disabilities classification by schools and variations in the meaning of discrepant achievement. *Learning Disabilities Research & Practice, 14*, 1–14.

Clay, M. (1987). Learning to be learning disabled. *New Zealand Journal of Educational Studies, 22*, 155–173.

Cronbach, L. J. (1975). Beyond two disciplines of scientific psychology. *American Psychologist, 30*, 116–127.

Denton, C., Vaughn, S., & Fletcher, J. (2003). Bringing research-based practice in reading intervention to scale. *Learning Disabilities Research & Practice, 18*, 201–211.

Donovan, S., & Cross, C. (2002). *Minority students in special and gifted education.* Washington, DC: National Academy Press.

Elliott, S. N., Witt, J. C., Kratochwill, T., & Stoiber, K. (2002). Selecting and evaluating classroom interventions. In M. Shinn, H. Walker, & G. Stoner (Eds.), *Interventions for academic and behavior problems II: Preventive and remedial approaches* (pp. 243–294). Bethesda, MD: National Association of School Psychologists.

Fletcher, J., Lyon, G. R., Barnes, M., Steubing, K., Francis, D., Olson, R., et al. (2002). Classification of learning disabilities: An evidence-based evaluation. In R. Bradley, L. Danielson, & D. Hallahan (Eds.), *Learning disabilities: Research to practice* (pp. 185–250). Mahwah, NJ: Erlbaum.

Foorman, B., Francis, D., Fletcher, J., Schatschneider, C., & Mehta, P. (1998). The role of instruction in learning to read: Preventing reading failure in at-risk children. *Journal of Educational Psychology, 90*, 37–55.

Fuchs, D., Fuchs, L., Mathes, P., Lipsey, M., & Roberts, P. H. (2002). Is "learning disabilities" just a fancy name for low achievement: A meta-analysis of reading differences between low achievers with and without the label. In R. Bradley, L. Danielson, & D. Hallahan (Eds.), *Learning disabilities: Research to practice* (pp. 737–762). Mahwah, NJ: Erlbaum.

Fuchs, D., Mock, D., Morgan, P., & Young, C. (2003). Responsiveness-to-intervention: Definitions, evidence, and implications for the learning disabilities construct. *Learning Disabilities Research & Practice, 18*, 157–171.

Gresham, F. M. (1989). Assessment of treatment integrity in school consultation and prereferral intervention. *School Psychology Review, 18*, 37–50.

Gresham, F. M. (2002). Responsiveness to intervention: An alternative approach to the identification of learning disabilities. In R. Bradley, L. Danielson, & D. Hallahan (Eds.), *Learning disabilities: Research to practice* (pp. 467–519). Mahwah, NJ: Erlbaum.

Gresham, F. M. (2006). Response to intervention. In G. Bear, K. Minke, & A. Thomas (Eds.), *Children's needs–III*. Bethesda, MD: National Association of School Psychologists.

Gresham, F. M., & Witt, J. C. (1997). Utility of intelligence tests for treatment planning, classification, and placement decisions: Recent empirical findings and future directions. *School Psychology Quarterly, 12*, 249–267.

Hale, J., Kaufman, A., Naglieri, J., & Kavale, K. (2006). Implementation of IDEA: Integrating response to intervention and cognitive assessment methods. *Psychology in the Schools, 43*, 753–770.

Holmbeck, G. N. (1997). Toward terminological, conceptual, and statistical clarity in the study of mediators and moderators: Examples from the child-clinical and pediatric psychology literatures. *Journal of Consulting and Clinical Psychology, 65*, 599–610.

Hoskyn, M., & Swanson, H. L. (2000). Cognitive processing of low achievers and children with reading disabilities: A selective meta-analytic review of the published literature. *School Psychology Review, 29*, 102–119.

Individuals With Disabilities Education Improvement Act (IDEA) of 2004. Pub. L. No. 108-446, 118 Stat. 2647.

Jenkins, J., & O'Connor, R. (2002). Early identification and intervention for young children with reading/learning disabilities. In R. Bradley, L. Danielson, & D. Hallahan (Eds.), *Learning disabilities: Research to practice* (pp. 99–149). Mahwah, NJ: Erlbaum.

Kaufman, A., & Kaufman, N. (2006). *Kaufman Assessment Battery for Children, second edition*. Bloomington, MN: Pearson Assessments.

MacMillan, D., & Siperstein, G. (2002). Learning disabilities as operationally defined by schools. In R. Bradley, L. Danielson, & D. Hallahan (Eds.), *Learning disabilities: Research to practice* (pp. 287–333). Mahwah, NJ: Erlbaum.

Mann, L. (1979). *On the trail of process*. New York: Grune & Stratton.

Meehl, P., & Rosen, A. (1955). Antecedent probability and the efficiency of psychometric signs, patterns, or cutting scores. *Psychological Bulletin, 52*, 194–216.

Mortenson, B., & Witt, J. C. (1998). The use of weekly performance feedback to increase teacher implementation of a prereferral intervention. *School Psychology Review, 27*, 613–627.

Naglieri, J., & Das, J. P. (1997). *Cognitive Assessment System*. Itasca, IL: Riverside.

National Association of State Directors of Special Education. (2005). *Response to intervention: Policy considerations and implementation*. Alexandria, VA: Author.

National Reading Panel. (2000). *Report of the National Reading Panel. Teaching children to read: An evidence-based assessment of the scientific research literature on reading and its implications for reading instruction* (NIH Publication No. 00-4769). Washington, DC: U.S. Government Printing Office.

Noell, G. H., Duhon, G., Gatti, S., & Connell, J. (2002). Consultation follow-up and behavior management intervention implementation in general education. *School Psychology Review, 31*, 217–234.

Noell, G. H., Witt, J. C., LaFleur, L., Mortenson, B., Ranier, D., & LeVelle, J. (2000). A comparison of two follow-up strategies to increase teacher intervention implementation in general education following consultation. *Journal of Applied Behavior Analysis, 33*, 271–284.

Perfetti, C., Beck, L., Bell, L., & Hughes, C. (1987). Phonemic knowledge and learning to read are reciprocal: A longitudinal study of first grade children. *Merrill-Palmer Quarterly, 33*, 283–319.

Reschly, D. J. (2002). Minority overrepresentation: The silent contributor to LD prevalence and diagnostic confusion. In R. Bradley, L. Danielson, & D. Hallahan (Eds.), *Learning disabilities: Research to practice* (pp. 361–368). Mahwah, NJ: Erlbaum.

Reschly, D. J., & Tilly, W. D. (1999). Reform trends and system design alternatives. In D. Reschly, W. D. Tilly, & J. Grimes (Eds.), *Special education in transition: Functional assessment and noncategorical programming* (pp. 19–48). Longmont, CO: Sopris West.

Reschly, D. J., & Ysseldyke, J. (2002). Paradigm shift: The past is not the future. In A. Thomas & J. Grimes (Eds.), *Best practices in school psychology IV* (pp. 3–20). Bethesda, MD: National Association of School Psychologists.

Rutter, M., & Yule, W. (1975). The concept of specific reading retardation. *Journal of Child Psychology and Psychiatry, 16,* 181–197.

Share, D., McGee, R., & Silva, P. (1989). IQ and reading progress: A test of the capacity notion. *Journal of the American Academy of Child and Adolescent Psychiatry, 28,* 97–100.

Shaywitz, S., Escobar, M., Shaywitz, B., Fletcher, J., & Makuch, R. (1992). Distribution and temporal stability of dyslexia in an epidemiological sample of 414 children followed longitudinally. *New England Journal of Medicine, 326,* 145–150.

Shaywitz, B., Fletcher, J., Holahan, J., & Shaywitz, S. (1992). Discrepancy compared to low achievement definitions of reading disability: Results from the Connecticut Longitudinal Study. *Journal of Learning Disabilities, 25,* 639–648.

Stanovich, K., & Siegel, L. (1994). The phenotypic performance profile of reading-disabled children: A regression-based test of the phonological core variable-difference model. *Journal of Educational Psychology, 86,* 74–85.

Steubing, K., Fletcher, J., LeDoux, J., Lyon, G. R., Shaywitz, S., & Shaywitz, B. (2002). Validity of IQ-discrepancy classifications of reading disabilities: A meta-analysis. *American Educational Research Journal, 39,* 469–518.

Torgesen, J. (1999). Phonologically-based reading disabilities: Toward a coherent theory of one kind of learning disability. In R. Sternberg & L. Spear-Swerling (Eds.), *Perspectives on learning disabilities* (pp. 231–262). New Haven, CT: Westview Press.

Torgesen, J., Alexander, A., Wagner, R., Rashotte, C., Voeller, K., & Conway, T. (2001). Intensive remedial instruction for children with severe reading disabilities: Immediate and long-term outcomes from two instructional approaches. *Journal of Learning Disabilities, 34,* 33–58.

Torgesen, J., & Burgess, S. (1998). Consistency of reading-related phonological processes throughout early childhood: Evidence from longitudinal-correlational and instructional studies. In J. Metsala & L. Ehri (Eds.), *Word recognition in beginning reading* (pp. 161–188). Hillsdale, NJ: Erlbaum.

Torgesen, J., Burgess, S., & Rashotte, C. (1996, April). *Predicting phonologically-based reading disabilities: What is gained by waiting a year?* Paper presented at the Scientific Study of Reading, New York.

U.S. Department of Education. (2002). *Twenty-fourth annual report to Congress on implementation of the Individuals With Disabilities Education Act.* Washington, DC: Author.

U.S. Department of Education. (1977). Assistance to states for education of handicapped children: Procedures for evaluating specific learning disabilities. *Federal Register, 42*(250), 65082–65085.

VanDerHeyden, A., Witt, J. C., & Naquin, G. (2003). Development and validation of a process for screening referrals to special education. *School Psychology Review, 32,* 204–227.

Vaughn, S., & Fuchs, L. S. (2003). Redefining learning disabilities as inadequate response to instruction: The promise and potential problems. *Learning Disabilities Research Practice, 18,* 137–146.

Vaughn, S., Linan-Thompson, S., & Hickman, P. (2003). Response to instruction as a means of identifying students with reading/learning disabilities. *Exceptional Children, 69,* 391–409.

Vellutino, F., Scanlon, D., & Lyon, G. R. (2000). Differentiating between difficult-to-remediate and readily remediated poor readers: More evidence against IQ-achievement discrepancy definition of reading disability. *Journal of Learning Disabilities, 33,* 233–238.

Vellutino, F., Scanlon, D., Sipay, E., Small, S., Pratt, A., Chen, R., et al. (1996). Cognitive profiles of difficult-to-remediate and readily remediated poor readers: Early intervention as a vehicle for distinguishing between cognitive and experiential deficits as basic causes of specific reading disability. *Journal of Educational Psychology, 88,* 601–638.

Watkins, M. (2000). Cognitive profile analysis: A shared professional myth. *School Psychology Quarterly, 15,* 465–479.

Witt, J. C., VanDerHeyden, A., & Gilbertson, D. (2004). Troubleshooting behavioral interventions: A systematic process for finding and eliminating problems. *School Psychology Review, 33,* 363–383.

Ysseldyke, J. (2001). Reflections on a research career: Generalizations from 25 years of research on assessment and instructional decision-making. *Exceptional Children, 67,* 295–309.

14

DAILY REPORT CARDS: HOME-BASED CONSEQUENCES FOR CLASSROOM BEHAVIOR

MARY LOU KELLEY AND NICHOLE JURBERGS

For decades, parents and teachers have used a variety of contingency management procedures to improve children's behavior (McMahon, Wells, & Kotler, 2006). Until recently, however, the systematic collaboration between parents and teachers to improve children's academic and classroom behavior has been negligible in comparison to interventions solely managed by school personnel. When collaboration does occur, communication by teachers to parents typically often is intermittent and negative (Kelley, 1990). The occasional note from the teacher often evokes fear in the child and dismay in the parent. This form of feedback generally is ineffective at altering behavior (Kelley, 2003).

Daily report cards, also referred to as *school–home notes*, represent an alternative approach for improving children's classroom behavior and academic performance (Jurbergs, Palcic, & Kelley, 2007a; Kelley, 1990). Daily report cards involve teachers evaluating a student's behavior daily and parents providing consequences on the basis of the evaluation. Children typically are responsible for bringing the note home. However, some clinicians and researchers have begun to use e-mail, thus eliminating the need for children to transport information.

Use of daily report cards reflects a larger movement toward increasing parent involvement in promoting children's classroom success. In part, this increased emphasis is due to legal changes governing school policy and to research findings supporting the strong contribution parents can make to student achievement (Christenson, Hurely, Sheridan, & Fenstermacher, 1997; Keith et al., 1998). For example, Public Law 94-142 legally and ethically obligates school personnel to incorporate parents into decision making regarding children's placements and educational goals.

USES AND ADVANTAGES OF DAILY REPORT CARDS

Daily report cards have been effective in improving a variety of target behaviors important to classroom success. Use of the procedure has resulted in increased homework completion, attentiveness, and appropriate participation in groups or class, as well as in reduced disruptive, noncompliant, or aggressive behavior (Blechman, Kotanchik & Taylor, 1981; Kelley, 1990). Although not documented in the literature, we have used daily report cards to increase a variety of interpersonal behaviors. For example, we have targeted social behaviors such as acknowledging others' opinions in group work in a bossy child, greeting teachers and classmates by a child with Asperger's syndrome, and working cheerfully with a child with separation anxiety.

Daily report cards have been used with children of varying ages. We have used them with children as young as 3 and as old as 16. Young children often require school- and home-based consequences or school reminders in order to bridge the time delay of reinforcement. With older students, weekly, rather than daily, evaluations may be sufficient. School–home notes often are used with children and adolescents with significant conduct problems (McMahon et al., 2006).

Recent research highlights the use of daily evaluations by teachers for data collection (Chafouleas, McDougal, Riley-Tilman, Panahon, & Hilt, 2005). Specifically, daily teacher ratings can be used for intervention planning or evaluating intervention effectiveness. For example, Chafouleas et al. (2005) recommended using daily teacher evaluations as an alternative to direct observation and rating scale data. The authors suggested that daily evaluations offer a reasonably objective measurement of behavior without the time demands of observational data collection. Similarly, we often recommend that daily report card data be used by parents and teachers to measure the success of the treatment as well as to guide treatment modifications and additions. For example, we often recommend that daily behavior ratings be obtained before and after beginning medication in children with attention-deficit/hyperactivity disorder (ADHD) in order to assess medication effectiveness.

The use of daily report cards provides numerous advantages over procedures managed solely by the teacher. The procedure provides daily, objective evaluations of children's positive and negative behavior. This type of feedback allows for the delivery of more immediate, planned, and effective consequences by parents. Positive feedback provided in a daily report card encourages parents and teachers to focus on skill building and reinforcing appropriate behavior, rather than simply decreasing negative behavior. The intervention distributes responsibilities between parents and teachers and requires minimal teacher time. Teachers often are more willing to use behavior management strategies when they share the responsibility with parents (Pisecco, Huzinec, & Curtis, 2001). Another prevalent but less recognized advantage is improvements in parent–child discussions about school performance. The procedure emphasizes reviewing the note with children in a neutral manner and providing consequences in a predetermined manner. Such a procedure gives parents a clear venue for promoting positive behavior. Children often find the use of a daily report card to be a positive alternative to parents' daily questioning about classroom behavior or the occasional negative note from their teacher that must be signed by their parents (Kelley, 2003).

RESEARCH ON TREATMENT OUTCOME AND ACCEPTABILITY

Ayllon, Garber, and Pisor (1975) used a "good behavior" daily report card targeting disruptive behaviors including out-of-seat, vocalizations, and any disruptive motor activity in a third-grade classroom. Parents provided appropriate rewards on days the child's behavior warranted a "good behavior" letter. The average level of disruption decreased from 90% during baseline to zero during the treatment phase. In another study, Blechman, Taylor, and Schrader (1981) used a "good news note" to increase the consistency of performance on math class work in a group of elementary students. Teachers sent a note home on days the student's math performance equaled or exceeded performance during baseline. Parents delivered positive reinforcement on days the child received a "good news note," and math performance consistency was significantly increased.

Research has consistently shown, however, that positive consequences alone often are insufficient to obtain and maintain desired behavior in children, particularly children with ADHD (Acker & O'Leary, 1987; Forehand, 1987; Pfiffner & O'Leary, 1987; Rosen, O'Leary, Joyce, Conway, & Pfiffner, 1984). Results of these studies suggest that both positive and negative consequences are necessary to achieve optimal levels of appropriate classroom behavior. Response cost is a technique that may be incorporated into a daily report card so that a child's classroom behavior may earn positive or negative consequences. Response cost is a punishment procedure involving the loss of positive reinforcers (privileges, points, rewards) contingent on misbehavior or failure to meet specified behavioral or academic criteria (Abramowitz & O'Leary, 1991). In the case of a school–home note, a child may be instructed by the teacher to cross off a smiley face from his note contingent on inappropriate behavior. The loss of the smiley face decreases the child's chance of bringing home a "good note" for the day and earning a reward. Children are rewarded at home for minimal loss of points or "smiley faces."

McCain and Kelley (1994) compared the effectiveness of a daily report card with and without response cost in improving the classroom performance of three fourth-grade boys. On-task, off-task, and disruptive behaviors were targeted. Parents were instructed to reward good notes with positive reinforcement according to a contract that outlined contingencies for reinforcement. In addition, the daily report cards with response cost required parents to provide consequences contingent on satisfactory on-task behavior and minimal loss of response cost points. All three students showed decreases in off-task behavior and exhibited low, stabilized levels of disruptive behavior during the response-cost intervention as compared with the traditional school–home note.

Kelley and McCain (1995) found similar results in a study that compared the effectiveness of a daily report card with and without response cost for increasing academic productivity and appropriate classroom behavior in five elementary-age children. Both notes included the target behaviors "completed classwork satisfactorily" and "used classtime well." The note used during the response-cost condition had the addition of five smiley faces on the page. Teachers instructed students to mark off a smiley face each time they were reprimanded for being off-task or behaving disruptively. Parents provided rewards contingent on satisfactory ratings and minimal loss of smiley faces in this condition. Both appropriate classroom behavior and academic productivity increased in all five children who received the intervention. In three of the subjects, the inclusion of the response cost component led to significantly greater improvement.

Jurbergs, Palcic, and Kelley (2007b) compared the effectiveness of similar daily report cards with and without response cost in improving the classroom performance of six African American first and second graders from impoverished backgrounds, who also were diagnosed with ADHD. Again, both on-task classroom behavior and academic productivity increased for all participants during treatment phases. In addition, accurate classwork completion increased substantially. However, there were no consistent added benefits of the response–cost component. The response–cost component was more effective in improving behavior for two participants, whereas the no-response–cost note was more effective for one participant. The other three, however, showed no differential effectiveness of the two treatments.

More recently, Jurbergs et al. (2007a) evaluated whether parent involvement is an essential component of daily report cards, or whether teacher evaluation and feedback is sufficient to improve children's behavior. The effectiveness of a daily report card with parent delivered consequences was compared with a daily report card with teacher feedback and no parent delivered consequences. The study evaluated the classroom behavior of 43 African American, low-income first through third graders with ADHD. The results indicated that the daily report card with home-based consequences was superior to the teacher-feedback-only condition, although both were significantly more effective than no treatment.

Palcic, Jurbergs, and Kelley (2007) compared the efficacy of daily report cards with home- or classroom-delivered consequences in increasing classroom on-task behavior and academic productivity of low-income African American children with ADHD. Results indicated that the two interventions were equally effective in improving children's on-task behavior and classwork productivity, suggesting that classroom-based interventions may be substituted for home-based daily report card interventions when parents are unable to provide consistent consequences.

A number of studies have examined the treatment acceptability of daily report cards. For example, Pisecco et al. (2001) found that teachers preferred daily report cards over other commonly used methods of managing children's classroom behavior (response cost, classroom lottery, and medication). Additionally, the interview data collected at the conclusion of the previously detailed two studies indicated that school–home notes were highly acceptable to all teachers, parents, and students involved. School–home notes with response cost, however, were preferred over notes without (Jurbergs et al., 2007b), and daily report cards with parent-delivered consequences were preferred over those without (Jurbergs et al., 2007a).

IMPLEMENTING A DAILY REPORT CARD

Kelley (1990) detailed procedures for establishing a daily report system. Additional reviews of the literature and discussions about implementing the procedure are found in later works (e.g., Kelley, 2003).

Step 1: Discuss the Procedure With Parents and Teachers

The possibility of using a daily report card typically begins when parents or teachers bring a concern about a student's behavior to a professional. After determining that the child is likely to respond to increased feedback and predictable consequences, use of the procedure is discussed with parents and teachers. During initial discussions, teachers should be encouraged to describe target behaviors. Both teachers and parents should be encouraged to focus on problem solving rather than diagnosis or etiology.

Step 2: Define Target Behaviors

Whenever possible, define target behaviors in terms of increasing good behavior, rather than decreasing bad behavior. For example, instead of targeting number of times tardy to class, target number of times the child arrived on time to class. Target behaviors should be relevant to academic success and occur frequently throughout the day. Common target behaviors include followed directions, turned in completed homework, completed classwork, used time wisely, talked only with permission, kept hands to self, played nicely at recess. Target behaviors should be defined specifically, and examples and nonexamples should be generated.

Step 3: Design the Note

Daily report cards generally are used to evaluate children's behavior throughout the day. As such, target behaviors often vary as a function of the setting. It is best to evaluate children's behavior at small intervals of time such as specific class periods or settings such as recess, lunch, or center time. Depending on the child's target behaviors, the intervals may include transition periods, such as walking in line or being prepared for class. Each behavior is evaluated using specific criteria. With younger children, we often use a happy, neutral, and sad face. For older children the evaluation criteria might be "good," "fair," and " poor" or "yes," "so-so" and "no." Each criterion should be defined and examples derived.

The actual report card should include the child's name and date as well as a space for parents to write comments or ask questions. We encourage parents to write a comment on the note each day so that the teacher is kept abreast of consequences provided at home on the basis of the evaluation. It is recommended that a group of blank notes be placed in a colorful folder. This allows for review of completed notes by parents and teachers so that progress can be monitored easily.

As discussed previously, response cost can be incorporated into the note. We recommend using a series of happy faces or numbers that are crossed off when the child exhibits a negative behavior. Teachers should be instructed to deliver reprimands in a calm manner and in close proximity to the child. With younger children, we sometimes place laminated happy faces in a small sack attached to the child. A face is removed from the sack when a targeted misbehavior occurs. The number of faces remaining during the interval is recorded on the note to be brought home.

Step 4: Prepare the Child

Before using a daily report card, the intervention should be explained thoroughly to the child. It is sometimes helpful to include children in the development of the procedure. Teacher, parent, and student responsibilities should be delineated and discussed in detail. Professionals should emphasize that daily report cards are intended to replace primarily negative discussions about school behavior with a more positive system. Some children are embarrassed about being singled out in the classroom. In these instances, care should be given to provide feedback discretely. Alternatively, teachers can e-mail parents the information, although this usually reduces teachers' feedback to students.

Step 5: Determine Consequences

Consequences should be determined by the child and parent and described in a behavioral contract. Behavioral contracting involves specifying specific behaviors that earn well defined consequences. Rewards often include activities or privileges typically enjoyed by the child, such as TV or computer time, dessert, or a slightly later bedtime. In addition, we recommend that rewards include additional privileges, such as money or special time with parents. Weekly rewards often consist of a preferred activity for consistently reaching daily goals. Often, daily report cards are welcomed by the child, as they can be used to reinstate privileges that were removed because of unacceptable classroom behavior.

Predetermined sanctions may be useful, such as writing an age-appropriate essay on the consequences of negative behavior exhibited and positive alternatives or performing an extra chore. Sanctions are helpful when the withdrawal of privileges is insufficient and are given when the child does not meet criteria for rewards.

Step 6: Begin Using the Daily Report Card

Copies of the daily report card should be placed in a notebook or folder. Leaving completed forms in the notebook allows for easy review of the child's progress. Initially, children should be rewarded for simply bringing the note home and discussing ratings constructively. We recommend obtaining a week of baseline data prior to establishing performance goals.

Step 7: Review the Note With the Child

Parents should review the note with the child from top to bottom. This allows parents to review all aspects of the child's day, rather than focus excessively on negative behavior. We suggest parents spend as much time discussing positive behavior and how the behavior can be repeated in the future as discussing negative behavior. Misbehavior should be discussed in a neutral manner, and parents should problem-solve with their children about how to improve their behavior. For example, if a student fails to hand in his homework, his parent might discuss how to improve the student's organizational system. As consequences are predetermined, there is no need to nag or excessively focus on negative behavior.

Step 8: Provide Promised Consequences

Parents should be strongly encouraged to provide promised consequences. It is helpful to record the consequences so that the child clearly knows how many days during the week she reached her performance goals. This also allows the therapist or counselor to review parent follow-through.

Generally, we recommend that children earn rewards for small improvements in behavior. One easy method of setting a performance criterion is to reward receiving no more than a specific number of "no's" for behavior ratings.

Step 9: Monitor Effectiveness

It is critical to review treatment effectiveness approximately 1 week after beginning the procedure. This allows for the therapist or counselor to make adjustments in the procedure and assist the family in determining performance criteria. The professional should discuss methods of improving behavior and encourage the continued use of the daily report card. For example, if the student tends to misbehave in a particular class, possible solutions, such as changing seats, are discussed. The therapist should also discuss whether the intervention was implemented with integrity. It is important to determine whether rewards are provided appropriately.

Daily report cards often lead to improved classroom behavior, more effective parent involvement, and reduced family conflict. However, when ineffective, professionals should reassess the appropriateness of the intervention and examine the reasons for the lack of progress. Sometimes, the procedure must be combined with other interventions, such as the use of medication for a child with ADHD.

Step 10: Fade the Note When Behavior Improves

When behavior improves to appropriate levels, the daily report card can be faded by first shifting to a weekly note. Using a weekly note, the teacher rates the child for the entire week, and the child earns weekly consequences. If success with the weekly system is maintained, the child should be able to earn complete cessation of the system. For some children, fading the daily report card is not possible. This is especially true with children with ADHD who often require salient, relatively immediate consequences to maintain desired behavior. Often, the daily report card is necessary to maintain optimal levels of positive behavior.

SUMMARY

Daily report cards may not be effective with all children. Use of the procedure requires children to respond to delayed consequences delivered at home. Children who require more consequences are not appropriate candidates for the procedure except when it is combined with other interventions. Also, daily report cards should only be used with children capable of performing the targeted behavior. Daily report cards also may be ineffective when parents are unable or unwilling to provide consequences in a contingent, predictable manner. Finally, daily reports are unlikely to be effective with depressed children or with those youth whose behavior generally is poorly managed by their parents.

REFERENCES

Abramowitz, A. J., & O'Leary, S. G. (1991). Behavioral interventions for the classroom: Implications for students with ADHD. *School Psychology Review, 20,* 220–234.

Acker, M. M., & O'Leary, S. G. (1987). Effects of reprimands and praise on appropriate behavior in the classroom. *Journal of Abnormal Child Psychology, 15,* 549–557.

Ayllon, T., Garber, S., & Pisor, K. (1975). The elimination of discipline problems through a combined school-home motivational system. *Behavior Therapy, 6,* 616–626.

Blechman, E. A., Kotanchik, N. L., & Taylor, C. J. (1981). Families and schools together: Early behavioral intervention with high-risk children. *Behavior Therapy, 12,* 308–319.

Blechman, E. A., Taylor, C. J., & Schrader, S. M. (1981). Family problem solving versus home notes as early intervention with high-risk children. *Journal of Consulting and Clinical Psychology, 49,* 919–926.

Chafouleas, S. M., McDougal, J. L., Riley-Tilman, T. C., Panahon, C. J., & Hilt, A. M. (2005). What do daily behavior report cards (DBRCs) measure? An initial comparison of DBRCs with direct observation for off-task behavior. *Psychology in the Schools, 42,* 669–676.

Christenson, S. L., Hurely, C. M., Sheridan, S. M., & Fenstermacher, K. (1997). Parents' and school psychologists' perspectives on parent involvement activities. *School Psychology Review, 26,* 111–130.

Forehand, R. (1987). Parental positive reinforcement with deviant children: Does it make a difference? *Child and Family Behavior Therapy, 8,* 19–25.

Jurbergs, N., Palcic, J., & Kelley, M. L. (2007a). *Daily behavior report cards with and without home-based consequences: Improving classroom behavior in low-income, African American children with ADHD.* Manuscript submitted for publication.

Jurbergs, N., Palcic, J., & Kelley, M. L. (2007b). School-home notes with and without response cost: Increasing attention and academic performance in low-income, ADHD children. *School Psychology Quarterly, 22,* 358–379.

Keith, T. Z., Keith, P. B., Quirk, K. J., Sperduto, J., Santillo, S., & Killings, S. (1998). Longitudinal effects of parent involvement on high school grades: Similarities and differences across gender and ethnic groups. *Journal of School Psychology, 36,* 335–363.

Kelley, M. L. (1990). *School-home notes: Promoting children's classroom success.* New York: Guilford.

Kelley, M. L. (2003). Daily report cards: Home-school contingency management procedures. In W. O'Donohue, J. E. Fisher, & S. C. Hayes (Eds.), *Cognitive behavior therapy: Applying empirically supported techniques in your practice* (pp. 114–120). Hoboken, NJ: Wiley.

Kelley, M. L., & McCain, A. P. (1995). Promoting academic performance in inattentive children: The relative efficacy of school-home notes with and without response cost. *Behavior Modification, 19,* 357–375.

McCain, A. P., & Kelley, M. L. (1994). Improving classroom performance in underachieving preadolescents: The additive effects of response cost to a school-home note system. *Child & Family Behavior Therapy, 16,* 27–41.

McMahon, R. J., Wells, K. C., & Kotler, J. S. (2006). Conduct problems. In E. J. Mash & R. A. Barkley (Eds.), *Treatment of childhood disorders* (3rd ed., pp. 137–268). New York: Guilford.

Palcic, J., Jurbergs, N., & Kelley, M. L. (2007). *Managing the classroom behavior of children with ADHD using home and classroom based contingencies: A low-income African American sample.* Manuscript submitted for publication.

Pfiffner, L. J., & O'Leary, S. G. (1987). The efficacy of all-positive management as a function of the prior use of negative consequences. *Journal of Applied Behavior Analysis, 20,* 265–271.

Pisecco, S., Huzinec, C., & Curtis, D. (2001). The effect of child characteristics on teachers' acceptability of classroom-based behavioral strategies and psychostimulant medication for the treatment of ADHD. *Journal of Clinical Child Psychology, 30,* 413–421.

Rosen, L. A., O'Leary, S. G., Joyce, S. A., Conway, G., & Pfiffner, L. J. (1984). The importance of prudent negative consequences for maintaining the appropriate behavior of hyperactive students. *Journal of Abnormal Child Psychology, 12,* 581–604.

15

SELF-MODELING

THOMAS J. KEHLE AND MELISSA A. BRAY

The intent of this chapter is to provide basic information about an intervention that involves spaced observations of video images of oneself engaged in adaptive behavior. The goal is to acquaint the reader with the design and application of self-modeling; to provide evidence for its efficacy, generalization, and maintenance; and to suggest why self-modeling is efficacious in altering behavior.

Dowrick (1999) convincingly argued that self-modeling is in concert with the assumptions of social cognitive, operant conditioning, and learned optimism theories. Consequently, it is appropriate to "consider the observation of one's behavior to be a learning mechanism in its own right, not a special case of observational learning . . . and that it functions to increase the future likelihood of that behavior" (Dowrick, p. 36).

Dowrick (1999) defined the term *self-modeling* as "an intervention procedure using the observation of images of oneself engaged in adaptive behavior" (p. 23). As Dowrick (1999) indicated, there are various forms of self-modeling, including imaginal self-modeling or mental rehearsal, imaginal peer-modeling, picture prompts or pictorial self-management, and self-observation afforded through in vivo, audio, and biblio self-modeling. These all evidence moderate positive effects, whereas video self-modeling consistently realizes substantially more pronounced effects. This is most probably

231

due to using the individual as his or her own model and consequently maximizing similarity to, and identification with, the model (Bandura, 1986; Braaksma, Rijlaarsdam, & van den Bergh, 2002; Dowrick, 1999). In addition, it is assumed that positive modification of one's behavior as a result of self-modeling may cause an alteration of cognitive processes such that these cognitions become consistent with the newly acquired observed behaviors (Kehle, Cressy, & Owen, 1990). For example, as Kehle, Hintze, and DuPaul (1997) suggested, children may enhance their feelings of self-efficacy by seeing themselves perform successfully in that such provides explicit information on how to behave, resulting in promoting the belief in one's capability (Bandura, 1997). "Observing an image of oneself produces a different reaction from observing someone else in the identical context. With a self-image, one pays much more attention, and if demonstrated behavior is valued, it provides an obvious source of self-belief" (Dowrick, 1999, p. 24). This notion that behavior precedes feeling, or in the case of self-modeling seeing oneself behave in an adaptive and successful manner, was a significant postulate of B. F. Skinner's (1964) behaviorism.

Specifically, Skinner harshly criticized and denied the ubiquitous belief that supports the "causal effect of self-concept on behavior, labeling it rather an epiphenomenon; that is, a set of self-descriptive verbal behaviors that follows rather than causes, crucial behaviors" (Kehle & Barclay, 1979, p. 47). Perhaps it is more efficacious to suggest that in order to effect meaningful and enduring behavioral change, one must first engineer the environment that allows the child to experience the behavior, or see him- or herself exhibiting the behavior, which then strengthens the child's belief that he or she can successfully execute the behavior in the future.

Typically, the child's behavior is recorded to video, which is then edited to construct a 2- to 4-minute treatment video depicting the desired outcome. The edited video is viewed by the child between six to eight times over a span of 4 to 6 weeks (Kehle, Bray, & Chafouleas, 2001). The rationale for spacing the viewings is based on the research finding that for a given amount of study time, spaced presentations of the material will yield substantially better results than would a single massed presentation. "The spacing effect is one of the most studied and remarkable phenomena to emerge in the 100-year history of research on learning" (Dempster, 1988, p. 627). The spacing effect is potent and reliable in that even as few as two spaced presentations are approximately twice as effective as two massed presentations; further, the effect is ubiquitous in that it occurs in almost all learning paradigms (Dempster, 1988).

In self-modeling research, the edited intervention videos are usually presented to the subject on several occasions over a space of time. It is assumed that there exists an optimal number of spacings and an optimal interval of time or gaps between them. Although this aspect of self-modeling has not yet been investigated, there is relevant evidence gleaned from studies on increasing retention without increasing study time. In experiments conducted by Rohrer and Pashler (2007), it was demonstrated "that powerful spacing effects occur over practically meaningful time periods" (p. 185). Furthermore, they found that performance is heavily dependent on the duration of the spacing gap. Brief gaps are less effective than longer gaps. It appears that the longer the spacing gap, the greater the long-term retention of previously learned material. Rohrer and Pashler also suggested that long-term retention is enhanced when the spacing gaps are distributed sporadically.

In addition to sporadically distributed spaced viewings of the edited intervention video, rather than showing the same identical video six to eight times to the child, several different brief edited segments depicting the same desired behavior are presented. On the basis of anecdotal evidence, Kehle, Bray, Margiano, Theodore, and Zhou (2002) believed that such increases the child's attention to the video.

Essentially, there are two types of self-models used, which Dowrick (1999) termed *positive self-review* and *feedforward*. In constructing a positive self-review intervention video, there is an attempt to maximize the performance or behavior by using rehearsal, prompts, incentives, etc., and then editing out any unwanted material. The resulting edited intervention video depicts exemplary and adaptive behavior: "the best the individual has been able to produce thus far" (Dowrick, 1999, p. 25). Dowrick believes positive self-review is "suited to improving the rate of a behavior that is below its desired level . . . whether it has been newly learned, or to reestablish a behavior that failed to maintain" (p. 25). Positive self-review can also be described as essentially the enhancement of existing behavior. As cited in Dowrick, B. F. Skinner stated that perhaps the best way to get a baseball player out of a batting slump is not to show videos of him striking out, but to show him instead "a short film of himself hitting home runs. A videotape device in the back of the dugout could have short cassettes for each player" (Epstein, 1980, p. 6).

Dowrick's (1999) feedforward implies the use of the self-modeling intervention to promote a skill or behavior "not yet acquired or previously demonstrated in a challenging context" (p. 25). Feedforward typically includes the components of existing behavior rearranged in a novel order or context (Dowrick, 1999). Feedforward can be described as using self-modeling to facilitate the acquisition of novel behaviors that the individual is capable of achieving.

As demonstrated by an early study conducted by Hosford and Johnson (1983), the effects of viewing an edited video of appropriate-only behavior are quite different from those of viewing a video that includes both the individual's appropriate and inappropriate behavior. Both procedures reduced some maladaptive behavior; however, the viewing of appropriate-only video resulted in immediate and substantial reduction of all inappropriate behavior. Hosford and Johnson suggested that viewing only positive or desired behaviors, in contrast to the more commonly used feedback method that includes both negative and positive comments, may be most effective.

EFFICACY OF SELF-MODELING

Self-modeling has been used successfully as an intervention to reduce stuttering (Bray & Kehle, 1996, 1999, 2001), increase reading fluency (Bray, Kehle, Spackman, & Hintze, 1998), reduce depressive symptoms in adolescents (Kahn, Kehle, Jenson, & Clark, 1990), increase on-task behavior (Clare, Jenson, Kehle, & Bray, 2000), increase classroom participation (Hartley, Bray, & Kehle, 1998), reduce disruptive classroom behavior (Kehle et al., 2002; Kehle, Clark, Jenson, & Wampold, 1986; Possell, Kehle, McLoughlin, & Bray, 1999), eliminate selective mutism (Kehle et al., 1990; Kehle, Madaus, Baratta, & Bray, 1998), reduce tic behavior in children with Tourette's syndrome (Clarke, Bray, Kehle, & Truscott, 2001), and improve basketball jump shooting skills in college athletics (Lee, Garrett, Kehle, & Douglas, 1997). In fact, the efficacy of self-modeling has been demonstrated in over 200 published studies examining myriad behaviors using varied research methodologies (see Dowrick, 1999, and Hitchcock, Dowrick, & Prater, 2003, for a comprehensive review of applications for self-modeling). Furthermore, it has been used to address behavior problems that have been historically resistant to change. Moreover, given the amount of time and effort on the part of either the subject or the interventionist, self-modeling is a relatively quick and nonintrusive intervention.

The following studies are presented to illustrate the procedures that we have used to address challenging behaviors that have been historically resistant to change.

Disruptive Classroom Behavior

Kehle et al. (1986) used self-modeling to reduce the disruptive, hyperactive, and aggressive behaviors of four 10- to 13-year-old boys placed in a self-contained special education classroom. The study used an A (baseline) B (intervention) A (withdrawal of intervention) design replicated across three children with a control child and follow-up phase. These children were selected by the teacher and described as the "most disruptive and inattentive in the class" (p. 290). They were in a class of 12 that included 9 boys and 3 girls. The special education teacher and her aide used a token economy with a response cost in an attempt to establish classroom control. This procedure was woefully ineffective in that baseline data indicated that the four boys evidenced maladaptive classroom behavior approximately 50% to 60% of the time. The three experimental children were videotaped in the classroom. These videotapes were then edited to remove all instances of touching, vocalizing, aggression, playing, disorienting, making noise, and being out of seat. These seven behaviors were collapsed and composed the dependent measure termed *disruptive behavior*. The occurrence of any one of the seven disruptive behaviors during a 30-minute session consisting of 120 continuous 15-second intervals was recorded.

The four data collection phases of the study were baseline, edited tape intervention, no tape, and follow-up. Baseline data were collected in vivo during regularly scheduled afternoon classes usually involving history, reading, and science. After baseline, each of the four students' behavior was videotaped during the afternoon class sessions. The three experimental students' videotapes were then edited to omit all instances of the seven disruptive behaviors. The intervention consisted of each student individually viewing their respective edited intervention tapes depicting exemplary classroom behavior on five occasions over a period of approximately 3 weeks. The control student on four occasions viewed his unedited tape, which depicted his typical disruptive, hyperactive, and aggressive behaviors. Immediately after viewing their respective tapes, the student was returned to the classroom and his behavior was recorded. "The self-modeling intervention had an immediate and dramatic effect on the experimental students' classroom behavior as evidenced by the observation that none of the data points in the edited tape intervention phase overlapped the baselines" (Kehle et al., 1986, p. 293). However, the control student, who viewed an unedited tape of his disruptive classroom behavior, evidenced almost total out-of-control behavior. This was anticipated in that he viewed his unedited tape, which included a substantial number of inappropriate classroom behaviors.

Moreover, during the subsequent third or no-tape phase of the study, the three experimental students maintained their appropriate classroom behavior. That is, their behavior did not return to baseline levels. This nonrecovery was most probably due to a "behavior trap," suggesting that the behavior was now under the control of different environmental contingencies and essentially irreversible (Hartmann & Atkinson, 1973, p. 590). Also, during phase three, the control student was presented an edited tape of himself depicting appropriate-only classroom behavior that immediately resulted in a substantial decrease of misbehavior and an increase of adaptive behavior. These treatment effects were maintained at a 6-week follow-up.

Selective Mutism

Selective mutism is characterized by the lack of speech in specific settings in which speech is expected; however, the individual is fully capable of normal speech and exhibits such in other settings. With regard to children, selective mutism is often associated with the school or school-related environments. It is a particularly intractable and rare disorder that tends to worsen the longer the condition persists (Kehle & Bray, 1998; Kehle, Bray, &

Theodore, 2006). Selective mutism is often accompanied with other features, including extreme shyness, withdrawal, social isolation, anxiety, and oppositional defiant behaviors (American Psychiatric Association, 2000). Although these instances are relatively rare, selective mutism has also been associated with diurnal enuresis, intentional vomiting, and reluctant and strained ambulation (Kehle et al., 1998).

Selective mutism's resistance to intervention, and consequently its persistence, makes it a very challenging condition to treat. Remschmidt, Poller, Herpertz-Dahlman, Hennighausen, and Gutenbrunner (2001), in a 12-year longitudinal study, noted that only 39% of children with selective mutism evidenced a complete remission. To complicate matters, the cause of selective mutism remains obscure but most probably involves a genetic predisposition (Black & Uhde, 1995) and likely does not involve trauma (Shipon-Blum, 2002).

Kehle and his colleagues (Kehle et al., 1990, 1997, 1998) have used a form of augmented self-modeling that has been relatively successful in addressing selective mutism. It was assumed that the augmentation of the self-modeling intervention with behavioral and cognitively based components improved the reliability and potency of the intervention. Suggestions for augmenting self-modeling include the use of "the spacing effect," "mystery motivator," "peer expectations," "controlled self-reinforcement," and "successive approximations."

Due to the dearth of published studies that have employed augmented self-modeling to treat children with selective mutism, the following step-by-step procedural outline is presented:

1. Consult with the child's parent in order to prepare approximately 10 to 12 questions that will be used in the production of the self-modeling edited videos. If possible, these questions should require more than a one-word response from the child. The parent is instructed to practice the questions in the home setting until the child readily responds to the questions. Also, the parent is instructed to use successive approximations to ensure that the child responds to the questions at increasingly closer proximity to the school grounds.

2. Near the end of the school day, and in a general class setting, the teacher is instructed to ask the questions beginning with #1 sequentially through #10 or #12 of classmates that have parental permission to be video recorded and involved in the intervention. Typically the procedure is to have the teacher ask the question #1 and call on one classmate to respond to question #1, than the same question is presented to the child with selective mutism (CSM), and finally the same question is asked of another classmate. This sequence is video recorded.

This procedure is repeated using other classmates until all 10 or 12 questions have been asked. To facilitate editing, it is important to instruct the teacher to pause for approximately 3 to 4 seconds after asking each question. This also allows the individual doing the video recording to focus back on the teacher asking the same question directed at the subsequent classmate. When recording the expected nonresponse of the CSM, the camera should focus on his or her head and shoulders. This whole sequence of videotaping should take approximately 20 to 30 minutes.

3. At the end of the school day and after the children have been dismissed and buses have left, have the mother or another person who freely converses with the CSM come into the classroom and ask the child the same questions, retaining the sequence and pausing approximately 3 to 4 seconds after the question is asked and after the child responds (e.g., the pausing makes the editing much easier). The camera is focused on the child's head and shoulders. More often than not, the camera will need to be positioned on a tripod and focused directly on the child with any recording indicator masked. The child's verbal responses should be comparable with the baseline that is most often evidenced in the home setting.

4. The video is edited to construct approximately five 2- to 3-minute edited intervention videos depicting the child appropriately responding supposedly to the teacher's questions during general class activities.

5. The first intervention session involves the interventionist, the school psychologist or social worker, having the child with selective mutism view his or her first 2- to 3-minute edited intervention video depicting exemplary responses to the teacher's questions. This viewing is conducted in a private office or room.

The child is instructed to pause the video whenever the child hears him- or herself responding to the teacher's questions. If this occurs, the child is then allowed to choose from six or seven small wrapped presents (selected, purchased, and wrapped by the parent) arrayed directly in front of the CSM (e.g., self-reinforcement).

Immediately after viewing the intervention video, the CSM is returned to the classroom and the interventionist addresses the class, with the CSM present, to explain to them why they were video recorded (e.g., to help the CSM to talk in school and have more fun) and also to explain the mystery motivator. A mystery motivator is a facsimile of a desired reinforcer (comparable to a birthday present, and selected and purchased by the parent) that is placed in a manila envelope with a question mark and the child's name on it. This envelope containing the reinforcer is taped to the blackboard. The child is instructed that he or she can gain access to the contents of the envelope on the condition that he or she displays the desired behavior as depicted on the edited intervention tape (i.e., asking the teacher in a normal conversational tone to allow him or her to have the contents of the mystery motivator). The mystery motivator is designed to increase the child's anticipation and value of the reinforcement (Jenson, Rhode, & Reavis, 1994).

6. The second intervention session occurs after a week or so has elapsed since the first intervention session. This sporadic spacing of the viewing takes advantage of the spacing effect. The CSM along with a classmate that has been judged as a friend, along with the interventionist and school psychologist or social worker, all view the second 2- to 3-minute intervention video. Assuming that the CSM pauses the video at those points where he or she is depicted on the video answering the teacher's questions, the CSM is allowed to choose one wrapped small gift that he or she is allowed to unwrap. The CSM is then asked to describe the gift to his or her friend. This procedure is repeated throughout the 2- to 3-minute video. The friend, at the end of the session, is also allowed to pick a wrapped gift (the parent of CSM selects, buys, and wraps the gift).

   Immediately after the session, the CSM and friend are returned to the classroom. However, before they enter the classroom, the two children are instructed to put their gifts into their backpacks. With prior permission from the CSM, and with a brief explanation to CSM's classmates, the entire class is shown the five brief intervention videos. This procedure tends to increase peer expectations for the CSM to engage in normal speech.

7. The self-modeling intervention sessions 3 through 6 are sporadically spaced over the next 6 to 8 weeks or until the CSM evidences expected speech within school-related settings that is comparable to the quality of speech evidenced in the home.

Behaviors Associated With Autism Spectrum Disorders

Autism spectrum disorders (ASD) have also been historically resistant to intervention. For the most part, applied behavior analysis has been the treatment of choice to address the myriad of disorders affecting the development of social communication, adaptive, and behavioral functioning characteristic of ASD. (See Wilczynski, Fisher, Christian, & Logue, chap. 20 of this volume, for a thorough review of school-based behavioral interventions for children with ASD.) However, interventions that have used self-modeling, which are less intrusive and require substantially less investment of time and financial resources, have also demonstrated impressive results. Specifically, self-modeling has been used to increase social initiations, verbal responsiveness, on-task and initiating behaviors (Buggery, 2005; Hagiwara & Myles, 1999; Sherer et al., 2001) and functional behaviors such as hand washing, shaving, making beds, and hanging clothing (Lasater & Brady, 1995). It has also been used to reduce off-task behaviors (Coyle & Cole, 2004), pushing, and tantrums (Buggery, 2005). These and other self-modeling studies were included in a meta-analysis that compared video self-modeling with video modeling (Bellini & Akullian, 2007). The results of their analysis indicated that both video modeling and video self-modeling were effective for "addressing social-communication skills, functional skills, and behavioral functioning" (Bellini & Akullian, 2007, p. 264) in children with autism spectrum disorders. Further, both video modeling and video self-modeling promoted skill acquisition, and these skills were maintained over time and transferred across persons and settings (Bellini & Akullian, 2007). It is perplexing why they did not find differences between these two different strategies in favor of video self-modeling. Of the 22 studies, only 7 examined the effects of video self-modeling, and this relatively small number of video self-modeling studies may not have been adequate to discern any differences between the two types of modeling interventions. Also, as discussed by Bellini and Akullian, a significant weakness of their study was that it included few studies that examined the unique effects of either video modeling or video self-modeling. Most of the studies included in their meta-analysis also had additional intervention strategies. Perhaps, as stated by Sherer et al. (2001), authors of one of the studies included in the meta-analysis, video self-modeling "was most effective for the children . . . who enjoyed watching themselves on video, and who demonstrated prior preference for visual learning, such as video viewing and the use of video support strategies" (Bellini & Akullian, 2007, p. 281).

Nevertheless, Bellini and Akullian's (2007) meta-analysis included 23 peer-reviewed studies involving 73 children with autism spectrum disorders. These studies were conducted by 20 primary researchers in 16 different geographical locations, and in accord with Horner et al. (2005), their results clearly surpass criteria for designation of both video modeling and video self-modeling as evidenced-based practices.

DOES SELF-MODELING ALTER MEMORIES?

Dowrick (1999) attributed the dramatic results brought about through self-modeling to a form of learning in its own right. This learning involves "the observation of one's adaptive or valued behavior, and that through self-observation the probability of the future occurrence of that behavior is increased" (Kehle et al., 2002, p. 205). However, Kehle et al. suggested a plausible alternative to Dowrick's explanation in that repeated and spaced observations of "oneself engaged in either valued or not valued behavior may alter the individual's memory of whether or not s/he previous performed that behavior. Moreover, this distortion of memory may function to increase the probability of the future occurrence of that behavior" (p. 205). Simply stated, self-modeling not only alters maladaptive behavior, it also alters the memory of that maladaptive behavior.

This assumption has gradually developed as a consequence of several 6- to 9-month follow-up interviews with children who were successfully treated for selective mutism. Amazingly, these children typically had little or no awareness of themselves actually being mute. A dramatic example of this alternation of memory was recently revealed in a case of a 7-year-old child with selective mutism named Vicky (pseudonym). By coincidence, Kehle also successfully treated Vicky's sister, Tammy (pseudonym) 10 years earlier. Tammy is now 17 and is a freshman in college. Vicky who is now in the second grade has not uttered, to anyone's knowledge, a single word in the classroom or any other school-related settings since enrolling in kindergarten. The mother stated that during the initial parent-teacher meeting, attended also by Vicky and Tammy, Vicky did not respond to any of the teacher's questions, nor would she respond to her mother's or Tammy's questions. Tammy became upset and shouted at her sister, "What is wrong with you? Are you nuts? Why don't you answer?" The mother was amazed and outside of the school setting queried Tammy with regard to her own selective mutism that was treated when she was also in the second grade. Tammy had no recollection of herself being selectively mute and remained irritated with her sister's nonresponsive and "embarrassing" behavior.

The alteration of memories of past events has been clearly demonstrated by numerous studies (Schacter, 1995, 1999); in fact, it is relatively easy to "create complex and elaborate false memories in the minds of research subjects, and that these subjects are confident that these false memories are real" (Loftus, 1997, p. 61).

As suggested by Kehle et al. (2002) and Margiano (2006), the procedure used in the self-modeling intervention is almost identical to that used in experiments that are designed to alter subjects' memories (Goff & Roediger, 1998). The edited intervention video (a) depicts sensory, perceptual, semantic, and contextual details and information; (b) conveys vivid imagery that approximates actual experience; (c) includes positive-only information and omits all negative information that may more readily influence impression formation and decision making; (d) involves spacing of repeated viewings of the positive behavior and thus allows time to elapse to attenuate the original memory trace; (e) conveys both images and narratives; (f) itself suggests a documented and objective source of reality; (g) promotes familiarity of misinformation; (h) depicts autobiographical events; and, finally, (i) exploits "choice supportive memory distortion" in remembering past decisions.

According to Margiano (2006), "self-modeling provides sufficient cognitive, perceptual, contextual, semantic, and affective information to closely approximate a 'true' memory, and facilitate source misattribution, suggestibility, biases, and thereby, memory alteration/implantation" (p. 1). As Kehle et al. (2002) indicated,

> behavior change elicited through self-modeling intervention may be mediated by alteration of the individual's memory for performance of the target behavior. That is, repeated observation of one's self engaged in adaptive or valued behavior may alter the individual's memory of having performed that behavior, with such memory distortion subsequently serving to increase the probability of the future performance of the target behavior." (Margiano, 2006, p. 3)

Perhaps all changes in human functioning (e.g., behavior, attitudes, values, knowledge,), brought about by any means including education, psychotherapy, chance, illness, result in a diminishment of memories of that functioning and enhancement of memories of newly acquired functioning.

SUMMARY

In summary, video self-modeling, a relatively quick and nonintrusive intervention is a form of learning that commonly results in substantial and relatively enduring change in a myriad of behaviors including those that have been historically resistant to change. The observation of oneself performing adaptive behaviors increases the likelihood of the future occurrence of those behaviors. Further, it is likely that self-modeling may also increase efficacious beliefs that parallel a simultaneous decrease in memories of oneself formally engaging in maladaptive behavior.

REFERENCES

American Psychiatric Association. (2000). *Diagnostic and statistical manual of mental disorders* (4th ed., text rev.). Washington, DC: Author.

Bandura, A. (1986). *Social foundations of thought and action: A social-cognitive theory.* Englewood Cliffs, NJ: Prentice Hall.

Bandura, A. (1997). *Self-efficacy: The exercise of control.* New York: Freeman.

Bellini, S., & Akullian, J. (2007). A meta-analysis of video modeling and video self-modeling interventions for children and adolescents with autism spectrum disorders. *Exceptional Children, 73,* 264–287.

Black, B., & Uhde, T. W. (1995). Treatment of elective mutism with fluoxetine: A double-blind, placebo-controlled study. *Journal of the American Academy of Child and Adolescent Psychiatry, 33*, 100–106.

Braaksma, M. A. H., Rijlaarsdam, G., & van den Bergh, H. (2002). Observational learning and the effects of model-observer similarity. *Journal of Educational Psychology, 94*, 405–415.

Bray, M. A., & Kehle, T. J. (1996). Self-modeling as an intervention for stuttering. *School Psychology Review, 25*, 358–369.

Bray, M. A., & Kehle, T. J. (1999). Self-modeling as an intervention for stuttering: A replication. *School Psychology Review, 27*, 587–598.

Bray, M. A., & Kehle, T. J. (2001). Long-term effects of self-modeling as an intervention for stuttering. *School Psychology Review, 30*, 131–137.

Bray, M. A., Kehle, T. J., Spackman, V. S., & Hintze, J. M. (1998). An intervention program to increase reading fluency. *Special Services in the Schools, 14*, 105–125.

Buggery, T. (2005). Video self-modeling applications with children with autism spectrum disorder in a small private school. *Focus on Autism and Other Developmental Disabilities, 20*, 52–63.

Clare, S. K., Jenson, W. R., Kehle, T. J., & Bray, M. A. (2000). Self-modeling as a treatment for increasing on-task behavior. *Psychology in the Schools, 37*, 517–522.

Clarke, M. A., Bray, M. A., Kehle, T. J., & Truscott, S. (2001). A school-based intervention designed to reduce the frequency of tics in children with Tourette's syndrome. *School Psychology Review, 38*, 403–411.

Coyle, C., & Cole, P. (2004). A videotaped self-modeling and self-monitoring treatment program to decrease off- task behavior in children with autism. *Journal of Intellectual and Developmental Disabilities, 29*, 3–15.

Dempster, F. N. (1988). The spacing effect: A case study in the failure to apply the results of psychological research. *American Psychologist, 43*, 627–634.

Dowrick, P. W. (1999). A review of self modeling and related interventions. *Applied and Preventive Psychology, 8*, 23–39.

Epstein, R. (1980). *Notebooks of B. F. Skinner*. Englewood Cliffs, NJ: Prentice Hall.

Goff, L. M., & Roediger, H. L., III. (1998). Imagination inflation for action events: Repeated imaginings lead to illusory recollections. *Memory & Cognition, 26*, 20–33.

Hagiwara, T., & Myles, B. S. (1999). A multimedia social story intervention: Teaching skills to children with autism. *Focus on Autism and Other Developmental Disabilities, 14*, 82–95.

Hartley, E. T., Bray, M. A., & Kehle, T. J. (1998). Self-modeling as an intervention to increase student classroom participation. *Psychology in the Schools, 35*, 363–372.

Hartmann, D. P., & Atkinson, C. (1973). Having your cake and eating it too: A note on some apparent contradiction between therapeutic achievements and design requirements in N = 1 studies. *Behavior Therapy, 4*, 589–591.

Hitchcock, C. H., Dowrick, P., & Prater, M. A. (2003). Video self-modeling in school-based settings. *Remedial and Special Education, 56,* 36–45.

Horner, R. H., Carr, E. G., Halle, J., McGee, G., Odom, A., & Wolery, M. (2005). The use of single-subject research to identify evidence-based practice in special education. *Exceptional Children, 71,* 165–179.

Hosford, R. E., & Johnson, M. E. (1983). A comparison of self-observation, self-modeling, and practice without video feedback for improving interviewing behaviors. *Counselor Education and Supervision, 23,* 62–70.

Jenson, W. R., Rhode, G., & Reavis, H. K. (1994). *The tough kid tool box.* Longmont, CO: Sopris West.

Kahn, J., Kehle, T. J., Jenson, W. R., & Clark, E. (1990). Comparison of cognitive-behavioral, relaxation, and self-modeling interventions for depression among middle-school students. *School Psychology Review, 19,* 196–211.

Kehle, T. J., & Barclay, J. R. (1979). Social and behavioral characteristics of mentally handicapped students. *Journal of Research and Development in Education, 12,* 46–56.

Kehle, T. J., & Bray, M. A. (1998). Selective mutism: A handout for parents and teachers. In A. S. Canter & S. A. Caroll (Eds.), *Helping children at home and school: Handouts from your school psychologist* (pp. 263–265). Silver Spring, MD: National Association of School Psychologists.

Kehle, T. J., Bray, M. A., & Chafouleas, S. M. (2001). Effectiveness of self-modeling as an intervention for behavioral change: Or is it really the alteration of memory? *The General Psychologist, 36,* 7–8.

Kehle, T. J., Bray, M. A., Margiano, S. G., Theodore, L. A., & Zhou, Z. (2002). Self-modeling as an effective intervention for students with serious emotional disturbance: Are we modifying children's memories? *Psychology in the Schools, 39,* 203–207.

Kehle, T. J., Bray, M. A., & Theodore, L. A. (2006). Selective mutism. In G. Bear & K. Minke (Eds.), *Children's needs III* (pp. 293–302). Washington, DC: National Association of School Psychologists.

Kehle, T. J., Clark, E., Jenson, W. R., & Wampold, B. E. (1986). Effectiveness of self-observation with behavior disordered elementary school children. *School Psychology Review, 15,* 289–295.

Kehle, T. J., Cressy, E. T., & Owen, S. V. (1990). The use of self-modeling as an intervention in school psychology: A case study of an elective mute. *School Psychology Review, 19,* 115–121.

Kehle, T. J., Hintze, J. M., & DuPaul, G. J. (1997). Selective mutism. In G. Bear, K. Minke, & A. Thomas (Eds.), *Children's needs II* (pp. 197–205). Washington, DC: National Association of School Psychologists.

Kehle, T. J., Madaus, M. M. R., Baratta, V. S., & Bray, M. A. (1998). Augmented self-modeling as a treatment for children with selective mutism. *Journal of School Psychology, 36,* 247–260.

Lasater, M. W., & Brady, M. P. (1995). Effects of video self- modeling and feedback on task fluency: A home-based intervention. *Education and Treatment of Children, 18,* 389–408.

Lee, H., Garrett, G., Kehle, T. J., & Douglas, J. (1997). Use of kinematic feedback and self-modeling intervention to improve basketball jump shooting skill [Abstract]. *Journal of Sport & Exercise Psychology, 19,* 80.

Loftus, E. F. (1997). Memories for a past that never was. *Current Directions in Psychological Science, 6,* 60–65.

Margiano, S. G. (2006). *Examination of the effects of self-modeling on autobiographical memory.* Unpublished doctoral dissertation, University of Connecticut, Storrs.

Possell, L. E., Kehle, T. J., McLoughlin, C. S., & Bray, M. A. (1999). Self-modeling as an intervention to reduce inappropriate classroom behavior. *Cognitive and Behavioral Practice, 6,* 99–105.

Remschmidt, H., Poller, M., Herpertz-Dahlman, B., Hennighausen, K., & Gutenbrunner, C. (2001). A follow-up study of 45 patients with elective mutism. *European Archives of Psychology and Clinical Neuroscience, 251,* 284–296.

Rohrer, D., & Pashler, H. (2007). Increasing retention without increasing study time. *Current Directions in Psychological Science, 16,* 183–186.

Schacter, D. L. (1995). *Memory distortion: How minds, brains, and societies reconstruct the past.* Cambridge, MA: Harvard University Press.

Schacter, D. L. (1999). The seven sins of memory: Insights from psychology and cognitive neuroscience. *American Psychologist, 54,* 182–203.

Sherer, M., Pierce, K. L., Paredes, S., Kisacky, K. L., Ingersoll, B., & Schreibmen, L. (2001). Enhancing conservation skills in children with autism via video technology: Which is better, "self" or "other" as a model? *Behavioral Modification, 25,* 140–158.

Shipon-Blum, E. (2002, February). "When the words just won't come out": Understanding selective mutism [Insert]. *NASP Communiqué, 30.*

Skinner, B. F. (1964). Behaviorism as a philosophy of psychology. In T. W. Wann (Ed.), *Behaviorism and phenomenology: Contrasting bases for modern psychology* (pp. 79–108). Chicago: University of Chicago Press.

IV

CUSTOMIZING BEHAVIORAL STRATEGIES FOR SPECIAL POPULATIONS

16

PRACTICAL STRATEGIES IN WORKING WITH DIFFICULT STUDENTS

WILLIAM R. JENSON, ELAINE CLARK, AND JASON BURROW-SANCHEZ

Given the challenges facing those who work with difficult students in the schools, it is essential that educators have available proven and practical strategies to improve student behavior and student learning. Because the topic of practical strategies is very broad, it is important to first define the terms *strategy*, *practical*, and *difficult student*. Although specific childhood disorders and additional behavior-change strategies are covered elsewhere in this book, this chapter focuses on some of the research-based strategies that have been found to be very practical and effective for use with difficult students in their school.

Strategies are interventions. The term *strategy* is used interchangeably with the term *intervention* in this chapter. We define an intervention as the systematic application of research-validated procedures to change behavior through either the teaching of new skills or the manipulation of antecedents and consequences (Bowen, Jenson, & Clark, 2004). Teaching new skills as an intervention involves teaching a set of skills that are adaptive and useful for a student. Simply teaching a set of skills does not meet this definition. Some skills are taught and learned by difficult students but seldom used outside of the instructional area (e.g., teaching social skills to difficult students in a pull-out group setting without planning for generalization of the skill; Kavale, Mathur, & Mostert, 2004). Most of the time, students do not use these skills outside of the group setting. Skills must be useful for the student and naturally rewarded in the student's environment for them to be useful as an intervention.

The manipulation of antecedents and consequences is integral to the definition of an intervention. An antecedent is anything that precedes and sets the occasion for a behavior. Antecedents can be places, times, people, or specific events. Antecedent manipulation has the advantage of being less labor intensive and more time efficient than consequence manipulation; therefore, it is one of the most practical forms of intervention. One example of antecedent manipulation described in this chapter is the use of precision requests (Jenson & Reavis, 1996; Rhode, Jenson, & Reavis, 1992). With precision requests, educators can significantly reduce student noncompliance by simply changing the way they give their requests.

Consequence manipulation is more involved than antecedent manipulation but is essential for some interventions. For our purposes, consequences can be defined in three basic ways: positive reinforcement, negative reinforcement, and punishers. Positive reinforcement is any stimulus that increases and maintains a behavior. The emphasis here is the phrase "any stimulus." The same stimulus can be a reinforcer for one student and a punisher for another student. Do not assume that a stimulus (e.g., M&Ms) is reinforcing unless it increases or maintains a behavior. Several suggestions for positive reinforcement techniques such as Mystery Motivators, Chart Moves, and Reinforcement Spinners are provided in this chapter.

Punishers are any stimulus that temporarily suppresses and decreases a behavior. Verbal reprimands, loss of privileges, and loss of positive reinforcers are common examples of mild punishers. Do not assume, however that a stimulus is always a punisher. Sometimes a stimulus can be a positive reinforcer depending on its effect on a student's behavior. For example, if a teacher yells at a student to stop a behavior but the behavior actually increases, then yelling is a positive reinforcer. If the behavior is suppressed and decreases, then it is a punisher. Several cautions should be used when implementing punishers. First, because problem behaviors decrease rapidly with an effective punisher, the person implementing it is rewarded, and therefore punishers can be overused with difficult students. When this happens, the person using punishers can become a negative stimulus to be avoided by the student. A good rule of thumb for educators is that the ratio of positive to punishers should be at least four positives to one punisher (Rhode et al., 1992). Difficult students also become "immune" to the effects of punishers because they are used so frequently. Many difficult students live in an educational "sea of negativity" (Jenson, Olympia, Farley, & Clark, 2004). Because of this developed immunity, only two punishment techniques are presented in this chapter—reprimands and the "What's It Going to Be Box."

The concept of negative reinforcement is possibly the most difficult for educators to understand and is commonly confused with punishment. Negative reinforcement is any stimulus that results in an increase in a behavior to escape or avoid that stimulus. For example, a student may increase a disruptive behavior to escape (get to leave) an algebra class he or she dislikes. It has been estimated that 75% of students who frequently end up in in-school suspension have engineered their own placement there to avoid something they dislike (Jenson, Rhode, Evans, & Morgan, 2007). One of the most problematic examples of a negatively reinforced behavior is coercion or pain control, which is explained in the discussion of difficult students that follows. One unique example of negative reinforcement is the "Dots for Motivation" program described later in this chapter.

What makes an intervention practical? Practicality is essential for the use of any intervention with difficult students. Several researchers (e.g., Elliott, 1988; chap. 4, this volume) have identified important practical variables when using interventions. These variables include the effectiveness of an intervention, simplicity of use, time efficiency, low cost, and social validity. Social validity (Kazdin, 1977; Schwartz & Baer, 1991; Wolf, 1978) means that the intervention is valued and acceptable in the educational environment (community). Next to effectiveness in changing a behavior, the time to prepare and implement an intervention is one of the most important variables (Bowen et al., 2004; Elliott, 1988).

What is a difficult student? Difficult students can include special education students with emotional, intellectual, or learning disabilities, and general education students. When defining difficult students, it is important to identify behaviors that are problematic and of top concern for educators. Noncompliance (i.e., not following an adult's request) leads the list of most teachers, followed by talk-outs, aggression, being off-task, disrupting the class, and arguing and defiance (Nicholas, 1998). These behaviors are considered externalizing behaviors because they affect others external to the student as opposed to internalizing behaviors (described in chap. 18, this volume). Excessive externalizing behaviors are usually followed by self-management deficits such as contingency-governed behaviors versus rule-governed behaviors, social skills deficits, academic problems, and nonmotivation.

Behavioral excesses such as noncompliance and disruptions are easier for educators to identify and understand. Behavioral and academic deficits of difficult students are more problematic and often overlooked. The self-management deficit of being contingency governed means that difficult students are impulsively controlled by the next stimulus they encounter in their environment, such as distractions outside of a classroom window, peer attention, or the opportunity to misbehave between classes. Most nondifficult students are rule- or value-governed in that they use internalized rules they have learned to help govern their behaviors. Difficult students are impulsively controlled by people, places, or events in their immediate environment. This implies two things about managing difficult students. First, educators must supply the rules for the school or class. Second, because difficult students are impulsively controlled by their environments, adult supervision of those environments is the first line of defense in reducing problem behaviors. It cannot be stressed enough that supervision is one of the most important preventative interventions educators should use.

Social and academic deficits are also critical areas for difficult students. These students are commonly several years behind their peers in the complexity and sophistication of their social skills (Patterson, Reid, & Dishion, 1992). They also tend to try to impulsively control social situations and peers, which often results in social rejection. Although traditional pull-out social skills instruction is not as effective, good social skills programs should (a) be taught across the whole school day, (b) include social correction procedures (i.e., the teaching interaction) that teach the correct skill at the time the student has a problem, and (c) include skills that are valued and naturally rewarded in the student's environment so the student is motivated to use them. Good examples of these types of programs are *Cool Kids: A Proactive Approach to Social Responsibility* (Fister-Mulkey, Conrad, & Kemp, 1998) and *Basic Social Skills for Youth: A Handbook from Boys Town* (Boy's Town, 1992).

Academic deficits are also fundamental when defining difficult students. Academic problems include deficits in reading, writing, and math computational skills. If a student has a deficit in an academic subject, the student will often misbehave to escape an academic environment that demands that academic skills. Problem behaviors such as being off-task, disruptive, or noncompliant can be linked to the inability to do the required academic task (Patterson et al., 1992). Educators should understand that grade retention for academic inability or immaturity is not an effective intervention. Retention generally makes things both academically and behaviorally worse for difficult students and often encourages them to drop out of school (Holmes, 1989; Jimerson, 2001).

Another "hidden" academic deficit, especially for students about to enter secondary school, is the area of study skills. When students transition from an elementary school with one teacher and enter a school with six or seven teachers, poor study skills can result in school failure. These skills are needed to extract and obtain academic information, organize that information, and return it in an acceptable form to a teacher. Some examples of important skills are note taking, reading for maximum information, time management, and test taking. There are several study skills programs available, including the *Skills for School Success* program (Archer & Gleason, 1991), which teaches all the essential skills needed by a student from the third grade through high school.

ANTECEDENT STRATEGIES AND COERCION/PAIN CONTROL

Coercion is an insidious process that can bring out some of the worst behaviors in both adults and students (Patterson et al., 1992). It is directly linked to yelling, making threats, noncompliance, arguing, temper tantrums, and several other disruptive behaviors. The coercive process starts when an adult gives a simple request to the student and the student ignores it; for example, "Rocky, wouldn't you like to take your seat so we can get started?" Next, the teacher tries to cajole or humor Rocky by saying, "Come on, Rocky, please take your seat and help me." In response, Rocky delays with a statement such as, "In a minute. I'm right in the middle of something." Now the teacher yells, "Now you had better do it! I'm not asking again." Rocky starts to argue and give excuses, such as, "Don't rush me, just a minute. I'm almost the winner in this video game." The exasperated teacher yells, "That's it! You have no business in this class—get to the principal's office." Rocky may explode, start a tantrum, and scream, "You always pick on me. I never have a chance to do anything fun in this stupid classroom." Now the startled and upset teacher thinks, "It's not worth pushing Rocky. Who cares if he learns?" and withdraws her request and walks away.

What has happened in this exchange? First, Rocky has been rewarded for noncompliance, delaying, arguing, excuse giving, and in the end for screaming and throwing a tantrum. When the teacher withdrew her command and walked away, Rocky was negatively reinforced (i.e., avoiding and escaping the request). As in this example, the adult withdraws the request approximately 60% of the time (Patterson et al., 1992). Second, over time, coercion interferes with Rocky's academic achievement because he uses this strategy to avoid difficult academic tasks. Third, coercion interferes with social skills acquisition and adjustment. If he has successfully used coercion with adults, then he will try and use it with peers to control social situations, which will eventually lead to peer rejection. The key is to stop this coercive exchange.

Antecedent Control as Precision Requests

Many adults want to jump directly to negative consequences to suppress coercive behavior. Mild negative consequences may eventually be needed; however, they should not be a first line of response. Consequences are expensive in terms of teacher's time, efforts, and emotions. Preventative antecedent control is a much more productive first-line approach to avoid the coercive process. If an antecedent sets the occasion for a behavior, then the reader needs to look at the antecedents that set the occasion for the coercive process. What happens just before the student is noncompliant, argumentative, and disruptive? It's simple—the antecedents come from the adult making the request and how the request is made.

Research has shown that small antecedent changes can significantly increase compliance (Mackay, McLaughlin, Weber, & Derby, 2001; Musser, Bray, Kehle, & Jenson, 2001). First, it is important that a request is not made using a question format. For example, "Wouldn't you like to get started?" or "Don't you want to get started?" are inappropriate requests made in a question format. Questions give a student a false sense of choice and an opportunity to say "no." Usually when teachers give these question formatted requests, "no" is an unacceptable response. It is much more effective to give a straightforward declarative request, such as "I want you to get started" or "It's time to get to work."

The second antecedent variable is distance. It has been estimated that the average teacher makes a request at 15 to 20 feet (Rhode et al., 1992). To increase compliance, get closer to the student. The appropriate distance from which to give a serious request to a student is 3 feet. Teachers, especially new teachers, should recognize that the desk is an enemy when it comes to compliance. Teachers must get out from behind the desk, move around the classroom, and make the request to a student from approximately 3 feet.

The third variable is tone of voice. Yelling does not improve compliance. Instead, it makes it worse because yelling is generally done from a distance. Requests made up close in a quiet voice are more effective. Yelling also elicits an emotional response from a student, and over time makes the teacher and the voice negative stimuli. As they used to say in the westerns, "Get up close, say it in a low voice, and don't say much" (Rhode, Jenson, & Morgan, 2003; Jenson et al., 2007). It was good advice for the western good guys, and it's good advice for teachers.

The fourth variable is eye contact. Requiring the student to look you in the eyes as you make the request will improve compliance (Hamlet, Axelrod, & Kuerschner, 1984). However, teachers often wonder how to get eye contact. There are two basic ways. First, get up close. As you near the student (5 to 6 feet), he or she will naturally look up and into your eyes (most of the time). When the student looks up, continue to make the request. It does not matter if the student looks away. You have his or her attention, and compliance will increase. A second way to get eye contact is to address the student by name and request that he or she look at you. In one study (Hamlet et al., 1984), the teacher said, "Look me in the eyes," then made the request. She knew it was working when the student said, "You can stop this look at me stuff. I've already hung up my coat and here is my homework!" It should be noted that making eye contact in some cultures is considered impolite or intimidating. For students from these cultures, the eye contact antecedent should be avoided.

The fifth variable is time. The compliance window of time is approximately 5 to 10 seconds. After making a request, the teacher should wait for 5 to 10 seconds without interruption and compliance will improve. Thirty-five to 40% of the time, the adult interrupts during this 5- to 10-second window by making more requests or repeating the original request unnecessarily (Forehand, 1977; Rhode et al., 1992).

The sixth variable includes two aspects. First, do not nag. The more you repeat the original request, the less compliance will increase. The general rule of thumb is to make only two requests and then follow through with a consequence. Second, do not make multiple requests. Giving a student a stream of different requests (like a machine gun) only reduces compliance. Get up close, get eye contact, give the request in a low tone, and wait.

The seventh antecedent variable is to describe what you want. Including a description of the behavior improves compliance. For example, instead of "Stop that," say "Don't touch other students." Or, instead of "Don't talk out in class," say "You need to raise your hand before you speak." Adding a little description can make a big difference.

Last, verbally reinforce compliance after a student has complied with the request. Research has shown (as reviewed by Jenson et al., 2004) that students are commonly ignored by teachers when they have appropriately followed a request. One study of difficult students indicted that teacher verbal reinforcement of a student who followed a request was at chance levels (Van Acker, Grant, & Henry, 1996). Such simple statements as "Thanks for following my directions" or "It helps me when you do what I say" can increase and then help maintain high rates of compliance.

A precision request is folding all of these antecedent compliance variables into one concept (Jenson & Reavis, 1996). When making a precision request, an educator makes a request (within 3 feet and with eye contact) and says "Please (and makes the request)" and waits 5 to 10 seconds. If the student complies, he or she is verbally rewarded. If the student does not comply, the educator makes a second request with a signal word imbedded. For example, the signal word might be *need*. For example, "Now I need you to (and make the request)." If the student complies, then he or she would be verbally rewarded. If not, a mildly aversive consequence should be delivered. In essence, the word *need* in the second request is a signal indicating to the student that no more requests will be made and a mild consequence will follow noncompliance.

Precision requests and reprimands have a lot in common. The punishment technique most frequently used by classroom teachers is the verbal reprimand (Jenson & Reavis, 1996; Van Houten, 1980). A reprimand is a specific and emphatic verbal statement used to stop an inappropriate behavior. Reprimands follow the same antecedent variables as effective precision commands, including close proximity, eye contact, and not repeating more than twice. Research has shown that, if a teacher uses the antecedent variables we discussed in conjunction with a reprimand, inappropriate classroom behavior will decrease and classroom academic performance will improve (Van Houten, 1980).

"Sure I Will": Combining Precision Commands With a Social Skill

If using precision commands will increase a student's compliance, then combining the command with a social skill that enhances compliance will be even more effective. The "Sure I Will" program is just such an intervention. In effect, students are taught that if they respond to the first part of a precision request by saying "Sure I will," and begin the requested behavior before the teacher has to repeat the precision command, "Now I need you to . . .," then they may be randomly rewarded. The "Sure I will" statement interferes with noncompliance and enhances follow through with the requested behavior. Research has shown that using the "Sure I Will" program can substantially increase compliance with difficult students (Kehle, Bray, Theodore, Jenson, & Clark, 2000; Neville & Jenson, 1984; Martin-LeMaster, 1990). The "Sure I Will" program has the added benefit that other adults (who may not be aware of the program) value the skill and will naturally reinforce it when difficult students use it (Martin-LeMaster, 1990). The "Sure I Will" program can also be used in classrooms with student teams and as a group contingency to improve overall classroom compliance. One team might be named the "Sure I Will" team, whereas others are called the "Okey Dokey" team, the "Glad You Asked" team, or the "No Problema" team. For a further discussion of this group contingency application, refer to the *Tough Kid Book* (Rhode et al., 1992).

RULES AS CLASSROOM EXPECTATION SETTERS

There are lots of opinions and anecdotal advice for teachers selecting and implementing rules in their classrooms; however, there is little research on their effectiveness. Some educators claim that for students to "buy into" the classroom rules, they need to have input into selecting the rules. Others feel that rules should reflect higher order societal and character values, such as being a good classroom citizen, being responsible, or being respectful and kind. We take exception with these two common beliefs. First, if students help write the rules, the teacher will not be ready the first day of class with a set of rules and a classroom rules program. Also, when students help write the rules, they are often ambiguous with unattainable high standards. We recommend that teachers determine the rules before school starts. To increase student buy in to the classroom rules system, let them help select the rewards they will get if they follow the rules.

High-order values like responsibility and respect rules are fine for adults; however, they are often ambiguous and meaningless, particularly for difficult students. Ask any five students individually what a rule means. If you get five different answers, then you have an ambiguous rule. All five students should be able to quickly state and give clear examples of a rule. Some teachers may object and say that responsibility is defined as being on time, being prepared, and following teacher's directions. If this is your response, then we suggest you scrap the word *responsibility* and use the three expectations to be your first three classroom rules. As for respect as a rule, remember who was the most respectful child on the *Leave it to Beaver* show? Eddie Haskell. Students can appear respectful and still be very problematic.

Classroom rules should reflect a teacher's expectations of students in a simple, easy-to-understand language. After surveying hundreds of teachers and their expectations of students, we suggest the following six rules: (a) Follow your teacher's directions; (b) Be in your seat before the bell rings; (c) Raise your hand and ask for permission to speak; (d) Be prepared; (e) Stay in your seat and keep your hands and feet to yourself; and (f) No roughhousing in the hall, bathrooms, lunchroom, or playground (Nicolas, 1998). These rules reflect common teacher expectations and are easily understood by all students (see Figure 16.1a). They should be posted, taught to students the first day of class, and reviewed each week. The icons on the bottom of the chart in Figure 16.1a represent qualities of good rules: they involve observable and measurable behaviors, they are positively stated, they are used in small numbers (no more than four or five), and they are not ambiguous.

Following rules and breaking rules should receive a consequence within the structure of a consistent classroom system. Figure 16.1b shows a What If Chart of positive consequences for following the rules and mildly punishing consequences for not following the rules. Have students nominate rewards (inexpensive and easy to locate) that the whole class will receive if everyone follows the rules. These rewards are listed as a menu on the left side of the What If Chart. On the bottom of the chart is an envelope shape labeled *Mystery Motivator* (discussed in the following section). To use this system, the teacher must keep a rules log that lists students' names and the rules those students broke that day. The teacher selects a random number each day that the students do not know. At the end of the day, this number is revealed. All the students with numbers of rule infractions that are less than the secret number get to vote on what the class will receive from the incentive menu on the What If Chart. Students with rule infractions at or above this number do not get to vote or receive the reward (this is an independent group contingency, described in chap. 10, this volume). One last twist with this system is that the winning students can be given a choice of voting on a particular reward from the incentive menu or selecting the Mystery Motivator.

On the right side of the What If Chart, list mildly punishing consequences for rule infractions in an increasing hierarchy. These consequences should be mild and not take a lot of teacher time. For example, one rule infraction results in the first consequence, two rule infractions result in the second consequence, and so on. Some mild consequences include a verbal warning from the teacher, the student's name written on a consequence list,

Classroom Rules

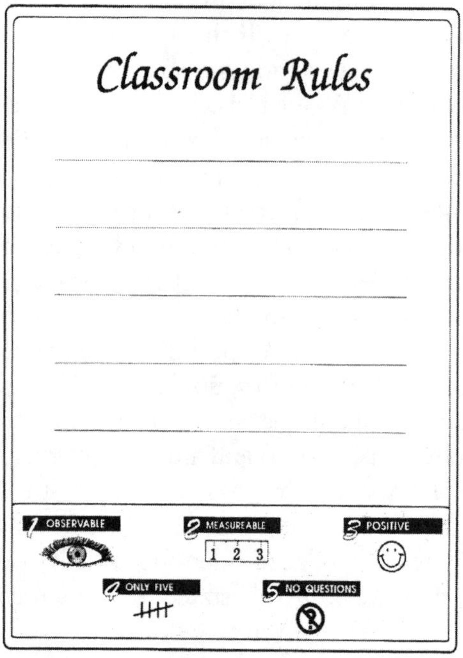

Classroom Rules
1 OBSERVABLE
2 MEASUREABLE
1 2 3
3 POSITIVE
4 ONLY FIVE
5 NO QUESTIONS

What If? Chart

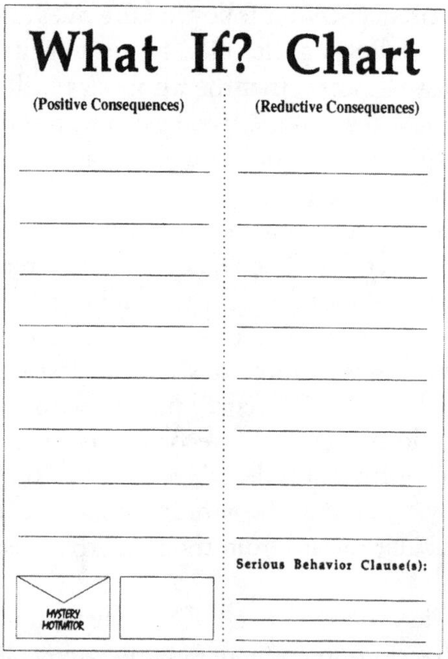

What If? Chart
(Positive Consequences)
(Reductive Consequences)
Serious Behavior Clause(s):
MYSTERY MOTIVATOR

Figure 16.1. Examples of a Rule Chart (a) and a What If Chart (b). From *Tough Kid Book: Practical Classroom Management Strategies* (pp. 21, 24), by G. Rhode, W. R. Jenson, and H. K. Reavis, 1992, Longmont, CO: Sopris West. Copyright 1992 by R. Jenson. Reprinted with permission of author.

a 30-second delay in class after the bell rings, shaving 5 minutes off of recess or a valued activity, a call home to the parent, or sitting near the teacher for the rest of the day.

We all want to know what is going to happen to us. We like certainty and we like to avoid uncertainty. The "What's It Going to Be Box" is based on this need for certainty and avoidance of uncertainty and is a collection of unknown simple consequences. The box contains about 20 sealed envelopes containing different mild consequences written on slips of paper. The consequences can include those listed on the What If Chart, or they can be other mild consequences, such as sitting in front of the classroom or near the teacher, or being last in line that day. If a student has a really difficult day during which he or she broke many rules, then as a consequence the student is instructed to randomly select an envelope from the box. This technique should be used sparingly and as the last of the consequence hierarchy on the What If Chart.

MOTIVATION AND THE DIFFICULT STUDENT

Difficult students are notoriously nonmotivated to perform in the classrooms, and their lack of motivation is a common teacher complaint. These teachers may be dealing with a combination of students who "won't do it" and who "can't do it." This type of nonmotivation gradually builds over time. For example, there are few nonmotivated kindergarteners. Most young children are happy to learn and excited about being in school. However, as some of these students get older, they repeatedly fail academic tasks. These failures do not leave the student's motivation system. Slowly, these failures build up and destroy a student's motivation. In essence, students become "poisoned" to performing academically and trying new academic tasks. This is why nonmotivation is so common in secondary students. Along with nonmotivation, difficult students also develop gaps in their basic academic skills and fall further and further behind. Over time, academic work itself takes on negative attributes that the student avoids or misbehaves to escape. Students who "won't do it" and "can't do it" are the very students who need to work more to catch up academically. Nonmotivated, difficult students need incentive systems to keep them working and to make their work experiences positive (Rawlins, 2007).

To select incentives for nonmotivated students, teachers have several techniques available to them. First, they can ask students what they would like to earn (with the stipulation that their choices can not take a lot of time or cost a lot of money). Or teachers can simply watch what students do. If they do something a lot, they like it and will work for it. Similarly, teachers can keep track of what students ask them for most frequently and use these items as incentives. Last but most important, teachers should "think like a kid." Things that to adults are silly, dumb, or absurd are often exactly what students want. Remember, however, that the simplest things can be the most potent incentives. Research has shown that the teacher's approval is one of the most powerful incentives in a classroom (as reviewed by Jenson et al., 2004). The following is a series of interventions that have been shown to be powerful incentive systems for nonmotivated students.

Mystery Motivators

This is a research-validated intervention that has been used to motivate students to improve academic performance in classrooms (Moore, Waguespack, Wickstrom, Witt, & Gaydos, 1994; Rhode et al., 1992), improve homework compliance (Madaus, Kehle, Madaus, & Bray, 2003; Olympia, Sheridan, & Jenson, 1994), and reduce disruptive classroom behaviors (Motram, Bray, Kehle, Broudy, & Jenson, 2002). A Mystery Motivator is simply an incentive written on a slip of paper that is sealed in an envelope. A big question mark can be written on the envelope to suggest "mystery" to the student who works for the unknown contents of the envelope. When the student meets the performance criterion, the envelope is opened and he or she receives the incentive written on the piece of paper.

Several variations of Mystery Motivators exist. One useful application is shown in Figure 16.2a (i.e., the envelope with days of the week listed underneath in boxes). Special pen sets (e.g., Crayola Color Changeables Markers) contain an invisible-ink pen along with colored pens. With the invisible-ink pen, Xs (two to three per week) are randomly printed in the days-of-the-week boxes as shown in Figure 16.2a. When the student demonstrates an appropriate behavior on a given day (i.e., turns in homework, finishes an academic assignment, or follows classroom rules), the student is allowed to take one of the colored pens and color in a box. If the X appears, the student is allowed to open the envelope and receive the incentive. The comment section can be used for positive statements about the child's progress and accomplishments.

Chart Moves to Rewards

This intervention is similar to the Mystery Motivator intervention (Jenson, Neville, Sloane, & Morgan, 1982). A picture is segmented into boxes, such as the snake in Figure 16.2b. Dots are randomly made with the invisible-ink pen in the segments, about one in every five squares. When the student performs a requested task, such as turning in a homework assignment, completing a unit of work, or being prepared and on time to class, he or she is allowed to color in a square. If the dot appears, the student gets the incentive in the Mystery Motivator envelope. Chart Moves are flexible in that several squares can be colored in each day for a variety of behaviors.

75 Scales Snake Chart

Figure 16.2. Examples of Mystery Motivator (a), Chartmoves (b), and Reward Spinner (c). From *Tough Kid Book: Practical Classroom Management Strategies* (pp. 45, 47), by G. Rhode, W. R. Jenson, and H. K. Reavis, 1992, Longmont, CO: Sopris West. Copyright 1992 by R. Jenson. Reprinted with permission of author.

Chart Moves also have other advantages. As the squares are filled in by the students, they can follow and track their progress.

Reinforcement Spinners

Spinners are another intervention that has the advantage of including several low-cost incentives along with a few high-cost incentives to motivate difficult students (Jenson et al., 1982; Peine, Darvish, Blakelock, Osborne, & Jenson, 1998). An example of a Reinforcement Spinner is given in Figure 16.2c. It is a circle (pie chart) with wedges of different sizes and with different incentives printed on them. In the middle of the spinner is a plastic arrow attached by a brad so it can be used to spin. When the student successfully demonstrates a desired behavior, he or she is allowed to spin the arrow. The wedge the arrow randomly lands in represents the reinforcer the student receives. Because thin wedges are less likely to be landed on than wide wedges, they can correspond to more expensive incentives. The wide wedges can be used for less expensive incentives or activity reinforcers.

Dots for Motivation

Research has shown the Dots for Motivation negative reinforcement incentive system to be effective in improving academic performance, particularly with older difficult students (Doyle, Jenson, Clark, & Gates, 1999). This technique is effective in increasing work completion on assignments that have a designated number of questions or problems, such as a math assignment. The only materials needed are small colored dots that are often used to label or color code files. Dots can be purchased at most office supply stores. Several dots come on a sheet and can be cut so that individual dots can be given to a student. The program works by awarding the student one dot for a designated number of problems solved correctly on his math sheet (e.g., every five problems). On the next assignment, the student can place the earned dots next to any math problems he does not want to do and can earn full credit for those problems. In essence, with the Dot program, students are working to get out of work.

CONCLUSION

Teaching difficult students is an inevitable part of everyday educational life. Understanding these students and their behavior excesses and deficits is a big step toward helping them improve their learning and behavior. Preventative approaches such as antecedent control with precision commands, posted rules that reflect teacher's expectations, and effective student supervision are key components of an effective program. Teachers should remem-

ber that positives, such as praise and positive attention, work best with difficult students who have become immune to punishment.

REFERENCES

Archer, A., & Gleason, M. (1991). *Skills for school success.* North Billerica, MA:
Curriculum Associates.

Bowen, J. A., Jenson, W. R., & Clark, E. (2004). *School-based. interventions for students with behavior problems.* New York: Kluwer Academic/Plenum.

Boy's Town. (1992). *Social skills for youth: A handbook from Boys Town.* Omaha, NE:
Boy's Town Press.

Doyle, P., Jenson, W. R., Clark, E., & Gates, G. (1999). Free time and dots as negative reinforcement to improve academic completion and accuracy for mildly
disabled students. *Proven Practice: Prevention, Remediation, Solutions for Schools,
2*, 10–15.

Elliott, S. (1988). Acceptability of behavioral treatments: Review of variables that
influence treatment selection. *Professional Psychology: Research into Practice, 19*,
68–80.

Fister-Mulkey, S., Conrad, D., & Kemp, K. (1998). *Cool kids: A proactive approach to
social responsibility.* Longmont, CO: Sopris West.

Forehand, R. (1977). Child noncompliance to parental requests: Behavior analysis
and treatment. In M. Hersen, R. M. Eisler, & P. M. Miller (Eds.), *Progress in
behavior modification* (Vol. 5, pp. 111–148). New York: Academic Press.

Hamlet, C. C., Axelrod, S., & Kuerschner, S. (1984). Eye contact as an antecedent
to compliant behavior. *Journal of Applied Behavior Analysis, 17*, 553–557.

Holmes, C. T. (1989). Grade level retention effects: A meta-analysis of research
studies. In L. Shepard & M. Smith (Eds.), *Flunking grades: Research and policies
on retention* (pp. 16–33). London: Falmer Press.

Jenson, W. R., Olympia, D., Farley, M., & Clark, E. (2004). Positive psychology and
externalizing students: Awash in a sea of negativity. *Psychology in the Schools,
41*, 67–80.

Jenson, W. R., Neville, M. H., Sloane, H., & Morgan, D. (1982). Spinners and chart
moves. *Child and Family Behavior Therapy, 4*, 81–85.

Jenson, W. R., & Reavis, K. (1996). Reprimands and precision requests. In K. Reavis,
S. J. Kukic, W. R. Jenson, D. Morgan, D. Andrews, & S. Fister (Eds.), *Best
practices: Behavioral and educational strategies for teachers* (pp. 49–58). Longmont:
CO: Sopris West.

Jenson, W. R., Rhode, G., Evans, C., & Morgan, D. (2007). *The tough kid principal's
briefcase: Practical behavior management for the whole school.* Longmont, CO: Sopris
West.

Jimerson, S. (2001). Meta-analysis of grade retention research: Implications for practice in the 21st century. *School Psychology Review, 30*, 420–437.

Kavale, K. A., Mathur, S. R., & Mostert, M. P. (2004). Social skills training and
teaching social behavior to students with emotional and behavioral disorders.

In R. B. Rutherford, M. M. Quinn, & S. R. Mathur (Eds.), *Handbook of research in emotional and behavioral disorders* (pp. 446–461). New York: Guilford.

Kazdin, A. E. (1977). Assessing the clinical or applied importance of behavior change through social validation. *Behavior Modification, 1*, 427–452.

Kehle, T., Bray, M., Theodore, L., Jenson, W., & Clark, E. (2000). A multi-component intervention designed to reduce disruptive classroom behavior. *Psychology in the Schools, 37*, 475–481.

Mackay, S., McLaughlin, T., Weber, K., & Derby, K. (2001). The use of precision requests to decrease noncompliance in the home and neighborhood: A case study. *Child & Family Behavior Therapy, 23*, 41–50.

Madaus, M., Kehle, T., Madaus, J., & Bray, M. (2003). Mystery motivator as an intervention to promote homework completion and accuracy. *School Psychology International, 24*, 369–377.

Martin-LeMaster, J. (1990). *Increasing classroom compliance of noncompliant elementary-age students.* Unpublished doctoral dissertation, University of Utah, Salt Lake City.

Moore, L., Waguespack, A., Wickstrom, K., Witt, J., & Gaydos, G. (1994). Mystery motivator: An effective and time efficient intervention. *School Psychology Review, 23*, 106–118.

Motram, L., Bray, M. A., Kehle, T. J., Broudy, M., & Jenson, W. R. (2002). Classroom-based intervention to reduce disruptive classroom behavior. *Journal of Applied School Psychology, 19*, 65–74.

Musser, E., Bray, M., Kehle, T., & Jenson, W. (2001). Reducing disruptive behaviors in students with serious emotional disturbance. *School Psychology Review, 30*, 294–305.

Neville, M., & Jenson, W. (1984). Precision commands and the "Sure I Will" program: A quick and efficient compliance training sequence. *Child & Family Behavior Therapy, 6*, 61–65.

Nicholas, P. (1998). *Teacher's and school psychologist's selection and use of classroom interventions for reducing behavioral excesses.* Unpublished doctoral dissertation, University of Utah, Salt Lake City.

Olympia, D., Sheridan, S., & Jenson, W. R. (1994). Using student-managed interventions to increase homework completion and accuracy. *Journal of Applied Behavior Analysis, 27*, 85–99.

Patterson, G. R., Reid, J. B., & Dishion, T. J. (1992). *Antisocial boys.* Eugene, OR: Castalia.

Peine, H., Darvish, R., Blakelock, H., Osborne, G., & Jenson, W. R. (1998). Non-aversive reduction of cigarette smoking in two men in a residential setting. *Journal of Behavior Therapy and Experimental Psychiatry, 29*, 55–65.

Rawlins, L. (2007). *The use of external reinforcement by teachers.* Unpublished doctoral dissertation, University of Utah, Salt Lake City.

Rhode, G., Jenson, W. R., & Morgan, D. P. (2003). *The tough kid new teacher kit: Practical classroom management survival strategies for the new teacher.* Longmont, CO: Sopris West.

Rhode, G., Jenson, W. R., & Reavis, K. (1992). *Tough kid book: Practical classroom strategies.* Longmont, CO: Sopris West.

Schwartz, I. S., & Baer, D. M. (1991). Social validity assessments: Is current practice state of the art? *Journal of Applied Behavior Analysis, 24,* 189–204.

Van Acker, R., Grant, S. H., & Henry, D. (1996). Teacher and student behavior as a function of risk for aggression. *Education and Treatment of Children, 19,* 316–334.

Van Houten, R. (1980). *How to use reprimands.* Lawrence, KS: H & H Enterprises.

Wolf, M. M. (1978). Social validity: The case for subjective measurement or how applied behavior analysis is finding its heart. *Journal of Applied Behavior Analysis, 11,* 203–214.

17

BEHAVIORAL INTERVENTIONS WITH EXTERNALIZING DISORDERS

GEORGE J. DUPAUL AND LISA L. WEYANDT

Externalizing disorders consist of a variety of problematic behaviors, such as inattention, hyperactivity, impulsivity, aggression, oppositional, and antisocial behaviors. Generally, two main approaches are used to classify disruptive behavior problems: empirically derived and clinical diagnostic categories such as those found in the *Diagnostic and Statistical Manual of Mental Disorders* (*DSM–IV–TR*; American Psychiatric Association [APA], 2000). Empirically derived syndromes are typically established with the use of rating scales developed for parents, teachers, or self-report instruments developed for children and adolescents. Statistical methods are used to determine salient or deviant symptoms. Achenbach and Rescorla (2001), for example, using empirically derived rating scales, have consistently found two syndromes that characterized behavioral problems: aggressive behavior and rule-breaking behavior. The *DSM* classification system is based on the presence or absence of clinical symptoms and the most commonly diagnosed externalizing disorders among children and adolescents include attention-deficit/hyperactivity

Preparation of this chapter was supported, in part, by National Institute of Mental Health grants R01-MH62941 and R01-61563.

disorder (ADHD), conduct disorder (CD), and oppositional defiant disorder (ODD; APA, 2000).

The actual prevalence of externalizing disorders is difficult to determine because of differing diagnostic criteria, assessment methods, and specific samples being studied. Fombonne (2002) reported that 5.4% to 35.5% of youth ages 4 to 18 years have behavior disorders, whereas Costello, Compton, Keeler, and Angold (2003) estimated that 15% to 20% of clinic-referred youth have externalizing problems. Prevalence rates also vary among specific externalizing disorders. For example, ADHD is estimated to affect 3% to 7% of the school-age population, whereas CD and ODD affect approximately 1% to 10% and 2% to 16%, respectively (APA, 2000). More recent findings using *DSM–IV* criteria suggest rates of 1.5% to 2.2% for CD and 2.3% to 5.5% for ODD (Canino et al., 2004). Prevalence rates for all externalizing disorders are higher among males than females with an average ratio of 3:1. Higher prevalence rates are reported in urban versus rural environments (Fleitlich-Bilyk & Goodman, 2004). It is important to recognize that externalizing disorders frequently co-occur. For example, most youth who are diagnosed with CD also meet diagnostic criteria for ODD, and 35% to 70% of children with ADHD develop ODD and/or CD (Biederman, Newcorn, & Sprich, 1991; Johnston & Ohan, 1999). Furthermore, disruptive behavior problems account for over 50% of referrals to mental health clinics (Waschbusch, 2002).

Interventions for externalizing problems vary depending on the specific concerns, but in general, pharmacological interventions are used more frequently with ADHD and less frequently with CD and ODD. Nonpharmacological interventions include behavioral strategies, classroom management and self-management techniques, social/peer interventions, and family interventions. The purpose of this chapter is to review the empirical literature concerning interventions for children with externalizing disorders. This review is not meant to be exhaustive but rather to highlight the major types of interventions currently available for externalizing problem behavior, with particular emphasis on behaviorally based treatment approaches.

BEHAVIORAL STRATEGIES IN CLASSROOM SETTINGS

A variety of behavioral interventions have been implemented to improve the classroom and social functioning of students with externalizing disorders. Strategies include teacher-mediated, parent-mediated, self-mediated, and peer-mediated interventions as well as treatment directed at social skills and peer relationships. Prior to reviewing each of these strategies, it is important to consider several important principles for designing classroom behavioral interventions with this population.

Important Principles for Designing Classroom Behavioral Interventions

Several principles are important to consider when designing school-based behavioral interventions for students with externalizing disorders (DuPaul & Stoner, 2003; DuPaul & Weyandt, 2006). First, interventions should include both proactive and reactive approaches. Proactive or preventive strategies involve changing antecedent conditions prior to a challenging behavior being exhibited. Alternatively, reactive strategies involve applying consequences following a specific target behavior. Optimal results are more likely to be obtained when a balanced treatment plan involving both approaches is used. Second, functional assessment data should be used to design interventions, particularly with respect to the selection of consequences (O'Neill et al., 1997). Assessment-based interventions are presumed to be more time- and cost-effective than a trial-and-error shotgun approach to treatment selection (Ervin, Ehrhardt, & Poling, 2001).

Given that many students with externalizing disorders exhibit academic performance difficulties (Nelson, Benner, Lane, & Smith, 2004), it is important to include treatment goals targeting both academic and behavioral outcomes. Interventions solely directed at improving classroom behavior rarely lead to concomitant improvement in academic achievement (DuPaul & Eckert, 1997). In addition, multiple mediators for treatment should be considered, including teachers, parents, peers, and the identified students themselves. An exclusive reliance on classroom teachers to implement all behavioral interventions can be problematic because of feasibility and resource issues. Finally, the intensity or "dosage" of intervention will vary across students on the basis of the severity of their challenging behaviors and the context of treatment. Therefore, a response to intervention approach should be used to determine the necessary dosage, wherein it is assumed that most students will respond to less intensive interventions. Those students who do not respond to a lower dosage can be provided with treatment that involves a higher frequency and/or denser reinforcement schedule.

Teacher-Mediated Interventions

Teacher-mediated interventions for students with externalizing behavior difficulties include both proactive and reactive strategies. Antecedent-based or proactive interventions include posting of classroom rules and providing choices for classroom tasks. The active teaching of classroom rules would involve (a) providing students with several simply-worded classroom rules (e.g., "raise your hand before speaking"); (b) reminding students of these rules on a regular basis through class discussion and demonstration; (c) regularly pointing out examples of students who are following rules (i.e., "catching students being good"); and (d) reminding students of expectations and rules prior to the start of a specific class activity (DuPaul & Stoner, 2003). Field studies have illustrated the association between classroom rule-following and successful school performance (e.g., Paine, Radicchi, Rosellini, Deutchmann, & Darch, 1983); thus, active teaching of rules should help all students to understand and follow directives on a more regular basis.

Choice-making interventions provide students with an opportunity to choose actions and/or tasks from a limited menu of options. For example, Dunlap et al. (1994) investigated the effects of choice making on the task engagement and disruptive behaviors of three middle school students with externalizing behavior difficulties. Using an ABAB reversal design, students were provided with a menu of academic tasks in spelling and English from which to choose. The results indicated that choice making led to significant increases in on-task behavior along with reductions in disruptive behavior.

Consequent-based or reactive strategies include contingent praise or reprimands, token reinforcement systems, and response cost. The most common teacher response to disruptive classroom behavior is a verbal reprimand; however, reprimands rarely are delivered in a manner that leads to effective behavior change. Investigations conducted by O'Leary and colleagues (e.g., Rosen, O'Leary, Joyce, Conway, & Pfiffner, 1984) have illustrated the ways in which reprimands can be delivered to effectively redirect students. Verbal reprimands are more effective when teacher concerns are communicated directly and when delivered immediately and consistently following the initial occurrence of disruptive behavior. In addition, reprimands should be brief and delivered privately with minimal emotion, while making eye contact with the child. Finally, praise should be delivered contingent on appropriate classroom behavior such that positive statements are delivered more frequently than reprimands (DuPaul & Stoner, 2003).

Token reinforcement is another consequence-based strategy in which students earn immediate contingencies (e.g., stickers, points) for appropriate behavior and immediate reinforcers can be exchanged later in the day or week for backup rewards (e.g., preferred home and school activities). There is an extensive empirical literature supporting classroom-based token reinforcement programs in reducing disruptive behavior exhibited by students with externalizing behavior difficulties (Kazdin & Weisz, 2003).

Two additional forms of token reinforcement are the use of home-based reinforcement for school behavior (i.e., daily school report card) and response cost. Daily report cards identify several classroom goals (e.g., complete assigned class work) that students must achieve to earn reinforcement at home (Chafouleas, Riley-Tillman, & McDougal, 2002; Kelley, 1990). Teachers provide numerical ratings (e.g., 1 ["did not meet goal"] to 5 ["met goal completely"]) for each behavior, with ratings serving as immediate reinforcement. Teacher ratings are translated to points at home and then used to "purchase" home-based rewards (e.g., access to television and/or video games). A daily report card system is one of the cornerstones of the classroom component within the Summer Treatment program developed by Pelham and colleagues (2002). As such, there is ample empirical support for the use of this system, especially in combination with classroom-based behavioral interventions (e.g., response cost) in the treatment of children with ADHD and related behavior disorders.

Response cost involves the removal of token reinforcement contingent on student display of disruptive behavior. The combination of positive reinforcement and response cost appears particularly effective for addressing classroom behavior of children with externalizing disorders. For example, several studies have documented the effectiveness of using mild penalties following inappropriate (i.e., off-task) behavior in maintaining consistent behavioral change following the use of an all-positive token system (Pfiffner & O'Leary, 1987; Rosen et al., 1984). Also, the concurrent use of token reinforcement and response cost has been found to improve on-task behavior, classwork completion, and academic accuracy of children with ADHD (DuPaul, Guevremont, & Barkley, 1992; Rapport, Murphy, & Bailey, 1980, 1982). In a classic study comparing response cost and stimulant medication for several children with ADHD, classroom improvement associated with response cost was equivalent to that obtained with methylphenidate (Rapport et al., 1982).

Self-Mediated Interventions

Two primary approaches have been studied with respect to self-mediated interventions for externalizing disorders. The traditional approach has involved the use of cognitive training to help students "stop, look, and listen" before responding to environmental stimuli. Cognitive training has limited efficacy with this population (DuPaul, Rutherford, & Hosterman, 2008). Alternatively, self-management strategies that involve students monitoring, evaluating, and/or reinforcing their own behavior have some data to support their use in classroom settings (Reid, Trout, & Schartz, 2005); therefore, the self-management approach is described in greater detail.

Self-management strategies such as self-monitoring, self-evaluation, and self-reinforcement are associated with improvements in classroom task engagement, peer interactions, and academic performance. In a classic study, Rhode, Morgan, and Young (1983) used the combination of self-monitoring and self-reinforcement to enhance the classroom behavior of six elementary students with "behavioral handicaps." The initial stages of the program involved the use of a token reinforcement program and verbal feedback from the teacher on the basis of teacher ratings of student behavior during specific intervals in the classroom. Ratings were provided using a six-point criterion on the basis of behavioral expectations (e.g., the degree to which students followed classroom rules). Teacher-provided points were exchanged for backup rewards in school or at home as in a standard token economy. Once students exhibited behavioral gains, they were trained in evaluating their own behavior using the same rating system as the teacher. At this stage, the teacher's ratings continued to be used to determine how many points that students earned; however, students could earn one bonus point for matching teacher ratings exactly. If student ratings deviated by more than one point from the teacher ratings, then no points were earned for that interval.

Over the course of time, teacher ratings were gradually faded such that the student ratings were the primary criterion for earning backup reinforcement. This was facilitated by (a) the use of random "matching challenges" that occurred on a periodic basis and (b) a gradual reduction in frequency of these matching challenges. The students eventually used self-ratings only with no backup reinforcers, and this led to maintenance of significant behavioral improvements across resource and general education classroom settings. This combination of self-monitoring and self-reinforcement has been extended to children with ADHD and related disruptive disorders in elementary (Hoff & DuPaul, 1998), middle (Shapiro, DuPaul, & Bradley, 1998), and high (Smith, Young, Nelson, & West, 1992) school settings.

Peer-Mediated Interventions

Interventions that involve classroom peers to deliver academic instruction (e.g., peer tutoring) or to implement components of a behavioral intervention have demonstrated efficacy for students with significant externalizing behaviors. For example, DuPaul, Ervin, Hook, and McGoey (1998) evaluated the effects of Class-Wide Peer Tutoring (CWPT; Greenwood, Maheady, & Delquadri, 2002) on the academic performance and classroom behavior of 19 students with ADHD and related disruptive behavior disorders who were attending first- through fifth-grade general education classrooms. A within-subject repeated measures design was used wherein each subject participated in two baseline (i.e., typical classroom activities such as the completion of independent seatwork) and two CWPT conditions in an ABAB reversal design format. Findings indicated that on-task behavior increased from an average of 21.6% during baseline to an average of 82.3% when CWPT was implemented. Associated reductions in disruptive behavior were also obtained. In addition, children's weekly posttest scores increased from an average of 55.2% during baseline to 73% for CWPT conditions. Similar, positive changes in behavior and academic performance were found for non-ADHD classmates, confirming previous findings that CWPT is helpful for all students, not just for those who are experiencing academic or behavior difficulties (Greenwood et al., 2002).

Social Relationship/Skills Interventions

Traditionally, interventions addressing peer relationship problems have focused on teaching students specific skills (e.g., taking turns and anger management) that are presumably missing from children's repertoires. Unfortunately, this approach has rarely been successful, particularly in relation to promoting generalization of use of social skills to settings outside of therapy sessions (Gresham, 2002). Thus, treatment strategies have been developed to encourage children to use skills already in their repertoire by promoting appropriate use and generalization across settings. For example, the Tough Kids Social Skills program developed by Sheridan (1995) involves three possible levels of social skills training including small group, class-wide, and school-wide. The small group training level may be particularly relevant for addressing the needs of children with externalizing disorders given their peer relationship difficulties. Twelve 60-minute group sessions address three overarching relationship components: social entry (e.g., conversation skills), maintaining interactions (e.g., playing cooperatively), and problem solving (e.g., resolving arguments). Several booster sessions are used to promote maintenance of gains in social performance. Sheridan, Dee, Morgan, McCormick, and Walker (1996) demonstrated preliminary empirical support for using the Tough Kids Social Skills program for students with disruptive behavior disorders such as ADHD.

BEHAVIORAL INTERVENTIONS IN HOME SETTINGS

In addition to classroom related interventions, a substantial body of literature exists regarding the role of the family in the development and continuance of externalizing problems. The development of externalizing disorders involves a complex interplay of numerous influences, including genetic and nongenetic factors. The family environment can certainly exacerbate and contribute to the genesis of externalizing problems, and research has found that family interventions, particularly parent training, is among the most effective approaches to reducing aggressive, noncompliant, and antisocial behavior in children and adolescents (Anastopoulos, Rhoads, & Farley, 2006; Cunningham, Bremner, & Boyle, 1995; Eyberg, Boggs, & Algina, 1995; Ghanizadeh & Shahrivar, 2005; McCabe, Turner, & Josephson, 2001; Nock, 2003). *Parent training* refers to "procedures in which a parent or parents are trained to interact differently with their child" (McCabe et al., 2001, p. 452). The primary emphasis of parent-training programs is on identifying and defining problem behavior and learning to anticipate and respond to problem behavior in a different manner. The content of parenting programs differs substantially, as do the methods used to assess the effectiveness of these programs. For example, parent-training programs may differ as to whether a structured or unstructured program is used, the delivery of the material, integration of token economies, homework assignments, documentation of progress, as well as the length of the parent training.

Using procedures originally developed by Hanf (1969) and Forehand and McMahon (1981), Barkley (1997) designed a parent-training program for defiant children (i.e., Defiant Children), and a number of studies have supported the program's effectiveness in decreasing problem behavior in children and adolescents. Various types of family intervention programs are available, and it remains unclear whether some of these programs are superior to others. Barkley, Guevremont, Anastopoulos, and Fletcher (1992) compared three family therapy programs (8 to 10 sessions) for treating family conflicts in adolescents with ADHD (most of whom had comorbid ODD) and found that all three interventions resulted in significant reductions in conflicts, negative communication, and anger during conflicts. All three programs were also associated with reduced internalizing and externalizing symptoms as well as improved rating of school adjustment and maternal depression. Robin (1981) compared two interventions with 31 families who were experiencing parent–adolescent conflict—problem-solving communication training, alternative family therapy, or wait list. Robin reported that both interventions resulted in significant reductions in parent–adolescent conflict but only problem-solving communication training resulted in improvements in problem-solving communication behavior.

More recently, Barkley, Edwards, Laneri, Fletcher, and Metevia (2001) compared the efficacy of problem-solving communication training, behavior management training, and a combination of problem-solving communication training and behavior management for parent and adolescent conflicts in adolescents with ADHD and ODD. The training took place over nine sessions, and results revealed significant improvement in ratings of parent–adolescent conflicts with intervention and there were no differences between intervention groups in terms of symptom change. Results also revealed that 42% to 80% of the families were in the "normal" range by the end of the sessions.

Sanders, Markie-Dadds, Tully, and Bor (2000) studied three variants of a behavioral family intervention known as Triple P (Positive Parenting Program) with a sample of 305 preschool children who were at high risk of developing conduct problems. Families were randomly assigned to one of these intervention groups (enhanced behavioral family intervention, standard behavioral family intervention, self-directed behavioral family intervention) or a wait list. Two of the groups, enhanced behavioral family intervention and standard behavioral family intervention, received active skills training and support from a trained practitioner. Unlike previous studies, findings indicated greater improvement in the enhanced family intervention group compared with the other groups. At follow-up 1 year later, however, all intervention groups showed similar improvement in behavior problems compared with the wait-list group.

Similar results were recently reported by Hoath and Sanders (2002), who studied the efficacy of Triple P intervention with parents who had children with ADHD. These studies suggested that parent-training programs designed to decrease parent–child conflict can be highly effective and that no particular program appeared superior to the other. A recent meta-analysis of parent-involved programs for externalizing problems associated with ADHD, however, raised questions about the effectiveness of parent training relative to other types of interventions. Specifically, Corcoran and Dattalo (2006) examined 16 studies and concluded that parent-training type programs were less effective at decreasing externalizing symptoms but were related to improvements in academic problems and internalizing symptoms. In addition, whether behavioral improvements can be sustained long term is unclear.

Danforth (1998) sought to determine whether behavioral improvements could be sustained over time and with parent training. Specifically, Danforth conducted eight individual parent-training sessions (1 hour each) with mothers of children with ADHD and comorbid ODD using the Behavior Management Flow Chart. Modeling, role-playing, and specific skills training for how to manage target behaviors (e.g., vocal rudeness, leaving the house without permission) were incorporated into the program. Outcome measures included direct observations of parent–child interactions, telephone interviews, and rating scales to assess maternal perceptions. Results revealed improved parenting behavior, reduced maternal stress, and reduced oppositional behavior, and these improvements were sustained over a 6-month period.

Long, Forehand, Wierson, and Morgan (1994) also explored whether parent training had long-term effects and studied interactions between mothers and young noncompliant children (2- to 7-year-olds). Mothers were taught to use clear commands, attention, and rewards for appropriate behavior, and time-out procedures for undesirable behavior. Increased compliance and reduction in problematic behavior was found immediately following treatment, and when followed up 14 years later, children who had participated were no different from matched community control participants with respect to measures of delinquency, academic progress, and parental relationships.

Results from Barkley et al. (2001) suggested that symptom improvement in parent–adolescent conflict persisted 2 months following treatment regardless of the type of parent-training (i.e., problem-solving communication training or behavior management training). Others, however, have reported differential improvement in parent-training programs over a 2-month period (e.g., Griest et al., 1982). Recently, Gardner, Burton, and Klimes (2006) conducted a community-based, parent-training intervention in children with conduct problems and reported improvement in child problem behavior at 6- and 18-months follow-up.

In addition to questions of effectiveness and sustainable improvements in behavior over time, researchers have questioned whether parent training can lead to behavioral improvements in the school setting. For example, Funderburk and colleagues (1998) introduced a 14-session parent-training program to families of boys between 2 and 7 years old who were referred by school personnel or mental health professional for conduct problems at home and at school. Findings indicated that children whose parents received training showed significant improvement in home and school behavior, and these improvements were sustained over 12 months. By 18-months follow-up, however, improvements were still found with compliance, but other behavioral measures declined to near pretreatment levels. More studies are needed to determine whether the positive effects of parenting programs will generalize to school-related behavior.

FUTURE DIRECTIONS FOR BEHAVIORAL INTERVENTIONS IN SCHOOL AND HOME SETTINGS

Empirical support for using behavioral interventions to address the challenging behaviors of students with externalizing disorders is relatively strong; however, there are several important directions for future treatment outcome studies. First, most available studies have been conducted with white, middle-class samples. The degree to which findings generalize to other racial and socioeconomic groups remains to be determined. Further, it may be fruitful to explore culturally sensitive adaptations of existing interventions in various subgroups of students. Second, over the past decade, educators have increased use of positive behavior support models in the context of a three-tiered service-delivery system (Sugai, Horner, & Gresham, 2002). Most of the interventions discussed in this chapter can be conceptualized as being at the most intensive end of the three-tiered continuum (i.e., interventions for those students in greatest need who have not responded to school-wide or class-wide interventions). Thus, there is a critical need to develop and evaluate interventions that can be effective at the first or second tier (i.e., universal and selected). Finally, cost-efficient methods for conducting valid functional analyses in classroom settings need to be developed and disseminated. Although functional behavioral assessment has a rich history in the applied behavior analytic field, the application of this methodology to school settings requires careful planning and consideration of feasibility issues (March & Horner, 2002). In particular, practical, user-friendly procedures to conduct experimental analyses in the development of behavioral interventions remain elusive.

Although preliminary research supports the effectiveness of family interventions in improving externalizing problems, several methodological issues remain (Kazdin, 1997). For example, information is lacking concerning the usefulness of these programs with girls. Farmer, Compton, Burns, and Robertson (2002), in a review of the literature concerning the treatment of externalizing disorders, found that boys composed nearly 70% of the samples studied. Small sample sizes characterize most studies, and very few are of a longitudinal design. Programmatic differences exist between the studies, and replication of studies is rare. Recent findings suggest that levels of parental stress are a strong predictor of children's improvement in externalizing behavior at 3, 6, and 12 months following discharge from an inpatient psychiatric treatment center, and the role of parental stress should also be further explored in outpatient parent-training programs (Blader, 2006). It is also important to note that research suggests families do not respond equally to parent-training programs, and family factors such as low socioeconomic status, personality variables, and ethnicity may be associated with different outcomes. Reid, Webster-Stratton, and Beauchaine (2001) were among the first to investigate the effectiveness of a parent-training program (The Incredible Years Parenting Program) in a low-income sample of Caucasian, African American, Hispanic, and Asian mothers whose children were enrolled in Head Start. Results revealed improvements in parent–child interactions and child behavior problems, and differences were not found across ethnic groups. Additional studies with children with documented behavior disorders are needed to further explore the role of ethnic background and parental response to intervention.

SUMMARY

Children and adolescents with externalizing disorders experience significant difficulties with behavior control, academic achievement, and development of appropriate interpersonal relationships. Behavioral interventions are effective in addressing the challenging behaviors exhibited by children with externalizing disorders in both home and school settings. Effective school-based interventions mediated by teachers include choice making, active teaching of classroom rules, contingent positive reinforcement, token reinforcement, and response cost. Daily report card systems that provide home-based reinforcement for appropriate school behavior also are effective. Peer-mediated and self-management interventions can enhance both behavioral and academic functioning while potentially promoting generalization of outcomes obtained through teacher-mediated strategies. A variety of parent-training programs have demonstrated success in helping parents to implement token reinforcement systems and related behavioral interventions in the home setting. Future research should focus on expanding samples across various demographic groups while placing interventions in the context of a broad-based, three-tiered service-delivery model.

REFERENCES

Achenbach, T. M., & Rescorla, L. A. (2001). *Manual for the ASEBA school-age forms and profiles.* Burlington: University of Vermont, Research Center for Children, Youth, and Families.

American Psychiatric Association. (2000). *Diagnostic and statistical manual of mental disorders* (4th ed., text rev.). Washington, DC: Author.

Anastopoulos, A. D., Rhoads, L. H., & Farley, S. E. (2006). Counseling and training parents. In R. A. Barkley (Ed.), *Attention deficit hyperactivity disorder: A handbook for diagnosis and treatment* (3rd ed., pp. 453–479). New York: Guilford.

Barkley, R. A. (1997). *Defiant children: A clinician's manual for assessment and parent training* (2nd ed.). New York: Guilford.

Barkley, R. A., Edwards, G., Laneri, M., Fletcher, K., & Metevia, L. (2001). The efficacy of problem-solving communication training alone, behavior management training alone, and their combination for parent-adolescent conflict in teenagers with ADHD and ODD. *Journal of Consulting and Clinical Psychology, 69,* 926–941.

Barkley, R. A., Guevremont, D. C., Anastopoulos, A. D., & Fletcher, K. E. (1992). A comparison of three family therapy programs for treating family conflicts in adolescents with attention-deficit hyperactivity disorder. *Journal of Consulting and Clinical Psychology, 60,* 450–462.

Biederman, J., Newcorn, J., & Sprich, S. (1991). Comorbidity of attention deficit hyperactivity disorder with conduct, depressive, anxiety, and other disorders. *American Journal of Psychiatry, 148,* 564–577.

Blader, J. C. (2006). Which family factors predict externalizing behaviors following discharge from psychiatric inpatient treatment? *Journal of Child Psychology and Psychiatry, 47,* 1133–1142.

Canino, G., Shrout, P. E., Rugio-Stipic, M., Bird, H. R., Bravo, M., Ramirez, R., et al. (2004). The *DSM-IV* rates of child and adolescent disorders in Puerto Rico. *Archives of General Psychiatry, 61,* 85–93.

Chafouleas, S. M., Riley-Tillman, T. C., & McDougal, J. (2002). Good, bad, or in-between: How does the daily behavior report card rate? *Psychology in the Schools, 39,* 157–169.

Corcoran, J., & Dattalo, P. (2006). Parent involvement in treatment for ADHD: A meta-analysis of the published studies. *Research on Social Work Practice, 16,* 561–570.

Costello, E. J., Compton, S. N., Keeler, G., & Angold, A. (2003). Relationships between poverty and psychopathology. *JAMA, 290,* 2023–2029.

Cunningham, C., Bremner, R., & Boyle, M. (1995). Large group community-based parenting programs for families of preschoolers at risk for disruptive behavior disorders: Utilization, cost-effectiveness, and outcome. *Journal of Child Psychology and Psychiatry and Allied Disciplines, 36,* 1141–1159.

Danforth, J. S. (1998). The outcome of parent training using the behavior management flow chart with mothers and their children with oppositional defiant disorder and attention-deficit hyperactivity disorder. *Behavior Modification, 22,* 443–473.

Dunlap, G., dePerczel, M., Clarke, S., Wilson, D., Wright, S., White, R., et al. (1994). Choice making to promote adaptive behavior for students with emotional and behavioral challenges. *Journal of Applied Behavior Analysis, 27,* 505–518.

DuPaul, G. J., & Eckert, T. L. (1997). The effects of school-based interventions for attention deficit hyperactivity disorder: A meta-analysis. *School Psychology Review, 26*, 5–27.

DuPaul, G. J., Ervin, R. A., Hook, C. L., & McGoey, K. E. (1998). Peer tutoring for children with attention deficit hyperactivity disorder: Effects on classroom behavior and academic performance. *Journal of Applied Behavior Analysis, 31*, 579–592.

DuPaul, G. J., Guevremont, D. C., & Barkley, R. A. (1992). Behavioral treatment of attention-deficit hyperactivity disorder in the classroom: The use of the Attention Training System. *Behavior Modification, 16*, 204–225.

DuPaul, G. J., Rutherford, L., & Hosterman, S. J. (2008). Attention-deficit hyperactivity disorder. In R. J. Morris & N. Mather (Eds.), *Evidence-based interventions for students with learning and behavioral challenges* (pp. 33–58). New York: Routledge.

DuPaul, G. J., & Stoner, G. (2003). *ADHD in the schools: Assessment and intervention strategies* (2nd ed.). New York: Guilford.

DuPaul, G. J., & Weyandt, L. L. (2006). School-based intervention for children with attention-deficit hyperactivity disorder: Effects on academic, social, and behavioural functioning. *International Journal of Disability, Development and Education, 53*, 161–176.

Ervin, R. A., Ehrhardt, K. E., & Poling, A. (2001). Functional assessment: Old wine in new bottles. *School Psychology Review, 30*, 173–179.

Eyberg, S. M., Boggs, S. R., & Algina, J. (1995). Parent-child interaction therapy: A psychosocial model for the treatment of young children with conduct problem behavior and their families. *Psychopharmacology Bulletin, 31*, 83–91.

Farmer, E. M. Z., Compton, S. N., Burns, B. J., & Robertson, E. (2002). Review of the evidence base for treatment of childhood psychopathology: Externalizing disorders. *Journal of Consulting and Clinical Psychology, 70*, 1267–1302.

Fleitlich-Bilyk, B., & Goodman, R. (2004). Prevalence of child and adolescent psychiatric disorders in southeast Brazil. *Journal of the American Academy of Child and Adolescent Psychiatry, 43*, 727–734.

Fombonne, E. (2002). Case identification in an epidemiological context. In M. Rutter & E. Taylor (Eds.), *Child and adolescent psychiatry*. Oxford, England: Blackwell.

Forehand, R. L., & McMahon, R. J. (1981). *Helping the noncompliant child: A clinician's guide to parent training*. New York: Guilford.

Funderburk, B. W., Eyberg, S. M., Newcomb, K., McNeil, C. B., Hembree-Kigin, T., & Capage, L. (1998). Parent-child interaction therapy with behavior problem children: Maintenance of treatment effects in the school setting. *Child & Family Behavior Therapy, 20*, 17–38.

Gardner, F., Burton, J., & Klimes, I. (2006). Randomised controlled trial of a parenting intervention in the voluntary sector for reducing child conduct problems: Outcomes and mechanisms of change. *Journal of Child Psychology and Psychiatry, 47*, 1123–1132.

Ghanizadeh, A., & Shahrivar, F. Z. (2005). The effect of parent management training on children with attention deficit hyperactivity disorder. *Journal of Child and Adolescent Mental Health, 17,* 31–34.

Greenwood, C. R., Maheady, L., & Delquadri, J. (2002). Classwide peer tutoring programs. In M. R. Shinn, H. M. Walker, & G. Stoner (Eds.), *Interventions for academic and behavior problems II: Preventive and remedial approaches* (pp. 611–649). Bethesda, MD: National Association of School Psychologists.

Gresham, F. M. (2002). Teaching social skills to high-risk children and youth: Preventive and remedial strategies. In M. R. Shinn, H. M. Walker, & G. Stoner (Eds.), *Interventions for academic and behavior problems II: Preventive and remedial approaches* (2nd ed., pp. 403–432). Washington, DC: National Association of School Psychologists.

Griest, D., Forehand, R., Rogers, T., Briener, J., Furey, W., & Williams, C. A. (1982). Effects of parent enhancement therapy on the treatment outcome and generalization of a parent training program. *Behaviour Research and Therapy, 20,* 429–436.

Hanf, C. (1969). *A two-stage program for modifying maternal controlling during mother-child (M-C) interaction.* Paper presented at the meeting of the Western Psychological Association, Vancouver, BC, Canada.

Hoath, F. E., & Sanders, M. R. (2002). A feasibility study of enhanced group Triple-P Positive Parenting Program for parents of children with attention-deficit/hyperactivity disorder. *Behaviour Change, 19,* 191–206.

Hoff, K., & DuPaul, G. J. (1998). Reducing disruptive behavior in general education classrooms: The use of self-management strategies. *School Psychology Review, 27,* 290–303.

Johnston, C., & Ohan, J. L. (1999). Externalizing disorders. In W. K. Silverman & T. H. Ollendick (Eds.), *Developmental issues in the clinical treatment of children.* Boston: Allyn & Bacon.

Kazdin, A. E. (1997). Parent management training: Evidence, outcomes, and issues. *Journal of the American Academy of Child and Adolescent Psychiatry, 36,* 1349–1356.

Kazdin, A. E., & Weisz, J. R. (2003). *Evidence-based psychotherapies for children and adolescents.* New York: Guilford.

Kelley, M. L. (1990). *School-home notes: Promoting children's classroom success.* New York: Guilford.

Long, P., Forehand, R., Wierson, M., & Morgan, A. (1994). Does parent training with young noncompliant children have long-term effects? *Behaviour Research and Therapy, 32,* 101–107.

March, R. E., & Horner, R. H. (2002). Feasibility and contributions of functional behavioral assessment in schools. *Journal of Emotional and Behavioral Disorders, 10,* 158–170.

McCabe, P. A., Turner, M. K., & Josephson, A. M. (2001). Parent management training. *Child and Adolescent Psychiatric Clinics of North America, 10,* 451–464.

Nelson, J. R., Benner, G. J., Lane, K., & Smith, B. W. (2004). Academic achievement of K-12 students with emotional and behavioral disorders. *Exceptional Children, 21,* 59–73.

Nock, M. K. (2003). Progress review of the psychosocial treatment of child conduct problems. *Clinical Psychology: Science and Practice, 10,* 1–28.

O'Neill, R. E., Horner, R. H., Albin, R. W., Sprague, J. R., Storey, K., & Newton, J. S. (1997). *Functional assessment and program development for problem behavior: A practical handbook.* Pacific Grove, CA: Brooks/Cole.

Paine, S. C., Radicchi, J., Rosellini, L. C., Deutchman, L., & Darch, C. B. (1983). *Structuring your classroom for academic success.* Champaign, IL: Research Press.

Pelham, W. E., Hoza, B., Pillow, D. R., Gnagy, E. M., Kipp, H. L., Greiner, A. R., et al. (2002). Effects of methylphenidate and expectancy on children with ADHD: Behavior, academic performance, and attributions in a summer treatment program and regular classroom settings. *Journal of Consulting and Clinical Psychology, 70,* 320–335.

Pfiffner, L. J., & O'Leary, S. G. (1987). The efficacy of all-positive management as a function of the prior use of negative consequences. *Journal of Applied Behavior Analysis, 20,* 265–271.

Rapport, M. D., Murphy, A., & Bailey, J. S. (1980). The effects of a response cost treatment tactic on hyperactive children. *Journal of School Psychology, 18,* 98–111.

Rapport, M. D., Murphy, A., & Bailey, J. S. (1982). Ritalin vs. response cost in the control of hyperactive children: A within-subject comparison. *Journal of Applied Behavior Analysis, 15,* 205–216.

Reid, M. J., Webster-Stratton, C., & Beauchaine, T. P. (2001). Parent training in head start: A comparison of program response among African American, Asian American, Caucasian, and Hispanic mothers. *Prevention Science, 2,* 209–227.

Reid, R., Trout, A. L., & Schartz, M. (2005). Self-regulation interventions for children with attention-deficit/hyperactivity disorder. *Exceptional Children, 71,* 361–377.

Rhode, G., Morgan, D. P., & Young, K. R. (1983). Generalization and maintenance of treatment gains of behaviorally handicapped students from resource rooms to regular classrooms using self-evaluation procedures. *Journal of Applied Behavior Analysis, 16,* 171–188.

Robin, A. L. (1981). A controlled evaluation of problem-solving communication training with parent-adolescent conflict. *Behavior Therapy, 12,* 593–609.

Rosen, L. A., O'Leary, S. G., Joyce, S. A., Conway, G., & Pfiffner, L. J. (1984). The importance of prudent negative consequences for maintaining the appropriate behavior of hyperactive students. *Journal of Abnormal Child Psychology, 12,* 581–604.

Sanders, M. R., Markie-Dadds, C., Tully, L. A., & Bor, W. (2000). The Triple-P Positive Parenting Program: A comparison of enhanced, standard, and self-directed behavioral family intervention for parents of children with early onset conduct problems. *Journal of Consulting and Clinical Psychology, 68,* 624–640.

Shapiro, E. S., DuPaul, G. J., & Bradley, K. L. (1998). Self-management as a strategy to improve the classroom behavior of adolescents with ADHD. *Journal of Learning Disabilities*, *31*, 545–555.

Sheridan, S. M. (1995). *The tough kid social skills book*. Longmont, CO: Sopris West.

Sheridan, S. M., Dee, C. C., Morgan, J. C., McCormick, M. E., & Walker, D. (1996). A multimethod intervention for social skills deficits in children with ADHD and their parents. *School Psychology Review*, *25*, 57–76.

Smith, D. J., Young, K. R., Nelson, J. R., & West, R. P. (1992). The effect of a self-management procedure on the classroom academic behavior of students with mild handicaps. *School Psychology Review*, *21*, 59–72.

Sugai, G., Horner, R., & Gresham, F. (2002). Behaviorally effective school environments. In M. R. Shinn, H. M. Walker, & G. Stoner (Eds.), *Interventions for academic and behavior problems II: Preventive and remedial approaches* (pp. 315–350). Bethesda, MD: National Association of School Psychologists.

Waschbusch, D. A. (2002). A meta-analytic examination of comorbid hyperactive-impulsive-attention problems and conduct problems. *Psychological Bulletin*, *128*,118–150.

18

INTERVENTIONS FOR INTERNALIZING DISORDERS

THOMAS J. HUBERTY

This chapter discusses internalizing disorders, primarily anxiety and depression, with an emphasis on identification, assessment, and intervention in the school setting. Internalizing disorders are primarily associated with anxiety, fear, and mood problems and are described as *over-controlled* patterns, such as withdrawal, inhibition of behavior, and social difficulties. Anxiety and depressive problems may occur in as many as 15% to 20% of children and youth (Garber, Keiley, & Martin, 2002; Shaffer et al., 1996), although only a small percentage of these are identified and treated. Much of the reason for underidentification is that these children typically are not disruptive and do not call attention to themselves. Because they are more likely to withdraw or be hesitant to interact, they may be perceived as "lazy," lacking in motivation, and have little interest in school performance and activities. Moreover, anxiety and depression are highly comorbid, co-occurring in as many as 50% of children and youth who are referred for either problem.

ANXIETY DISORDERS

The central cognitive characteristic of anxiety is *worry*, which Vasey, Crnic, and Carter (1994) defined as "an anticipatory cognitive process involving repetitive thoughts related to possible threatening outcomes and their potential consequences" (p. 530). People with high levels of anxiety worry excessively and are more likely to perceive more situations as potentially threatening than do others. Moreover, they focus excessive attention on potential negative outcomes, which may or may not be based on actual circumstances. Whether the situation is genuine or imagined, the highly anxious person shows developmentally inappropriate anticipatory reactions to perceived threatening situations. Consequently, anxious children have an attributional bias toward perceiving more situations as threatening and anxiety-producing compared with their peers.

Spielberger (1973) advanced the concepts of *trait anxiety* and *state anxiety*, which refer to stable versus situational anxiety, respectively. Trait anxiety is characterized by high levels of anxiety that are pervasive across situations and is the basis for anxiety disorders. State anxiety is situation-specific, such as when being evaluated or giving a speech (Huberty & Dick, 2006). When the task is completed, anxiety returns to its initial level. Not all people who have state anxiety have trait anxiety, but highly trait-anxious children are more likely to experience state anxiety. Table 18.1 lists the primary cognitive, behavioral, and physiological symptoms of anxiety that children might experience. Not all children will experience all the symptoms at the same time or at the same level of intensity, but likely will show some symptoms from each category.

Prevalence and Developmental Patterns

Because anxiety occurs in all children as a normal developmental pattern, differentiating it from anxiety disorders can be challenging. Rather than being unique characteristics, most often the symptoms are the same as those of everyday anxiety but more intense, more frequent, and of longer duration than is everyday anxiety. Also, because anxious children typically are not disruptive, their symptoms may go undetected unless severe, or they may be mistaken for another problem. For example, inattention is common to both anxiety and attention-deficit problems. Although the behaviors may appear similar, the reasons for the inattention are different and require different intervention approaches. Prevalence rates for anxiety disorders in children and youth are estimated to range from 10% to 20% (Gurley, Cohen, Pine, & Barrett, 1996). In general, girls are about twice as likely as boys to develop anxiety disorders, beginning in early adolescence. In childhood, gender prevalence rates are similar. Anxiety disorders, although treatable, tend to persist in some form into adulthood, again more often in women than men. Of all anxiety disorders listed in the *Diagnostic and Statistical Manual of Mental Disorders (DSM–IV–TR*; American Psychiatric Association, 2000), only separation anxiety disorder is unique to children.

TABLE 18.1
Characteristics of Anxiety

Cognitive	Behavioral	Physiological
Concentration problems	• Motor restlessness	• Tics
Memory problems	• "Fidgety"	• Recurrent, localized
• Attention problems	• Task avoidance	pain
• Oversensitivity	• Rapid speech	• Rapid heart rate
• Problem solving	• Erratic behavior	• Flushing of the skin
• Worry	• Irritability	• Perspiration
• Cognitive dysfunctions	• Withdrawal	• Headaches
○ Distortions	• Perfectionism	• Muscle tension
○ Deficiencies	• Lack of participation	• Sleeping problems
• Attributional style	• Failing to complete	• Nausea
problems	tasks	• Vomiting
	• Seeking easy tasks	• Enuresis

Etiology of Anxiety Disorders

The causes of anxiety disorders have been investigated across genetic, temperamental, social, and parenting factors. Genetic patterns appear to account for about one third of the variance for anxiety as a risk factor (Barlow, 2002), and heritability for specific anxiety disorders is unlikely (Eley, 2001). Last, Hersen, Kazdin, Orvaschel, and Perrin (1991) found no significant evidence to suggest that specific anxiety disorders in children also existed in their relatives. Therefore, a tendency toward general anxiety rather than specific disorders appears to be more transgenerational.

Some children are temperamentally prone to developing anxiety disorders. Children who show extreme behavioral inhibition (BI) are more likely to develop anxiety disorders and are less sociable, more withdrawn, and show more avoidance than approach behavior (Kagan, Reznick, & Snidman, 1987, 1988). Although shy children are prone to experiencing anxiety, behaviorally inhibited children are especially susceptible to developing anxiety disorders. High-BI children tend to maintain these patterns into adolescence and adulthood.

The degree to which psychosocial factors directly cause anxiety disorders or contribute to a predisposition to experience anxiety is unclear. As anxious children encounter more situations that create a perception of lack of control, the effects accumulate, creating a stable pattern of apprehension (Chorpita, 2001). Over time, specific events tend to have less direct effect on social and emotional development than does the accumulation of multiple events. In a similar manner, parenting factors contribute to the development of anxiety. Chorpita, Albano, and Barlow (1998) found that parents with high degrees of anxiety tend to create anxiety in their children, presumably as a result of modeling and promoting of anxious behaviors. There is some evidence that anxious mothers engage in highly controlling and overly protective behaviors, causing their daughters to feel incompetent, insecure, unassertive, and lacking control over events. These findings suggest that, in some cases, working with the family and the child in treatment would be beneficial.

Cultural Considerations

To a large degree, culture influences how one experiences and expresses social and emotional concerns. Anxiety occurs in virtually all cultures, but there is relatively little research available about non-Caucasian children. For example, *ataque de nervios* is a term that refers to a feeling of distress and anxiety in Hispanic populations and appears similar to the concept of anxiety reaction (López & Guarnaccia, 2000). Although cultural factors are important considerations for assessment and intervention, it is beyond the scope of this chapter to review them in detail. Nevertheless, the clinician should carefully assess and incorporate the child's cultural background in the assessment and intervention process.

DEPRESSIVE DISORDERS

Depression and related mood disorders comprise the second largest clinical group of internalizing disorders, occurring in up to 7% of adolescents (Hankin et al., 1998), but only about 1% to 2% of children experience major depressive disorders (Keenan, Hipwell, Duax, Stouthamer-Loeber, & Loeber, 2004). Depression and anxiety are comorbid in as many as 50% of cases. Similar to those of anxiety, characteristics of depression can be viewed as cognitive, behavioral, and physiological symptoms. Some of these symptoms also occur in anxiety, which helps to explain their high degree of comorbidity. Table 18.2 lists the primary cognitive, behavioral, and physiological symptoms of depressive and mood disorders. Similar to anxiety, not all children will show all of the symptoms or show them at the same level of intensity, but likely will show some symptoms from each category. The reader should note that many of the symptoms of anxiety and depression are similar, demonstrating the comorbidity of the two disorders.

Prevalence and Developmental Pathways

Rates of depression in children increase with age, with a relatively rapid increase at adolescence. Depression in preschool children is rare, occurring in less than 1% of the population (Kashani & Carlson, 1987), although data are limited. In preadolescent children, the rate is about 1.5%, increasing to about 8% to 10% in adolescents. During the elementary years, rates of de-

TABLE 18.2
Characteristics of Depression

Cognitive	Behavioral	Physiological
• "All or none" thinking • Catastrophizing • Memory problems • Concentration problems • Attention problems • Internal locus of control • Negative view of self, world, and future • Automatic thinking • Negative attirbutional style • Negative affect • Feelings of helplessness • Feelings of hopelessness • Low self-esteem • Difficulty making decisions • Feels loss of control • Suicidal thoughts	• Depressed mood • Social withdrawal • Does not participate in usual activities • Shows limited effort • Decline in self-care or personal appearance • Decreased work or school performance • Appears detached from others • Crying for no apparent reason • Inappropriate responses to events • Irritability • Apathy • Uncooperative • Suicide attempts	• Psychomotor agitation or retardation • Somatic complaints • Poor appetite or overeating • Insomnia or hypersomnia • Low energy or fatigue

pression are about the same for boys and girls. Beginning at about 13 to 15 years of age, girls' prevalence rates begin to increase. The reasons for these differences have been discussed from multiple perspectives, including hormonal and biological differences, different stressors, variances in gender social and role expectations, girls being more likely to report their symptoms, and that boys and girls cope with depression differently. Overall, the ratio of depressive disorders in girls to boys is about 2:1 to 3:1. Thus, in a class of 30 middle school students, up to three are at risk of major depression, with two of them being girls.

The typical onset of depression is about 11 to 14 years of age, which corresponds to late elementary and early middle school years. Because many social and biological changes are occurring, it is easy to view symptoms of depression as developmental changes and fail to identify significant mood problems. The duration of major depressive disorders is about 7 to 9 months, but approximately 6% to 10 % may last up to a few years. Dysthymic disorders typically have a longer duration of about 1 year, although there is some question about the validity of the diagnosis of dysthymia (Goodman, Schwab-Stone, Lahey, Shaffer, & Jensen, 2000).

Etiology of Depressive Disorders

Research has shown a moderate to high genetic predisposition toward depression, although the degree of heritability varies across samples. When parents rate their adolescents' depressive symptoms, heritability ranges from 30% to 80%, whereas youths' own ratings range from 15% to 80% (Rice, Harold, & Thapar, 2002). Moderate heritability of some causal risk factors exists, such as a propensity toward experiencing negative life events.

Clark, Watson, and Mineka (1994) and others have described *negative emotionality*, which refers to a tendency for a child to perceive and react to the world as chronically threatening or distressing. Symptoms of this pattern include anger, depression, feelings of inadequacy, and experiences of constant stress and is associated with the development of anxiety and depression. Thus, these children may have a biologically based attributional bias toward experiencing the world negatively that has its beginnings in early childhood and develops over time.

Psychosocial problems, which tend to be cyclical, occur with depressed children. These children tend to have social skills deficits, which create more social difficulties and add to the likelihood of developing additional mood problems. Therefore, depressed children often engage in a cycle of contributing to interpersonal difficulties with peers and adults (Joiner, Coyne, & Blalock, 1999).

There is considerable evidence that depression occurs in children of depressed parents. Having a depressed parent increases the risk of adolescent depression by as much as 45% (Silk et al., 2007). Depressed mothers tend to have more punitive parenting styles, reject their children, and be overprotective. They also set higher expectations for their children, are less emotionally supportive, and are less positive (Sheeber & Sorenson, 1998). There tends to be more conflict in families with depressed youth, who are less effective problem-solvers and communicate less well with parents.

Effects on Academic and Social Performance

Depressed children tend to have lower grades in school (Forehand, Brody, Long, & Fauber, 1988), which suggests that affective problems should be considered when academic performance declines, especially from late elementary school forward. Depressed children have been shown to have compromised academic achievement and low self-perceptions of academic competence, affecting their task initiative and persistence (Ialongo, Edelsohn, Werthamer-Larson, Crockett, & Kellam, 1996). Because depressed children tend to have low initiative and psychomotor retardation, they may be seen as "lazy," unmotivated, and uninterested in school. Over time, they may start to feel academically incompetent, despite having average or above ability. Depressed children are at risk of increased isolation from others, restricted range of interests, inappropriate social interactions, irritability, and impatience, and they may be impaired in their ability to receive positive feedback from others. If this cycle persists, feelings of helplessness and hopelessness may occur, increasing the risk of suicidal ideation.

Cultural Considerations

The research on the nature and prevalence of clinical depression across cultures tends to be inconclusive, but it is reasonable to assume that persons in all cultures are likely to feel unhappy, sad, or dysphoric at times. In a study that compared depression prevalence rates between white and African American children, few differences were found (Costello et al., 1996). There is some evidence that African American adolescent girls have lower rates of depression than do their European-American peers. Lower socioeconomic status (SES) is associated with increased rates of depression. Children at the lowest SES levels show two to three times the rate of depression of nonpoor children. There is no reason to believe, however, that these children are more genetically or biologically vulnerable to depression. Rather, poverty and disadvantage contribute to the likelihood of greater family stress, discrimination, and adverse living conditions (Costello et al., 1996). Silk et al. (2007) found that elevated neighborhood adversity may constrain or limit the impact of protective factors at other levels and contribute to an increased risk of depression.

ASSESSMENT OF INTERNALIZING DISORDERS

Assessment and identification of internalizing problems in children can be difficult for several reasons: (a) these children tend not to be disruptive, thereby not calling attention to themselves; (b) their behaviors may be mistaken for typical variations of childhood and adolescence; (c) their behaviors may be mistaken for other problems, such as low motivation, "laziness", attention deficits, and low ability; (d) they tend to be difficult for adults to identify accurately; (e) younger children have a difficult time expressing internal mood states; and (f) children typically do not refer themselves for psychological help.

To accurately assess internalizing problems in children and youth, the clinician must have a thorough understanding of the normal manner of expression of anxiety and mood at different ages, gender differences, and cultural and environmental factors that may contribute to their development. For example, separation anxiety in children from caretakers at 1 year of age is developmentally appropriate. At 14 years of age, such separation anxiety would not be expected and may indicate the presence of anxiety warranting assessment and intervention.

Because internalizing problems tend to be difficult to identify in the school setting, particularly if they are mild or moderate, the best approach to identification is to screen all or the majority of at-risk children at the start of an academic year. Routine screening for internalizing disorders in school settings is not common, however, which contributes to their underidentification.

A first step is to provide in-service training to teachers, administrators, specialists, and other personnel to learn how to identify the signs of extreme anxiety and depression. All teachers could be asked to complete brief behavior rating scales of internalizing problems, and those children who score above a preset score, such as one standard deviation above the mean, could be referred for more in-depth evaluation. An effective approach is the Systematic Screening for Behavior Disorders (SSBD; Walker & Severson, 1992). The SSBD is a three-stage, multiple-gating procedure. In the first stage, a teacher completes a rating scale for all children for internalizing and externalizing behaviors. At the second stage, the three children ranked high in internalizing or externalizing behaviors are further assessed with two teacher rating scales. The authors of the SSBD concluded that this number of children identified for further assessment present the greatest likelihood of having significant problems. Individual users of the SSBD could choose to increase the number of children referred for additional evaluation to increase the likelihood of identifying children whose internalizing problems might otherwise go undetected. Structured observations in classroom and nonclassroom settings are also conducted. Cutoff criteria are set for Stage II, and children who exceed these criteria are referred for in-depth psychological evaluations as Stage III activities.

An alternative approach is for teachers to rate the top 20% of children who have these patterns with a psychometrically sound behavior rating scale, such as the Behavioral Assessment Scale for Children—2 (BASC–2; Reynolds & Kamphaus, 2004) or the Child Behavior Checklist (CBCL; Achenbach, 2001). In a class of 30 students, for example, up to 6 students would likely be rated at the maximum rate of 20%. At the elementary level, there likely would be an equal number of boys and girls. At the middle school and high school levels, more girls than boys are likely to be identified. Following identification of these students, thorough psychological evaluations would be conducted using a multimethod approach.

Structured Observations

The student should be observed in both classroom and nonclassroom settings, using operationalized behavioral criteria for assessing frequency, intensity, and duration of behaviors. Because children with internalizing problems tend to show withdrawn and reserved behaviors, measurement approaches should focus on behaviors such as latency of response (e.g., how long before a child responds to a question or command), duration (e.g., how long on or off-task), or frequency (e.g., how often the child needs reminders to work).

Behavior Rating Scales

Multidimensional behavior rating scales often are completed by teachers and parents to assess the frequency and nature of behavior patterns. Although behavior rating scales have some disadvantages in that they reflect the perspective of one person, they have been shown to be effective screeners and indicators of emotional and behavioral problems in children and youth. They are especially useful for assessing young children who cannot complete self-report measures due to factors such as necessary reading and language ability levels. Behavior rating scales completed by multiple informants also provide information about the frequency, intensity, and duration of behaviors from multiple settings and circumstances. This information can be especially useful for developing interventions for behaviors that vary across settings. The results can be informative about typical behaviors and can offer assistance in understanding the child. A frequent issue with rating scales, however, is that informants' ratings often do not show high agreement. In their classic study, Achenbach, McConaughy, and Howell (1987) found only modest correlation among different informants. Ratings of internalizing behaviors tend to show less agreement because of their subjective nature. Furthermore, children's self-ratings of internalizing problems often do not correspond well with adult ratings. Nevertheless, behavior rating scales such as the BASC-2 and CBCL should be part of the assessment process. To help reduce problems associated with cross-instrument variance, different informant forms of the same instrument should be used.

Self-Report Measures

Self-report measures of anxiety and depression should be included in the individual assessment, as appropriate. Children younger than about 8 years old may have difficulty understanding and responding to these measures and may give unreliable information. For those children who can respond to self-report measures, anxiety scales such as the Revised Children's Manifest Anxiety Scale for Children (Reynolds & Richmond, 1983) and the Multidimensional Anxiety Scale for Children—Revised (March, 1999) have been shown to have adequate psychometric properties. Well-established self-report depression measures are the Children's Depression Inventory (Kovacs, 1981), the Reynolds Children's Depression Scale (Reynolds, 1994), and the Reynolds Adolescent Depression Scale—2 (Reynolds, 2002).

A distinguishing characteristic between anxiety and depression is the nature of affect. Clark and Watson (1991) proposed their tripartite model of anxiety and depression as a way to understand the often-found association between anxiety and depressive symptoms in adults. They found that depression is associated with low positive affect and anxiety with physiological hyperarousal, and that both anxiety and depression are associated with negative affect. Lonigan, Phillips, and Hooe (2003) found evidence that this model applies to children and adolescents. A useful scale to assess affect is the Positive and Negative Affect Scale for Children (Laurent et al., 1999).

Some children may have anxiety or depression of such severity that school-based interventions may be necessary to help them cope with academic demands and maintaining interpersonal relationships. Several direct interventions have been developed that can be used or adapted in the school setting to improve functioning. If direct interventions are to be used, a thorough assessment using the methods described earlier is essential. After the assessment has been completed, developing interventions should follow a problem-solving approach: (a) problem identification, (b) development of interventions, (c) implementation of interventions, and (d) evaluation of intervention effectiveness.

Problem Identification

Using the assessment data, interventions for the anxious or depressed child should be formulated. In developing interventions for anxiety, the clinician should remember that it is neither advisable nor feasible to attempt to eliminate it entirely. Rather, the overall treatment goal should be to teach the child strategies to reduce it to a manageable level across a variety of situations. For the depressed child, the primary focus of interventions is to increase responsiveness, reduce anger and irritability, and to improve social functioning. It may not be possible in a school setting to eliminate dysphoria and negative affect, but improved social and academic functioning is a realistic goal in most cases.

Development of Interventions

The interventions for anxiety and depression can be similar, particularly if they co-occur. Anxiety interventions include (Huberty, in press) the following:

- self-monitoring,
- relaxation techniques,
- systematic desensitization,
- cognitive self-control techniques,
- graduated exposure therapy,
- social reinforcement,
- self-reinforcement for successful anxiety reduction, and
- self-instruction techniques.

Intervention techniques for depression (Huberty, in press) include the following:

- pleasant activity scheduling,

- problem-solving techniques,
- self-monitoring techniques,
- identifying and changing cognitive distortions,
- self-instructional approaches, and
- reattribution training.

Although many of these techniques may not be feasible in the school setting, they can be adapted for specific purposes and implemented using a problem-solving approach. Cognitive–behavioral approaches are among the most evidence-based interventions for anxiety and depression in children. Many of these approaches use manualized treatments, which incorporate multiple, structured sessions designed to teach the child strategies to identify the interaction of cognitive, behavioral, and physical symptoms and to develop methods to change distorted or deficient cognitions. Examples of these programs include Coping Cat (Kendall, Choudhury, Hudson, & Webb, 2002; Kendall & Hedtke, 2006) and Taking ACTION by Stark and Kendall (1996) to treat depression. Friedberg and McClure (2001) is an excellent source for practical cognitive–behavioral interventions that do not require extensive manualized treatment.

Implementation of Interventions

Once interventions have been determined, they should be implemented in a specific, planned sequence that is directly linked with the target behaviors or cognitions. Which persons are involved in the intervention, for example, teachers, should be made clear, and their roles and responsibilities should be clearly delineated.

Evaluation of Interventions

When developing interventions, it is important to include the corresponding method of evaluating the interventions. This phase is important for two reasons: (a) it permits formative evaluation of the intervention to determine when changes need to be made, and (b) it provides for summative evaluation to determine whether the intervention is effective.

In most cases, the student with anxiety or depression will have academic or social problems in the classroom, necessitating working with the teacher and classroom aides. It is my experience that teachers may feel uncomfortable addressing anxiety and depression problems because they may see them as mental health issues that fall outside their training. Many of the interventions listed above can be adapted for classroom implementation with the teacher serving in a collaborative role. Before attempting to formalize classroom interventions, the school psychologist should consider several factors: (a) the teacher's knowledge of the signs and symptoms of anxiety and depression, (b) whether the teacher believes that such problems can or should be addressed in the classroom, (c) whether the teacher attributes the problems to the child or considers that school setting variables are contributors, (d) whether the teacher is willing to be a partner in working with a consultant, and (e) whether the identified interventions are acceptable. If the first four issues can be clarified effectively, then interventions should be developed in a collaborative manner using a problem-solving approach. Without a collaborative relationship, implementation and monitoring is less likely to occur. Some interventions may have group applicability, whereas others may be student-specific. For example, teachers can be taught to use relaxation techniques with an entire class, whereas an individual student may need help coping with social anxiety.

SPECIAL EDUCATION ELIGIBILITY AND INTERVENTIONS

A child whose anxiety and depression significantly impair social or academic functioning in the school setting may be eligible for special education services as a student with an emotional disturbance or emotional disability (ED) under the auspices of the Individuals With Disabilities Education Improvement Act of 2004 (IDEA). Identification of eligibility for students with ED is arguably the most challenging area of special education, in part due to the difficulty with operationalizing the criteria of the federal definition of emotional disturbance. The school psychologist can help to identify these children and assist in developing Individualized Education Programs (IEPs).

Because of the nature of anxiety and depression and their relative subjectivity, translating the behaviors into instructional strategies in an IEP can be challenging. Target behaviors selected should be those most directly affecting functioning and may require individual counseling and program or instructional modifications. The committee members should be reminded that the child will not "grow out of it," that it is not normal, or that it is not merely resistance, but that help is necessary.

Assessment and eligibility for children with emotional and behavioral problems often are issues in special education due process hearings. For many years, I have been an administrative law judge/independent hearing officer for special education due process hearings under the auspices of the IDEA (2004), as well as for Section 504. Having presided over numerous hearings, my experience has shown that assessment of and determining eligibility for children with internalizing problems is one of the most challenging areas for school psychologists and other school personnel to document and defend. Therefore, the school psychologist should focus on best practices and current research when assessing, explaining, and making recommendations for children with internalizing disorders who require special education services.

CONCLUSION

Anxiety and depression in children and youth are two of the most common clinical problems that can have significant effects on personal, social, and academic functioning. In the school setting, these problems can be difficult to detect, but they can nevertheless cause significant difficulties that require intervention. The school psychologist can be a valuable contributor to the team working with these children through assessment, intervention, and consultation with teachers, other school personnel, and parents.

REFERENCES

Achenbach, T. M. (2001). *Manual for the child behavior checklist*. Burlington, VT: University Associates in Psychiatry.

Achenbach, T. M., McConaughy, S., & Howell, C. T. (1987). Child/adolescent behavioral and emotional problems: Implications of cross-informant correlations for situational specificity. *Psychological Bulletin, 101*, 213–232.

American Psychiatric Association. (2000). *Diagnostic and statistical manual of mental disorders* (4th ed., text rev.). Washington, DC: Author.

Barlow, D. H. (2002). *Anxiety and its disorders: The nature and treatment of anxiety and panic* (2nd ed.). New York: Guilford.

Chorpita, B. F. (2001). Control and the development of negative emotions. In M. W. Vasey & M. R. Dadds (Eds.), *The developmental psychopathology of anxiety* (pp. 112–142). New York: Oxford University Press.

Chorpita, B. F., Albano, A. M., & Barlow, D. H. (1998). The structure of negative emotions in a clinical sample of children and adolescents. *Journal of Abnormal Psychology, 107*, 74–85.

Clark, L. A., & Watson, D. (1991). Tripartite model of anxiety and depression: Psychometric evidence and taxonomic implications. *Journal of Abnormal Psychology, 100*, 316–336.

Clark, L. A., Watson, D., & Mineka, S. (1994). Temperament, personality, and the mood and anxiety disorders. *Journal of Abnormal Psychology, 103*, 103–116.

Costello, E. J., Angold, A., Burns, B. J., Stangl, D. K., Tweed, D. L., Erkanli, A., et al. (1996). The Great Smoky Mountains Study of Youth: Goals, design, methods, and the prevalence of *DSM-III-R* disorders. *Archives of General Psychiatry, 53*, 1129–1136.

Eley, T. C. (2001). Contributions of behavioral genetics research: Quantifying genetic, shared environmental and nonshared environmental influences. In M. W. Vasey & M. R. Dadds (Eds.), *The developmental psychopathology of anxiety* (pp. 45–59). New York: Oxford University Press.

Forehand, R., Brody, G. H., Long, N., & Fauber, R. (1988). The interactive influence of adolescent and maternal depression on adolescent social and cognitive functioning. *Cognitive Therapy and Research, 12*, 341–350.

Friedberg, R. D., & McClure, J. M. (2001). *Clinical practice of cognitive therapy with children and adolescents: The nuts and bolts.* New York: Guilford.

Garber, J., Keiley, M. K., & Martin, N. C. (2002). Developmental trajectories of adolescents' depressive symptoms: Predictors of change. *Journal of Consulting and Clinical Psychology, 70,* 79–95.

Goodman, S. H., Schwab-Stone, M., Lahey, B., Shaffer, D., & Jensen, P. (2000). Major depression and dysthymia in children and adolescents: Discriminant validity and differential consequences in a community sample. *Journal of the American Academy of Child and Adolescent Psychiatry, 39,* 761–770.

Gurley, D., Cohen, P., Pine, D. S., & Barrett, O. L. (1996). Discriminating anxiety and depression in youth: A role for diagnostic criteria. *Journal of Affective Disorders, 39,* 191–200.

Hankin, B. L., Abramson, L. Y., Moffitt, T. E., Silva, P. A., McGee, R., & Angell, K. E. (1998). Development of depression from preadolescence to young adulthood: Emerging gender differences in a 10-year longitudinal study. *Journal of Abnormal Psychology, 107,* 128–140.

Huberty, T. J. (in press). Best practices in school-based interventions for anxiety and depression. In A. Thomas & J. Grimes (Eds.), *Best practices in school psychology-V.* Bethesda, MD: National Association of School Psychologists.

Huberty, T. J., & Dick, A. C. (2006). Performance and test anxiety. In G. Bear & K. Minke (Eds.), *Children's needs-III* (pp. 281–291). Bethesda, MD: National Association of School Psychologists.

Ialongo, N., Edelsohn, G., Werthamer-Larson, L., Crockett, L., & Kellam, S. G. (1996). Social and cognitive impairment in first-grade children with anxious and depressive symptoms. *Journal of Clinical Child Psychology, 25,* 15–24.

Individuals With Disabilities Education Improvement Act of 2004, 20 U.S.C. § 1400 et seq.

Joiner, T. E., Coyne, J. C., & Blalock, J. (1999). On the interpersonal nature of depression: Overview and synthesis. In T. E. Joiner & J. C. Coyne (Eds.), *The interactional nature of depression* (pp. 3–19). Washington, DC: American Psychological Association.

Kagan, J., Reznick, J. S., & Snidman, N. (1987). The physiology and psychology of behavioral inhibition. *Child Development, 58,* 1459–1473.

Kagan, J., Reznick, J. S., & Snidman, N. (1988). Biological bases of childhood shyness. *Science, 240,* 167–171.

Kashani, J. H., & Carlson, G. A. (1987). Seriously depressed preschoolers. *American Journal of Psychiatry, 144,* 348–350.

Keenan, K., Hipwell, A., Duax, J., Stouthamer-Loeber, M., & Loeber, R. (2004). Phenomenology of depression in young girls. *Journal of the American Academy of Child and Adolescent Psychiatry, 43,* 1098–1106.

Kendall, P. C., Choudhury, M., Hudson, J., & Webb, A. (2002). *"The C.A.T Project" workbook for the cognitive-behavioral treatment of anxious adolescents.* Ardmore, PA: Workbook.

Kendall, P. C., & Hedtke, K. A. (2006). *Coping cat workbook* (2nd ed.). Ardmore, PA: Workbook.

Kovacs, M. (1981). *Children's Depression Inventory*. Minneapolis, MN: Pearson Assessments.

Last, C. G., Hersen, M., Kazdin, A., Orvaschel, H., & Perrin, S. (1991). Anxiety disorders in children and their families. *Archives of General Psychiatry, 48,* 928–934.

Laurent, J., Catanzaro, S. J., Joiner, T. E., Rudolph, K. D., Potter, K. I., & Lambert, S. (1999). A measure of positive and negative affect for children: Scale development and preliminary validation. *Psychological Assessment, 11,* 326–338.

Lonigan, C. J., Phillips, B. M., & Hooe, E. S. (2003). Relations of positive and negative affectivity to anxiety and depression in children: Evidence from a latent variable longitudinal study. *Journal of Consulting and Clinical Psychology, 71,* 465–481.

López, S. R., & Guarnaccia, P. J. J. (2000). Cultural psychopathology: Uncovering the social world of mental illness. *Annual Review of Psychology, 51,* 571–598.

March, J. S. (1999). *Multidimensional anxiety scale for children*. North Tonawanda, NY: Multi-Health Systems.

Reynolds, C. R., & Kamphaus, R. W. (2004). *Behavior Assessment System for Children, Second Edition (BASC-2)*. Minneapolis, MN: Pearson Assessments.

Reynolds, C. R., & Richmond, B. O. (1983). *Revised Children's Manifest Anxiety Scale*. Los Angeles: Western Psychological Publishing.

Reynolds, W. M. (2002). *Reynolds Adolescent Depression Scale—2*. Lutz, FL: Psychological Assessment Resources.

Reynolds, W. M. (1994). *Reynolds Child Depression Scale*. Lutz, FL: Psychological Assessment Resources.

Rice, R., Harold, G. T., & Thapar, A. (2002). Assessing the effects of age, sex and shared environment on the genetic etiology of depression in childhood and adolescence. *Journal of Child Psychology and Psychiatry and Allied Disciplines, 43,* 1039–1051.

Shaffer, D., Fisher, P., Dulcan, M. K., Davies, M., Piacentini, J., Schwab-Stone, M. E., et al. (1996). The NIMH Diagnostic Interview Schedule for Children Version 2.3 (DISC): Description, acceptability, prevalence rates, and performance in the MECA study. *Journal of the American Academy of Child and Adolescent Psychiatry, 161,* 865–877.

Sheeber, L., & Sorenson, E. (1998). Family relationships of depressed adolescents: A multimethod assessment. *Journal of Clinical Child Psychology, 27,* 268–277.

Silk, J. S., Vanderbilt-Adriance, E., Shaw, D. S., Forbes, E. E., Whalen, D. J., Ryan, N. D., & Dahl, R. E. (2007). Resilience among children and adolescents at risk for depression: Mediation and moderation across social and neurobiological contexts. *Development and Psychopathology, 19,* 841–865.

Spielberger, C. D. (1973). *Manual for the State-Trait Anxiety Inventory for Children*. Palo Alto, CA: Consulting Psychologists Press.

Stark, K., & Kendall, P. C. (1996). *Treating depressed children: Therapist manual for "Taking ACTION."* Ardmore, PA: Workbook.

Vasey, M. W., Crnic, K. A., & Carter, W. G. (1994). Worry in childhood: A developmental perspective. *Cognitive Therapy and Research, 18,* 529–549.

Walker, H. M., & Severson, H. H. (1992). *Systematic screening for behavior disorders (SSBD)* (2nd ed.). Longmont, CO: Sopris West.

19

BEHAVIORAL INTERVENTIONS
FOR PRESCHOOLERS

DAVID W. BARNETT AND RENEE O. HAWKINS

For consulting professionals, preschool challenges often include disruptive and aggressive behaviors, nonproductive activity engagement, and related stress-producing situational disturbances for parents and teachers. Educational and social risks frequently require environmental interventions with corresponding teacher and parent support. This chapter focuses on the importance of keeping behavior plans positive. Most of the interventions here are positive and instructional, the first alternatives for consideration.

Research strongly links early challenges to later problems of adjustment, so waiting for children who are at risk to begin schooling could mean more effort and expense in intervention services and points to the need for prevention programs. Models of challenging behaviors include (a) early coercive and ineffective parenting (Patterson & Bank, 1986); and (b) at-birth or early detected conditions (e.g., autism) that may require supportive, instructional, and function-based interventions for behavioral or learning challenges. The coercion model (challenging child plus ineffective parenting) is powerful and can work in two ways. To simplify: (a) child whines, parent gives in,

Appreciation is extended to Ed Daly for sharing ideas on productive practice.

child is reinforced; and (b) child whines, parent explodes, child quiets temporarily, parent is reinforced. Rapid learning and generalization may result from either.

IDENTIFYING PRESCHOOL TARGET VARIABLES

Target variable selection is based on functional assessments and intervention research. The measurement is contextualized (What functionally is happening in specific situations? What variables can and should be changed?) and changes in performance (i.e., level and trend) are what matters. Teams often need a starting place and a way to sequence intervention objectives. *Keystones* are relatively narrow target variables that have widespread positive consequences (see Barnett, Bauer, Ehrhardt, Lentz, & Stollar, 1996, for sources and related concepts). Keystone variables are individualized, but examples often include compliance with adult requests, rule learning and self-regulation, functional communication, social competence (i.e., appropriate play can be a replacement behavior for aggression), and early academic competence that may be analyzed at various levels (i.e., learning activity quality and engagement; early literacy skills). The benefits of selecting keystone targets potentially include effective and sustained interventions with broad (i.e., collateral) positive effects.

For example, for a child not engaging in appropriate play, a keystone strategy based on functional assessment may include instruction on specific contextual play skills and analysis of performance variables. Skills may include behavior and language for play bouts (i.e., adding high-interest social activities and scripting choices for "play plans"; teacher's instructing, practicing with children, and reinforcing play bids, turn taking, and sharing) and class-wide introduction of appropriate activities, prompts, and other supports (modeling). Measurement of the keystone variable occurs at appropriate levels: (a) evidence of successful play for classmates; (b) progress monitoring of social engagement for at-risk children using micro-norms (i.e., sampling typical children's play for the same activity) for goal setting and evaluation; (c) functional and developmental analyses of related skills and performance as needed; and (d) teacher's acceptance, adherence, and adaptation of instructional skills. Keystones for the teacher also may include increasing effective instruction and reducing ineffective managerial techniques that trigger classroom disruptions and weaken intervention effects.

Targeted variables may address classroom, group, or individual learning or behavior even when a referral concerns an individual child (i.e., curriculum, routines, peers, as well as developmental questions). Home concerns can include dissatisfaction with parenting techniques, sibling interactions, family routines (e.g., bedtime), and elopement (running from adults or activities), as well as developmental concerns. Community concerns might add disruptions while shopping and dangerous car behavior. The prevention efforts, intervention, or instruction goes where the behavior occurs. Methods include predicting troublesome situations and developing adults' plans for effectively instructing children concerning appropriate behaviors in settings, practicing behavior, and applying reinforcement and contingencies (i.e., mild consequences) that work, and thus managing various settings for achieving appropriate behavioral and developmental outcomes.

CONSIDERATIONS FOR PLANNING PREVENTIVE INTERVENTIONS AT THE PRESCHOOL LEVEL

Prevention is used in two ways: (a) long-term prevention of risk through early intervention and (b) specific prevention of challenging behaviors through instructional and antecedent environmental interventions. Positive prevention efforts such as teaching effective parenting skills, implementing class-wide social problem solving, and managing triggering antecedents can occur at various times with individuals who have meaningful contact with a child (e.g., Strain & Joseph, 2004).

Decision Rules and Intervention Permissions

Parents and professionals team in making decisions. Decision rules are based on agreements to carefully try an intervention for a set time (or number of trials, etc.) to see what changes in plans may be needed. Prior research can be used to help set immediate goals (i.e., determine what results can be expected at that point). The intervention is evaluated and further decisions are made on the basis of the data. To obtain informed consent by parents, communications would include comprehensible explanations of intervention steps, the intervention's scientific status, and data use, as well as other legal and ethical requirements. Also, for "high-stakes" interventions, we recommend obtaining informed consent from persons carrying out the intervention because data are kept and used on the performance of the intervention (termed intervention *adherence* or *integrity*) as well as the child's behavior or performance.

Empirically Based, Scripted, and Supportive Interventions

Research-based interventions are preferred if possible in making plans, but they can be challenging for teachers as well as for parents to carry out. At the same time, intervention failures may have cumulative deleterious effects for all involved. Scripted interventions are one way for teams to improve researched-based plans by addressing both the research fidelity (i.e., accuracy of components) and adherence or integrity (accuracy of implementation), and ultimate self-regulation of plans. Scripts serve as (a) personalized and detailed guidelines for providing instruction, intervention, or management to meet specific setting goals, and (b) prompts and models for children (Barnett, Bauer, et al., 2007). Scripted plans are derived from observations about successful interactions, as well as intervention design principles and specific researched interventions. Scripts may be tight (i.e., differential reinforcement), loose (i.e., incidental teaching), and multicomponent and comprehensive. Scripts are modified for appropriate levels of support to help teachers, parents, or others in reaching and maintaining fluency. Script use is eventually faded with desirable intervention components becoming routinized or self-regulated.

Supportive environmental interventions are based on specific changes in routines, activities, interactions (teacher or parent, peer or sibling), and contingencies, among other variables. Environmental interventions address a common parent's or teacher's question: "But I referred this child, so why are you observing me too?" To reduce the risk of intervention failure, high-quality data are typically needed on basic interactions (i.e., adult–child, and so on) in activities and routines that are keystones for success.

Evaluation: Brief Trials and Accountability Designs

Brief intervention trials are used as basics of evaluation. Intervention trials consist of sequences of hypothesis-derived interventions (having internal validity evidence) ordered by intensity (i.e., intrusiveness, ease) and tried out carefully, as needed, to help build sound plans. Data are graphed for intervention teams using accountability designs (A is baseline; B, C, and BC are sequential or combined conditions) and form the basis of next steps in decisions. Sequences, including an early script fluency condition for parents or teachers, allow for intervention refinement that is often needed in consulting with challenging behaviors (as opposed to "here is an intervention, see if it works").

FOUNDATIONAL PRACTICES IN INTERVENTIONS WITH YOUNG CHILDREN

Foundations of interventions with young children include observing accurately (parents, teachers, as well as consultants), creating productive instructional practice opportunities (a part of improving "time-in"), and often improving coercive or ineffective interactions.

Scanning, Positive Attention, and Instructional Management

Accurate observations are the bedrock of intervention designs. Effective teachers continuously move and scan, "spot check" likely trouble-prone activities or times at greater frequency, use positive attention accurately and abundantly, and follow up on redirections (parents' methods are similar; Paine, Radicchi, Rosellini, Deutchman, & Darch, 1983). In using positive scanning with instruction, teachers anticipate problems; encourage replacement behaviors; and use choice making, brief instruction, and/or practice as needed. A desirable ratio is a range of five to seven positive scans for every negative scan (i.e., a reprimand without an effective instructional objective; Strain & Joseph, 2004).

Increasing Opportunities to Learn and Practice

Young children are taught needed skills including social problem solving and self-regulation naturally and effectively, or not. Social learning interventions embedded in activities and routines or structured programs can help accomplish this goal (Vaughn et al., 2003; Webster-Stratton & Reid, 2003). Through the instructional hierarchy, children progress through acquisition, fluency, generalization, and adaptation as they become proficient with skills (Haring, Lovitt, Eaton, & Hansen, 1978). Reinforcement may be needed to help initiate and sustain learning trials.

Time-in and Choice Making

Adding interesting activities and materials and rotating them (removing and reintroducing at a later time), guiding use, setting limits, and using mild consequences (i.e., brief loss of time with highly preferred activity by selecting a less-preferred activity for one session) are ways to improve time-in. Choice making adds quality to interactions and helps enrich environments, and it may be used to help manage behavior (i.e., Peck et al., 1996). Choices can include reinforcement, activities, and task sequences (what gets done first) or when breaks from activities are needed.

Incidental Teaching

This significant and adaptable intervention can be applied to language as well as social problem solving. The adult "seeds" the environment (i.e., adds activities to promote social engagement), waits for children's responses, and uses these natural occurrences to extend children's skills and performances (Hart & Risley, 1982).

Switching Routines

Transitions can be troublesome, or they can be planned as learning opportunities. Expanding "grandma's law" and adding the unifying idea that brief but potent learning trials have powerful cumulative effects can lead to other flexible intervention plans. Productive learning or practice can naturally result from planning changes, interrelationships, or children's "work" or positive behavior practice related to the brief "switching" occurring between routines and high-interest activities. For example, a brief deliberate pause (time delay of 5 to 15 seconds) gives a child the opportunity for practicing a functional request for participating in an activity of interest and builds competencies in communication. Individualized transition routines (i.e., adding a brief rewarding transition task) for an upset child may make natural classroom activities more rewarding (see neutralizing routines, Horner, Day, & Day, 1997). Before switching from one activity to another, children may be requested to briefly (in seconds) practice a new curricular skill (Jacobson, Bushell, & Risley, 1969). All know grandma's law, but a contrasting general principle is that children will work to achieve previous status in preferred activities if time in preferred activities is reduced even by small amounts.

Compliance With Adult Requests

Compliance is a keystone of successful parent–child and teacher–child interactions. Training may involve practice with accurate observations and with components of interactions that improve activities and routines. Consulting can then focus on compliance and reducing coercive cycles. Components may include proximity (not shouting from another room) and eye contact, direct and developmentally appropriate requests, brief wait time, accurately applied and mild consequences, and continued monitoring for follow through, among other components. Providing support for compliance interventions sounds easy, but it may require significant expertise (e.g., McMahon & Forehand, 2003).

Interspersing Easy Tasks and Sequencing High-Probability Requests

Interspersing easy tasks among more difficult ones and presenting high-probability requests prior to low-probability requests are simple antecedent strategies that may effectively increase the likelihood that a child will comply and display appropriate behavior. Interspersing easier tasks among more challenging tasks may result in increased engagement and compliance with the difficult task (Horner, Day, Sprague, O'Brien, & Heathfield, 1991). The interspersal of easy tasks among more difficult ones can occur within a given activity or through the scheduling of activities throughout the day. For example, known items can be interspersed among unknown items when presenting learning tasks. Over the course of the day, preferred activities (i.e., free play time) can be interspersed among more arduous curricular tasks. Presenting children with a series of high-probability requests (i.e., requests with which they comply ≥ 80% of the time) followed by brief reinforcement also can result in increased compliance to low-probability requests (i.e., requests with which they comply ≤ 40–50% of the time; Mace et al., 1988). Although outcomes in research are mixed, in some cases this can set the stage for increased compliance.

EXAMPLES OF HIGH-IMPACT INTERVENTIONS

This section describes interventions that effectively teach children appropriate and functional replacement behaviors and that structure the environment to support and promote positive behaviors.

Functional Communication

Functional communication training (FCT), which is based on the premise that some challenging behaviors are forms of communications, teaches children effective and appropriate ways to communicate their needs and preferences (Carr & Durand, 1985). FCT has been used successfully to decrease aggression, self-injurious behavior, and stereotypy (e.g., repetitive behaviors), and to improve communication disorders across a variety of settings (Durand & Merges, 2001). The first step to this approach is to identify the function of the challenging behavior using various functional assessment methods (e.g., obtain or avoid something). Once the function is identified, a communicative replacement behavior can be taught (i.e., child's request or sign). The consequences identified as maintaining the problem behavior then are used to reinforce the replacement response.

For example, a child may display tantrum behavior when asked to engage in a difficult task. Assuming the function of the tantrum behavior is escape from task demands, the child can be taught to ask for help as an alternative behavior. Just as the tantrum behavior was reinforced by the task becoming less challenging, asking-for-help behavior would be reinforced as teacher assistance would make the task less difficult.

Research support for FCT continues to grow, and researchers have identified some key findings across studies that can guide intervention development and increase chances for success (Durand & Merges, 2001). First, it is imperative that the replacement behavior serve the same function as the original problem behavior. Again, the premise of FCT is that challenging behaviors are a means of communication, and the newly taught behavior should be a more appropriate way of communicating the same information. If there is not a match between the trained response and the function of the problem behavior, the child may continue to rely on the challenging behavior to access desired consequences. Second, the replacement behavior should be more effective and efficient for the child in accessing the desired consequences than the problem behavior. If the replacement behavior requires greater effort and/or does not result in the same schedule of reinforcement, the child is likely to continue displaying the challenging behavior. The trained responses should be easily recognized and acceptable to others in the environment who will respond to the behavior. If the response is not readily noticed and accepted, there is a low probability that it will be reinforced and a high probability that the challenging behavior will persist.

Finally, when applying FCT, there needs to be a plan for how to address the challenging behavior (Durand & Merges, 2001). The goal of FCT is to make the problem behavior essentially nonfunctional, so, to the extent possible, the problem behavior should be ignored. In some cases, mild negative consequences may be needed initially. However, ensuring that the replacement behavior is more effective and efficient at attaining desired outcomes will decrease the need for punishment.

Social Stories

Social Stories appear to be a simple strategy for increasing social behavior and decreasing problem behavior (Reynhout & Carter, 2006; Sansosti, Powell-Smith, & Kincaid, 2004). The rationale for the use of Social Stories is that children with challenging behaviors, particularly children diagnosed with an autism spectrum disorder, have difficulties interpreting social cues and developing appropriate behavioral responses. Social Stories provide children with an individualized guide for behavior, given a set of social circumstances (Gray & Garand, 1993). After identifying the specific problem behavior displayed by the child and specifics regarding the context of the social situation, a story is created, detailing for the student appropriate behaviors in the problematic situation.

Typically, Social Stories include picture cues and text describing the situation; meanings of important social cues; desired social responses, thoughts, feelings, and reactions of the characters involved in the story; and general social rules. Gray (2000) developed guidelines for writing Social Stories and emphasized that stories be more descriptive than directive. The stories can be rehearsed using modeling, role-play, and feedback just before the child is presented with the targeted situation. Written at the comprehension level of the child, Social Stories can be presented to the child in a variety of ways, from independent reading to videotape. Social Stories provide children with explicit learning opportunities for identifying social cues as well as appropriate interpretations and responses to those cues. The modeling, practice, and feedback incorporated in Social Stories teaches children behaviors that are likely to access them the natural and positive consequences associated with appropriate social interactions.

Despite the strong rationale for the use of Social Stories, the research base is limited and highly variable (Reynhout & Carter, 2006; Sansosti et al., 2004). However, Social Stories have been used to increase social greetings, sharing, positive social interactions, compliance, on-task behavior, and hand-washing behavior. Decreases in aggressive behavior, inappropriate vocalizations, tantrums, and obsessive behaviors have followed implementation of Social Stories. Applicable to a wide range of challenging behaviors and easy to implement, Social Stories are a promising intervention or supportive option. Teams may want to consider behavioral function when creating stories.

Peer-Mediated Social Interventions

Serving as relevant and meaningful models of appropriate behavior, peers can be essential components of effective interventions to promote social skills (Mathur & Rutherford, 1991; Odom, Hoyson, Jamieson, & Strain, 1985). Although this sometimes presents challenges to plan and carry out, peers can be trained to initiate and reinforce appropriate social interactions with children who are isolated or demonstrate problem behaviors. Less socially skilled children can benefit from the direct modeling of appropriate social behavior by more socially skilled or trained peers. Peer-mediated interventions may promote greater generalization of social skills than interventions implemented solely by teachers or other adults. Peers may interact with each other more than they interact with adults in the environment, allowing for more continuous feedback in natural settings.

Through direct instruction (Play, Stay, & Talk; Kohler, Greteman, Raschke, & Highnam, 2007), role-play, and feedback, peers have been trained to be effective behavior change agents. To implement interventions, peers have learned specific social interaction behaviors, including making eye contact, inviting another student to play, and initiating appropriate responses to negative behaviors. Selection of peers may be guided by specific criteria, including compliance with teacher requests, willingness to help with the intervention plan, age-appropriate social skills, and a neutral or positive interaction history with the target student. Although one trained peer can have positive effects on target student behavior, using multiple peers in the intervention may enhance logistics and generalization. Peer-mediated social interventions have increased positive social interactions, peer reciprocity, social responding, social initiations, and sustained interactions of target children (Mathur & Rutherford, 1991).

Activity Schedules

Many challenging behaviors displayed by children serve the function of escape—more specifically, escape from task demands. However, when individuals have information about upcoming task demands, they may experience less aversion to the demands, and the occurrence of escape-maintained problem behavior may decrease (Flannery & Horner, 1994). Furthermore, improving self-regulated performance is a fundamental early childhood goal, and activity schedules may help.

The use of activity schedules in the school and home environments is one way to clearly communicate future task demands to children, help promote activity completion, and increase functional independence. Pictures are used to represent activities scheduled throughout the day. Children are taught what activities the pictures represent and how to read the schedule. Activity schedules can help students deal with transition times in the classroom, a common setting event for problem behavior. In addition, the activity schedule can prepare students for changes in daily routines. In the home environment, activity schedules can be used to increase child independence and provide children a guide for using unstructured time (Hall, Krantz, & McClannahan, 1995).

Multicomponent Consequence Hierarchies

Ongoing and/or more intense occurrences of problem behavior may result in unnecessarily severe consequences (i.e., intensity of reprimands may increase without effect, children may be sent home without an effective plan). Consequence hierarchies are step-by-step plans for dealing with challenging behaviors at varying levels of frequency and intensity by delivering consequences along a continuum (Bull & Solity, 1987). Minor, singular occurrences of problem behavior may result in a small consequence (i.e., disapproving look from teacher; rule reminder). However, by laying out the specific consequences that will result from problem behaviors, teachers are more likely to apply consistent consequences for problem behavior. Rather than waiting for a problem behavior to occur and thinking of appropriate consequences reactively, teachers address behavior proactively and preventatively by establishing a consequence hierarchy. The hierarchy can be shared with children to help self-regulate behavior by reminding them of the specific consequences associated with misbehavior.

Consequences included in a hierarchy are individualized to the teacher and classroom environment. Introduced earlier, initial positive steps may address improving learning activities and routines as well as clarifying and practicing class-wide and specific activity rules, expectations, and consequences. Strategies used early on in the hierarchy may include differential reinforcement of appropriate behavior, eye contact, ignoring of minor disruptions (e.g., accidental, self-corrected, not sustained), and reminders of goals and rewards. For ongoing problem behavior or moderate disruptions, teachers may move closer in proximity to the student and provide brief verbal direction. If problem behavior continues, teachers may provide students with a cue that is associated with consequences but allows the teacher to continue with the instruction or activity. In preschools, consequence hierarchies can be built on preferred activities such as "teacher helper," novel or "bonus" activities, and planned routines for access and use of preferred activities. For example, play tickets (i.e., individualized by child's name, attached by Velcro to activity charts) are brought to activities by children to manage access and behavior (number of children, appropriate limits; by K. Mackiewicz, see Barnett, Bauer, et al., 2007, for a complete version). All children have continued access to preferred activities (i.e., loss of privilege, a punishment, is very brief; contingencies include positive instruction to regain access; threats are not used).

Other interventions may be integrated; examples include contingent observation (or school–home notes, and so on). Contingent observation ("sit and watch") can be effective for misbehavior in interest-rich environments (Porterfield, Herbert-Jackson, & Risley, 1976) and involves the following steps: (a) appropriate/inappropriate behaviors are described to the child; (b) the child is guided to the edge of the activity; (c) the child is told to watch how the other children play; (d) in less than 1 minute, the child is asked whether he or she is ready to rejoin the activity and use appropriate behavior; (e) if the child replies affirmatively, he or she rejoins the group; (f) if the child does not indicate readiness to rejoin, "sit and watch" is continued for 30 seconds to 1 minute; and (g) if the child rejoins the activity, positive reinforcement is given. If this cycle is not effective, the child is guided to a quiet and safe/supervised place in the room, and choice making continues. High-quality data are important because effective consequence hierarchies would rapidly reduce the need to use the more intense steps of the hierarchy or functional analysis and replanning should occur, and some procedures viewed as "aversive" can have negative side effects. Out of the scope of this chapter, full consequence hierarchies may be needed for dealing with highly disruptive or dangerous behaviors that require other safeguards and permissions. However, if positives (instruction and reinforcement for alternative appropriate behaviors) and early consequences (technically, mild punishment) are well planned, the need for more intense consequences is greatly reduced.

EMERGING USE OF POSITIVE BEHAVIOR SUPPORT AND RESPONSE TO INTERVENTION IN PRESCHOOLS

Positive behavior support (PBS) provides a system of school-wide prevention and service delivery. PBS was developed originally for improving quality of life for students with developmental disabilities and challenging behaviors but has now been expanded to aspects of school social environment for all children. Response to intervention (RtI) adds the use of a technically adequate prevention and intervention history as evaluation data for disability questions (currently, specific learning disabilities in the Individuals With Disabilities Education Improvement Act of 2004). PBS and RtI have been integrated into models for organizing school services into tiers and making instructional decisions that can fit preschools and promote parent roles (e.g., Barnett, VanDerHeyden, & Witt, 2007).

Prevention and intervention may be organized as tiers by sequencing and combining valid interventions by intensity variables. Tier 1 includes agency-wide PBS programs, class-wide core curriculum (this would include social problem solving), and low-intensity ("typical") individualized efforts commonly used by effective teachers. Tier 2 provides supplemental intervention for children who need more comprehensive programming. Tier 3 adds more frequent progress monitoring and structured problem solving by applying functional assessment methods for children not responding to Tier 2 interventions or who need more immediate comprehensive programming. For children with extremely challenging behaviors, programming can take place initially within all tiers simultaneously, with the RtI design goal being that of decreasing intensity.

CONCLUSION

Effective preschool consulting services for parents and teachers are based on accurately assessing and prioritizing challenges faced by children, parents, and teachers in natural environments; developing empirically-based intervention plans; and carefully trying plans out. Often high on the list of concerns are disruptive and aggressive behaviors, lack of engagement in activities, and resulting developmental questions. Successful outcomes for young children frequently require that environments be changed and that teachers and parents are well supported in carrying out positive interventions. Plans target activities and routines that promote children's learning as well as parenting and teaching success. Systematic prevention and intervention services can be structured through RtI and PBS models. The focus is on data-based decision making leading to appropriately tiered interventions carried out as classwide, group, and individualized plans for supporting children and teachers as well as parents.

REFERENCES

Barnett, D. W., Bauer, A., Bell, B., Elliott, N. E., Haski, H., Barkley, E., et al. (2007). Intervention scripts: What we've learned in 20 years of research and practice in preschools. *Journal of Speech-Language Pathology and Applied Behavior Analysis*, 2, 158–181.

Barnett, D. W., Bauer, A., Ehrhardt, K., Lentz, E., & Stollar, S. (1996). Keystone targets for change: Planning for widespread positive consequences. *School Psychology Quarterly, 11*, 95–117.

Barnett, D. W., VanDerHeyden, A. M., & Witt, J. C. (2007). Achieving science-based practice through response to intervention: What it might look like in preschools. *Journal of Educational and Psychological Consultation, 7*, 31–54.

Bull, S., & Solity, J. (1987). *Classroom management: Principles to practice*. New York: Croom Helm.

Carr, E. G., & Durand, M. (1985). Reducing behavior problems through functional communication training. *Journal of Applied Behavior Analysis, 18*, 111–126.

Durand, V. M., & Merges, E. (2001). Functional communication training: A contemporary behavior analytic intervention for problem behaviors. *Focus on Autism and Other Developmental Disabilities, 16*, 110–119.

Flannery, K. B., & Horner, R. H. (1994). The relationship between predictability and problem behaviors for students with severe disabilities. *Journal of Behavioral Education, 4*, 157–176.

Gray, C. A. (2000). *The new social story book*. Arlington, TX: Future Horizons.

Gray, C. A., & Garand, J. D. (1993). Social stories: Improving responses of students with autism with accurate social information. *Focus on Autistic Behavior, 8*, 1–10.

Hall, L. J., Krantz, P. J., & McClannahan, L. E. (1995). Promoting independence in integrated classrooms by teaching aides to use activity schedules and decreased prompts. *Education and Training in Mental Retardation and Developmental Disabilities, 30*, 208–217.

Haring, N. G., Lovitt, T. C., Eaton, M. D., & Hansen, C. L. (1978). *The fourth R: Research in the classroom*. Columbus, OH: Merrill.

Hart, B., & Risley, T. R. (1982). *How to use incidental teaching for elaborating language*. Austin, TX: Pro-Ed.

Horner, R. H., Day, H. M., & Day, J. R. (1997). Using neutralizing routines to reduce problem behavior. *Journal of Applied Behavior Analysis, 30*, 601–614.

Horner, R. H., Day, H. M., Sprague, J. R., O'Brien, M., & Heathfield, L. T. (1991). Interspersed requests: A nonaversive procedure for reducing aggression and self-injury during instruction. *Journal of Applied Behavior Analysis, 24*, 265–278.

Jacobson, J. M., Bushell, D., Jr., & Risley, T. (1969). Switching requirements in a Head Start classroom. *Journal of Applied Behavioral Analysis, 2*, 43–47.

Kohler, F. W., Greteman, C., Raschke, D., & Highnam, C. (2007). Using a buddy skills package to increase the social interactions between a preschooler with autism and her peers. *Topics in Early Childhood Special Education, 27*, 155–163.

Mace, F. C., Hock, M. L., Lalli, J. S., West, B. J., Belfiore, P., Pinter, E., et al. (1988). Behavioral momentum in the treatment of noncompliance. *Journal of Applied Behavior Analysis, 21*, 123–141.

Mathur, S. R., & Rutherford, R. B. (1991). Peer-mediated interventions promoting social skills of children and youth with behavioral disorders. *Education and Treatment of Children, 14*, 227–242.

McMahon, R. J., & Forehand, R. L. (2003). *Helping the noncompliant child* (2nd ed.). New York: Guilford.

Odom, S. L., Hoyson, M., Jamieson, B., & Strain, P. S. (1985). Increasing handicapped preschoolers' peer social interactions: Cross-setting and component analysis. *Journal of Applied Behavior Analysis, 18*, 3–16.

Paine, S. C., Radicchi, J., Rosellini, L. C., Deutchman, L., & Darch, C. B. (1983). *Structuring your classroom for academic success*. Champaign, IL: Research Press.

Patterson, G. R., & Bank, L. (1986). Bootstrapping your way in the nomological thicket. *Behavioral Assessment, 8*, 49–73.

Peck, S. M., Wacker, D. P., Berg, W. K., Cooper, L. J., Brown, K. A., Richmond, D., et al. (1996). Choice-making treatment of young children's severe behavior problems. *Journal of Applied Behavior Analysis, 29*, 263–290.

Porterfield, J. K., Herbert-Jackson, E., & Risley, T. R. (1976). Contingent observation: An effective and acceptable procedure for reducing the disruptive behavior of young children in a group setting. *Journal of Applied Behavior Analysis, 9*, 55–64.

Reynhout, G., & Carter, M. (2006). Social Stories for children with disabilities. *Journal of Autism and Developmental Disorders, 36*, 445–469.

Sansosti, F. J., Powell-Smith, K. A., & Kincaid, D. (2004). A research synthesis of social story interventions for children with autism spectrum disorders. *Focus on Autism and Other Developmental Disabilities, 19*, 194–204.

Strain, P. S., & Joseph, G. E. (2004). Engaged supervision to support recommended practices for young children with challenging behavior. *Topics in Early Childhood Special Education, 24*, 39–50.

Vaughn, S., Kim, A., Sloan, C. V. M., Hughes, M. T., Elbaum, B., & Sridhar, D. (2003). Social skills interventions for young children with disabilities: A synthesis of group designs. *Remedial and Special Education, 24*, 2–15.

Webster-Stratton, C., & Reid, M. J. (2003). Treating conduct problems and strengthening social and emotional competence in young children. *Journal of Emotional and Behavior Disorders, 11*, 130–143.

20

BEHAVIORAL INTERVENTIONS AND AUTISM IN THE SCHOOLS

SUSAN M. WILCZYNSKI, LAURA FISHER,
LAUREN CHRISTIAN, AND JESSE LOGUE

Autism spectrum disorders (ASDs), also known as pervasive developmental disorders (PDDs), are a cluster of developmental disorders that are characterized by deficits in communication, poor social interactions, and repetitive behaviors or fixed routines. Five different diagnostic labels fall under the category of pervasive developmental disorder: autistic disorder, Asperger's disorder, pervasive developmental disorder–not otherwise specified (PDD-NOS), Rett's disorder, and childhood disintegrative disorder (*Diagnostic and Statistical Manual of Mental Disorders; DSM–IV–TR*; American Psychiatric Association [APA], 2000). Children with autistic disorder demonstrate a delay in language acquisition, have moderate to severe deficits in social functioning, and may have lower cognitive skills. In contrast, children with Asperger's disorder do not demonstrate a delay in language, cognitive, or adaptive functioning. Rather, they experience qualitative impairments in social interactions, including communicating effectively in a complex social world. PDD-NOS is given as a diagnosis when children do not meet the full criteria for either Asperger's disorder or autistic disorder but exhibit symptoms of impaired communication, social interaction, or repetitive behaviors.

Rett's disorder and childhood disintegrative disorder are both very rare and involve severe delays in cognitive, social, adaptive, and communicative abilities. Due to the prognosis for these disorders and likely genetic etiology, there is some controversy about whether Rett's disorder and childhood disintegrative disorder should be considered on the autism spectrum.

The prevalence of ASDs appears to be on the rise. According to the Centers for Disease Control and Prevention, 1 in 150 children currently living in the United States has an ASD (Rice, 2007). ASDs are now more common than pediatric cancer, diabetes, and AIDS combined (Autism Speaks, 2007). Between 1992 and 2003, there was an 805% cumulative growth of children with autism in public schools. Across the United States, the average annual increase of autism-related cases in the school systems was almost 20%. This means 1 out of every 264 children in the nation's public school system in 2003 required an individualized education plan (IEP) and related services for autism in the school setting (Hollenbeck, 2004). Clearly, it is and will continue to be important for school professionals to be aware of this disorder and be knowledgeable about treatment options available to these children in the public school setting.

According to the No Child Left Behind Act of 2001 (2002), school professionals need to select interventions that have evidence supporting their effectiveness. A broad array of behavioral interventions have substantial research support for ASDs. Due to space limitations, the focus on this chapter will is restricted to early intensive behavioral interventions (EIBIs), naturalistic strategies, and social skills development. A wide variety of interventions designed to target academic, communication, adaptive, social, play, and vocational skills have been developed. In addition, a large number of behavioral interventions have also been developed to decrease behaviors that interfere with life functioning (e.g., self-injury, aggression, sexually inappropriate, hazardous or stereotypic behaviors, symptoms of anxiety or depression). Clearly this chapter cannot address all of these domains. We strongly encourage readers to review the chapters in this volume on academic interventions by Eckert, Codding, Truckenmiller, and Rheinheimer (chap. 7); functional behavioral assessment by Noell and Gansle (chap. 3); working with difficult students by Jensen, Clark, and Burrow-Sanchez (chap. 16); and reductive procedures by Little, Akin-Little, and Cook (chap. 11). The foundation of good assessment and intervention remains the same for children with autism and other children facing difficulties in school, and these resources will serve as a solid starting point. Our selection of social skills as a focus of this chapter is based on the fact that social skills are defining features of ASDs and, probably due to the complexity of the social world, they seem least responsive to remediation. Yet there are easily implemented behavioral interventions such as video modeling and scripting that hold promise for improving critical social and communication skills. In addition, generalization, teacher-training standards, and evidence-based practice are briefly addressed.

APPLIED BEHAVIOR ANALYSIS, DISCRETE TRIAL INSTRUCTION, AND EARLY INTENSIVE BEHAVIORAL INTERVENTIONS

There are many misconceptions about applied behavior analysis. Unfortunately, these misconceptions often lead to unnecessary conflict. To avoid these misconceptions, we begin with a definition of three distinct concepts. Applied behavior analysis (ABA) is a field of study that is dedicated to helping individuals reach their potential by improving socially relevant skills (Baer, Wolf, & Risley, 1968). This is accomplished by (a) targeting specific, observable, and measurable behaviors and (b) systematically establishing that a relationship exists between the treatment and positive change by collecting data on socially relevant behaviors through replication. A large number of intervention approaches (e.g., token economy, picture schedules, functional equivalence training, social scripting, video modeling) have come directly from the field of ABA.

In contrast to ABA, discrete trial instruction (DTI) is a teaching technique that relies on a great deal of control within the learning environment (Ghezzi, 2007). Specifically, teachers maintain control over the events that occur before, during, and after the presentation of a task. This most often occurs by (a) introducing a command, (b) providing an opportunity for the student to respond, (c) delivering an appropriate consequence (e.g., a "high five" for an appropriate response or withdrawing attention for an incorrect response), and (d) giving a short break before the next teaching opportunity. DTI does not occur exclusively in one environment (e.g., at a table), nor does it focus on a small range of skills (e.g., many social and communication skills can be taught with this method). This teaching methodology often involves the educator providing a broad range of carefully timed prompts that are systematically faded so that the child can perform tasks independently (Mueller, Palkovic, & Maynard, 2007). Interested readers are referred to Ghezzi (2007) for a detailed description of discrete trial training (DTT). A primary distinguishing factor between DTT and ABA is that there are a broad number of interventions that fall under the umbrella of ABA, one of which is DTT.

Finally, EIBIs are comprehensive programs that focus on the needs of young children and use a broad range of ABA techniques. They often rely more on DTT when a child first enters the program and gradually expand to a wider host of intervention techniques as the child moves through the program. A more detailed description of EIBI follows.

The controversies surrounding DTI, ABA, and EIBI are largely the result of misconceptions about these different approaches. It is important to look beyond the controversies and consider the data. School professionals are expected to select interventions that have research support, and it is clear that EIBI has been shown to be effective in improving life functioning for young children who participate in these programs. Improvements in IQ, communication, and social interaction have all been evidenced when young children participate in EIBI programs. Additional studies must be conducted to establish the extent to which consistent findings are evidenced when (a) the treatment program is established by researchers outside Lovaas's circle of colleagues (Lovaas, 1987), (b) parents direct the treatment program instead of professionals, (c) all program components are delivered in a traditional school setting, (d) follow-up data are collected throughout the school years, and (e) data targeting socially complicated behaviors are collected in lieu of teacher reports of social improvements. However, it is clear that school professionals serving young children with ASDs should receive the appropriate training in regards to these interventions.

The extent to which an intervention is adult-directed or child-directed is another controversy in the area of autism. Substantial evidence has been forwarded to support EIBI (a largely adult-directed approach) as well as incidental teaching and/or pivotal response treatment (largely child-directed approaches). It is true that more large-scale studies have been conducted to support EIBI, but the preponderance of evidence supporting these child-directed, naturalistic strategies is compelling. It is interesting that these interventions share many features. For example, a quality teaching interaction involves (a) structuring the antecedent condition required to initiate the learning opportunity, (b) giving the child a chance to respond, (c) providing reinforcers for correct responding, and (d) offering a quick respite before the next teachable moment.

An EIBI is a comprehensive program for young children (usually under the age of 8) that targets the core characteristics of autism. Although additional areas for improvement may be targeted (e.g., problem behaviors), therapists or educators provide programming in the areas of communication; social interaction; and restrictive, repetitive, maladaptive patterns of behavior, interest, or activities. In addition, EIBI programs are provided for a substantial number of hours each week (e.g., at least 20 hours) and are sustained over a protracted period of time (e.g., often for 2 to 3 years).

The most well-known EIBI program was developed by Ivar Lovaas. Lovaas (1987) published a study in which 19 young children (under the age of 4) with ASD were provided 40 hours of treatment per week for approximately 2 to 3 consecutive years. In comparison with students receiving approximately 10 hours of special education services per week, the individuals receiving the EIBI treatment performed substantially better. In fact, the IQ scores of 47% of individuals participating in the EIBI treatment were in the average range, whereas none of the children in the special education obtained this level of functioning. Furthermore, on the basis of teacher report, these children were perceived as indistinguishable from their peers in a school setting. A follow-up study published in 1993 showed that these effects were maintained over time (McEachin, Smith, & Lovaas, 1993).

Additional studies supporting the effectiveness of EIBI have been published in recent years. For example, significant improvements were evidenced for an EIBI group in terms of IQ and adaptive functioning, as compared with a special education group. However, no significant differences emerged in terms of language comprehension (Cohen, Amerine-Dickens, & Smith, 2006). Eighty-one percent of children in the EIBI group were served in the general education classroom after the completion of the project (65% required some level of support) as opposed to less than 5% of the special education group.

The differences between the experimental groups in the studies described here lie both in the number of treatment hours provided and the type of intervention implemented. This has left many professionals wondering whether it would really matter what type of treatment was used if a sufficient number of hours were provided. The answer appears to be yes. Howard, Sparkman, Cohen, Green, and Stanslaw (2005) compared a 30-hour eclectic treatment program, a 25- to 40-hour EIBI program, and a 15-hour traditional preschool program. The EIBI group improved significantly in terms of cognitive functioning, nonverbal skills, receptive and expressive language, and adaptive skills, whereas the 30-hour eclectic group showed no significant differences from the 15-hour traditional preschool group. Similarly, Eikeseth, Smith, Jahr, and Eldevik (2002, 2007) demonstrated that children in a EIBI program set in the schools showed significant improvement in IQ, communication, and adaptive skills in comparison with children receiving an eclectic program; this improvement was sustained at a 3-year follow-up. These data suggest that the type of treatment, in this case a behavioral intervention, is a critical component of treatment effectiveness. Of course, this does not rule out the possibility that future research will identify alternative early intensive intervention approaches that also produce gains.

NATURALISTIC STRATEGIES

Whereas DTI involves the use of highly structured teaching conditions that are carefully orchestrated by the instructor, naturalistic procedures involve less structured teaching conditions that are often guided by the child's interests (Cowan & Allen, 2007). Naturalistic procedures involve capitalizing on naturally occurring teaching opportunities that occur in a child's everyday life. This teaching process emerged as a way to maximize a child's spontaneous use of language, to generalize speech, and to improve vocabulary growth curves for children with communication delays (Hart & Risley, 1968, 1995). The most well-known and established naturalistic behavioral interventions include incidental teaching and pivotal response treatments (PRT).

Incidental Teaching

Incidental teaching involves creating or contriving environmental conditions that are likely to be of interest to the child (e.g., toy selection is based on the child's known interest as opposed to what the adult believes the child should like). Once the child initiates (e.g., often reaching for an object), the teacher requires an utterance and, as appropriate, an elaboration of the sound or words the child initially used. The teacher thereby confirms the child's request and the child gains access to the object (Hart & Risley, 1995). Of course, this requires the teacher to have a level of control over many different materials in the child's environment and involves simultaneously and frequently placing preferred objects into transparent containers (Wilczynski et al., 2003). In contrast to DTI, in which the interaction is typically adult directed, incidental teaching involves child-directed interactions. Incidental teaching procedures have been extended to include peers as facilitators. In this way, not only is communication enhanced but social interaction with same-age peers is also improved (McGee, Almeida, Sulzer-Azaroff, & Feldman, 1992).

Pivotal Response Treatment

PRTs also capitalize on naturally occurring teaching opportunities and involves targeting pivotal behaviors (i.e., behaviors that yield improvement in skills beyond those immediately taught) to produce generalized responding in the natural environment. The five pivotal behaviors identified to date include motivation, responsivity to multiple cues (i.e., the ability to respond appropriately in similar but somewhat different situations, such as responding "hello" when peers wave or say "hi"), self-management, self-initiations, and empathy (Koegel & Koegel, 2006). PRT holds many characteristics in common with incidental teaching. For example, each approach focuses on creating conditions in which children are likely to initiate interactions because each considers motivation to be a central component of effective teaching. However, PRT goes beyond the target skill to enhance motivation by interspersing mastered tasks throughout the learning session (Dunlap & Koegel, 1980) and offering choices in a wide variety of ways. For example, a child can be given the option to select math or reading or to choose to describe a truck versus a house. Another crucial distinction is the inclusion of self-management as a strategy for improving life functioning. All human beings need to be able to regulate their own behavior without the continued mediation of others to maintain a reasonable level of responding. By incorporating self-management, PRT is likely to lead to a higher level of independence over time. Finally, whereas incidental teaching generally focuses on very young children, PRT has been extended to older students as well (Koegel & Koegel, 2006); however, a substantially larger percentage of studies supporting PRT as an effective intervention have included younger participants.

A large number of studies have been conducted to support the effectiveness of the various components of PRT. Specifically, studies suggest PRT is effective in enhancing communication (Koegel, Camarata, Koegel, Ben-Tall, & Smith, 1998) and social interactions (Koegel, Carter, & Koegel, 2003; Koegel, Werner, Vismara, & Koegel, 2005). However, no large-scale studies comparing PRT to an alternate treatment group have been published to date. Large-scale studies comparing different treatments significantly enhance our understanding of the efficacy of a given treatment. In addition, we look forward to studies showing how improvements associated with PRT are sustained over a protracted period of time. The interested reader is referred to *Pivotal Response Treatments for Autism* by Koegel and Koegel (2006) for a more exhaustive review of this intervention.

SOCIAL SKILLS

As noted previously, qualitative impairments in social interactions are one of the defining features of ASDs. Not surprisingly, many different behavioral approaches have been offered to address this significant concern. Evidence of improvements in social functioning is available within the context of comprehensive programs (Lovaas, 1987) and, as has been noted previously, naturalistic strategies have been effective at improving social interactions. Unfortunately, the majority of the literature focusing exclusively on social skill programs is less impressive. Bellini, Peters, Benner, and Hopf (2007) conducted a meta-analysis of 55 school-based studies that targeted social skills for children and adolescents with ASDs. Overall, low to moderate effects were noted in terms of skill acquisition, maintenance, and generalization. These authors concluded that practitioners and researchers should follow the recommendations of Gresham, Sugai, and Horner (2001). These recommendations included: (a) social skills training at a sufficient level of intensity within an environment in which the skill must be demonstrated, (b) the teaching strategy should be matched to the nature of the deficit (e.g., skill versus performance deficit), and (c) the social skill intervention program should be implemented with a high degree of integrity. Considering the lack of evidence suggesting social skill intervention programs are effective with most populations (Gresham et al., 2001), it is not surprising that substantial support for social skill programs for children with ASDs is not available. Despite the limitations of the current literature base, it is important to be familiar with a few intervention approaches that have some level of research support.

Video Modeling

Video modeling involves the visual (i.e., video) presentation of specific social and communication skills that are performed to facilitate the imitation of the skill by the child with ASD (Charlop & Milstein, 1989). The video is not typically used in isolation. That is, extravideo prompting and delivery of tangible reinforcers are frequently used in the context of practice opportunities following presentation of the video. Although the target child can serve as the "star" of the video with positive effects (Buggey, 2005), this is not a requirement because there is not a significant difference between video modeling involving peers and video self-modeling (Sherer et al., 2001). Thus, children with ASDs who exhibit skill deficits (i.e., have not developed the requisite skills to perform a task) as opposed to performance deficits (i.e., have the capacity to perform a task but are insufficiently motivated to do so) may develop the skills with the peer serving as the video model faster and more efficiently. It is interesting that when compared with live modeling (i.e., in vivo), video modeling has proved superior for a variety of social skills, including play and conversation (Charlop-Christy, Le, & Freeman, 2000). See chapter 15 of this volume for a more detailed description of this evidence-based practice.

Scripting

Scripting involves a written presentation of what to say under a specified social situation. Much like an actor would follow a script, individuals with ASDs can learn their "lines" so that they can perform under the necessary conditions. Scripts have been developed to improve play interactions (Goldstein & Cisar, 1992), social initiations (Krantz & McClannahan, 1993), and conversations (Charlop-Christy & Kelso, 2003). In addition to increasing scripted social interaction, scripting leads to improvements in unscripted social interactions as well (Krantz & McClannahan, 1993). Scripting is sometimes used in conjunction with other behavioral supports (e.g., visual schedules; Krantz & McClannahan, 1998).

GENERALIZATION OF SKILLS

Although not a defining feature of ASDs according to the *DSM–IV–TR* (2000), generalization represents a major educational impediment for many students with ASDs (Koegel, Koegel, & O'Neill, 1989). Generalization occurs when the effects of training spread across conditions that are different from the original training situation. Stimulus generalization occurs when a child has fully developed a skill that he or she can correctly perform in more than one setting, with more than one set of materials, and with more than one person. Furthermore, to function most effectively in the social world, individuals sometimes must demonstrate more than one response that serves the same purpose (e.g., waving and saying hello is an example of response generalization).

Children with ASDs are generally not good at generalizing the skills they develop, nor are they likely to spontaneously develop multiple skills that serve the same purpose. Therefore, it is critical that educational professionals program for generalization. There are a broad number of strategies available when programming for generalization (Stokes & Baer, 1977), and the different approaches described in this chapter often do so in somewhat different ways. For example, EIBI often begins with DTT in which a skill is taught in isolation and efforts to address generalization are often not initiated until a later time (i.e., days, weeks, or months later). In contrast, naturalistic procedures typically program for generalization from the beginning by teaching a skill in one or more environments in which a child will need to demonstrate the skill from the onset. It is interesting that if naturalistic procedures are taught in only one environment, a skill is not technically generalized. Even if it is regularly demonstrated in the same "natural" environment, a skill is not generalized unless it is demonstrated with more than one person or with more than one stimulus. It is important to note that all of these approaches directly program for generalization as opposed to the "train and hope" model of generalization (i.e., train a skill and then hope it generalizes).

SUMMARY AND CONCLUSION

There is a substantial body of evidence supporting the effectiveness of behavioral interventions for individuals with ASDs. These interventions either represent comprehensive programs, which are designed to address the core characteristics of ASDs, or they represent focused interventions, which are designed to target specific educational and behavioral needs of individuals with ASDs. In fact, the research literature supporting a range of interventions is so extensive it would be impossible to consider in the context of this concise chapter. We hope this brief synopsis of critical intervention approaches gives readers cause for excitement—quality of life can be significantly improved through the use of behavioral interventions for individuals diagnosed with an ASD. Treatment of ASDs is complex, which means educators whose services are governed by a desire to provide best practices must also become familiar with (a) controversies regarding treatment options, (b) the need to understand the broad range of interventions that target specific skills or problem behaviors, and (c) the importance of evidence-based practice in providing educational services.

Given the importance of engaging in evidence-based practice, it is unfortunate that most teachers receive little or insufficient training in treatments that work for ASDs (National Research Council, 2001). It is important for school professionals who are providing services to children with ASDs to become familiar with the upcoming Network of Autism Training and Technical Assistance Programs teacher training standards. These standards were based on a broad consensus that teachers deserve to receive adequate training in treatments that work. Once teachers are familiar with the autism training expectations for their profession, the next step is to identify where such training is available. The good news is that training is often available at regional universities. For example, Lerman, Vorndram, Addison, and Kuhn (2004) demonstrated that teachers were able to develop a large number of skills critical to providing effective behavioral interventions with individuals with autism in a brief intensive university-based summer program.

We are reluctant to close this chapter without mentioning that although understanding which interventions have research support is a critical component of engaging in evidence-based practice, it is not enough. In addition to being confident that an intervention enjoys research support, we encourage readers to select treatments on the basis of (a) data-based clinical decision making, (b) values and preferences of key constituents (e.g., parents, educators, specialists, students), and (c) establishing and improving the capacity of the system to implement an intervention with integrity. Reviewing this volume's chapter on behavioral assessment by Watson and Watson (chap. 2) and the chapter on acceptability and treatment integrity by Martens and McIntyre (chap. 4) should support readers in engaging in true evidence-based practice. Moreover, we encourage readers to become familiar with the National Standards Project when the results are announced in spring 2009. The National Standards Project, an unprecedented effort to review educational and behavioral intervention treatment literature for individuals with ASDs under the age of 22, will serve as a guiding force in evidence-based practice. The strength of evidence (based on quality, quantity, and consistency) of educational and behavioral interventions will be available so that readers can identify which treatments of interest enjoy solid research support.

REFERENCES

American Psychiatric Association. (2000). *Diagnostic and statistical manual of mental disorders* (4th ed., text rev.).Washington, DC: Author.

Autism Speaks. (2007). *What is autism? An overview.* Retrieved July 18, 2007, from http://www.autismspeaks.org /whatisit/index.php?WT.svl+Top_Nav

Baer, D. M., Wolf, M. M., & Risley, T. (1968). Current dimensions of applied behavior analysis. *Journal of Applied Behavior Analysis, 1*, 91–97.

Bellini, S., Peters, J., Benner, L., & Hopf, A. (2007). A meta-analysis of school-based social skill interventions for children with autism spectrum disorders. *Remedial and Special Education, 28*, 153–162.

Buggey, T. (2005). Video self-modeling applications with students with autism spectrum disorder in a small private school setting. *Focus on Autism and Other Developmental Disabilities, 20*, 52–63.

Charlop, M. H., & Milstein, J. P. (1989). Teaching autistic children conversational speech using video modeling. *Journal of Applied Behavior Analysis, 22*, 275–285.

Charlop-Christy, M. H., & Kelso, S. E. (2003). Teaching children with autism conversational speech using a cue card/written script program. *Education and Treatment of Children, 26*, 108–127.

Charlop-Christy, M. H., Le, L., & Freeman, K. A. (2000). A comparison of video modeling with in vivo modeling for teaching children with autism. *Journal of Autism and Developmental Disorders, 30*(6), 537–552.

Cohen, H., Amerine-Dickens, M., & Smith, T. (2006). Early intensive behavioral treatment: Replication of the UCLA model in a community setting. *Developmental and Behavioral Pediatrics, 27*, 145–155.

Cowan, R. J., & Allen, K. D. (2007). Using naturalistic procedures to enhance learning in individuals with autism: A focus on generalized teaching within the school setting. *Psychology in the Schools, 44*, 701–715.

Dunlap, G., & Koegel, R. L. (1980). Motivating autistic children through stimulus variation. *Journal of Applied Behavior Analysis, 13*, 619–627.

Eikeseth, S., Smith, T., Jahr, E., & Eldevik, S. (2002). Intensive behavioral treatment at school for 4- to 7-year-old children with autism. *Behavior Modification, 26*, 49–68.

Eikeseth, S., Smith, T., Jahr, E., & Eldevik, S. (2007). Outcome for children with autism who began intensive behavioral treatment between ages 4 and 7. *Behavior Modification, 31*, 264–278.

Ghezzi, P. (2007). Discrete trial teaching. *Psychology in the Schools, 44*, 667–679.

Goldstein, H., & Cisar, C. (1992). Promoting interaction during sociodramatic play: Teaching scripts to typical preschoolers and classmates with disabilities. *Journal of Applied Behavior Analysis, 25*, 289–305.

Gresham, F. M., Sugai, G., & Horner, R. H. (2001). Interpreting outcomes of social skills training for students with high-incidence disabilities. *Teaching Exceptional Children, 67*, 331–344.

Hart, B. M., & Risley, T. R. (1968). Establishing use of descriptive adjectives in the spontaneous speech of disadvantaged preschool children. *Journal of Applied Behavior Analysis, 1*, 109–120.

Hart, B., & Risley, T. R. (1995). *Meaningful differences in the everyday experiences of young American children.* Baltimore: Paul H. Brookes.

Hollenbeck, D. F. (2004). *Public schools autism prevalence report series, 1992–2003, fighting autism.* Retrieved October 31, 2007, from http://www.fightingautism.org/ idea/ reports/OR-Autism-Statistics-Prevalence-Incidence-Rates.pdf

Howard, J. S., Sparkman, C. R., Cohen, H., Green, G., & Stanslaw, H. (2005). A comparison of intensive behavior analytic and eclectic treatments for young children with autism. *Research in Developmental Disabilities, 26,* 359–383.

Koegel, L. K., Carter, C. M., & Koegel, R. L. (2003). Teaching children with autism self-initiations as a pivotal response. *Topics in Language Disorders, 23,* 134–145.

Koegel, R. L., Camarata, S., Koegel, L. K., Ben-Tall, A., & Smith, A. E. (1998). Increasing speech intelligibility in children with autism. *Journal of Autism and Developmental Disorders, 28,* 241–251.

Koegel, R. L., & Koegel, L. K. (2006). *Pivotal response treatments for autism: Communication, social, & academic development.* Baltimore: Paul H. Brookes.

Koegel, R. L., Koegel, L. K., & O'Neill, R. (1989). Generalization in the treatment of autism. In L. V. McReynolds & J. E. Spradlin (Eds.), *Generalization strategies in the treatment of communication disorders* (pp. 116–131). Toronto, Canada: B. C. Decker.

Koegel, R. L., Werner, G. A., Vismara, L. A., & Koegel, L. K. (2005). The effectiveness of contextually supported play date interactions between children with autism and typically developing peers. *Research & Practice for Persons With Severe Disabilities, 30,* 93–102.

Krantz, P. J., & McClannahan, L. E. (1993). Teaching children with autism to initiate to peers: Effects of a script-fading procedure. *Journal of Applied Behavior Analysis, 26,* 121–132.

Krantz, P. J., & McClannahan, L. E. (1998). Social interaction skills for children with autism: A script-fading procedure. *Journal of Applied Behavior Analysis, 31,* 191–202.

Lerman, D. C., Vorndran, C. M., Addison, L., & Kuhn, S. C. (2004). Preparing teachers in evidence-based practices for young children with autism. *School Psychology Review, 33,* 510–526.

Lovaas, O. I. (1987). Behavioral treatment and normal educational and intellectual functioning in young autistic children. *Journal of Consulting and Clinical Psychology, 55,* 3–9.

McEachin, J. J., Smith, T., & Lovaas, O. I. (1993). Long-term outcome for children with autism who received early intensive behavioral treatment. *American Journal on Mental Retardation, 97,* 359–372.

McGee, G. G., Almeida, C., Sulzer-Azaroff, B., & Feldman, R. (1992). Promoting reciprocal interactions via peer incidental teaching. *Journal of Applied Behavior Analysis, 25,* 117–126.

Mueller, M. M., Palkovic, C. M., & Maynard, C. S. (2007). Errorless learning: Review and practical application for teaching children with pervasive developmental disorders. *Psychology in the Schools, 44,* 691–700.

National Research Council and Committee on Educational Interventions for Children With Autism, Division of Behavioral and Social Sciences and Education. (2001). *Educating children with autism.* Washington, DC: National Academy Press.

No Child Left Behind Act of 2001, Pub. L. No. 107–110, 115 Stat. 1425 (2002). Retrieved October 31, 2007, from http://www.ed.gov/policy/elsec/leg/esea02/107-110.pdf

Rice, C. (2007). Prevalence of autism spectrum disorders. Autism and developmental disabilities monitoring network, 14 sites, United States, 2002. *Morbidity and Mortality Weekly Report Surveillance Summaries, 56*(SS01), 1–28.

Sherer, M., Pierce, K. L., Paredes, S., Kisacky, K. L., Ingersoll, B., & Schreibman, L. (2001). Enhancing conversation skills in children with autism via video technology. Which is better, "self" or "other" as a model? *Behavior Modification, 25,* 140–158.

Stokes, T. F., & Baer, D. M. (1977). An implicit technology of generalization. *Journal of Applied Behavior Analysis, 10,* 349–367.

Wilczynski, S. M., Cowan, R. J., Wolf, K., Vause, T., Lewis, L. J., Hayes, A., et al. (2003). Project BEST-CASE: A model for structuring an intensive early childhood intervention program for children with autistic spectrum disorders. *Proven Practice, 5,* 23–36.

21

TRAUMA-FOCUSED COGNITIVE BEHAVIOR THERAPY

STEVEN G. LITTLE AND ANGELEQUE AKIN-LITTLE

Trauma is not an uncommon experience among children and adolescents. Abuse, domestic and community violence, natural disasters, and grief are all examples of childhood traumatic experiences. Felitti et al. (1998) conducted a retrospective study of over 17,000 adults and found that more than one half of their sample reported at least one adverse event in childhood. According to the Bureau of Justice Statistics (2006), 13.8 adolescents per 1,000 (ages 12 to 17) were victims of serious violent crimes (aggravated assault, rape, robbery, and homicide) in 2005. In addition, more than one million people were displaced by Hurricane Katrina in 2005, with many remaining displaced today (Akin-Little & Little, in press). Other natural disasters, such as Hurricanes Ivan in 2004 and Rita and Wilma in 2005, floods in the northeast and Texas in 2006, and the California wildfires of 2007, all left thousands of families homeless. It is clear that exposure to traumatic events is not uncommon in childhood and adolescence, and psychologists working with children and in schools should have some training in meeting the needs of this segment of the population.

According to the *Diagnostic and Statistical Manual of Mental Disorders* (*DSM–IV–TR*; American Psychiatric Association [APA], 2000), an extreme traumatic stressor is one that involves

> direct personal experience of an event that involves actual or threatened death or serious injury, or other threat to one's physical integrity; or witnessing an event that involves death, injury, or threat to the physical integrity of another person; or learning about unexpected or violent death, serious harm, or threat of death or injury experienced by a family member or other close associate. (p. 463)

Symptoms that result from traumatic stressors can be grouped into four main categories: affective, behavioral, cognitive, and physical (Cohen, Mannarino, & Deblinger, 2006). Affective symptoms include fear, depression, and anger. Behavioral symptoms usually involve avoidance of reminders of the traumatic experiences, and cognitive symptoms involve distorted cognitions the child may have about him- or herself, others, the event, or the world, with the main cognition being the belief that the event is the child's fault. Finally, physical symptoms are related to the chronic stress of the traumatic experience and include elevated pulse and blood pressure, increases in muscle tension, and hypervigalence. However, it should also be noted that not every child exposed to a traumatic event will develop trauma symptoms. Many children demonstrate resiliency, the ability to thrive and excel even when exposed to severe stressors (Leckman & Mayes, 2007).

One intervention that has been empirically supported for use with children and adolescents experiencing symptoms as a result of trauma exposure is trauma-focused cognitive–behavior therapy (TF-CBT). An extensive body of research has supported the efficacy of TF-CBT with sexually abused children (e.g., Cohen, Deblinger, Mannarino, & Steer, 2004; Cohen, Mannarino, & Knudsen, 2005), and an emerging literature indicates it can be just as effective for other types of trauma (Cohen, Mannarino, & Deblinger, 2006; Cohen, Mannarino, & Staron, 2006). In fact, TF-CBT is one of only three interventions that have been identified as meeting the criteria for evidence-based practice by the Kauffman Best Practices Project (Chadwick Center for Children and Families, 2004), and it is the only trauma treatment for children with a scientific rating of 1, meaning it is well-supported effective practice by the California Evidence-Based Clearinghouse for Child Welfare (2006–2007). TF-CBT is used with children and adolescents exposed to trauma in an attempt to develop a collection of core skills that build on one another (Cohen, Mannarino, & Deblinger, 2006). Treatment is designed to match the needs of the individual child and family and, to be effective, must be consistent with the family's religious, community, and cultural values. In addition, the therapist must be flexible and creative; the family must be actively involved with treatment; and the therapist must model trust, empathy, and acceptance throughout the course of therapy. The goal of TF-CBT is an optimally functioning individual and family well after treatment has been terminated. To accomplish this, the therapist attempts to establish a sense of self-efficacy in the client's affect, behavior, and cognitions (Cohen, Mannarino, & Deblinger, 2006).

SPECIFIC COMPONENTS OF TRAUMA-FOCUSED COGNITIVE BEHAVIOR THERAPY

TF-CBT is a short-term treatment that involves individual sessions with children and parents as well as joint parent–child sessions. The main components of TF-CBT are psychoeducation, parenting skills, relaxation, affective modulation, cognitive coping and processing, trauma narrative, in vivo mastery of trauma reminders, conjoint child–parent sessions, and the enhancement of future safety and development. Although this chapter summarizes these components, a more complete description of each component can be found in Cohen, Mannarino, and Deblinger (2006).

Psychoeducation is the initial component of TF-CBT and continues throughout therapy for both the child and parent. Information about trauma, its effects, and its treatment should be included. It is important to individualize the information so that it is specific to the type of trauma that was experienced and the child's developmental level. Educating parents and children about treatment helps form expectations and prepares them for the types of activities that will be conducted during therapy.

The second component is the development of parenting skills; these skills focus on helping parents deal with their child's behavior problems (Cohen, Deblinger, Mannarino, & Steer, 2004). Parenting skills taught include the use of praise, selective attention, time-out, and contingency management. Relaxation techniques are taught to the child in an effort to help the child reduce the physiological symptoms of stress and to sleep. No one relaxation technique is recommended, but the developers of TF-CBT use a combination of focused breathing, meditation, and progressive muscle relaxation. Therapists who do not have a background in the use of relaxation techniques may want to consider referring to the relaxation program developed by Cautela and Groden (1978).

Affective expression and affective modulation involve teaching children to manage their emotions and deal with their anxiety. Children who have experienced a traumatic event may find it hard to identify emotions, differentiate between emotions, or express their feelings appropriately. If the child is able to express and control his or her feelings, the child may be less likely to use avoidance as a coping strategy. Techniques that are used during this component include thought interruption, positive imagery, positive self-talk, and social skills training.

Cognitive coping and processing involves teaching children and parents about the relationships among thoughts, feelings, and behavior. This component helps children and parents identify and correct maladaptive thoughts.

Developing a narrative version of their traumatic experiences is believed to be an essential component in TF-CBT and is designed to help the client control intrusive and upsetting trauma-related imagery. The goal of the trauma narrative is to separate unpleasant associations between thoughts, reminders, or discussion of the trauma from overwhelming negative emotion. Over the course of several sessions, the child is encouraged to describe what happened, as well as his or her thoughts and feelings before, during, and after the trauma in greater and greater detail. Eventually the child will share this narrative with parent(s) or a caregiver.

In vivo mastery of trauma reminders are designed to help resolve generalized avoidant behaviors. Frequently, innocuous cues in the environment bring up unpleasant emotions and can lead to avoidance of those cues. This does not mean the child should be desensitized to all perceived trauma cues. Many are legitimate and serve to prevent retraumatization. Part of this component is getting the child to recognize important cues from innocuous conditioned cues.

TF-CBT also includes conjoint child–parent sessions to review information, read the trauma narrative, and facilitate communication. The goal is to get the child comfortable in talking with parent(s) or a caregiver about his or her traumatic experiences and other significant events. These sessions tend to occur toward the end of therapy because the child first needs sufficient time to cognitively process the trauma.

The final component of TF-CBT is designed to enhance the child's future safety and development. In many cases the child will be unlikely to face a similar trauma in the future. Although it is acceptable to stress the possibility that the trauma will not occur, the therapist should never assure any child that he or she will not experience trauma again. The goal, however, is to ensure that the child has the skills necessary to minimize the likelihood of future trauma and to cope with trauma effectively should it occur again.

EMPIRICAL SUPPORT FOR TRAUMA-FOCUSED COGNITIVE BEHAVIOR THERAPY

Although TF-CBT is relatively new therapeutic technique, it has been empirically validated and is recognized by multiple sources as an empirically based intervention. TF-CBT has consistently been demonstrated as an efficacious treatment for posttraumatic stress disorder (PTSD), depression, anxiety, and other related symptoms. There is also an abundance of evidence to support the efficacy of TF-CBT over treatments such as nondirective play therapy and supportive therapies for children who were the victims of sexual abuse (Cohen, Deblinger, & Mannarino, 2004). In addition, although the majority of studies have focused on child sexual abuse, evidence also suggests that it is effective for children exposed to other types of trauma as well as for children who are multiply traumatized (Cohen, 2005).

Cohen and Mannarino (1996) conducted the first treatment outcome study for sexually abused children using TF-CBT and compared TF-CBT with a nondirective supportive therapy (NST) for sexually abused preschool children and their parents. Treatment consisted of 12 individual sessions for both the child and parent. Results indicated that the TF-CBT group demonstrated improvement on most outcome measures, whereas the NST group did not exhibit similar outcomes. In a follow-up to this study, Cohen and Mannarino (1997) evaluated treatment outcome 6 and 12 months after initial treatment. Results indicated that the TF-CBT group exhibited significantly more improvement over time than did the NST group. Results also indicated the superior effectiveness of TF-CBT over NST in reducing sexually inappropriate behavior.

Cohen, Deblinger, Mannarino, and Steer (2004) compared the efficacy of TF-CBT with child centered therapy (CCT) for the treatment of PTSD and related emotional and behavioral problems in children who have been sexually abused. Participants were randomly assigned to a manualized treatment consisting of TF-CBT or CCT. Results indicated that parents in the TF-CBT reported lower levels on each of the outcome measures (except parental support) than did those who received CCT. Specifically, children and parents in the TF-CBT group reported improvement in PTSD symptoms, depression, feelings of shame, behavioral problems, and dysfunctional abuse attributions. Results also indicated that two times as many children in the CCT group continued to have PTSD on the basis of DSM–IV–TR (APA, 2000) criteria. TF-CBT also appeared to improve children's feelings of trust, perceived credibility, and shame. This study is important because it supports the use of a shorter version of TF-CBT.

Deblinger, Mannarino, Cohen, and Steer (2006) assessed the maintenance effects of TF-CBT and CCT in participants in the Cohen, Deblinger, Mannarino, and Steer (2004) study. Participants were followed for 6 additional months while being provided with booster sessions. Results indicated that children in the TF-CBT group maintained the gains made at posttreatment; that is, the children who received TF-CBT continued to show fewer PTSD symptoms and fewer symptoms of shame compared with children in the CCT group. In addition, parents in the TF-CBT group reported less emotional distress than did parents in the CCT group. This study is important because it provides support that a shortened version of the TF-CBT protocol has benefits that persist (at least for 6 months) after treatment has concluded. That children experienced less abuse-related shame during follow-up is also important, as shame may mediate the impact of sexual abuse and hinder long-term recovery.

Cohen, Mannarino, and Knudsen (2004) examined a 16-session (8 trauma-based sessions and 8 grief-based sessions) trauma-focused cognitive–behavioral therapy for childhood traumatic grief (CBT-CTG). Traumatic grief occurs when trauma symptoms interfere with a child's ability to successfully deal with the normal grieving process. Results indicated that children experienced significant improvements in CTG, PTSD, depression, and anxiety symptoms and a reduction in behavior problems. PTSD symptoms improved only during the trauma-focused treatment components, whereas CTG improved during both trauma-focused and grief-focused components. In addition, parents also experienced significant improvement in PTSD and depressive symptoms. In a follow-up study, Cohen, Mannarino, and Staron (2006) examined the effectiveness of a 12-session CBT-CTG model in treating trauma and grief symptoms. Despite the relative effectiveness of the 16-session approach, this study sought to examine the impact of a shortened version of the CBT-CTG protocol used in Cohen, Mannarino, and Knudsen. Participants included 39 children and adolescents who had experienced the loss of a parent or sibling because of accidental death, medical reasons, homicide, suicide, or drug overdose. Significant improvements in children's self-reported symptoms of CTG, PTSD, depression, and anxiety were reported. In addition, parents reported improvement in their child's PTSD, internalizing and externalizing symptoms, and total behavior problems, but they themselves did not report improvement in their depressive symptoms. Similar to the outcomes in Cohen, Mannarino, and Knudsen, a decline in PTSD symptoms and improvement in adaptive functioning was observed only during the trauma-focused phase of CBT, whereas CTG symptoms improved for both the traumatic- and grief-focused CBT interventions. Cohen, Mannarino, and Staron concluded that trauma-focused and a shortened version of a grief-focused CBT protocol is effective at reducing PTSD and CTG, anxiety, behavioral problems, and depressive symptoms. This study has practical utility because it demonstrated that a shortened version of a trauma- and grief-focused CBT can be effective at improving childhood trauma and grief symptoms. It also involved a collaborative approach with children and parents so the information gained from therapy could be transferred between home and clinic and could potentially improve generalization and maintenance.

Kitchiner, Phillips, Roberts, and Bisson (2007) conducted a pilot study to evaluate the effectiveness of a TF-CBT educational training package coupled with a mental health practitioner clinical group supervision (CGS) component for the treatment of PTSD. Ten professionals ranging in experience levels from certified psychiatrists to a midwife with no experience participated as therapists. Therapists received between 6 and 23 sessions of TF-CBT training, and each therapist provided services to at least one participant.

Results indicated that PTSD symptoms improved significantly on the Beck Depression Inventory (Beck, Steer, & Garbing, 1988) and a secondary measure. In addition, participants also reported slight increases in adjustment related to being alone and at work. Despite the fact that improvements were reported in the pilot study, these improvements may need to be viewed with a cautious eye because of minimal control and comparison groups. It would be important to assess the relative impact of the TF-CBT+CGS against TF-CBT alone to determine whether CGS added more strength to TF-CBT. Further exploration should be conducted to assess the benefit of coupling GCS with TF-CBT.

In the only study in schools published to date, Kataoka et al. (2003) used group TF-CBT with Latino immigrant students who had been exposed to community violence. Participants included 198 students in Grades 3 through 8 with trauma-related depression and/or PTSD symptoms. The therapy was delivered in Spanish. Results indicated that students in the intervention group had significantly greater improvement in PTSD and depressive symptoms compared with wait-list controls at 3-month follow-up. Findings suggest that this program can be implemented in school settings and is associated with a decline in trauma-related mental health problems.

CONCLUSIONS

Clearly, children and adolescents experience traumatic events. However, most psychologists working in schools are not receiving specific training in efficacious service delivery for children exposed to trauma. TF-CBT is an effective therapeutic technique that can be used in many different types of traumatic situations. In an attempt to provide additional training to psychologists, the National Crimes Treatment and Research Center at the Medical College of the University of South Carolina, with a grant from the Substance Abuse and Mental Health Services Administration, developed a 10-hour Web-based, multimedia, distance education course for mental health professionals seeking to learn TF-CBT. The only requirements for participating in the training are that individuals have a master's degree or higher in a mental health discipline or are currently enrolled in a graduate training program in a mental health discipline. Interested individuals can find the training program at http://tfcbt.musc.edu (Medical University of South Carolina, 2005).

REFERENCES

Akin-Little, K. A., & Little, S. G. (2008). Our Katrina experience: Providing mental health services in Concordia Parish, Louisiana. *Professional Psychology: Research and Practice, 39*, 18–23.

American Psychiatric Association. (2000). *Diagnostic and statistical manual of mental disorders* (4th ed., text rev.). Washington, DC: Author.

Beck, A. T., Steer, R. A., & Garbing, M. G. (1988). Psychometric properties of the Beck Depression Inventory: Twenty-five years of evaluation. *Clinical Psychology Review, 8*, 77–100.

Bureau of Justice Statistics. (2006). *National crime victimization survey: Violent crime trends, 1973-2005*. Washington, DC: U.S. Department of Justice Office of Justice Programs. Retrieved September 14, 2007, from http://www.ojp.usdoj.gov/bjs/glance/tables/viortrdtab.htm

California Evidence-Based Clearinghouse for Child Welfare. (2006-2007). *Trauma treatment for children*. Retrieved September 13, 2007, from http://www.cachildwelfareclearinghouse.org/search/topical-area/7

Cautela, J. R., & Groden, J. (1978). *Relaxation: A comprehensive manual for adults, children, and children with special needs*. Champaign, IL: Research Press.

Chadwick Center for Children and Families. (2004). *Closing the quality chasm in child abuse treatment: Identifying and disseminating best practices*. San Diego, CA: Author.

Cohen, J. A. (2005). Treating traumatized children: Current status and future directions. In E. Cardeña & K. Croyle (Eds.), *Acute reactions to trauma and psychotherapy: A multidisciplinary and international perspective* (pp. 109–121). New York: Haworth Press.

Cohen, J. A., Deblinger, E., & Mannarino, A. P. (2004). Trauma-focused cognitive-behavioral therapy for sexually abused children. *Psychiatric Times, 21*(10), 109–121. Retrieved October 10, 2007, from http://www.psychiatrictimes.com/p040952.html

Cohen, J. A., Deblinger, E., Mannarino, A. P., & Steer, R. A. (2004). A multi-site, randomized controlled trial for sexually abused children with PTSD symptoms. *Journal of the American Academy of Child and Adolescent Psychiatry, 43*, 393–402.

Cohen, J. A., & Mannarino, A. P. (1996). A treatment outcome study for sexually abused preschool children: Initial findings. *Journal of the American Academy of Child & Adolescent Psychiatry, 35*, 42–50.

Cohen, J. A., & Mannarino, A. P. (1997). A treatment study for sexually abused preschool children: Outcome during a one-year follow-up. *Journal of the American Academy of Child & Adolescent Psychiatry, 36*, 1228–1235.

Cohen, J. A., Mannarino, A. P., & Deblinger, E. (2006). *Treating trauma and traumatic grief in children and adolescents*. New York: Guilford.

Cohen, J. A., Mannarino, A. P., & Knudsen, K. (2004). Treating childhood traumatic grief: A pilot study. *Journal of the American Academy of Child & Adolescent Psychiatry, 43*, 1225–1233.

Cohen, J. A., Mannarino, A. P., & Knudsen, K. (2005). Treating sexually abused children: One year follow-up of a randomized controlled trial. *Child Abuse & Neglect, 29*, 135–145.

Cohen, J., Mannarino, A. P., & Staron, V. R. (2006). A pilot study of modified cognitive-behavioral therapy for childhood traumatic grief (CBT-CTG). *Journal of the American Academy of Child & Adolescent Psychiatry, 45*, 1465–1473.

Deblinger, E., Mannarino, A. P., Cohen, J. A., & Steer, R. A. (2006). A follow-up study of a multisite, randomized, controlled trial for children with sexual abuse-related PTSD symptoms. *Journal of the American Academy of Child & Adolescent Psychiatry, 45*, 1474–1484.

Felitti, V. J., Anda, R. F., Nordenberg, D., Williamson, D. F., Spitz, A. M., Edwards, V., et al. (1998). Relationship of childhood abuse and household dysfunction to many of the leading causes of death in adults. The Adverse Childhood Experiences (ACE) Study. *American Journal of Preventive Medicine, 14*, 245–258.

Kataoka, S. H., Stein, B. D., Jaycox, L. H., Wong, M., Escudero, P., Tu, W., et al. (2003). A school-based mental health program for traumatized Latino immigrant children. *Journal of the American Academy of Child Psychiatry, 42*, 311–318.

Kitchiner, N. J., Phillips, B., Roberts, N., & Bisson, J. I. (2007). Increasing access to trauma focused behavioural therapy for post traumatic stress disorder through a pilot feasibility study of a group clinical supervision model. *Behavioural and Cognitive Psychotherapy, 35*, 251–254.

Leckman, J. F., & Mayes, L. C. (2007). Nurturing resilient children. *Journal of Child Psychology and Psychiatry, 48*, 221–223.

Medical University of South Carolina. (2005). *A web-based learning course for trauma-focused cognitive-behavioral therapy.* Retrieved December 29, 2008, from http://tfcbt.musc.edu

INDEX

with home- or classroom-delivered consequences, 225
implementation steps for, 225–229
parent involvement with, 225
treatment acceptability of, 225
uses and advantages of, 222–223
using response cost with, 223–224
Data, in SWPBS, 127
Deblinger, E., 329
Deci, E. L., 76, 84–85
Decision making, linking assessment to, 28
Decision rules, 299
Deficit models (SLDs), 213–214
Defining problems, 197–198
Delayed reinforcement, 195
Demandingness, 103–104
Dependent group-oriented contingencies, 162
Depression, anxiety vs., 289
Depressive automatic thoughts, 104–106
Depressive disorders, 284–287
    cultural influences on, 287
    effects on academic/social performance, 286
    etiology of, 285–286
    prevalence and developmental pathways of, 284–285
    school-based interventions for, 290–292
Descartes, René, 99
Description, of desired behavior, 253
Descriptive functional behavioral assessments, 51–52
Desk, distance and, 252
Developmental models, in cognitive behavior therapy, 99–107
Diagnostic and Statistical Manual of Mental Disorders (DSM-IV-TR), 265–266, 326
Dickinson, A. M., 81
Differential reinforcement of alternative behaviors (DRA), 54, 61, 175
Differential reinforcement of incompatible behavior (DRI), 175
Differential reinforcement of low rates of behavior (DRL), 174
Differential reinforcement of other behavior (DRO), 174
Difficult students, 247–261
    antecedent control with, 251–253
    and coercion, 251
    defined, 249
    motivation of, 257–260

precision requests to, 253–254
problematic behaviors of, 249–250
rules as expectation setters for, 254–257
Dimensions of behavior, measuring, 30–32
Direct descriptive assessment, in functional assessment, 35, 36
Direct instruction, in math, 115
Direct (behavior) observation, 29
    in functional assessment, 35
    in functional behavioral analysis, 51
Disconvergent data, 28
Discounting the positives, 105
Discrete trial instruction (DTI), 313, 314
Discriminative stimuli, 81
Distance, 252
Dobes, R. W., 198
Dots for Motivation, 260
Dowrick, P. W., 231–233
DRA. *See* Differential reinforcement of alternative behaviors
DRI. *See* Discrete trial instruction
DRI (differential reinforcement of incompatible behavior), 175
DRL (differential reinforcement of low rates of behavior), 174
DRO (differential reinforcement of other behavior), 174
DSM-IV-TR. See Diagnostic and Statistical Manual of Mental Disorders
DuPaul, G. J., 270
Duration of behaviors, 30, 31
Dysfunctional cognitions models
    in cognitive behavior therapy, 100, 103–106
    in cognitive therapy, 105–106
    in rational emotive behavior therapy, 103–105
D'Zurilla, T. J., 15–16

Early intensive behavioral interventions (EIBIs), 312–315
ED (emotional disability), 292
Education of the Handicapped Act Amendments (1990), 45
Efficacy
    of behavioral interventions, 4
    of cognitive–behavioral interventions, 4–5
    of self-modeling, 235
EIBIs (early intensive behavioral interventions), 312–315

Elementary and Secondary Education Act of 1965 amendments, 126
Ellis, A., 96, 97, 103–105
Embarrassing behaviors, as reinforcers, 164–165
Emergent reading skills, improving, 113
Emotional disability (ED), 292
Emotional disturbance, 98, 292
Emotional reasoning, 106
Empirically derived syndromes, 265
Empirical research, 4
Environment, FBA assumptions about, 46–47
Environmental variables, in FBA, 49
Error of association, 37
Error of inaccurate functional behavioral assessment, 36
Error of misplaced precision, 36–67
Ervin, R. A., 270
Evidence-based interventions, 111–121
    mathematics, 114–118
    reading, 112–114
    requirement for, 63
    spelling, 119–121
    writing, 118–119
Evidence-based practice, guidelines for, 5
Exchangeable rewards, 164
Exclusionary time-out, 179
Externalizing disorders, 265–275
    classroom behavioral strategies for, 266–271
    designing interventions for, 267
    future directions for interventions for, 274–275
    home behavioral interventions for, 271–274
    peer-mediated interventions for, 270
    pharmacological interventions for, 266
    prevalence of, 266
    self-mediated interventions for, 269–270
    social relationship/skills interventions for, 270–271
    teacher-mediated interventions for, 267–269
External validity, 65
Extinction
    defined, 175
    to modify consequences, 134–135
    and reductive procedures, 175–176
Extinction burst, 176

Extra-environmental events assessment, 33–35
Extreme traumatic stressors, 326
Extrinsic reinforcement, 73–86
    and behavioral criticisms of cognitive research, 80–85
    best practices in use of, 85–86
    concern over, 73–74
    intrinsic motivation vs., 74–76
    reinforcer/reward effects, 76–80
    use of, 73
Eye contact, 252

Family intervention programs, 271–272
FBA. See Functional behavioral assessment
FCT. See Functional communication training
Feedforward models, of self-modeling, 233
Flora, S. R., 74
Fortune-telling, 105
Frequency of behaviors, 30, 31
Functional analysis (in FBA), 47, 52–53
Functional assessment, 43–45. See also Functional behavioral assessment
    defined, 35
    for externalizing disorders, 267
Functional Assessment Informant Record-Teacher, 29
Functional behavioral assessment (FBA), 35–37, 43–55
    conceptual framework of, 46–48
    controversy about, 44–46
    descriptive, 51–52
    essential goal of, 44
    as family of methods, 45–46
    functional analyses in, 52–53
    indirect, 49–50
    linking assessment data to treatment plans in, 53–54
    observational test conditions in, 52–53
    target of assessment within, 48–53
    technologies for, 47
    as tertiary tier SWPBS intervention, 138
    traditional assessment vs., 43–44
Functional communication training (FCT), 47, 54, 303–304
Future safety and development, as TF-CBT component, 328

General interest theory, 77–78
Generalizability of results, 65

Quiet voice, 252

Random selection
 of criteria, 166–167
 of rewards, 164
 of target students, 167
Rate of behaviors, 30, 31
Rating scales
 for behavioral assessment, 29–30
 in functional assessment, 50
 for internalizing disorders, 288–289
Rational emotive behavior therapy (REBT),
 103–105
Reactive strategies, for externalizing disorders, 267
Reading, evidence-based interventions for,
 112–114
Reading comprehension, improving, 114
Reading fluency, improving, 113–114
Real-time recording, 31
REBT (rational emotive behavior therapy),
 103–105
Recency error of perception, 36
Recognition, as reinforcer, 164
Reductive procedures, 171–183
 and behavioral momentum, 172–173
 defined, 171
 positive, proper, and proactive, 180–
 183
 punishments, 173, 176–178
 reinforcement-based, 173–176
 time-out, 178–180
Rehearsal. See Mental rehearsal
Reinforcement
 and acceptability of treatment, 62
 automatic, 49
 best practices in use of, 85–86
 delayed, 195
 differential, 54, 61
 extrinsic. See Extrinsic reinforcement
 of generalization, 192
 for implementation integrity, 67–68
 intermittent, 191, 195
 naturally occurring, 193
 negative, 49, 249
 noncontingent, 54
 positive, 6, 49, 248
 rewards vs., 82
 verbal, 253
Reinforcement-based reductive procedures,
 173–176
Reinforcement contingencies

 in functional behavioral analysis, 48–
 49
 in interventions, 59
Reinforcement Spinners, 259, 260
Reinforcer/reward effects
 behavioral investigations of, 79–80
 in cognitive evaluation theory, 76–78
 and overjustification hypothesis, 78–79
Reinforcers, rewards vs., 79
Relaxation techniques, in TF-CBT, 327
Repeated readings practice, 114
Representation techniques, for math problem-solving, 117
Reprimands, 253, 268
Requests
 high-probability, 147–149
 multiple, 253
 in question format, 252
Response class, 190
Response cost, 177–178
 with daily report cards, 223–224
 for externalizing disorders, 268, 269
Response generalization, 191–192
Response to intervention (RTI, RtI), 206,
 209–216
 advantages from using, 213–215
 behavioral consultation as vehicle for,
 22
 models of, 209–211
 with preschoolers, 307–308
 with specific learning disabilities, 211–
 215
Restitutional overcorrection, 178
Restitution training, 178
Rett's disorder, 311, 312. See also Autism
 spectrum disorders
Revised Children's Manifest Anxiety Scale
 for Children, 289
Rewards. See also Extrinsic reinforcement
 contingent, 160
 performance-independent, 81, 85
 quality-dependent, 76
 reinforcement vs., 79, 82
 reinforcer/reward effects, 76–80
 task-contingent, 76–77, 85
 varying criteria for, 166
Reynolds Adolescent Depression Scale-2,
 289
Reynolds Children's Depression Scale, 289
Rhode, G., 269–270
Risk model (RTI), 214
RTI, RtI. See Response to intervention

Trauma-focused cognitive behavior therapy (TF-CBT), 325–331
  components of, 327–328
  empirical support for, 328–331
  goal of, 326–327
Trauma narrative, in TF-CBT, 328
Traumatic grief, 330
Traumatic stressors, 325–326
Treatment effectiveness
  and adoption of behavioral interventions, 61–62
  and behavioral assessments, 37–38
Treatment evaluation (behavioral consultation model), 17
Treatment implementation (behavioral consultation model), 17
Treatment integrity, 59–68
  and acceptability of treatment, 62
  and best practices in implementation support, 66–68
  defined, 60
  as degree of contingent application, 61
  dimensions of, 60–61
  as percentage of behaviors consequated, 60–61
  as percentage of correct steps, 60
  in practice, 63–64
  for preschooler interventions, 299–300
  in research, 64–66
  and treatment effectiveness, 61–62
  and treatment outcome, 63
  using problem-solving methods, 210
Triadic relationship, in consultation, 14–15
Triple P (Positive Parenting Program), 272–273

Unconscious motivation, 97
Understanding, as mechanism of change, 98–99

Validity
  convergent, 28
  external, 65
  internal, 65
  social, 62
Value-governed students, 250
Variable interval (VI) schedule of reinforcement, 195
Variable ratio schedule of reinforcement, 195
Vellutino, F., 211
Verbal reinforcement, 253
Verbal rewards, 78, 84. See also Praise
Video modeling. See also Self-modeling
  for autism spectrum disorders, 318
  effectiveness of, 231–232
VI (variable interval) schedule of reinforcement, 195
Voice, tone of, 252
Vygotsky, L. S., 102

"Wait-to-fail" approach, 213
Watson, John, 4
wDRO (whole-interval DRO), 174
Wetzel, R. J., 16
What If chart, 255–257
"What's It Going to Be Box," 257
Whole-interval DRO (wDRO), 174
Whole-interval recording, 31
Worry, 281–282
Writing, evidence-based interventions for, 118–119

Yelling, 252
Young, K. R., 269–270

ABOUT THE EDITORS

Angeleque Akin-Little, PhD, lives in Auckland, New Zealand, and is president of the consulting company Behavioral, Educational, and Research Consultants. She also consults with internationally based centers, specializing in applied behavior analysis training and service delivery. She earned her PhD in school psychology from the University of Southern Mississippi in Hattiesburg in 1999 and is a board-certified behavior analyst. She has served on the faculty of Hofstra University in Hempstead, New York, and the University of the Pacific in Stockton, California, and is a fellow of Division 16 (School Psychology) of the American Psychological Association. Her main research and practice interests are in the area of behavioral interventions in homes and schools and applied behavior analysis, particularly the effects of extrinsic reward on intrinsic motivation.

Steven G. Little, PhD, is a professor in educational (school) psychology at Massey University in Auckland, New Zealand. A native of the United States, Dr. Little received his PhD in school psychology from Tulane University in New Orleans, Louisiana, in 1987, and he taught at various school psychology programs in the United States for 22 years before moving to New Zealand in 2009. He has published extensively in the school psychology literature, served as president of Division 16 (School Psychology) of the American Psychological Association, and served on the editorial boards of numerous school psychology journals. He is a board-certified behavior analyst and his main research and practice interest is in behavioral interventions with children in homes and schools.

Melissa A. Bray, PhD, is a faculty member in the school psychology program at the University of Connecticut in Storrs. She is a fellow of the American Psychological Association (APA), the Association for Psychological

Science, and an elected member of the Society for the Study of School Psychology. She is licensed as a psychologist in the State of Connecticut and also holds national certification in school psychology. Since receiving her doctorate in 1997, she has published or has in press 90 books, articles, chapters, and reviews in the professional literature. Of particular significance, Dr. Bray was the 2003 recipient of the prestigious APA Division 16 (School Psychology) Lightner Witmer Award, the Division's highest honor given to early career scholars. Dr. Bray has been involved in state, national, and international professional associations and has served as vice-president for social and ethical responsibility and ethnic minority affairs, Division 16 Executive Committee.

Thomas J. Kehle, PhD, is the director of school psychology at the University of Connecticut in Storrs. He is a fellow of the American Psychological Association, the Association for Psychological Science, and the American Association of Applied and Preventive Psychology. Dr. Kehle is licensed as a psychologist in the State of Connecticut, a member of the National Register of Health Service Providers in Psychology, a charter member of the Society for the Study of School Psychology, and an honorary member of the American Academy of School Psychology. He serves as an associate editor for *Psychology in the Schools* and is on the editorial board of the *Journal of Psychoeducational Assessment*. Professor Kehle's publication record is substantial in that he has published or has in press over 150 books, articles, chapters, and reviews in the professional literature.